W. E. B. Du Bois and the Problems of the Twenty-First Century

W. E. B. Du Bois and the Problems of the Twenty-First Century

An Essay on Africana Critical Theory

Reiland Rabaka

LEXINGTON BOOKS

A division of
ROWMAN & LITTLEFIELD PUBLISHERS, INC.
Lanham • Boulder • New York • Toronto • Plymouth, UK

LEXINGTON BOOKS

A division of Rowman & Littlefield Publishers, Inc.
A wholly owned subsidary of The Rowman & Littlefield Publishing Group, Inc.
4501 Forbes Boulevard, Suite 200
Lanham, MD 20706

Estover Road
Plymouth PL6 7PY
United Kingdom

British Library Cataloguing in Publication Information Available

Library of Congress Cataloging-in-Publication Data

The hardback edition of this book was previously catalogued by the Library of Congress
as follows:

Rabaka, Reiland, 1972–
  W.E.B. Du Bois and the problems of the twenty-first century : an essay on Africana
critical theory / Reiland Rabaka.
    p. cm.
  Includes bibliographical references and index.
  1. Du Bois, W. E. B. (William Edward Burghardt), 1868–1963—Political and social
views. 2. Du Bois, W. E. B. (William Edward Burghardt), 1868–1963—Philosophy.
3. African Americans—Study and teaching. 4. African American philosophy.
5. Critical theory. 6. Racism—United States. 7. United States—Race relations.
8. African Americans—Politics and government. 9. African Americans—Social
conditions. 10. African Americans—Social conditions—21st century. I. Title.
E185.97.D73R33 2007
305.896'0730092—dc22   2006030821

ISBN-13: 978-0-7391-1682-1 (cloth : alk. paper)
ISBN-10: 0-7391-1682-7 (cloth : alk. paper)
ISBN-13: 978-0-7391-1683-8 (pbk. : alk. paper)
ISBN-10: 07391-1683-5 (pbk. : alk. paper)

Printed in the United States of America

∞™ The paper used in this publication meets the minimum requirements of American
National Standard for Information Sciences—Permanence of Paper for Printed Library
Materials, ANSI/NISO Z39.48-1992.

For my mother, grandmothers, and great aunt

Contents

Preface and Acknowledgments

"Dr. Du Bois's greatest virtue was his committed empathy with all the oppressed and his divine dissatisfaction with all forms of injustice." — M. L. King Jr., 1970, 28

"W. E. B. Du Bois is the towering black scholar of the twentieth century. The scope of his interests, the depth of his insights, and the sheer majesty of his prolific writings bespeak a level of genius unequaled among modern black intellectuals. . . . As with any great figure, to grapple with Du Bois is to wrestle with who we are, why we are what we are, and what we are to do about it." — West, 1996, 55, 57

"W. E. B. Du Bois is important to the study of blacks and the development of black thought in the New World because he articulated most of the important themes of this area of inquiry. If there is any doubt, a consultation of nearly every text in the field would reveal his influence." — Gordon, 2006, 5

"There is no need to subscribe to all that Dr. Du Bois has said and done. . . . Only the future can tell to what degree the historical audacities of Du Bois are viable. . . . Dr. Du Bois has always been put forward as one of the great black men and one of the great leaders of the black people. But I have said that he is one of the great intellectuals — American intellectuals — of the twentieth century, and today and in years to come his work will continue to expand in importance while the work of others declines." — C. L. R. James, 1977, 202, 211

I was in junior high school the first time I read, or rather attempted to read, the weighted words of W. E. B. Du Bois. The book was, of course, *The Souls of Black Folk*. I will never, ever, forget it. It was the cover of the book that drew me to it, that soulfully summoned me in a special, almost alchemic way. I feel sort of embarrassed saying it, but *The Souls of Black Folk* is the first book with a black person on the cover that my twelve-year-old eyes had ever seen. Sure, my mother read me fiction and poetry by black writers growing up, and she certainly encouraged me to read books by black authors, but their pictures weren't on the covers of their books. Something happened to me when I saw Du Bois and, as I felt back then and still feel now, he saw me. I stared at him and studied that determined look on his face and the fire in his eyes, and he stared back at me, I imagined, with wild wonder. We went on like this for what seemed a lifetime, and then at last I opened the book. Along with *The Autobiography of Malcolm X* and *Angela Davis: An Autobiography*, both of which I read the summer before I began high school, *The Souls of Black Folk* is a touchstone in my life and has traveled with me from adolescence to adulthood.

Growing up in a poor and extremely poverty-stricken family of peasants and petty-farmers scattered throughout the South, and being the son of a Southern Baptist minister, I was immediately taken by the candid discussion of racism and black spirituality in *The Souls of Black Folk*. Du Bois, it seemed to me, was writing about my life as much as he was writing about his, and he did so in such an extremely eloquent and lyrical manner that I found myself in his words. I too lived behind "the Veil," and pondered the world beyond it. I was all too familiar with that omnipresent question, which liberal and well-meaning white folk always seemed to ask more with their actions than their words: "How does it feel to be a problem?"

Certainly my life stands as a testament to the fact that black people at the dawn of the twenty-first century are still approached more as problems than as persons—that is, human beings with rights to be respected and protected. When and where I read Du Bois's blistering criticisms of racial domination and discrimination in *The Souls of Black Folk*, I found myself thinking, even in junior high, that finally I had found someone who not only lived through the horror and harrowing experience of what it means to be black in an utterly anti-black and white supremacist world, but who unequivocally advocated anti-racist resistance in thought and action. He articulated, what appeared to me at twelve or thirteen years of age, some special secret truth that only he and I were privy to. I did not know it then, but what Du Bois shared with me in that initial encounter, in those tattered and repeatedly read pages of *The Souls of Black Folk*, would alter my intellectual and political life forever.

Coming of age in the Deep South in the early 1990s I was baffled by the constant displays of racism, and particularly "white supremacy," as Du Bois dubbed it in classic essays, such as "The Souls of White Folk" (1910) and "Of the Culture of White Folk" (1917). Throughout high school and undergraduate the more I read Du Bois, the more special secret truths he shared with me, and only adolescent me, or so I possessively thought. Our special secret truths transcended and, I am tempted to say, transgressed the rubric(s) of race and the harsh realities of racism to quickly include Pan-Africanism, anti-colonialism, black Marxism, democratic socialism, male-feminism, and pacificism, among others. Increasingly I began to interpret him as more than merely a "race man" or "race leader." In the fertile ground of my mind he blossomed into a revolutionary humanist intellectual and political chameleon who spoke in novel and much-needed ways to my burgeoning and deep-seated desire to simultaneously become a radical political activist, insurgent intellectual, and avant-garde artist. However, it was not simply Du Bois the insurgent intellectual, political radical, and littérateur who intrigued me. There were also the intense, often painfully autobiographical moments strewn throughout his corpus that endeared him to me and fostered a special, extra-intellectual kinship. For instance, the fact that he grew up poor, without a father, had a close and loving relationship with his mother, was fascinated with Africa and its diaspora from an early age, read voraciously, told vivid stories, and respected but was extremely critical of the black church and other forms of organized religion, endeared him to me and aided me in my quest to make sense of the world and the "problems," not only that he identified and to which he sought solutions, but also the new "problems" of contemporary culture and society. As an undergrad, I was particularly moved when I read the often-overlooked passage from his "Last Message," which the then ailing octogenarian, nearly nonagenarian Du Bois composed sensing his imminent death:

> I have loved my work, I have loved people and my play, but always I have been uplifted by the thought that what I have done well will live long and justify my life; that what I have done ill or never finished can now be handed on to others for endless days to be finished, perhaps better than I could have done. (Du Bois, 1971b, 736)

After reading this, I simply couldn't keep the secret truths he shared with me to myself; I had to tell someone else. I wondered if there were others who had found themselves in his words, who were mesmerized by his magic message, who possessed the intellectual audacity to attempt to finish in the twenty-first century what he initiated in the nineteenth century. Once I got to graduate school I began to systematically and critically study his lifework and intellectual legacy, and I, consequently, wrote my master's thesis and doctoral dissertation on his intellectual history and social and political philosophy.

In graduate school I quickly realized that if and when Du Bois was read, even in an Africana Studies Ph. D. program, *The Souls of Black Folk* was usually his only book engaged. Nary a word was uttered about the intellectual historical fact that Du Bois, as Lewis Gordon (2000b) perceptively put it, defied "the adage of radicalism in youth and conservatism in old age by reversing its order" (p. 94). I would be the first to earnestly admit that Du Bois began as a black bourgeois social reform theorist who was even willing to work with Booker T. Washington up until the turn of the twentieth century. However, I would also, perhaps in the same breath, point out that Du Bois spent more of his intellectual life and energy criticizing black (and white) conservatism than contributing to that insidious ideological tradition, which I must bemoaningly admit continues to plague the remnants of radical politics and revolutionary social movements in (post)modern twenty-first century America.

Contemporary intellectuals and activists who start and stop with Du Bois's early work, such as *The Philadelphia Negro*, *The Souls of Black Folk*, and "The Talented Tenth," do Du Bois a disservice when they praise or criticize these works as though he never wrote another word. In other words, and in essence, contemporary critics customarily intellectually assassinate Du Bois at thirty-five, the age at which he wrote his most famous work, *The Souls of Black Folk*. It is as if he did not live another sixty years and die at the ripe old age of ninety-five with the socialist President of Ghana, Kwame Nkrumah, at his bedside. It is as if he did not spearhead the Niagara Movement and put forward intellectual history-making criticisms of Booker T. Washington and his accommodationist philosophy. It is as if he did not go on to establish the NAACP, the first national civil rights organization in United States history, and edit one of the most popular periodicals in African American history, *The Crisis*. It is as if he was not the special guest of Mao Tse-tung in communist China, or Nikita Khrushchev in Soviet Russia. And, finally, it is as if his passport was not revoked by the U.S. government for half a decade and he was not harassed and ultimately jailed for advocating peace and associating with communists and socialists. Indeed, it is intellectually disingenuous to quarantine our criticisms to the first thirty-five years of the life of an activist-intellectual who not simply continued to contribute to radical politics and revolutionary social movements for another sixty years, but who, as Manning Marable observed, left an intellectual and political legacy that ranks with and rivals those of Frederick Douglass and Martin Luther King Jr. Marable (1986) declared:

> Only Frederick Douglass and Martin Luther King, Jr., equaled Du Bois's role in the social movement for civil rights in the United States. But, in other respects, Du Bois's diverse activities over nearly a century left a larger legacy. Du Bois was the "father of Pan-Africanism" and a central theoretician of African independence; the major social scientist, educator, critic, and political journalist of black America for two generations; and an important figure in the international movements for peace and socialism. (p. viii)

For over a decade my primary theoretical preoccupation has been to chart Du Bois's contributions to radical politics and critical social theory. Not only have I read and reread his early work—of course, *The Philadelphia Negro*, *The Souls of Black Folk*, and "The Talented Tenth" among them—but, in order to coherently and comprehensively chronicle his contributions to critical theory of contemporary society, I have turned time and time again to his other, some might even go so far to say "more obscure," albeit groundbreaking, scholarly books, such as *The Negro*, *Darkwater*, *The Gift of Black Folk*, *Black Reconstruction*, *Black Folk, Then and Now*, *Color and Democracy*, and *The World and Africa*, among others; his innumerable efforts at autobiography, for instance, *Darkwater*, *Dusk of Dawn*, *In Battle for Peace*, and *The Autobiography of W. E. B. Du Bois*; his edited volumes, specifically the Atlanta University studies; his editorship of and publications in periodicals, such as *The Moon*, *The Horizon*, *The Crisis*, and *Phylon*; his, literally, hundreds of critical essays and scholarly articles on a staggeringly wide range of topics; his public intellectualism, political activism, and participation in national and international social movements, such as Pan-Africanism, the Niagara Movement, the NAACP, the Harlem Renaissance, the Civil Rights Movement, the Women's Liberation Movement, and the Peace Movement, among others; and his countless creative writings, which encompass novels, short stories, poetry, and plays.

In the American academy, amid the current intellectual trepidation and word-wizardry of many of the more noted intellectuals and theorists, Du Bois's discourse on racism, capitalism, colonialism, civil rights, social justice, women's liberation, world peace, and democratic socialism exist furtively in the radical intellectual imagination, stripped of its critical potency, and even mocked by postmodernists and post-Marxists (among many others) who argue that his thought is outdated or old fashioned. However, for those of us with unquenchable commitments to continuing the fight for freedom, for those of us deeply disturbed by what is going on in our war-torn world, and for those of us who desperately search for solutions to our most pressing social problems, Du Bois's anti-imperial ideas and actions, his increasing commitment(s) to gender justice, his radical political vision, and his theory of social change offer a much needed *Africana* alternative to and through the mazes of postmodernism, postcolonialism, postfeminism, and post-Marxism, among other contemporary conceptual distractions and disruptions.

Along with other black radical figures, like Fannie Lou Hamer, Malcolm X, Frantz Fanon, Amilcar Cabral, Ella Baker and C. L. R. James, the example of Du Bois can serve as a means of rethinking the possibilities of resistance to, and transformation of, the new (global) imperialisms of our age. His work cuts across several disciplines and, therefore, closes the chasm between Africana Studies and critical theory, constantly demanding that intellectuals not simply think deep thoughts, develop new theories, and theoretically support radical politics, but *be* and constantly *become* political activists, social organizers and cultural workers—folk the Italian philosopher, Antonio Gramsci referred to as "organic intellectuals" (see Gramsci, 1971, pp. 3–23; 2000, pp. 300–22). In this sense, the studies gathered in *W. E. B. Du Bois and the Problems of the Twenty-First Century* contribute not only to Africana American, Cultural, Ethnic, and Women's Studies, but also to contemporary critical theoretical discourse across an amazingly wide range of "traditional" disciplines, and radical political activism outside of (and sometimes even *against*) the academy.

W. E. B. Du Bois and the Problems of the Twenty-First Century discursively moves beyond *The Souls of Black Folk* and Du Bois's other important early work, and engages his intellectual and political activities for their import to radical politics and the reconstruction of critical social theory. It does not privilege Du Bois's later thought and texts over his early work, or middle period, in as much as it levels the interpretive terrain and performs an archaeology of the full range of his unique intellectual history and political evolution. This book is primarily preoccupied with what Du Bois identified as the most pressing "problems" of the nineteenth and twentieth centuries, and what his lifelong search for solutions to those "problems" provides radical political activists and critical social theorists facing, unfortunately, many of the same (or, at the least, very similar) "problems" in the twenty-first century.

Similar to the thought and texts of Karl Marx, Du Bois's work provides no guarantees, but it does present blueprints for a better world and an alternate model and method of intellectual and political struggle, one that could, and I believe should, be employed in contemporary efforts to reinvigorate radical political thought and revolutionary social movements. Although he lived ninety-five years and accomplished much during his highly productive lifetime, a dying Du Bois knew that the quest for human freedom must go on. He acknowledged in his "Last Message" that there was still much to be done, and it is there, in that epitaphic moment where he humbly "handed on to others" what he "never finished," it is there that this book finds its locus.

W. E. B. Du Bois and the Problems of the Twenty-First Century is not simply about Du Bois, but also about what the many people who have contributed to my personal, professional, and political development have taught me. W. E. B. Du Bois, as I will repeat throughout the text, represents a radical political intellectual ancestor who provides me with several paradigms and points of departure to explore Africana Studies' contributions to critical theory of contemporary society. Though his thought is the primary point of departure, the critical thought of many, many others has influenced and informed my conceptions of radical politics and critical social theory. Each chapter bears the imprint of the diverse, though often disconnected, intellectual and political arenas and agendas I draw from and endeavor to establish critical dialogue with. As a consequence, the list of individuals and institutions to which I am indebted is, indeed, enormous. Such being the case, I hope I may be forgiven for deciding that the most appropriate way in which to acknowledge my sincere appreciation is simply to list them below without the comments each has so solemnly earned. My deepest gratitude and most heartfelt *asante sana* (a thousand thanks) are offered to: my mother, Marilyn Giles; my grandmothers, Lizzie Mae Davis and Elva Rita Warren; my great aunt, Arcressia Charlene Connor; my older brother and his wife, Robert Smith II and Karen Smith; my younger brother, Dwight Clewis; my nieces and nephews, Robert Smith III, Ryan Smith, Kalyn Smith, Remington Smith, and Dominique Clewis; my father, Robert Smith I; my grandfather, Joseph Warren; Lucius Outlaw; Molefi Asante; Maulana Karenga; Kristine Lewis; Rhonda Tankerson; De Reef Jamison; Tashala Jamison; Mark Christian; Stacey Smith; Patrick DeWalt; Lamya Al-Kharusi; Allison Dill; Kimberly Marshall; Anthony Lemelle; Julian Kunnie; Nelson Keith; James Conyers; Gregory Stephens; Katherine Bankole; Sigmund Washington; Ursula Lindqvist; Toroitich Chereno; Troy Barnes; Jamarah Amani; Timothy Allen; April Sweeney; Nicole Barcliff; Elzie Billops; Adam Clark; Lakisha Williams; Brandy Durham; Zachary Epps; Nicole Houston; Denise Lovett; Kilja Kim; Andrew Smallwood; Ronald Stephens; Bakari Kitwana; and Nuwumba.

I am also indebted to several institutions for research fellowships and funds. I must begin by thanking my colleagues, especially Maulana Karenga, in the Department of Black Studies at California State University–Long Beach, where I was provided with a reduced teaching load and research grant which enabled me to initiate this study. The Department of Black Studies at California State University–Long Beach, in addition, generously supported a research leave, which allowed me to participate in the Visiting Scholars Initiative at the Center for African American Studies at the University of Houston during the 2003–2004 academic year and complete the research and writing of the manuscript. The faculty, staff, and students of the Center for African American Studies at the University of Houston were especially unselfish and supportive throughout the most critical year in the research and writing of this book. *Nashukuru sana* (special thanks) to James Conyers, Angela Williams, Phyllis Bearden, Ahati Toure, and Paul Easterling. Also, thanks to the wonderful students who took my seminar on W. E. B. Du Bois at the University of Houston and helped me work through many of the ideas and arguments that form the foundation of this book. The faculty, staff, and students in the Department of Ethnic Studies and the Center for Studies of Ethnicity and Race in America (CSERA) at the University of Colorado at Boulder deserve special thanks for their patience and critical support. *Nashukuru sana* (special thanks) to Susan Armstrong and Chelsea Lane for always being there and lending a brother a helping hand. Also, thanks to the insightful students who took my seminar on W. E. B. Du Bois at the University of Colorado at Boulder. This book has greatly benefited from the critical questions and eloquent answers they offered me (and Du Bois).

Several research libraries, special collections, and archives hosted and helped me transform this book from a schoolboy's dream into grown man's reality. I am indelibly indebted to the directors and staffs of: the W. E. B. Du Bois Papers, Department of Special Collections and University Archives, W. E. B. Du Bois Library, University of Massachusetts at Amherst; W. E. B. Du Bois Institute for African and African American Research, Harvard University; Arthur A. Houghton Jr., Library, Harvard University; Center for African American Studies, Wesleyan University; Schomburg Center for Research in Black Culture, New York Public Library; Nicholas Murray Butler Library, Columbia University; John Henrik Clarke Africana Library, Africana Studies and Research Center, Cornell University; African American Collection, Hillman Library, University of Pittsburgh; Africana Research Center, Pennsylvania State University; Charles L. Blockson African American Collection, Temple University; Center for African American History and Culture, Temple University; Center for Africana Studies, University of Pennsylvania; Moorland-Spingarn Research Center, Howard University; African American Studies Research and Resource Center, George Mason University; John Hope Franklin Collection for African and African American Documentation, Rare Book, Manuscript, and Special Collections Library, Duke University; Carter G. Woodson Center for African American and African Studies, University of Virginia; Robert W. Woodruff Library, Atlanta University Center Archives; Manuscript Sources for African American History, Special Collections, Emory University; Fisk University Library, Fisk University; Amistad Research Center, Tulane University; Center for African and African American Studies, University of Texas at Austin; St. Clair Drake Center for African and African American Studies, Roosevelt University; Center for African American and African Studies, University of Michigan; Neal-Marshall African American Cultural Center, Indiana University; African and African American Collection, University Library, University of California–Berkeley; Ralph J. Bunche Center for African American Studies, University of California–Los Angeles; Center for Black Studies, University of California–Santa Barbara;

Blair-Caldwell African American Research Library, Denver Public Library; and Center for African American Policy, University of Denver.

My editor, Joseph Parry, and the Lexington Books editorial board deserve very special thanks for seeing the potential in this book project and prodding me along during the many months it took me to revise the manuscript and prepare it for production. I honestly believe that I could not have had a better publishing experience. Kind permission was granted by publishers and journals to publish several of the book's chapters that appeared in very early versions elsewhere:

Chapter 1 is a substantially revised and expanded version of "Africana Critical Theory of Contemporary Society: Ruminations on Radical Politics, Social Theory, and Africana Philosophy," which appeared in Molefi K. Asante and Maulana Karenga (Eds.), *The Handbook of Black Studies* (pp. 130–52). Thousand Oaks, CA: Sage, 2006. Reprinted by permission of Sage Publications Inc.

Chapter 2 contains a substantially revised and expanded version of "W. E. B. Du Bois's 'The Comet' and Contributions to Critical Race Theory," which appeared in *Ethnic Studies Review: Journal of the National Association for Ethnic Studies* 29 (1), 22–48.

Chapter 3 is a revised version of "'Deliberately Using the Word *Colonial* in a Much Broader Sense': W. E. B. Du Bois's Concept of 'Semi-Colonialism' as Critique of and Contribution to Postcolonialism," which appeared in *Jouvert: A Journal of Postcolonial Studies* 7 (2), 1–32.

Chapter 5 contains a substantially revised and expanded version of "W. E. B. Du Bois and 'The Damnation of Women': An Essay on Africana Anti-Sexist Critical Social Theory," which appeared in *Journal of African American Studies* 7 (2), 39–62.

Chapter 5 also contains a substantially revised and expanded version of "The Souls of Black Female Folk: W. E. B. Du Bois and Africana Anti-Sexist Critical Social Theory," which appeared in *Africalogical Perspectives* 1 (2), 100–41.

Chapter 6 is a condensed version of "The Souls of Black Radical Folk: W. E. B. Du Bois, Critical Social Theory, and the State of Africana Studies," which appeared in *Journal of Black Studies* 36 (5), 732–63. Reprinted by permission of Sage Publications Inc.

This book is lovingly dedicated to my mother, Marilyn Giles; my grandmothers, Lizzie Mae Davis and Elva Rita Warren; and my great aunt, Arcressia Charlene Connor, and they individually and collectively know the many millions of reasons why. If, then, my gentle readers, any insights are gathered from my little book, I pray you will attribute them to the aforementioned. However, if (and when) you find foibles and intellectual idiosyncrasies, I humbly hope you will neither associate them with any of the forenamed nor, most especially, W. E. B. Du Bois. I, and I alone, am responsible for what herein is written.

—Reiland Rabaka
Philadelphia, Pennsylvania
Dallas, Texas
Los Angeles, California
Houston, Texas
Denver, Colorado

Chapter One

Introduction:
W. E. B. Du Bois and
Africana Critical Theory

"Du Bois detected early, along with and presumably independently of his German contemporaries associated with the Frankfurt Institute, the fundamental homology uniting Fascism, Bolshevism, and the New Deal; he expressed a need to adjust the orthodox critique of capitalism to account for the rise of a 'new class of technical engineers and managers' and other internal systemic changes in the twentieth century, and he demonstrated a sense of the significance of the mass-culture apparatus, planned obsolescence and intensified marketing in the contemporary social management synthesis."—Reed, 1997, pp. 217–18

"With a politics remarkably progressive for his time (and ours), Du Bois confronted race, class, and gender oppression while maintaining conceptual and political linkages between the struggles to end racism, sexism, and war. . . . In his analysis integrating the various components of African American liberation and world peace, gender and later economic analyses were indispensable."—J. A. James, 1997, pp. 36–7

"He [Du Bois] virtually, before anyone else and more than anyone else, demolished the lies about Negroes in their most important and creative periods of history. The truths he revealed are not yet the property of all Americans but they have been recorded and arm us for our contemporary battles. . . . Dr. Du Bois was not only an intellectual giant exploring the frontiers of knowledge, he was in the first place a teacher. He would have wanted his life to teach us something about our tasks of emancipation."—M. L. King Jr., 1970, pp. 20, 24

DU BOIS, AFRICANA STUDIES, AND CRITICAL THEORY

The African holocaust and anti-colonial struggle; Pan-Africanism and the Peace movement; Marxism and male-feminism; the African American struggle for human and civil rights; intellectual adoration of, and admiration for, Frederick Douglass and Alexander Crummell; disputations with Booker T. Washington and Marcus Garvey—an enigmatic and eclectic combination of critical ideas and interests unfolds across the landscape of William Edward Burghardt Du Bois's life and work. For many he represents one of the most critical and contradictory race theorists of the twentieth century. Another host argues that he is "the father of Pan-Africanism" and a pioneering architect of anti-colonial theory and praxis. For others, such as Cedric Robinson (2000) in *Black Marxism*, Du Bois was one of the most sophisticated Marxist theorists in American radical history, though "his work had origins independent of the impulses of Western liberal and radical thought" (p. 186). Still others, such as Joy James, Beverly Guy-Sheftall, Cheryl Townsend Gilkes, and Nellie McKay contend that Du Bois's name, along with that of Charles Lenox Remond and Frederick Douglass, belongs on that very short list of men who openly advocated gender equality and spoke out against female domination and discrimination. His work, in many senses similar to that of C. L. R. James and Frantz Fanon, and due no doubt to its highly porous nature, has been critically analyzed and appropriated by scores of academics and political activists who harbor harrowingly different intellectual and ideological agendas.

Though his thought took several crucial (and critical!) philosophical and political twists and turns in his eighty-year publishing career (from 1883 to 1963), it is Du Bois's concepts of race and anti-racism, Pan-Africanism and anti-colonialism, critique of capitalism and critical Marxism and, most recently, his anti-sexism and male-feminism that have come under the greatest scholarly scrutiny and can be said to have ushered in the contemporary Du Bois renaissance.[1] But, I should bellow from the beginning, rarely if ever have these central themes in Du Bois's oeuvre been juxtaposed and examined for their import to *critical theory*. That is, theory that, first, transverses traditional academic boundaries (disciplines) by synthesizing the most emancipatory elements of philosophy, politics, the arts, and the social sciences; second, provides comprehensive criticisms of a wide range of imperial impulses in social, political, and cultural phenomena and practices—from racism to religion, sexism to sexuality, aesthetics to athletics, and mass movements to the mass media; and, finally, projects alternatives to *what is* (domination and discrimination) by arguing on ethical grounds for *what ought to be* and/or *what could be* (human liberation via social transformation). To be sure, Du Bois's thought has traveled an almost unfathomable tract of intellectual terrain, receiving commentary and criticism from philosophers, historians, political scientists, economists, literary theorists, feminists, Pan-Africanists, and Marxists, to name only a few scholarly and political communities. However, on no occasion have his thought and texts been critically engaged for their contribution to critical theory of contemporary society.

This book will analyze W. E. B. Du Bois's thought for its contribution to contemporary critical theory in particular, and Africana Studies theory and methodology more generally. Consequently, it is not my intention to offer a definitive or even exhaustive treatment of his biography or life-work, which would seem rather redundant coming so quickly on the heels of David Levering Lewis's Pulitzer Prize-winning volumes (see Lewis 1993, 2000). I am concerned here primarily, and almost exclusively, with Du Bois's theoretical and political legacy—that is, with the ways he constructed, deconstructed, and reconstructed theory and the aims, objectives, and outcomes of his theoretical applications and discursive practices. He consistently appropriated, revised and rejected disparate concepts, always integrating what he perceived to be the most radical (and later *revolutionary*) thought into his critical sociotheoretical discourse. His work in several senses lends itself to critical social theory because it provides a model and methodology to affect and chart social change.[2]

Commencing with a discussion of some of the central issues involved in critical socio-theoretical discourse in continental and diasporan African (i.e., Africana) intellectual history, the following studies will focus on Du Bois's four key contributions to critical theory, and specifically critical theory in the interest of continental and diasporan Africans—what I have referred to elsewhere as *Africana critical theory*.[3] Though he made many theoretical breakthroughs and, as we will see, covered and crisscrossed a great deal of uncharted and ofttime treacherous intellectual terrain, many of Du Bois's major positions arise and recur as he addressed issues involving race, gender, and the dual dimensions of class exploitation and oppression in Africana life-worlds and lived-experiences. In an effort to focus exclusively, but not superficially, on what I have identified as Du Bois's seminal and most significant donations to the discourse and development of critical social theory, I undertake extended analysis of his concepts of race, anti-racism, and critical race theory; his critique of sexism, and particularly patriarchy; his anti-colonialism and (proto) postcolonial theory; and his concept of a race-centered and racism-conscious critique of capitalism and Marxism.

In order to understand Du Bois's contributions to critical theory, and his contributions to the discourse and development of Africana critical theory in specific, one must first engage the discursive formations of Africana Studies and the history of Africana thought. Why, we are quick to ask? Because Du

Bois is almost unanimously acknowledged as an important architect of Africana Studies and a doyen in Africana philosophical discourse (see Anderson and Zuberi, 2000; Bell, Grosholz and Stewart, 1996; Clarke, Jackson, Kaiser and O'Dell, 1970; Marable, 2000, 2005; Stewart, 1984; Warren, 1984; Williams, 1983). His thought and texts contribute to virtually every major area of inquiry in Africana Studies. Therefore, to get a grasp of Du Bois's thought, let alone grapple with the issues it addresses, we have to critically engage the classical thought-traditions that fueled and formed it, as well as the contemporary thought-traditions that it gave rise to and laid a foundation for. More than any other intellectual arena, Africana Studies has consistently given Du Bois's thought and texts its highest commendations and its most meticulous criticisms. It is also the academic discipline, perhaps, most modeled on his extensive and diverse intellectual activity because it is a *transdisciplinary discipline* (i.e., a discipline that transverses and transcends traditional single phenomenon-focused disciplines) that seeks solutions to Africana peoples' problems by employing the theoretic breakthroughs of both the social sciences and humanities.

Africana Studies has long had a ragged relationship with Du Bois and his discourse. There have been times throughout the history of modern Africana thought when it was intellectually en vogue to vituperatively criticize various intellectual and political positions he held. At other times it has been intellectually fashionable to uncritically praise Du Bois for being prophetic and foresighted on certain issues. There was even a period when his biography was privileged over his philosophy, and another when his European influences were indomitably argued to be more influential on his ideas than his Africana influences. In the present volume I am concerned with this discourse only insofar as it will enable me to illuminate ways in which Du Bois's thought and texts can be utilized to develop a critical theory of contemporary society more thoroughly and compassionately concerned with the life-worlds and lived-experiences of continental and diasporan Africans. This book, then, is principally concerned with paradigmatic shifts and theoretic revolutions in Du Bois's intellectual history and the ways these thought-transformations provide a new and novel paradigm and distinct theoretical point of departure for contemporary philosophy, radical politics, and critical social theory.

The central focus of this book will be Du Bois's donations to the discourse and development of a critical theory of contemporary society that highlights and accents the major issues of modern Africana existence. From his doctoral dissertation, *The Suppression of the African Slave Trade* (1896), to his posthumously published autobiography, *The Autobiography of W. E. B. Du Bois* (1968a), Du Bois theorized and documented continental and diasporan African history, culture, and struggle, increasingly emphasizing black radical thought and black revolutionary practices. In exploring his life-work from a critical theoretical frame of reference, we are faced with the fact that the bulk of his body of writings fall within the conceptual parameters and academic context(s) of what is currently called Africana Studies.

Part of my task in the remainder of this introduction entails elaborating on the distinct conception of critical theory that will be employed in the chapters to follow. This conception of critical theory, Africana critical theory, is grounded in and grows out of Africana Studies, and specifically the discourses of Africana philosophy, Africana social and political theory, and Africana intellectual history. Contrary to the plethora of polemics, simplifications, mystifications, and misinterpretations of Du Bois, his thought makes several significant contributions to the discourses of Africana Studies and contemporary critical theory. In an effort to emphasize these contributions, I shall discuss the history of Africana thought, the role and tasks of theory in Africana Studies, critical social theory in general, and, ultimately, my conception of Africana critical theory. By analyzing and criticizing Du Bois's thought and the politico-economic and socio-cultural situations to which it responds, his ideas and actions can be accessed and assessed for their contribution to: (1) contemporary Africana philosophy and social theory; (2) modern mass movements calling for radical social transformation, from the Civil Rights and Black Power movements to the brewing anti-war and peace movements at the dawn of the twenty-first century; and (3) future moral and multicultural social thought and practices. In what follows I will, first, engage the discourse and development of Africana Studies. Then, I discuss the nature and nuances of philosophy and critical theory in Africana Studies discourse. Third, I introduce my conception of Africana critical theory and reintroduce Du Bois from this new frame of reference. And, finally, I conclude this introduction by emphasizing the book's recurring theme of the radical reconstruction of contemporary critical social theory and outlining the distinct theoretical thrusts of each of the subsequent chapters.

DISCIPLINARY DEVELOPMENTS AND NEW DISCURSIVE DIRECTIONS IN AFRICANA STUDIES

Africana Studies blurs the lines between disciplines and offers interdisciplinarity in the interest of continental and diasporan Africans. Drawing from and contributing to the natural and social sciences, and the arts and humanities, Africana Studies is a broadly construed *interdisciplinary discipline* which critically interprets and analyzes classical and contemporary continental and diasporan African thought and practice. The agnomen *Africana* has come to represent many things to many different people, and not all of them of African descent. It has a long and discontinuous history of use, from W. E. B. Du Bois's 1909 contraction of the term for a proposed encyclopedia "covering the chief points in the history and condition of the Negro race," with contributions by a board of one hundred "Negro American, African and West Indian" intellectuals (1997b, p. 146); to James Turner's (1984) assertion that "the concept *Africana* is derived from the 'African continuum and African consociation' which posits fundamental interconnections in the global Black experience" (p. viii); to Lucius Outlaw's (1997) utilization of the term as a "gathering" and/or "umbrella" notion "under which to situate the articulations (writings, speeches, etc.)" of continental and diasporan Africans "collectively . . . which are to be regarded as philosophy" (p. 64); to Emmanuel Eze's (1997b) employment of the heading to emphasize, in a "serious sense," the historical and cultural range and diversity of continental and diasporan African thought in consequence of "*the single most important factor that drives the field and the contemporary practice of African/a Philosophy . . . the brutal encounter of the African world with European modernity*" (p. 4; emphasis in original); and, finally, to Lewis Gordon's (2000a) recent adoption of the term to refer to "an area of thought that focuses on theoretical questions raised by struggles over ideas in African cultures and their hybrid and creolized forms in Europe, North America, Central and South America, and the Caribbean" (p. 1). Whether "thought," "philosophy," or "studies" accompanies *Africana*, the term and its varying conceptual meanings have, indeed, traveled a great deal of social, political, historical, cultural, philosophical, and physical terrain. However, if there is one constant concerning the appellation "Africana," it is the simple fact that for nearly a century intellectuals and activists of African origin and descent have employed the term to indicate and include the life-worlds and lived-experiences of continental *and* diasporan Africans.

Disciplinary development is predicated on discursive formations to which *Africana Studies*—that is, African, African American, Afro-Latino, Caribbean, Pan-African, and Black Studies—is not immune.[4] Discursive formations, meaning essentially knowledge production and dissemination, what we would call in Africana Studies epistemologies or theories of knowledge, provide the theoretical thrust(s) that help to guide and establish interdisciplinary arenas while simultaneously exploding traditional disciplinary boundaries. As a consequence of the over-emphasis on experience and emotion in the study of continental and diasporan African life there has been a critical turn toward Africana thought or, more properly, Africana philosophy.[5]

After five hundred years of the Europeanization of human consciousness, it is not simply European imperial thought and texts that stand in need of

Africana critical analysis. Africana theorists, taking a long and critical look at Africana history and culture, argue that consequent to holocaust, enslavement and, as Fanon (1965, 1967, 1968, 1969) and Ngũgĩ (1986, 1993, 1997) note, physical *and* psychological colonization, Africana people have been systematically socialized and ideologically educated to view and value the world, and to think and act employing a European imperial *modus operandi*. This means, then, that many Africana people, many of Du Bois's most beloved "black folk" in the modern moment, have internalized not simply imperial thought and practices but, to put it plainly, *anti-African* thought and practices.

Internalized anti-African thought and practices have problematicized and plagued Africana Studies almost since its inception. It has led to a specific species of intellectual reductionism that turns on an often clandestine credo which warrants that black people ante up experience and emotion where white people contribute theory and/or philosophy. The internalization of this thought expressed itself most notably in the work of Negritude poet and theorist Leopold Sedar Sénghor (1995), who infamously asserted that reason is Europe's great contribution to human culture and civilization where rhythm is Africa's eternal offering. In Sénghor's ironic infamous words: "'I think therefore I am,' wrote Descartes, who was the European *par excellence*. The African could say, 'I feel, I dance the Other, I am'" (p. 120).[6]

The implication, and what I wish to emphasize here is not that there is no place for discussions of the experiential aspects of black life in Africana Studies, but that this *experiential/emotional approach* has become, in many scholars' and students' minds, the primary and most privileged way of doing Africana Studies. On the one hand, one of the positives of the experiential/emotional approach to black life obviously revolves around the historical fact that people of African descent have long been denied an inner life and time and space to explore and discover their deep (social, political, and spiritual, among other) desires, what black feminist theorist bell hooks (1990, 1995) has referred to as "radical black subjectivity." Even the very thought, let alone serious consideration of an Africana point of view would be an admission of consciousness, which would in turn call for the dynamism and dialecticism of reciprocal recognition and some form of (hopefully *critical*) reflection. On the other hand, one of the many negatives of privileging the experiential/emotional approach is that we end up with a multiplicity of narratives and biographies of blacks' experience of the world, but with no theoretical tools (*developed* and/or *developing*) in which to critically interpret these distinctly black experiences. In some senses this situation forces Africana Studies scholars and students to turn to the theoretical breakthroughs and analytical advances of other (read: "traditional," white/Eurocentric) disciplines in order to interpret black life-worlds and lived-experiences. Thus, this reproduces

intellectually what Africana men, women and children have long been fighting against physically and psychologically: a dependency and/or colonial
complex.[7]

A *disciplinary dependency complex* collapses and compartmentalizes the
entirety of black existence into the areas of experience, emotion, intuition,
and creative expression, and advances white theory, white philosophy, white
science, and white concepts of culture and civilization as the normal and neutral sites and sources of intellectual acumen and cutting-edge criticism. This
conundrum takes us right back to Du Bois's (1986a) contention in *The Souls
of Black Folk* that black people not be confused with the problems they have
historically confronted and continue currently to confront (pp. 363-371; see
also Anderson and Zuberi, 2000). "Africanity," or blackness, to put it bluntly,
has so much more to offer the human and social sciences than merely its ex-
periential/emotional aspects.[8] Without conscious and conscientious *conceptual generation* Africana Studies will be nothing more than an academic
ghetto. By "academic ghetto," I mean a place where Africana intellectuals exist in intellectual poverty, on the fringes of the white academy, and eagerly ac-
cepting the dominant white intellectuals' interpretations of reality.

If, indeed, Africana Studies seeks to seriously engage continental and diasporan African thought *and* practice, it cannot with the experiential/emotional
approach alone, which almost by default emphasizes Africana practice, and
privileges it over Africana thought. The experiential/emotional approach in
Africana Studies has a tendency to employ white theoretical frameworks to interpret and explore Africana practice(s); meaning essentially that it uses white
theory to engage black behavior, negating black thought on, and black critical
conceptual frameworks created for the interpretation of, black behavior. What
is more, the experiential/emotional approach, by focusing on black actions and
emotions and relying on white theory to interpret these actions and emotions,
handicaps and hinders the development of Africana Studies, because disciplines cannot and do not develop without some form of conceptual generation
that is internal and endemic to their distinct disciplinary matrices and ongoing
academic agendas. This *disciplinary dependency complex* on white theory, instead of aiding in the development of Africana Studies as an independent interdisciplinary discipline, unwittingly helps to confirm the age-old anti-African
myth that thought or philosophy should be left to whites, and that blacks should
stick to the arts, entertainment, and athletics. The negation or, at the least, the
neglect of thought or philosophy in the systematic and scientific study of continental and diasporan Africans' experience and *thought*ful and/or *thought*-
filled engagement of the world has led to several counter-discursive formula-
tions and formations, two of the more recent being *Africana philosophy* and
what I have humbly chronicled and called *Africana critical theory*.

AFRICANA PHILOSOPHY AND
CRITICAL THEORY OF/IN AFRICANA STUDIES

In order to theorize blackness—and some might even argue in order to practice blackness, which is to say, to actually and fully *live* our Africanity—some type of thought, or rather more to the point, some form of philosophy will be required. "Days are gone," the Nigerian philosopher Emmanuel Eze (1997a) asserts, "when one people, epoch, or tradition could arrogantly claim to have either singularly invented philosophy, or to have a monopoly over the specific yet diverse processes of search for knowledge typical to the discipline of philosophy" (p. ix). And I think that it is important for us to extend this critical caveat further to encompass, in specific, the work of contemporary Western European-trained philosophers of African descent in relation to the discursive formations of Africana philosophy. Being biologically black, or of African origin and/or descent, and having received training in Western European philosophy does not necessarily make one and one's thought and texts Africana philosophy. A critical distinction, then, is being made at this juncture between *philosophers of African origin and descent* and *Africana philosophers*. The former grouping has more to do with biology, phenotype, and academic training than any distinct philosophical focus that would warrant an appellation of a "school" or "tradition," while the latter grouping is consciously concerned with discursive formations and practices geared toward the development of thought and thought-traditions that seek solutions to problems plaguing people of African origin and descent. The latter grouping also, like Africana critical theory, does not adhere to the protocols and practices of racialism(s) and traditional disciplinary development, but harbors an epistemic openness toward the contributions of a wide range of thinkers (and doers) from transethnic, multiracial and multicultural backgrounds, various academic disciplines, and assorted activist-traditions.[9]

All of this brings us to the questions recently raised by the discursive formation of *Africana critical theory of contemporary society*. Africana critical theory is *theory critical of domination and discrimination in classical and contemporary, continental and diasporan African life-worlds and lived-experiences*. It is a style of critical theorizing, inextricably linked to progressive political practice(s), that highlights and accents Africana radicals' and revolutionaries' answers to the key questions posed by the major forms and forces of domination and discrimination that have historically and continue currently to shape and mold our modern/postmodern and/or neo-colonial/postcolonial world.

Africana critical theory involves not only the critique of domination and discrimination, but also a deep commitment to human liberation and radical social transformation. Similar to other traditions of critical social theory, Africana critical theory is concerned with thoroughly analyzing contemporary society "in light of its used and unused or abused capabilities for improving the human [and deteriorating environmental] condition" (Marcuse, 1964, p. xlii). What distinguishes and helps to define Africana critical theory is its emphasis on the often-overlooked continental and diasporan African contributions to critical theory. It draws from critical thought and philosophical traditions rooted in the realities of continental and diasporan African history, culture, and struggle. Which, in other words, is to say that Africana critical theory inherently employs a methodological orientation that highlights and accents Africana theories and philosophies "born of struggle" (Harris, 1983). And, if it need be said at this point, Africana struggle is simultaneously national and international, transgender and transgenerational and, therefore, requires multidimensional and multiperspectival theory in which to interpret and explain the various diverse phenomena, philosophical motifs and social and political movements characteristic of—to use Fanon's famous phrase—*l'expérience vécue du Noir* ("the lived-experience of the black"), that is, the reality of constantly wrestling simultaneously with racism, sexism, colonialism and capitalism, among other forms of imperialism (Fanon, 2001; see also Gordon, Sharpley-Whiting, and White, 1996; Sekyi-Otu, 1996; Weate, 2001).

Why, one may ask, focus on Africana radicals' and revolutionaries' theories of social change? An initial answer to this question takes us directly to Du Bois's dictum, in the "Conservation of Races" (1897), that people of African origin and descent "have a contribution to make to civilization and humanity" that their historic experiences of holocaust, enslavement, colonization, and segregation have long throttled and thwarted (1986a, p. 825). He maintained that, "[t]he methods which we evolved for opposing slavery and fighting prejudice are not to be forgotten, but learned for our own and others' instruction" (Du Bois, 1973, p. 144). Hence, Du Bois is suggesting that Africana liberation struggle(s)—i.e., the combined continental and diasporan African fight(s) for freedom—may have much to contribute to critical theory, and his comments here also hit at the heart of one of the core concepts of critical theory, the *critique of domination and discrimination* (Agger, 1992; O'Neill, 1976; Rasmussen and Swindal, 2004).

From a methodological point of view, critical theory seeks to simultaneously: (1) comprehend the established society; (2) criticize its contradictions and conflicts; and (3) create egalitarian (most often democratic socialist) alternatives (Morrow, 1994). The ultimate emphasis on the creation and offering of alternatives brings to the fore another core concept of critical theory, its *theory of liberation and social transformation* (Marcuse, 1968, 1969; Marsh, 1995, 1999; Ray, 1993). The paradigms and points of departure for critical theorists vary depending on the theorists' race, gender, sexual orientation, religious affiliation, nationality, intellectual interests, and political persuasions. For instance, many European critical theorists turn to Hegel, Marx, Freud, Gramsci, Sartre, and/or the Frankfurt School (Adorno, Benjamin, Fromm, Habermas, Horkheimer, and Marcuse), among others, because they understand these thinkers' thoughts and texts to speak in special ways to modern and/or "postmodern" life-worlds and lived-experiences (see Held, 1980; Jay, 1996; Kellner, 1989; Wiggerhaus, 1995). My work, Africana critical theory, utilizes the thought and texts of Africana intellectual ancestors as critical theoretical paradigms and points of departure because so much of their thought is not simply problem-posing but solution-providing where the specific life-struggles of persons of African descent (or "black people") are concerned—human life-struggles, it should be said without hyperbole and high-sounding words, which European critical theorists (who are usually Eurocentric and, often unwittingly, white supremacist) have woefully neglected in their classical and contemporary critical theoretical discourse; a discourse that ironically has consistently congratulated itself on the universality of its interests, all the while, for the most part, side-stepping the centrality of racism and colonialism within its own discursive communities and out in the wider world. Moreover, my conception of critical theory is critically preoccupied with classical Africana thought-traditions not only because of the long unlearned lessons they have to teach contemporary critical theorists about the dialectics of being simultaneously radically humanist and morally committed agents of a specific nation or cultural groups' liberation and social(ist) transformation, but also because the ideas and ideals of continental and diasporan African intellectual-activists of the past indisputably prefigures and provides a foundation for contemporary Africana Studies, and Africana philosophy in specific. In fact, in many ways, Africana critical theory, besides being grounded in and growing out of the discourse of Africana Studies, can be said to be an offshoot of Africana philosophy, which according to the acclaimed African American philosopher Lucius Outlaw (1997), is:

a "gathering" notion under which to situate the articulations (writings, speeches, etc.), and traditions of the same, of Africans and peoples of African descent collectively, as well as the sub-discipline or field-forming, tradition-defining, tradition-organizing reconstructive efforts which are (to be) regarded as philosophy. However, "Africana philosophy" is to include, as well, the work of those persons who are neither African nor of African descent but who recognize the legitimacy and importance of the issues and endeavors that constitute the disciplinary activities of African or [African Caribbean or] African American philosophy and contribute to the efforts—persons whose work justifies their being called "Africanists." Use of the qualifier "Africana" is consistent with the practice of naming intellectual traditions and practices in terms of the national, geographic, cultural, racial, and/or ethnic descriptor or identity of the persons who initiated and were/are the primary practitioners—and/or are the subjects and objects—of the practices and traditions in question (e.g., "American," "British," "French," "German," or "continental" philosophy). (p. 64)

✔ Africana critical theory is distinguished from Africana philosophy by the fact that critical theory cannot be situated within the world of conventional academic disciplines and divisions of labor. It transverses and transgresses boundaries between traditional disciplines and accents the interconnections and intersections of philosophy, history, politics, economics, the arts, psychology and sociology, among other disciplines. Critical theory is contrasted with mainstream, monodisciplinary social theory through its multidisciplinary methodology and its efforts to develop a comprehensive dialectical theory of domination and liberation specific to the special needs of contemporary society (see Agger, 1998; Habermas, 1984, 1987a, 1988, 1989b; Outlaw, 1983a, 1983b, 1983c, 1983d; Wilkerson and Paris, 2001). Africana philosophy has a very different agenda, one that seems to me more meta-philosophical than philosophical at this point, because it entails theorizing-on-tradition and tradition-construction more than tradition extension and expansion through the production of normative theory and critical pedagogical praxis aimed at application (i.e., immediate self and social transformation).[10]

The primary purpose of critical theory is to relate radical thought to revolutionary practice, which is to say that its focus—philosophical, social, and political—is always and ever the search for ethical alternatives and viable moral solutions to the most pressing problems of our present age. Critical theory is not about, or rather *should not* be about allegiance to intellectual ancestors and/or ancient schools of thought, but about using *all* (without regard to race, gender, class, sexual orientation, and/or religious affiliation) accumulated radical thought and revolutionary practices in the interest of liberation and social(ist) transformation. With this in mind, Cornel West's (1982) contentions concerning "Afro-American critical thought" offer an outline for the type of theorizing that Africana critical theory endeavors:

> The object of inquiry for Afro-American critical thought is the past and present, the doings and the sufferings of African people in the United States. Rather than a new scientific discipline or field of study, it is a genre of writing, a textuality, a mode of discourse that interprets, describes, and evaluates Afro-American life in order comprehensively to understand and effectively to transform it. It is not concerned with "foundations" or transcendental "grounds" but with how to build its language in such a way that the configuration of sentences and the con-

stellation of paragraphs themselves create a textuality and distinctive discourse which are a material force for Afro-American freedom. (p. 15)

Though Africana critical theory encompasses and is concerned with much more than the life-worlds and lived-experiences of "African people in the United States," West's comments here are helpful, as they give us a glimpse at the kind of connections critical theorists make in terms of their ideas having an impact and significant influence on society. Africana critical theory is not thought-for-thought's sake (as it often seems is the case with so much contemporary philosophy—Africana philosophy notwithstanding), on the contrary, Africana critical theory is thought-for-life-and-liberation's sake. It is not only a style of writing which focuses on radicalism and revolution, but a new way of *thinking* and *doing* revolution that is based and constantly being built on the radicalisms and revolutions of the past.

From West's frame of reference, "Afro-American philosophy expresses the particular American variation of European modernity that Afro-Americans helped shape in this country and must contend with in the future. While it might be possible to articulate a competing Afro-American philosophy based principally on African norms and notions, it is likely that the result would be theoretically thin" (p. 24). Contrary to West's comments, Africana critical theory represents and registers as that "possible articulat[ion] of a competing [Africana] philosophy based principally on African norms and notions," and though he thinks that the results will be "theoretically thin," Africana critical theory—following Fanon (1968, 1969)—understands this risk to be part of the price the oppressed ("the wretched of the earth") must be willing to pay for their (intellectual, political, and physical) freedom. Intellectually audacious, especially considering the widespread Eurocentricism and white supremacism of contemporary conceptual generation, Africana critical theory does not acquiesce or give priority and special privilege to European history, culture, or thought. It turns to the long overlooked thought and texts of women and men of African descent who have developed and contributed radical thought and revolutionary practices that could possibly aid us in our endeavors to continuously create a theory critical of domination and discrimination in contemporary culture and society.

Above and beyond all of the aforementioned, Africana critical theory is about offering alternatives to *what is* (domination and discrimination), by projecting possibilities of *what ought to be* and/or *what could be* (human liberation and revolutionary social transformation). It is not afraid, to put it as plainly as possible, to critically engage and dialogue deeply with European and/or other cultural groups' thought-traditions. In fact, it often finds critical cross-cultural dialogue necessary considering the historical conundrums and current shared conditions and crises of the modern, almost completely transethnic and multicultural world (see Goldberg 1994; Goldberg and Solomos, 2002). Africana critical theory, quite simply, does not privilege or give priority to European and/or other cultural groups' thought-traditions since its philosophical foci and primary purpose revolve around the search for solutions to the most pressing social and political problems in continental and diasporan African life-worlds and lived-experiences in the present age.

EPISTEMIC OPENNESS AND THEORETIC WEAKNESSES IN AFRICANA THOUGHT

Africana critical theory navigates many theoretic spaces that extend well beyond the established intellectual boundaries of Africana Studies. At this point, it is clearly characterized by an *epistemic openness* to theories and methodologies usually understood to be incompatible with one another. Besides providing it with a simultaneously creative and critical tension, Africana critical theory's *antithetical conceptual contraction* (i.e., its utilization of concepts perceived to be contradictory to, and in conflict and competing with one another) also gives it its theoretic rebelliousness and untamable academic quality. Which is to say that Africana critical theory exists or is able to exist well beyond the boundaries of the academy and academic disciplines because the bulk of its theoretic base, its primary points of departure, are radical and revolutionary Africana political practices and social movements. The word "theory," then, in the appellation "Africana critical theory" is being defined and, perhaps, radically refined, for specific discursive purposes and practices. This is extremely important to point out because there has been a long intellectual history of chaos concerning the nature and tasks of "theory" in Africana Studies.

To an Africana critical theorist, it seems highly questionable, if not just downright silly at this juncture in the history of Africana thought, to seek a theoretical Holy Grail that will serve as a panacea to our search for the secrets to being, culture, politics or society. Taking our cue from Du Bois and C. L. R. James, it may be better to conceive of theory as an "instrument" or, as Frantz Fanon and Amilcar Cabral would have it, a "weapon" used to attack certain targets of domination and discrimination. Theories are, among many other things, optics, ways of seeing; they are perspectives which illuminate specific phenomena. However, as with any perspective, position or standpoint, each theory has its blind spots and lens limitations, what we call in the contemporary discourse of Africana philosophy, *theoretical myopia*.

Recent theoretical debates in Africana Studies have made us painfully aware of the fact that theories are discipline-specific constructs and products, created in particular intellectual contexts, for particular intellectual purposes (see Aldridge and Young, 2000; Asante and Karenga, 2006; Conyers, 1997; Hall, 1999; Marable, 2000, 2005; Norment, 2001). Contemporary Africana thought has also enabled us see that theories are always grounded in and grow out of specific social discourses, political practices, and national and international institutions. In *The Hermeneutics of African Philosophy*, the Eritrean philosopher Tsenay Serequeberhan (1994) correctly contends that "political 'neutrality' in philosophy, as in most other things, is at best a 'harmless' naïveté, and at worst a pernicious subterfuge for hidden agendas" (p. 4). Each discipline has an academic agenda. Therefore, the theories and methodologies of a discipline promote the development of that particular discipline. Theories emerging from traditional disciplines that claim to provide an eternal philosophical foundation or universal and neutral knowledge transcendent of historical horizons, cultural conditions and social struggles, or a metatheory (i.e., a theory about theorizing) that purports absolute truth that transcends the interests of specific theorists and their theories, have been and are being vigorously rejected by Africana Studies scholars and students. Theory, then, as Serequeberhan says of philosophy, is a "critical and explorative engagement of one's own cultural specificity and lived historicalness. It is a critically aware explorative appropriation of our cultural, political, and historical existence" (p. 23).[11]

Theoretic discourse does not simply fall from the sky like wind-blown rain, leaving no traces of the direction from which it came and its initial point of departure. On the contrary, it registers as and often radically represents critical concerns interior to epistemologies and experiences arising out of a specific cultural and historical horizon within which it is located and discursively situated. In other words, similar to a finely crafted woodcarving or hand-woven garment, theories retain the intellectual and cultural markings of their makers, and though they can and do "travel" and "cross borders," they are optimal in their original settings and when applied to the original phenomena that inspired their creation (Said, 1999, 2000; Giroux, 1992).

A more modest conception of theory sees it, then, as an instrument (or, as Michel Foucault would have it, a "tool") to help us illuminate and navigate specific social spaces, pointing to present and potential problems, interpreting and criticizing them, and ultimately offering ethical and egalitarian alternatives to them (e.g., see Foucault, 1977a, 1977b, 1984, 1988, 1997, 1998, 2000). At their best, theories not only illuminate social realities, but they help individuals make sense of their life-worlds and lived-experiences. To do this effectively, theories utilize images, arguments, symbols, concepts, and narratives. Modern metatheory often accents the interesting fact that theories have literary components and qualities: they narrate or tell stories, employ rhetoric and semiotics and, similar to literature, often offer accessible interpretations of classical and contemporary life. However, theories also have cognitive and kinship components that allow them to connect with other theories' concepts and common critical features, as when a variety of disparate theories of Africana Studies discourse raise questions of race and racism, or questions of identity and liberation.

There are many different types of theory, from literary theory to linguistic theory, cultural theory to aesthetic theory, and political theory to postmodern theory. Africana critical theory is a critical conceptual framework that seeks an ongoing synthesis of the most emancipatory elements of a wide-range of *social theory* in the interest of continental and diasporan Africans. This means Africana critical theory often identifies and isolates the social implications of various theories, some of which were not created to have any concrete connections with the social world (and certainly not the African world), but currently do as a consequence of the ways they have been appropriated and articulated.

Here it is extremely important to recall the history of theory. Theories are instruments and, therefore, can be put to use in a multiplicity of manners. Historically, theories have always traveled outside of their original contexts, but two points of importance should be made here. The first point has to do with something Edward Said (1999, 2000) said long ago, that theories lose some of their original power when taken out of their original intellectual and cultural contexts, because the sociopolitical situation is different, the suffering and/or struggling people are different, and the aims and objectives of their movements are different. The second point is reflexive and has to do with the modern moment in the history of theory: Never before have so many theories traveled so many mental miles away from their intellectual milieux. This speaks to the new and novel theoretical times that we are passing through. Part of what we have to do, then, is identify those theories ("instruments" and/or "weapons") that will aid us most in our struggles against racism, sexism, capitalism, and colonialism, among other epochal imperial issues.

The turn toward and emphasis on social theory suggests several of Africana critical theory's key concerns, such as the development of a synthetic sociopolitical discourse that earnestly and accessibly addresses issues arising from: everyday black life in white supremacist societies; women's daily lives in male supremacist societies; and the commonalities of and the distinct differences between black life in colonial and capitalist countries. Social theoretical discourse is important because it provides individuals and groups with topographies of their social terrains. This discourse also often offers concepts and categories that aid individuals and groups in critically engaging and radically altering their social worlds (see Calhoun, 1995; R. Collins, 2000; Habermas, 1988; B. Turner 1996).

Social theories, in a general sense, are simultaneously heuristic and discursive devices for exploring and explaining the social world. They accent social conditions and can often provoke social action and political praxis. Social theories endeavor to provide a panoramic picture that enables individuals to conceptualize and contextualize their life-worlds and lived-experiences within the wider field of sociopolitical relations and institutions. Additionally, social theories can aid individuals in their efforts to understand and alter particular sociopolitical events and artifacts by analyzing their receptions, relations, and ongoing effects.

In addition to socio-theoretical discourse, Africana critical theory draws directly from the discourse of *dialectics* because it seeks to understand and, if necessary, alter society as a whole, not simply some isolated or culturally confined series of phenomena. The emphasis on dialectics also sends a signal to those social theorists and others who are easily intellectually intimidated by efforts to grasp and grapple with the whole of human history, that Africana critical theory is not in any sense a traditional social theory but *a social activist and political praxis-promoting theory* that seriously seeks the radical redistribution of social wealth and political power. The dialectical dimension of Africana critical theory enables it to make connections between seemingly isolated and unrelated parts of society, demonstrating how, for instance, neutral social terrain, such as the education industries, the entertainment industries, the prison industrial complex, the political electoral process, or the realm of religion are sites and sources of ruling race, gender, and/or class privilege and power.[12]

Dialectics, the art of demonstrating the interconnectedness of parts to each other and to the overarching system or framework as a whole, distinguishes Africana critical theory from other theories in Africana Studies because it simultaneously searches for progressive and retrogressive aspects of Africana, Eurocentric, and other cultural groups' thought-traditions. This means, then, that Africana critical theory offers an external and internal critique, which is also to say that it is *a self-reflexive social theory*: a social theory that relentlessly reexamines and refines its own philosophical foundations, methods, positions, and presuppositions. Africana critical theory's dialectical dimension also distinguishes it from other traditions and versions of critical theory because the connections it makes between social parts and the social whole are those that directly and profoundly affect Africana life-worlds and lived-experiences. No other tradition or version of critical theory has historically claimed or currently claims to highlight and accent sites of domination and sources of liberation in the interest of continental and diasporan Africans.

WEAPONS OF THEORY AND
THOUGHT-TRADITIONS OF PRAXIS

In "The Weapon of Theory," the Guinea-Bissaun freedom fighter Amilcar Cabral (1979) asserted: "every practice gives birth to a theory. If it is true that a revolution can fail, even though it be nurtured on perfectly conceived theories, no one has yet successfully practiced revolution without a revolutionary theory" (p. 123). Africana critical theory is a "revolutionary theory" and a beacon symbolizing the birth of a theoretical revolution in Africana Studies. Its basic aims and objectives speak to its radical character and critical qualities. It promotes social activism and political practice geared toward the development of an ethical and egalitarian society by pointing to: what needs to be transformed; what strategies and tactics might be most useful in the transformative efforts; and which agents and agencies could potentially carry out the social transformation.

Following Cabral (1972, 1973, 1979), Africana critical theory conceives of theory as a "weapon," and the history of Africana thought as its essential arsenal. As with any arsenal, a weapon is chosen or left behind based on the specifics of the mission, such as the target, terrain and time-sensitivity. The same may be said concerning "the weapon of theory." Different theories can be used for different purposes in disparate situations. The usefulness or uselessness of a particular theory depends on the task at hand and whether the theory in question is appropriate for the task. Theory can be extremely useful, but it is indeed a great and grave mistake to believe that there is a grand narrative, super-theory, or theoretical god that will provide the interpretive or explanatory keys to the political and intellectual kingdom (or queendom). Instead of arguing for a new super-theory, Africana critical theory advocates an ongoing synthesis of the most moral and radical political elements of classical and contemporary, continental and diasporan African thought-traditions with other cultural groups' progressive thought and political practices.

Contemporary society requires a continuous and increasingly high level of socio-political mapping because of the intensity of recent politico-ideological maneuvers—what the Italian critical theorist, Antonio Gramsci (2000, pp. 222–45), identified as "wars of position" and "wars of maneuver"—and the urgency of present socio-economic transformations.[13] History has unfolded to this in-between epoch of immense and provocative change, and many theories of contemporary society outline and attempt to explain an aspect of this change, and, as a result, are relevant with regard to certain social phenomena. But no single theory captures the complete socio-political picture, though there are plethoras that religiously claim to, and promise to provide their adherents with theoretical salvation in the sin-sick world of theory. It should be stated outright: *All theories have blind spots and lens limitations, and all theories make critical contributions as well.* Consequently, Africana critical theory advocates combining classical and contemporary theory from diverse academic disciplines and activist-traditions; though Africana thought, it must be made clear, is always and ever Africana critical theory's primary point of departure. My conception of critical social theory keeps in mind that the mappings of each theory provide some novel insights, but that these insights alone are not enough to affect the type of social change needed. It is with this understanding that Africana critical theory draws from the diverse discursive formations and practices of a wide range of Africana thought-traditions, such as African, African Caribbean, Afro-Latino, and African American philosophy; black postmodernism; black existentialism; black feminism; black Marxism; black nationalism; black liberation theology; womanism; critical race theory; philosophy of race; Negritude; and Pan-Africanism.

Africana critical theory relentlessly examines its own aims, objectives, positions, and methods, constantly putting them in question in an effort to radically refine and revise them. It is thus epistemically open, flexible and non-dogmatic, constantly exhibiting the ability to critically engage opposing theories and appropriate and incorporate progressive strains and reject retrogressive strains from them. It is here that Africana critical theory exhibits its theoretical sophistication and epistemological strength and stamina. Along with the various Africana theoretical perspectives which Africana critical theory employs as its primary points of departure, it also often critically engages many of the other major theoretical discourses of the modern moment, such as feminism, Marxism, pragmatism, existentialism, historicism, phenomenology, hermeneutics, semiotics, Frankfurt School critical theory, critical pedagogy, poststructuralism, postmodernism, and postcolonialism.

Africana critical theory engages other discursive formations because it is aware of the long history of appropriation and rearticulation in Africana thought. This takes us right back to the point made earlier about black people employing white theory to explore and explain black experiences. Instead of simply side-stepping this important intellectual history, Africana critical theory confronts it in an effort to understand and, if need be, alter it in an attempt to actualize black liberation on terms interior to contemporary Africana life-worlds and lived-experiences. This brings to mind the Caribbean philosopher Lewis Gordon's (1997a) contention that,

[T]heory, any theory, gains its sustenance from that which it offers *for* and *through* the lived-reality of those who are expected to formulate it. Africana philosophy's history of Christian, Marxist, Feminist, Pragmatist, Analytical, and Phenomenological thought has therefore been a matter of what specific dimensions each had to offer the existential realities of theorizing blackness. For Marxism, for instance, it was not so much its notion of "science" over all other forms of socialist theory, nor its promise of a world to win, that may have struck a resonating chord in the hearts of black Marxists. It was, instead, Marx and Engels' famous encomium of the proletarians' having nothing to lose but their chains. Such a call has obvious affinity for a people who have been so strongly identified with chattel slavery. (p. 4, emphasis in original)

It is important to understand and critically engage *why* continental and diasporan Africans have historically embraced and continue currently to embrace Eurocentric theory. Saying simply that blacks who did or who do embrace some aspects of white theory are intellectually insane or have an intellectual inferiority complex logically leads us to yet another discourse on black pathology. Persons of African origin and descent have been preoccupied in the modern moment with struggles against various forms and forces of domination, oppression, and exploitation. They, therefore, have been and remain attracted to theories that they understand to promise or provide tools to combat their domination, oppression, and/or exploitation. Though blacks in white supremacist societies are often rendered anonymous and/or are virtually invisible, they do not have a "collective mind" and have reached no consensus concerning which theories make the best weapons to combat their domination, oppression, and/or exploitation.[14] This means then that the way is epistemically open, and that those blacks who embrace or appropriate an aspect of white theory are not theoretically "lost" but, perhaps, simply employing the theoretical tools they understand to be most applicable and most readily available to them in their emancipatory efforts. Fanon speaks to this issue in a special way in both *Black Skin, White Masks* and *The Wretched of the Earth*, where he declares "the discoveries of Freud are of no use to us here" in the hyper-racialized and hyper-colonized life-worlds and lived-experiences of black folk, and "Marxist analysis should always be slightly stretched every time we have to do with the colonial problem. Everything up to and including the very nature of precapitalist society, so well explained by Marx, must here be thought out again" (1967, p. 104, 1968, p. 40). Fanon (1967) did not find anything of use in Freud for the particular kind of critical theoretical work he was doing in *Black Skin, White Masks*, and he even went so far to say that "there is a dialectical substitution when one goes from the psychology of the white man to that of the black" (p. 151). However, he was able to employ some aspects of Marxism for the kind of critical theoretical work he was doing in *The Wretched of the Earth*, but—and this is the main point—he critically engaged Marxism from his own critical subjective and radical political position as a hyper-racialized and hyper-colonized black man in a white supremacist capitalist and colonial world. In other words, his

Africanity, or non-Europeanness, was never left in abeyance or abandoned for the sake of Eurocentric theoretical synthesis. Approaching Marxism from this Africana critical theoretical angle, essentially employing it as a tool and not as a tenet, Fanon was able to extend and expand the critical theoretical and radical political range and reach of Marxism; more than merely Africanizing it, but seminally building on and moving beyond it to critically engage phenomena, life-worlds, and lived-experiences that Marx and his Eurocentric heirs have shamefully shoved to the intellectual outposts of their quite quarantined racial and colonial (and patriarchal) world of ideas.

It is quite possible, even with the advent and academization of Africana Studies from the mid-1960s to the present, that many contemporary intellectuals and activists of African descent are unaware of Africana intellectual history, and especially Africana critical thought-traditions, which is very different from saying that they are unattracted to or find little or nothing of use in Africana critical thought-traditions. Contemporary Africana theorists must take as one of their primary tasks making classical and contemporary Africana critical thought more accessible and attractive, particularly to blacks but also to non-African others. There simply is no substitute for the kinds of easily intelligible and epistemically open critical theoretical genealogies and contemporary conceptual generations that Africana Studies scholars must produce and propound to the Africana intelligentsia, the masses of black folk, well-meaning whites, and transethnic others if not simply Africana Studies but the souls of humble and hard-working black folk are to survive and continue to contribute to human culture and civilization.

Africana critical theory engages a wide and diverse range of theory emerging from the insurgent intellectuals of the academy and the activist-intellectuals of revolutionary socio-political movements. It understands each theory to offer enigmatic and illuminating insights because the more theory a theorist has at her/his disposal, the more issues and objects they can address, the more tasks they can perform, and the more theoretical targets they can terminate. As stated above, theories are optics or perspectives, and it is with this understanding that Africana critical theory contends that bringing a multiplicity of perspectives to bear on a phenomenon promises a greater grasp and a more thorough engagement and understanding of that phenomenon. For instance, many theories of race and racism arising from the discourse of Africana Studies have historically exhibited a serious weakness where sexism, and particularly patriarchy, is concerned. This situation was (to a certain extent) remedied and these theories were strengthened when Africana Women's Studies scholars diagnosed these one-dimensional and uni-gendered theories of race and racism, and coupled them with their own unique anti-racist interpretations of women's domination and discrimination and gender relations (see Butler and

Walter, 1991; Guy-Sheftall, 1995; Hull, Scott and Smith, 1982; James and Sharpley-Whiting, 2000; Nnaemeka, 1998). Indeed this is an ongoing effort, and clearly there is no consensus in Africana Studies as to the importance of critically engaging gender domination and discrimination in continental and diasporan African life-worlds and lived-experiences. But, whether we have consensus or not, which we probably never will, the key concern to keep in mind is that though it may not be theoretically fashionable to engage certain phenomena it does not necessarily mean that it is not theoretically important to engage that phenomena. As theorists part of our task is to bring unseen or often overlooked issues to the fore. In order to do this we may have to develop new concepts and categories so that others might be able to coherently comprehend these enigmatic issues.

In calling for bringing many theories to bear on a phenomenon, Africana critical theory is not eliding the fact that in many instances a single theory may be the best source of insight. For example, Pan-Africanism offers a paradigm for analyzing the history of Africana anti-colonialism and decolonization; where black Marxism accents the interconnections of racism and capitalism in black life; while black feminism often speaks to the intersection(s) of racism and sexism in black women's life-worlds. Africana critical theory chooses to deploy a theory based on its overarching aims and objectives, which are constantly informed by the ongoing quest for human freedom. It is not interested in an eclectic combination of theories—that is, *theoretical eclecticism*—simply for the sake of theoretical synthesis and contributing to the world of ideas, but its earnest interest lies in revolutionary social(ist) transformation in the interest of Africana and other oppressed people. Hence, at the heart of Africana critical theory there is simultaneously a revolutionary democratic socialist and revolutionary anti-racist humanist impulse which recurringly heeds the hallowed words of Du Bois (1971c) when he daringly declared in his often overlooked 1933 essay, "Where Do We Go from Here?":

[I]nstead of our facing today a stable world, moving at a uniform rate of progress toward well-defined goals, we are facing revolution. I trust you will not be scared by this word . . . I am not discussing a coming revolution, I am trying to impress the fact upon you that you are already in the midst of a revolution; you are already in the midst of war; that there has been no war of modern times that has taken so great a sacrifice of human life and human spirit as the extraordinary period through which we are passing today. Some people envisage revolution as a matter of blood and guns and the more visible methods of force. But that, after all, is merely the temporary and outward manifestation. Real revolution is within. That comes before or after the explosion—is a matter of long suffering and deprivation, the death of courage and the bitter triumph of despair. This is the inevitable prelude to decisive and enormous change, and that is the thing that is on us now. We are not called upon then to discuss whether we want revolution or not. We have got it. . . . [I]ndeed unless we suffer a spiritual revolution by which men are going to envisage small incomes and limited resources and endless work for the larger goals of life, unless we have this, nothing can save civilization either for white people or black. (pp. 150–51, 154)

As an early interdisciplinarian with strong socio-theoretical leanings and deep connections to the discourse of Africana Studies, Du Bois offers Africana critical theory an ideal point of departure to present and develop its discourse. This encounter will also allow us to radically reinterpret Du Bois as a critical social theorist whose extensive theoretical legacy has been omitted from the history of critical theory. Part of this omission, I have a sneaking suspicion, has to do with what is perceived as Du Bois's theoretical eclecticism—that is, his contraction of both Africana and European theory believed to be antithetical by thinkers interior to both thought-traditions. However, claims such as these fall flat when Du Bois's discourse is viewed from the epistemically open Africana critical theoretical framework, which accents the purposes and intended outcomes of theorists' intellectual appropriations and combinations. Africana critical theory, then, is not as concerned with *which* theories Du Bois used, as much as it seeks to discover and learn from *how* or the ways in which he creatively connected and used them.

Du Bois has been hailed as an historian, philosopher, sociologist, Marxist and political activist, but rarely if ever as an early interdisciplinary social theorist with concrete radical political commitments not simply to blacks, civil rights, and social justice, but to the multicultural masses, transethnic working-classes, women's liberation, and (neo)colonized and/or struggling people of color worldwide. He has long been praised and criticized by legions of scholars who have interpreted and rigorously reinterpreted his work, often overlooking its deep theoretical dimensions. In this book Du Bois's multifarious and ever-evolving social theory is situated at the center and examined for the first time for its significance to contemporary radical political thought and revolutionary social movements.

DU BOIS AND THE DISCOURSE OF AFRICANA CRITICAL THEORY

Interpretations of Du Bois are enormously varied and widespread throughout traditional and nontraditional disciplines. Previous books on Du Bois have neglected to present his complex and sometimes seemingly contradictory relationship to the wide range of theory he contracted and to demonstrate how he constructed, deconstructed, and reconstructed theory in light of changing politico-economic and socio-cultural conditions. Because he is widely considered, as Cornel West (1996) contends, "the towering black scholar of the twentieth century" whose "prolific writings bespeak a level of genius unequaled among modern black intellectuals," Du Bois has been the target of polemics and many misinterpretations that have frequently distorted his discourse and obscured his corpus's contributions to critical social theory (p. 55).

Critics with various academic agendas and political programs have made many efforts to refute Du Bois and illustrate the inadequacies of his thought. Work in this vein has a tendency to elide the political and intellectual origins and inspirations of Du Bois's thought. These kinds of criticisms also often fail to discuss Du Bois's work in relation to the history of Africana thought and dialectically (i. e., critically and appreciatively) observe *how* and *which* limitations internal to his project, as well as historical obstacles, led Du Bois to constantly revise and redevelop his social and political theory and praxis. Moreover, many of the books and studies published in the last quarter of the twentieth century frequently focus on a specific stage of Du Bois's thought and, therefore, are often intellectually disingenuous as they practice a type of theoretical freeze-framing that Du Bois long and loudly opposed. Although there have been several watershed works in Du Bois studies that urbanely engage a stage of his project or an aspect of his intellectual history, most interpretations have been deficient in their presentation of the broad range and reach of his social thought and political practices.

In the succeeding chapters I move beyond one-dimensional interpretations of Du Bois and analyze in detail syntheses, ambiguities, and modifications in his thought by employing the Africana critical theoretical framework. This framework will allow me to trace the developments and revisions of his thought rather than reproduce the conventional flat-footed analyses that approach or, rather, reproach his work as though it were ideology or a completed thought-complex. Utilizing the Africana critical theoretical framework will also enable me to chart both the conceptual ruptures and theoretical revolutions in Du Bois's thinking, and the intellectual constants and long-held political positions at the core of his corpus.

In the spirit of his life-long advocacy of critical thought, I develop detailed discussions of Du Bois's work which address the success or failure of his efforts to provide new theories and praxes to help human beings understand and alter contemporary society. From this angle his work can be simultaneously evaluated based on the goals he himself set for it and based on the aims and objectives of developing an Africana critical theory of contemporary society. We will observe how the aforementioned tensions within his project either hindered him from and/or helped him to rethink and redesign his social theory. And we will also witness instances where Du Bois turns phenomena that initially presented theoretical and political obstacles into theoretical and political putty in his hands.

In our effort to illuminate the itinerary of Du Bois's thought as it passes through several series of stages of development that appropriate Africana and European ideas, we must examine how his theory reaches, or fails to reach, the outcomes he initially envisioned. This method of closely reading his theory in light of its objectives will enable us to perceive how Du Bois deepens and develops critical social theory, infusing it with elements from thought-traditions that engage issues and prioritize problems that critical theory (especially that of the Frankfurt School, including Habermas) has historically downplayed and diminished, if not outright ignored and omitted. Du Bois's contributions to philosophy, radical politics, and social theory, among other areas, enhance and extend critical theory of contemporary society by offering a compelling and comprehensive body of writings comparable in scope to the monumental work of Karl Marx, C. L. R. James, Antonio Gramsci, Frantz Fanon, and Herbert Marcuse.

Because Du Bois's work represents a series of responses to complex and quickly changing historical conditions and social crises, an adequate interpretation of his thought requires a creative combination of intellectual history, intellectual biography, philosophy of race, sociology of race, critical race theory, feminist theory, womanist theory, postcolonial theory, hermeneutics, semiotics, polemics, Marxist-humanism, epistemological investigation, philosophical exploration, social and political analysis, and critical evaluation of both its theoretical and political dimensions. Prior studies of Du Bois's thought have been vitiated by their failure to sufficiently situate his works within their multidimensional historical, political and intellectual milieux, and have failed to demonstrate how the diverse stages and works fit into his overarching intellectual history and constantly evolving radical political project. To overcome this problem I will interpret Du Bois's writings in relation to their classical and our contemporary contexts and shall show how history and various theoretical and practical questions and critiques point to the limitations of his theories and inspire (and sometimes incite) Du Bois to revise and re-articulate his positions. The following chapters, then, seek to provide interpretations and criticisms of Du Bois's thought and texts in an effort to develop a discussion of his contributions to critical theory of contemporary society and emphasize Africana thought-traditions' gifts to modern movements geared toward human liberation and radical social transformation.

The next chapter examines Du Bois as a foundational figure in philosophy of race and an important contributor to the contemporary discursive formations and practices of critical white studies and critical race theory. Similar to race, I suggest that Du Bois's critical race and anti-racist thought frequently shifted and changed due to scientific data, or the lack of scientific data, and continental and diasporan Africans' collective historical experiences and dynamic socio-cultural conditions and crises. In an effort to counter disparaging claims that quarantine his critical race and anti-racist thought to his early, turn of the twentieth century years, I offer a detailed discussion of the genesis and protracted history of Du Bois's philosophy of race and his development of, conceivably, the first critical theory of race and racism.

In chapter 3, I argue that Du Bois's conception of colonialism prefigures and provides a paradigm for and a critique of contemporary postcolonial discourse. I question and criticize the racial and racist nature of not only classical colonialism, but also of contemporary colonial discourse, particularly postcolonialism. Du Bois's anticolonial theory and praxis (especially via his leadership role in Pan-African politics and movements) are demonstrated to be powerful points of departure for theorizing the nebulous character of colonialism and the nuances of neocolonialism in our supposedly simultaneously postcolonial condition and postmodern moment. This chapter, then, builds on the theoretical momentum of chapter 2 and charts the role of race and racism in colonialism and how contemporary theorists of colonialism often overlook its racial or, rather, racist dimensions.

Chapter 4 turns to Du Bois's much-mangled critiques of capitalism and Marxism and offers a fresh look at *how* and sometimes *why* he simultaneously criticized, innovated and employed Marxist, anti-Marxist, and non-Marxist methodology to critique capitalism and develop his homespun half a century-spanning discourse on democratic socialism. Further, I identify Du Bois as a doyen in race/class critical discourse and one of the (if not the very) first theorist(s) to creatively couple anti-racist theory with Marxian methodology. I side-step well-worn and often empty arguments as to whether Du Bois was a Marxist and/or what kind of Marxist he was by emphasizing his extensions and expansions of Marxian theory, and thus the philosophical foundation of most forms of contemporary critical theory. Many of the issues addressed in this chapter are directly connected to the concerns of the two previous chapters because, as I pointedly observe throughout chapter 2, it is virtually impossible to discuss Africana philosophies of race and anti-racist struggles without linking them to white supremacist capitalism and colonialism, which in Africana critical theory translates into the dual dimensions of black politico-economic exploitation and socio-cultural oppression.

In chapter 5 I examine the complexity and contradictions of the anti-sexist aspects of Du Bois's social theory in an effort to tease out its contributions to critical theory of contemporary society. I contend that in contrast to most of the theorists of the Frankfurt School tradition of critical theory, though flawed and subtly sexist in some instances, Du Bois's critical theoretical discourse did not downplay gender domination and discrimination. On the contrary, his social theory consistently advocated the critique of sexism right alongside the critique of racism, capitalism, and colonialism. Moreover, I demonstrate that Du Bois long held the position that black women serve as a sort of litmus test for social theorists because they not only grapple with economic exploitation, but also white *and* male supremacism(s). This chapter, therefore, brings the broad theoretical work of each of the previous chapters into dialogue and climatically seeks to develop an anti-racist, anti-sexist, anti-capitalist, and anti-colonial critical theory of contemporary society, using Du Bois's thought and texts as a paradigm and point of departure.

The concluding chapter engages Du Bois's oeuvre as an unfinished project of human liberation and radical social transformation. It points to some of the pitfalls and problematics of previous interpretations and criticisms of Du Bois and strongly stresses the necessity of future studies to examine his work as theory as opposed to ideology. I also make note of many of the remaining tasks for redeveloping critical theory of contemporary society and argue that henceforth it must be much more multicultural, transethnic, transgender, sexuality-sensitive, and have a broader base than classical and/or conventional critical theory. Contemporary critical theory, I contend, must initiate the arduous and intricate task of simultaneously and dialectically redeveloping and revising its classical philosophical foundation(s), move beyond its now inadequate and/or obsolete positions, and constantly synthesize itself with the most critical and cutting-edge social and political theory available. Du Bois's discourse, I end the book asserting, offers an almost ideal source of and site for the radical reconstruction of critical theory and contemporary society.

NOTES

1. With regard to what I am referring to as "the contemporary Du Bois renaissance," I have in mind not only the plethora of recent reprints by Du Bois, but also David Levering Lewis's Pulitzer Prize-winning volumes and the spate of works in Du Boisia that preceded those texts and closed the twentieth and opened the twenty-first centuries. See, for example, Andrews (1985), Bloom (2001), Byerman (1994), Durr (2001), Horne (1986), Juguo (2001), Lewis (1993, 2000), Marable (1986), Reed (1997), Wolters (2001), and Zamir (1995). A number of noteworthy doctoral dissertations were produced during this period as well, see Alridge (1997), Braley (1994), Chandler (1997), Drake (1985), Drummer (1995), Edelin (1981), Edwards (2001), Gabbidon (1996), Greco (1984), Higbee (1995a), Hwang (1988), Makang (1993),

Meade (1987), Moore (1998), Morrison (2000), Neal (1984), Nwankwo (1989), Okoro (1982), Quainoo (1993), Warren (1984), Wortham (1997), Wright (1985), and Yuan (1998). There were also several conferences on and commemorations and centennial celebrations of his books and classic essays which rekindled intellectual and politic interest in Du Bois, see Anderson and Zuberi (2000), Bell, Grosholz and Stewart (1996), Crouch and Benjamin (2003), Fontenot (2001), and Katz and Sugrue (1998). Moreover, many of Du Bois's speeches and his audio autobiography have been recently reissued on compact disc, see Du Bois (1960a, 1960b, 2000c). Finally, curiosity concerning Du Bois's long-buried radical legacy has been revived by two documentaries produced in the last decade of the twentieth century, see Baulding (1992) and Massiah (1995). The Massiah documentary is far superior to the Baulding production and is considered the definitive work in this genre, but Baulding paints a more nuanced picture of Du Bois's early years, family life, and initial intellectual formation. Taken along with the aforementioned studies, dissertations, conference proceedings, and compact discs, these documentaries (which both aired on PBS multiple times) have brought Du Bois back to intellectual life and introduced him to yet another youthful generation of social justice seekers.

2. For a more detailed discussion of Du Bois's life and work, see first and foremost his own adventures in autobiography: "The Celebration of My Twenty-fifth Birthday" (1893), *The Souls of Black Folk* (1903), "Credo" (1904), "I Am Resolved" (1912), *Darkwater: Voices from Within the Veil* (1920), "So the Girl Marries" (1928), "On Being Ashamed of Oneself: An Essay on Race Pride" (1933), *A Pageant in Seven Decades, 1868–1938* (1938), *Dusk of Dawn: An Essay Toward an Autobiography of a Race Concept* (1940), "My Evolving Program for Negro Freedom" (1944), "My Golden Wedding" (1946), "I Bury My Wife" (1950), "I Take My Stand" (1951), *In Battle for Peace: The Story of My 83rd Birthday* (1952), "A Vista of Ninety Fruitful Years" (1958), "My Last Message to the World" (1958), "To an American Born Last Christmas Day" (1958), "Advice to a Great-Grandson" (1958), "A Negro Student at Harvard at the End of the Nineteenth Century" (1960), *W. E. B. Du Bois: A Recorded Autobiography* (1960), and *The Autobiography of W. E. B. Du Bois: A Soliloquy on Viewing My Life from the Last Decade of Its First Century* (1968), see Du Bois (1938, 1952, 1960a, 1968a, 1968b, 1969a, 1969b, 1970d, 1985a, 1997a). One should also consult his posthumously published *Against Racism: Unpublished Essays, Papers, Addresses, 1887–1961*, and the three-volume collection of his correspondence, *The Correspondence of W. E. B. Du Bois, 1877–1963*, see Du Bois (1985a, 1997b, 1997c, 1997d). Also helpful in this regard are several secondary sources which often reveal more about various trends and traditions in Africana social and political theory and praxis than they do Du Bois's intellectual development and biography, see, for example, Broderick (1955, 1958a, 1958b, 1959, 1974), Cain (1990a), Chandler (1997), Clarke, Jackson, Kraiser, and O'Dell (1970), Davis (1974), DeMarco (1974), Drake (1985), Drake (1986/87), Drummer (1995), Durr (2001), Franklin (1995), Golden (1966), Guzman (1961), Higbee (1995b), Katznelson (1999), Lester (1971), Lewis (1993, 2000), Logan (1971), Marable (1985a, 1986, 1996, 1998), Moore (1981), Moses (1975, 1978, 1993a, 1996, 1998), Rampersad (1990), Reed (1985, 1997), Rudwick (1956, 1960, 1968, 1982), Stuckey (1987), Sundquist (1993, 1996), Tuttle

(1957, 1973), Tyner (1997), Walden (1966, 1977), Williams (2001), Wolters (2001), Woodard (1976), Wright (1985), and Zamir (1995).

3. I advance this book, then, as a continuation of the Africana Critical Theory (ACT) project which was initiated with my doctoral dissertation, "Africana Critical Theory: From W. E. B. Du Bois and C. L. R. James's Discourse on Domination and Liberation to Frantz Fanon and Amilcar Cabral's Dialectics of Decolonization" (2001). It need be noted at the outset, and in agreement with David Held (1980), "[c]ritical theory, it should be emphasized, does *not* form a unity; it does not mean the same thing to all its adherents" (p. 14, emphasis in original). For instance, Steven Best and Douglas Kellner (1991) employ the term "critical theory" in a general sense in their critique of post-modern theory, stating: "We are using 'critical theory' here in the general sense of critical social and cultural theory and not in the specific sense that refers to the critical theory of society developed by the Frankfurt School" (p. 33). Further, Raymond Morrow (1994) has forwarded that the term *critical theory* "has its origins in the work of a group of German scholars [of Jewish descent] (collectively referred to as the *Frankfurt School*) in the 1920s who used the term initially (*Kritische Theorie* in German) to designate a specific approach to interpreting Marxist theory. But the term has taken on new meanings in the interim and can be neither exclusively identified with the Marxist tradition from which it has become increasingly distinct nor reserved exclusively to the Frankfurt School, given extensive new variations outside the original German context" (p. 6). Finally, in his study of Marx, Foucault, and Habermas's philosophies of history and contributions to critical theory, Steven Best (1995) uses the term *critical theory* "in the most general sense, designating simply a critical social theory, that is, a social theory critical of present forms of domination, injustice, coercion, and inequality" (p. xvii). He, therefore, does not "limit the term to refer to only the Frankfurt School" (p. xvii). This means, then, that the term "critical theory" and the methods, presuppositions, and positions it has come to be associated with in the humanities and social sciences: (1) connote and continue to exhibit an epistemic openness and style of radical cultural criticism that highlight and accent the historical alternatives and emancipatory possibilities of a specific age and/or sociocultural condition; (2) are not the exclusive domain of Marxists, neo-Marxists, post-Marxists, feminists, post-feminists, poststructuralists, postmodernists, and/or Habermasians; and, (3) can be radically reinterpreted and redefined to identify and encompass *classical and contemporary, continental and diasporan African liberation theory and praxis*. For a few of the more noteworthy histories of the Frankfurt School and their philosophical project and various sociopolitical programs, see Bernstein (1995), Bottomore (1985), Bubner (1988), Dews (1987), Freundlieb, Hudson and Rundell (2004), Geuss (1981), Held (1980), Ingram (1990), Jay (1996), Kellner (1989), Kohlenbach and Geuss (2005), McCarthy (1991), McCarthy and Hoy (1994), Mendieta (2005), Morrow (1994), Nealon and Irr (2002), O'Neill (1976), Pensky (2005), Rasmussen (1999), Rasmussen and Swindal (2004), Stirk (2000), Thompson (1990), Wiggerhaus (1995), and Wolin (1992, 1995, 2006). And, for further discussion of the Africana critical theory project, see Rabaka (2002, 2003a, 2003b, 2003c, 2003d, 2004, 2005a, 2006a, 2006b, 2006c, forthcoming).

4. The literature on Africana Studies, which, to reiterate, includes African, African American, Afro-Latino, Caribbean, Pan-African, and Black Studies, is diverse and

extensive. The most noteworthy overviews and analyses are: Aldridge (1988), Aldridge and Young (2000), Alkalimat (1986, 1990), Allen (1974), Anderson (1990), Asante (1987, 1988, 1990), Asante and Karenga (2006), Azevedo (1993), Bailey (1970), Ba Nikongo (1997), Bates, Mudimbe and O'Barr (1993), Blassingame (1973), Butler (1981, 2000, 2001), Conyers (1997, 2003), Cortada (1974), Crouchett (1971), Daniels (1980, 1981), Ford (1973), Fossett and Tucker (1997), Frye (1978), Gordon and Gordon (2006a, 2006b), Hall (1999), Hare (1972, 1998), Harris, Hine and McKay (1990), Hayes (1997), Johnson and Lynne (2002), Karenga (1988, 2001, 2002), Kelley (1997b), Kershaw (1989, 1992, 2003), Kilson (1973, 2000a), Marable (2000, 2005), Marable and Mullings (2000), Mercer (1994), Norment (2001), Robinson, Foster and Ogilvie (1969), Stewart (1979, 1992), Turner and McGann (1980), Turner (1984), and Walton (1969).

5. My interpretation of Africana philosophy is grounded in and grows out of the thought and texts of several classical and contemporary continental and diasporan African theorists whose works lend themselves to a critical theoretical framework and/or discursive formations regarding the history, nature and tasks of Africana thought-traditions and how these thought-traditions can be used in the interest of human liberation and radical social transformation. The most noteworthy and major texts in this regard are: Babbitt and Campbell (1999), Birt (2002), Cabral (1972, 1973, 1979), Coetzee and Roux (1998), P. H. Collins (1998, 2000), A. Y. Davis (1981, 1989, 1998), English and Kalumba (1996), Eze (1997a, 1997b, 2001), Fanon (1965, 1967, 1968, 1969), Gooding-Williams (2005), Gordon (1997a, 1997b, 1998, 2000a, 2006a, 2006b), Gyekye (1995, 1996, 1997), Harris (1983, 1989, 1999a, 1999b), Henry (2000), hooks (1981, 1984, 1990, 1991, 1995), Hord and Lee (1995), Hountondji (1996), Imbo (1998), Irele (1990, 2001), Irele and Gikandi (2004), C. L. R. James (1980, 1984, 1992, 1994, 1995, 1996, 1999), J. A. James (1996a, 1997, 1999), Kwame (1995), Lawson (1992), Lawson and Kirkland (1999), Locke (1983, 1989, 1992), Lott (1998, 1999, 2002), Lorde (1984, 1988), Lott and Pittman (2003), Masolo (1994), McGary (1999), McGary and Lawson (1992), Mills (1997, 1998, 2003), Mosley (1995), Mudimbe (1988, 1994), Outlaw (1996a, 1997, 2005), Pittman (1997), Serequeberhan (1991, 1994, 1997, 2000), West (1982, 1988a, 1988b, 1999), Wiredu (1980, 1995, 1996, 2004) and Wright (1984).

6. My criticism of Sénghor here does not negate my critical appreciation of some aspects of his conception(s) of "African Socialism." For further discussion, see my "Negritude's Connections and Contributions to Africana Critical Theory" (and especially the subsection "A Sartrean African Philosopher?: Leopold Sedar Senghor, Negritude, Cultural Mulattoism, Africanity, and the Adventures of African Socialism"), in which I critically discuss Senghor's, as well as Aimé Césaire's, advances and retreats with regard to the development of Africana philosophy and Africana critical theory (see Rabaka 2001, pp. 129-178, esp. pp. 144-151).

7. My analysis here smacks of black existentialism or Africana philosophy of existence, which afforded me the theoretical tools to tease out the issues involved in the experiential/emotional approach in Africana Studies. Interpreting experience, that is, investigating any lived-reality, almost inherently entails a confrontation with existential and ontological questions and claims. These questions and claims, as quiet as they are

kept, differ for each human group because each human group's historical horizon and cultural contexts, which were either created by them or some other human group, are wide and varied and always vacillating between human homogeneity and heterogeneity, often ultimately giving way in our postmodern moment to hybridity. For further discussion of Africana philosophy of existence or black existentialism, see Lewis Gordon's groundbreaking *Existence in Black: An Anthology of Black Existential Philosophy* (1997) and *Existentia Africana: Understanding Africana Existential Thought* (2000).

8. The conception of "Africanity" that I invoke and employ here involves a combination of African identity and African personality theory and is drawn primarily from the work of the Eritrean philosopher Tsenay Serequeberhan (1998), in his article "Africanity at the End of the Twentieth Century." It should be noted that Sénghor (1971) theorized and helped to popularize this term in Africana philosophical discourse with his work, *"The Foundations of "Africanité" or "Negritude" and "Arabite"*, which more or less uses European thought and culture as a paradigm to develop a racially reactionary, and therefore extremely essentialist, African identity. For my more detailed criticisms of Senghor and his version of Negritude, see Rabaka (2001).

9. With regard to my conception of a "philosopher," I follow Lewis Gordon's (1997b) lead in making a critical distinction between "philosophers" and "scholars of or on philosophy." In his words:

> "Philosopher" here means something more than a person with a doctorate in philosophy. I regard many individuals with that title to be scholars of or on philosophy instead of philosophers. Philosophers are individuals who make original contributions to the development of philosophical thought, to the world of ideas. Such thinkers are people whom the former study. It is no accident that philosophers in this sense are few in number and many of them did not [and do not] have doctorates in philosophy, for example, René Descartes, David Hume, Søren Kierkegaard, William James, Edmund Husserl, Karl Jaspers, Jean-Paul Sartre, Simone de Beauvoir, and Alfred Schutz. (pp. 48-49)

This distinction between "philosophers" and "scholars of or on philosophy" is also in line with Lucius Outlaw's (1997) articulation of *Africana* philosophy and *Africana* philosophers. Within the world of this discursive formation, "persons past and present, who were and are without formal training or degrees in philosophy are being worked into developing canons as providing instances of reflections, on various matters, that are appropriately characterized as philosophical" (p. 63). In addition, Outlaw's timely tome, *On Race and Philosophy* (1996a), also offers critical insights on the academic tasks and some of the social and political challenges confronting Africana philosophers, as well as philosophers of African descent, as they increasingly transgress the boundaries of the "traditional" white philosophy discipline/department and their training in Western European and European American philosophy.

10. Part of Africana philosophy's current meta-philosophical character has to do with both its critical and uncritical appropriation of several Western European philosophical concepts and categories. As more philosophers of African origin and descent receive training in and/or dialogue with Africana Studies theory and methodology, the basic notions and nature of Africana philosophy will undoubtedly change. Needless to say, Africana philosophy has an intellectual arena and engages issues that are often

distinctly different from the phenomena that preoccupy and have long plagued Western European and European American philosophy. I am not criticizing the meta-philosophical motivations in the discourse of contemporary Africana philosophy as much
as I am pleading with workers in the field to develop a "division of labor"—à la Du
Bois's classic caveat(s) to continental and diasporan Africans in the face of white supremacy (see Du Bois, 1973, 2002). A move should be made away from "philoso-
phizing on Africana philosophy" (i.e., meta-philosophy), and more Africana philosophical attention should be directed toward the cultural crises and social and political
problems of the present age. In order to do this, Africana philosophers will have to
turn to the advances of Africana Studies scholars working in history, cultural criticism, economics, politics, and social theory, among other areas. For a more detailed
discussion of the nature and tasks of Africana philosophy, see Lucius Outlaw's
groundbreaking "Africana Philosophy" and "African, African American, Africana
Philosophy" (Outlaw 1996a, 1997). For more examples of Africana philosophy, see
endnote number 5.

11. Here, and throughout the remainder of this section of the introduction, I draw
heavily from the discourse of Africana hermeneutics, or Africana philosophy of interpretation, in an effort to emphasize the importance of culturally grounded inquiry and
interpretation in Africana critical theory. As Okondo Okolo (1991) observed in his
classic essay "Tradition and Destiny: Horizons of an African Philosophical Hermeneutics," Africana hermeneutics, as with almost all hermeneutical endeavors, centers on
the ideas of tradition and destiny and how successive generations interpret, explain,
and embrace their historical, cultural, and intellectual heritage. In his own words:

> For our part, we want to test the resources but also the limits of our hermeneutical mod-
> els and practices, by examining the two notions that encompass our interpretative efforts
> in an unconquerable circle—the notions of Tradition and Destiny. These notions simulta-
> neously define the object, the subject, the horizons, and the limits of interpretation. To in-
> terpret is always to close the circle of the subject and the object. We cannot, however,
> make this circle our own if we do not lay it out beyond the thought of the subject and the
> object, toward a thinking of our horizons and the limits of our interpretation defined by
> the reality of our traditions and the ideality of our destiny. (p. 202)

Okolo, among other Africana hermeneutics, highlights the abstruse issues that arise in
interpretative theory and praxis in our present social world and world of ideas. Historical and cultural experiences determine and, often subtly, define what we interpret and
the way we interpret. If, for instance, Africana thought-traditions are not known to, and
not shared with, theorists and philosophers of African descent and other interested
scholars, then they will assume there is no history of theory or philosophy in the
African world (see Eze, 1997a; Gordon and Gordon 2006a, 2006b; Harris, 1983; Lott
and Pittman, 2003; Wiredu, 2004). These would-be Africana theorists will draw from
another cultural group's schools of thought, because human existence, as the Africana
philosophers of existence have pointed out, is nothing other than our constant confrontation with ontological issues and questions. What is more, the nature of theory, especially in the current postcolonial/postmodern period, is that it incessantly builds on
other theories. In other words, a competent theorist must not only be familiar with the

history and evolutionary character of theory, but the intellectual origins of theories—that is, with *who*, *where*, and *why* specific theories were created to describe and explain a particular subject and/or object. For further discussion of Africana hermeneutics, see Okere (1971, 1991), Outlaw (1974, 1983a, 1983c), and Serequeberhan (1991, 2000).

12. Most notably, my interpretation of dialectics has been influenced by Herbert Marcuse's studies in dialectical thought, see his *Reason and Revolution* (1960), *Negations: Essays in Critical Theory* (1968), *Studies in Critical Philosophy* (1973), "On the Problem of the Dialectic (Part 1)" (1976a), "On the Problem of the Dialectic (Part 2)" (1976b), and "A Note on Dialectic" (1997b).

13. Here and throughout this section in addition to Amilcar Cabral's critical theory, I am generously drawing from Antonio Gramsci's conceptual contributions: "ideological hegemony," "organic intellectual," "historical bloc," "war of position," "war of maneuver," and "ensemble of ideas and social relations," and so on. His work has deeply influenced my conception of critical theory as a form of ideological and cultural critique, as well as a radical political praxis-promoting social theory. In particular, Gramsci's assertion that class domination is exercised as much through popular and unconscious consensus (or the internalization of imperialism) as through physical coercion (or the threat of it) by the state apparatus—especially in advanced capitalist societies where politics, education, religion, law, media, and popular culture, among other areas, are controlled by the ruling class—his work innovatively emphasizes the ideological and counter-hegemonic dimension that radical politics and critical social theory today must deepen and further develop. However, in terms of Africana critical theory of contemporary society and the life-worlds of people of African origin and descent, and people of color in general, class domination and capitalism represent one of many interlocking systems of domination and discrimination that must be ideologically and physically combated and discontinued. Therefore, Gramsci's work provides several insights, but must be synthesized with other theory, especially critical race theory, anti-racist feminist theory, postcolonial theory, critical pedagogy, and liberation theology, among others, if it is to aid in the (re)construction of a new, more multicultural, radical anti-racist and gender justice-seeking critical theory of contemporary society. For further discussion, see Gramsci (1967, 1971, 1975, 1977, 1978, 1985, 1992, 1994a, 1994b, 1995a, 1995b, 1996, 2000).

14. My interpretation of black invisibility and anonymity has, of course, been deeply influenced by Ralph Ellison's *Invisible Man* (1980) and Toni Morrison's *Playing in the Dark: Whiteness and the Literary Imagination* (1990), but has been enhanced most by Lewis Gordon's *Bad Faith and Anti-Black Racism* (1995a), "Existential Dynamics of Theorizing Black Invisibility" (1997a, pp. 69–79), "Context: Ruminations on Violence and Anonymity" (1997b, pp. 13–24), and "Existential Borders of Anonymity and Superfluous Invisibility" (2000a, pp. 153–63). On the black collective mind and African communal thought theses, see Robin Horton's *Patterns of Thought in Africa and the West: Essays on Magic, Religion, and Science* (1993) and Paulin Hountondji's *African Philosophy: Myth and Reality* (1996). And for solid criticisms of these theses, see Kwasi Wiredu's *Philosophy and an African Culture* (1980) and Kwame Gyekye's *An Essay on African Philosophical Thought* (1995).

Chapter Two

Du Bois's Concepts of Race, Critiques of Racism, and Contributions to Critical White Studies and Critical Race Theory

"White folks know niggers talk, an they dont mind jes so long as nothing comes of it, so here goes." —Toomer, 1993, p. 90

"A people that undertakes a struggle for liberation rarely legitimizes race prejudice. Even in the course of acute periods of insurrectional armed struggle one never witnesses the recourse to biological justifications. The struggle of the inferiorized is situated on a markedly more human level. The perspectives are radically new. The opposition is the henceforth classical one of the struggles of conquest and of liberation." —Fanon, 1969, p. 43

"It would be well to remind white America of its debt to Dr. Du Bois. When they corrupted Negro history they distorted American history because Negroes are too big a part of the building of this nation to be written out of it without destroying scientific history. White America, drenched with lies about Negroes, has lived too long in a fog of ignorance. Dr. Du Bois gave them a gift of truth for which they should eternally be indebted to him." —M. L. King Jr., 1970, p. 27

"This race talk is, of course, a joke, and frequently it has driven me insane and probably will permanently in the future; and yet, seriously and soberly, we black folk are the salvation of mankind." —Du Bois, 1995a, p. 470

INTRODUCTION:
DU BOIS'S DISCOURSE ON RACE AND RACISM

Du Bois's corpus contains an astounding body of literature on and knowledge of race and racism. His philosophy of race figures prominently, and has consistently been featured, in racial discourse. Moreover, race theorists have chronicled his concepts of race from a multiplicity of disciplinary and theoretic perspectives, often arguing against and, at other times, agreeing with his critical writings on race and racism, which have been documented to have dominated racial discourse for the first half of the twentieth century (Bay, 1998; Bobo, 2000; Bruce, 1995; Chaffee, 1956; Holt, 1990, 1998; Meade, 1987; Mostern, 1996; Rampersad, 1996b; C. M. Taylor, 1981).

The history of Du Bois's philosophy of race and anti-racist theory is not an easy tale to tell, but one that must be told. Why? One may ask. Why do we need another (re)interpretation of Du Bois's concept(s) of race and critique(s) of racism? Why should we revisit the discourse of race and racism anyway? Isn't race, and therefore racism, a thing of the past or, at the least, a superstitious social construction that science tells us has never existed, or certainly no longer exists? Didn't Anthony Appiah's analytic philosophical assault debunk Du Bois's philosophy of race once and for all, exposing its pseudo-scientific and narrow nationalistic underpinnings? And, after all the smoke has cleared and the dust settled, isn't Du Bois just another over-engaged "race man" posthumously positioned as a radical theorist?[1]

Throughout this chapter I will address these questions (and probably problematize and raise many others) by arguing that Du Bois's writings on race are relevant and contribute to contemporary racial discourse for four fundamental reasons. First, his philosophy of race is often interpreted as an "ideology of race"—that is, an inert, inflexible, fixed and fast, singular notion of what race is, and which groups constitute constituent races. This is not only a gross misinterpretation of Du Bois's constantly evolving philosophy of race, but an example of the type of intellectual disingenuousness and invisibility that plagues Africana intellectuals of every political persuasion and social station.

Critically engaging Du Bois's philosophy of race offers objective interpreters and critics of race and racism an opportunity to analyze a theoretically rich and thoroughgoing series of ruminations on race and racism by a pioneer race theorist who almost infinitely harbored a hardnosed skepticism toward the supposed scientific and/or biological bases of race. This skepticism, coupled with his own homegrown pragmatism, often led Du Bois to contradictory conclusions regarding race (West, 1989). However, he repeatedly reminded his readers that he was not searching for a sound, scientific concept of race as much as he was on a quest to either locate or create a vehicle for Africana cultural development and social survival.

The meaning of race has always moved, as the very idea of race has consistently traveled far and wide since its inception. Du Bois has the distinction of being one of the first persons of African descent to scientifically research and write on race (Durr, 2001; B. S. Edwards, 2001; Juguo, 2001; Lewis, 1993, 2000; Lott, 1999, 2001). His Africanity or blackness is important inso-far as Africans or blacks have historically been and continue currently to be considered one of the most thoroughly and oppressively racialized groups—though under-theorized from their own cultural perspectives and radical po-litical positions—in the history of race and racism (Gordon, 1995a; Kelley, 1997a; Marable, 1983, 1993, 2002). From an increasingly Africana history-, culture-, and philosophy-informed critical perspective, he studied the history of race with an intense interest in its origins and originators, and the pur-pose(s) of its origination. This alone should distinguish Du Bois's writings on race as more than mere intellectual artifacts, but there is much more.

His concepts of race harbor an inherent and radical humanism that is often complex and seemingly contradictory, but which nonetheless is part and par-cel of his overarching philosophy of race. In specific, Du Bois developed what I will crudely call a "gift theory" which, in short, elaborated that each race has specific and special "gifts" to contribute to national and international culture and civilization. In works such as *The Souls of Black Folk* (1903), "The Peo-ple of Peoples and Their Gifts to Men" (1913), and *Darkwater* (1920), and most especially in later works like *The Gift of Black Folk* (1924), "The Black Man Brings His Gifts" (1925), *Black Reconstruction of Democracy in Amer-ica* (1935), *Black Folk, Then and Now* (1939), *Dusk of Dawn: An Essay To-ward an Autobiography of a Race Concept* (1940) and *The World and Africa* (1947), Du Bois put forward concepts of race that were not biologically based, but predicated on political, social, historical, and cultural "common" charac-teristics and experiences shared by continental and diasporan Africans (see Du Bois, 1913, 1939, 1965, 1968a, 1970b, 1989, 1995a, 1995b). In Du Bois's gift theory, these characteristics represent Africana peoples' "gifts" or race- and culture-specific contributions to the forward flow of human history.

Second, and falling fast on the heels of the first point, it is important for us to revisit Du Bois's concepts of race because what we now know of his race theory is almost utterly predicated on and relegated to his early writings. For instance, most contemporary critics of Du Bois's theory of race begin and of-ten end with his 1897 address to the American Negro Academy, "The Con-servation of Races." Some critics go as far as his early career classics, "The Study of the American Negro Problem" (1898), *The Philadelphia Negro* (1899), and, of course, *The Souls of Black Folk* (1903). Further than these texts, however, contemporary race critics do not dare venture, which to my mind seems absurd considering the fact that Du Bois continued to publish for another 60 years. Scant attention has been given to Du Bois's writings on race and racism after *The Souls of Black Folk*, and, when on rare occasions they are engaged, more is made of his infamously alleged and highly controversial collapsing of race into class in his 1935 classic, *Black Reconstruction of Democracy in America*. Maybe those who argue that Du Bois collapsed race into class and that he uncritically accepted communism have never read his 1936 essay, "Social Planning for the Negro, Past and Present," where he roars against the supposed racelessness and political panacea thesis of the socialists and communists: "There is no automatic power in socialism to override and suppress race prejudice. . . . One of the worst things that Negroes could do today would be to join the American Communist Party or any of its many branches" (1982c, p. 38). Du Bois then, as I will demonstrate in chapter 4, was a much more astute interpreter of Marxian philosophy and class theory than many contemporary race theorists may be aware of. Without a thorough understanding of why, and the ways in which he critically engaged, as opposed to openly embraced, Marxism many critics of his concepts of race are doomed to do Du Bois a disservice by misinterpreting his motivations for emphasizing certain aspects of race and racism at specific socio-historic and politico-economic intervals. It may not be too much of an overstatement to say that Du Bois developed a discourse on race in order to critique racism and provide a philosophical foundation for anti-racist struggle. This is the second reason his work has import for contemporary race and racism discourse: because it may offer models for us to further our critiques of race and to combat racism.

The third reason Du Bois's writings on race are important for contemporary race and racism discourse is because of the recent emergence of critical white studies and the emphasis on whiteness, white racelessness or white racial neutrality and universality, and white supremacy. In several pioneering publications in historical sociology, sociology of race, and political economy he deftly and defiantly hit at the heart of whiteness, chronicling its rise alongside the concept of race, noting that to be white is to be raceless, to be powerful or, at the least, to have access to power or people in positions of power. In the logic of the white world, race is something that soils the social status of sub-humans, that is, non-whites; it politically pollutes their thinking, thus rendering them powerless, irrational, and in need of clear conceptions concerning themselves and the world. Since whites are the only group that is not plagued by race, they then have been burdened by God (who, within the racist logic of the white supremacist world, is also, of course, white) with the task of leading the lost, raced "natives," "barbarians," "savages," and sub-humans to the higher level or lily-white "heaven" of humanity. Du Bois resented whites' racial mythmaking, and directed a significant portion of his writings on race and racism to critiquing whiteness and white supremacy. His writings, such as "Race Friction Between Black and White" (1908), "The Souls of White Folk" (1910), "Of the Culture of White Folk" (1917), "White Co-

Workers" (1920), "The Superior Race" (1923), "The White Worker" (1935), "The White Proletariat in Alabama, Georgia, and Florida" (1935), "The White World" (1940) and "The White Folk Have a Right to Be Ashamed" (1949), represent and register as early and sustained efforts that critique and combat whiteness and white supremacy. Du Bois's work in this area, then, can be said to prefigure and provide a point of departure for the contemporary discourse and debates of critical white studies.

Finally, Du Bois's writings on race are relevant with regard to contemporary race and racism criticism as they contribute significantly to the discourse of critical race theory. No longer considered the exclusive domain of legal studies scholars and radical civil rights lawyers and law professors, critical race theory has blossomed and currently encompasses and includes a wide range of theory and theorists from diverse academic disciplines. In a nutshell the core concerns of critical race theory include: race and racism's centrality to European imperial expansion and modernity; racism's interconnection(s) with sexism, capitalism, and colonialism; white supremacy; white normativity and white neutrality; state-sanctioned (or, legal) racial domination and discrimination; and revolutionary anti-racist race and cultural consciousness amongst people of color (Crenshaw, Gotanda, Peller and Thomas, 1995; Delgado, 1995; Delgado and Stefancic, 2001; Essed and Goldberg, 2001; Goldberg, Musheno and Bower, 2001; Goldberg and Solomos, 2002). Du Bois's philosophy of race in many senses foreshadows contemporary critical race theory and, therefore, contributes several paradigms and points of departure. However, as with so many other aspects of his thought, Du Bois's writings on race and racism have been relegated to the realm, at best, of sociology, which downplays and diminishes their interdisciplinarity and significance for contemporary critical social theory and radical politics. Therefore, his writings on race have been virtually overlooked and/or rendered intellectually invisible by critical race theorists.

As Joy James (1997) and Cheryl Townsend Gilkes (1996) argue, and as I will discuss in greater detail in chapter 5, Du Bois was critically conscious of some of the ways that race is gendered and gender is raced. Emerging in the fifteenth century, and coinciding with European imperial expansion around the globe, racial domination threw fuel on the wildfire of preexisting gender discrimination. An astute student of gender relations, Du Bois accented the interconnections of racism and sexism, specifically white supremacy and patriarchy. This means, then, that at the least some of his anti-racist social theorizing may serve as a model for critical race theory in the sense that it seeks a similar goal: To make visible the long invisible connections between racial and gender domination and discrimination, not only in law but in medicine, politics, education, and religion, among other aspects and areas of contemporary society (see Rabaka, forthcoming). What is intellectually amazing and seminally significant is that Du Bois developed *a sexism-sensitive conception of race and racism* almost a hundred years prior to the current critical race theory movement, which is to say that Du Bois's work for all theoretical and practical purposes could (and, I think, should) be considered *classical critical race theory*.

Du Bois was also an early exponent of the race/class thesis that contended that though class struggle had been a part of human history for several centuries, the modern concept of race and the sociopolitical practice of racism, coupled with capitalism and colonialism exacerbated class conflicts (amongst both colonizers and the colonized). Though often unacknowledged, similar to C. L. R. James (1994, 1996, 1999) and Oliver C. Cox (1959, 1987), Du Bois was a pioneer in terms of analyzing the political economy of race and racism, which is to say that he often argued against studying race independent of class (see chapter 4). Race and class, as we have seen with race and gender in Du Bois's *sexism-sensitive* and/or *gender-centered conception of race*, are inextricable and incessantly intersecting and reconfiguring, constantly forming and reforming, creating a racist dimension in modern class theory and struggle, and a classist or economically exploitive dimension in racial politics and struggle.

Race and racism were European modernity's weapons of choice. A (sub)person, from the modern white world's frame of reference, was economically exploited based on biology or ethnicity. That is, the degree(s) to which one was dominated and/or discriminated against was predicated on European-invented racial classifications and ethno-cultural categorizations (Goldberg, 1993, 1994, 2001). Du Bois's writings on the political economy of race and racism provide another paradigm for contemporary critical race theory to build on and bolster its calls for racial, economic, and gender justice.

In what follows, I will further elaborate on each of the four fundamental reasons Du Bois's writings on race are relevant to contemporary critical race discourse. Devoting a section to each issue, the remainder of the chapter is divided into four sections and begins with a discussion of Du Bois's philosophy of race. In the subsequent sections, I treat his critiques of racism and white supremacy, respectively. Then I conclude the chapter by examining his contributions to critical race theory and contemporary struggles for racial justice.

DU BOIS'S CONCEPT(S) OF RACE

There have been so many interpretations, reinterpretations, and misinterpretations of Du Bois's "The Conservations of Races" over the last century that I am tempted to forgo a discussion of it here (Appiah, 1985, 1992; Broderick, 1959; Goodin, 2002; Gooding-Williams, 1996; Holt, 1998; Lott, 1999, 2001; Meier, 1963; Moore, 1981; Moses, 1993a; Outlaw, 1995, 1996b; Reed, 1997; Rudwick, 1960, 1968, 1982; P. C. Taylor, 2000; Zamir, 1995). However, as Tommy Lott in *The Invention of Race* (1999) tells us, it remains one of the best points of departure for the undaunted contemporary philosopher of race who dares venture into the vortex of Du Bois's discourse on race and racism and the barrage of commentary and criticism it has elicited. In "The Conservation of Races" Du Bois set out to simultaneously deconstruct and reconstruct "race." In 1897, when he delivered this address, race was something for which science had no "final word," and no "definite conclusion[s]" (Du Bois, 1986a, pp. 815–16). Race science was actually *racist* science, a bunch of purportedly biologically-determined, "scientific" categories created by white supremacist "scientists" with an eye aimed at maintaining and magnifying white world supremacy (Eze, 1997c; Goldberg, 1993; Mosse, 1978; Poliakov, 1974; Stephan, 1982, 1990). Du Bois's (1986a) deconstruction of race, then, was geared toward debunking nineteenth century pseudo-scientific notions of race based on "physical characteristics" and white supremacy (p. 815).

Though this very well may have been Du Bois's intention, and I think it was, when he rendered his reconstruction of race he was caught in a quagmire and series of contradictions because he relied on the very "physical characteristics" he claimed had no biological basis for race. Many critics have questioned why Du Bois did not leave the language of race altogether (Appiah, 1985, 1992; Gilroy, 1993a; Gooding-Williams, 1996; Jones, 1997; Zamir, 1995). Where others have asked if it would not have been better for him to emphasize politics or social alternatives outside of the racial arena (Broderick, 1959; DeMarco, 1983; Meier, 1963; Moore, 1981; Rudwick, 1982; Wolters, 2001). To these queries Du Bois's (1986a) text seems quick to quip: because "there can be no doubt, first, as to the widespread, nay, universal, prevalence of the race idea, the race spirit, the race ideal, and as to its efficiency as the vastest and most ingenious invention for human progress" (p. 817). The "vastest and most ingenious invention for human progress"? But, didn't race lead to racism? Hasn't "the race idea" harmed more than it has ever helped people of African origin and descent, and humanity as a whole, for that matter? What, with high tones, is he talking about? Has Du Bois gone off the deep end? I answer emphatically: no! No, Du Bois didn't lose it. No, he is not a narrow-minded nationalist (at least not in this instance). And no, just for the hell of it, to the white supremacists and liberal racists who would fix their faces to say this sounds remotely like "reverse racism."

In order to understand why Du Bois deconstructed and reconstructed race, as opposed to creating or advocating another alternative for black radical politics, social development, and cultural survival, we will have to quickly examine his concepts of race and critiques of racism. This section will be devoted to his concepts of race, and the subsequent section will treat his critiques of racism, though I should observe that it will be very difficult, if not impossible, to discuss race without discussing racism to a certain extent. Also, I must admit, it would be backbreaking to discuss classical concepts of race without comparing them, however unconsciously, to contemporary concepts of race. Therefore, this section, much like each of the chapters in this book, uses Du Bois's thought and texts as a point of departure to revisit and revise modern discourse on domination and liberation.

"The Conservation of Races" is an almost ideal essay to engage Du Bois's critical theory of race because he maintained and routinely revised many of the views he espoused here throughout his career (Chaffee, 1956; Green and Smith, 1983; Mostern, 1996; Sundquist, 1996). In this sense, "The Conservation of Races" not only serves contemporary critical race theorists as an entrée to Du Bois's philosophy of race, but it served a similar function for Du Bois as well. For instance, in *Dusk of Dawn*, in the chapter "The Concept of Race," he reflected:

> I was born in the century when the walls of race were clear and straight; when the world consisted of mutually exclusive races; and even though the edges might be blurred, there was no question of exact definition and understanding of the meaning of the word. One of the first pamphlets that I wrote in 1897 was on "The Conservation of Races" wherein I set down as the first article of a proposed racial creed: "We believe that the Negro people as a race have a contribution to make to civilization and humanity which no other race can make." (1986a, p. 639)

Forty years after he penned "The Conservation of Races" Du Bois was still clinging to some of the "essential" (as opposed to "essentialist") ideas he set down in it, ideas that continue to impact and influence critical race discourse and debates to this day. Du Bois (1986a) begins the essay asking: "What is the real meaning of Race; what has, in the past, been the law of race development, and what lessons has the past history of race development to teach the rising Negro people?" (p. 815). He then proceeds to deconstruct prevalent nineteenth century notions of race based on biology, i.e., "physical characteristics" and "physical differences," such as "cranial measurements . . . color, hair, [and] bone" (pp. 815–816). All these "physical characteristics," Du Bois declares, "are patent enough, and if they agreed with each other it would be very easy to classify mankind. Unfortunately for scientists, however, these criteria of race are most exasperatingly intermingled" (p. 816). On the one hand, the "final word of science, so far, is that we have at least two, perhaps

three great families of human beings—whites and Negroes, possibly the yellow races" (p. 816). On the other hand, he perplexingly pondered:

> We find upon the world's stage today eight distinctly differentiated races, in the
> sense in which History tells us the word must be used. They are the Slavs of
> eastern Europe, the Teutons of middle Europe, the English of Great Britain and
> America, the Romance nations of Southern and Western Europe, the Negroes of
> Africa and America, the Semitic people of Western Asia and Northern Africa,
> the Hindoos of Central Asia and the Mongolians of Eastern Asia. (pp. 817–18)

Within each of the "eight distinctly differentiated races," Du Bois reports,
there are "minor race groups," which seem to confound him as much as I am
almost certain they will contemporary critical race theorists (p. 818). The science of race, he concludes at the outset of his essay, is predicated on confusing and "contradictory criteria" that may never be clear-cut because of the
socio-historic reality of racial "intermingling" (p. 816). Early in his essay,
then, Du Bois makes it clear that he is not interested in rendering a biologically determined or pseudo-scientific definition of race, and that it has been
and remains "racial intermingling" that has dumbfounded what would be *pure*
race discourse.

According to Du Bois, stepping outside of the realm of race science and
taking an enormous intellectual risk: A race is "a vast family of human beings,
generally of common blood and language, always of common history, traditions and impulses, who are both voluntarily and involuntarily striving together for the accomplishment of certain more or less vividly conceived
ideals of life" (p. 817). As I intimated earlier, part of Du Bois's reconstructed
concept of race rests on biological factors, i.e., a claim of "common blood."
But we would do well to note that he wrote that persons who belong to a specific race are "*generally* of common blood" and "*always* of common history,
traditions and impulses." Du Bois put more emphasis on peoples' "common
history, traditions and impulses" than he did on their "common blood and language" in his definition of race because his definition was neither for scientific nor biological intentions, but social and political purposes.

In Du Bois's philosophy of race, "common history, traditions and impulses"
mattered much more than "common blood and language" because, as he makes
clear in *The Health and Physique of the Negro American* (1906), he was well
aware of racial "intermingling" and the socio-historic fact that there are now
and historically have been few, if any, "pure" and "unmixed" races (1906, pp.
13–18; see also Fegerson, 1987). This is an extremely important and—at the
time and, perhaps, even today—*radical* point to make because, as he put it in
his often overlooked 1935 essay, "Miscegenation": "Most American students
have the curious habit of studying Negroes indiscriminately without reference

to their blood mixture and calling the result a study of the Negro race" (1985a, p. 98). Du Bois (1986a) sought to sidestep biology-based concepts of race because he knew that "all members of the Negro race were not black," or purely or completely of African origin or descent (p. 627). By which he further meant that all blacks are not black. Or, put another way, all people classified and categorized as "black" do not have "the rich, dark brown [skin] of the Zulu[s]" (p. 816). What is more, the texture of their hair and the size and shape of their heads, noses, lips, etc., vary widely and are not always similar or shared common or characteristic physical features. After this devastating deconstruction of race, we are left exasperatingly wondering exactly what Du Bois did a century ago: "What, then, is a race?"

This question is meant to be rhetorical more than it is meant to be anything else, though much else has been made of it. As he illustrated, Du Bois was critically conscious of the ways in which white race scientists conceived of race (Durr, 2001; B. S. Edwards, 2001; Liss, 1998). Referring to many of the major turn of the twentieth century white race theorists such as Darwin, Blumenbach, Huxley, and Raetzel, Du Bois exposed inconsistencies in their biology-based theories of race and offered what has been repeatedly referred to by several, at times, sophisticated philosophers of race as a "socio-historical" reconception of race (Appiah, 1985, 1992; Goodin, 2002; Gooding-Williams, 1996; Lott, 1999, 2001; Outlaw, 1995, 1996b; P. C. Taylor, 2000). In response to his rhetorical question, "What, then, is a race?," Du Bois (1986a) infamously answered: "It is a vast family of human beings, generally of common blood and language, always of common history, traditions and impulses, who are both voluntarily and involuntarily striving together for the accomplishment of certain more or less vividly conceived ideals of life" (p. 817). Above I examined his use of "generally" and "always" in this passage, so I will not spend much time on it here. What I am more interested in at this point is the latter part of Du Bois's definition of race and its simultaneously problematic and promising theoretical, social, and political possibilities.

According to Du Bois, members of a specific race *always* share history, culture ("traditions"), and socio-political views and values ("impulses" and "striving[s]") that, though "subtle, delicate and elusive," are "clearly defined to the eye of the Historian and Sociologist" (pp. 816–17). Biologists and racist scientists, Du Bois is hinting at here, have missed perhaps the most significant element of race: its historical, cultural, social and political points of intersection and interconnection. Races are only *generally* of "common blood," but *always* of "common history, traditions and impulses." The "common blood" or biological bit of Du Bois's definition of race is just that, a small or minor piece of the puzzle, of the riddle of race, of his overall antiracist racial reconstruction project that is easily eclipsed by major historical, cultural, and socio-political factors. A claim of "common blood" is *not* a necessary factor for ascertaining racial membership and/or ethno-cultural inclusion. When and where Du Bois uses "always" above to measure and magnify the "subtle, delicate and elusive" differences of history and culture, "which have silently but definitely separated men into groups," he is simultaneously sidestepping and critiquing white supremacist conceptions of race and demonstrating that his redefinition of race is *primarily* predicated on historical, cultural, and socio-political factors as opposed to purely physiological phenomena. In a word, persons are members of the same race if, and only if, they share or have in common history, culture, and socio-political struggle(s). But it is not the case, in Du Bois's conception of race, that persons are members of the same race if, and only if, they share "common blood and language."

The latter part of Du Bois's definition of race stated above, which reads "always of common history, traditions and impulses, who are both voluntarily and involuntarily striving together for the accomplishment of certain more or less vividly conceived ideals of life," reveals his major motivation for maintaining the language and accoutrements of race. Here, Du Bois is directing his readers to the "deeper differences" that distinguish one race from another, the "spiritual" and "psychical" differences (p. 818). Recall, Du Bois stated that "the race idea [is] . . . the vastest and most ingenious invention for human progress." This is so because to "the eye of the Historian and Sociologist," "the history of the world is the history, not of individuals, but of groups, not of nations but of races, and he who ignores or seeks to override the race idea in human history ignores and overrides the central thought of all history" (p. 817). Aside from the fact that Du Bois may have overstated his case by claiming that "the race idea" is "the central thought of *all* history"—because race really was not "invented" and put to racist purposes in the manner in which we are currently familiar with it until European modernity, which also spawned capitalism to accompany the age-old practices of sexism and colonialism—his statement, nevertheless, highlights the anti-racist and radical political dimension(s) of his definition of race.

Flying in the face of biology based concepts of race, Du Bois declares, "so far as purely physical characteristics are concerned, the differences between men do not explain all the differences of their history," and "physical differences of color, hair and bone go but a short way toward explaining the different roles which groups of men have played in Human Progress" (p. 816). When and where Du Bois writes of the "different roles which groups of men have played in Human Progress," he clearly reveals that he conceives of race as a socio-political vehicle. Though many philosophers of race have remarked on Du Bois's "socio-historical" reconception of race, I do not think that this characterization does his anti-racist concept of race justice, since it also contained a definite and distinct political and, as we will soon see, ethical dimension. The political dimension of Du Bois's definition of race has been commented on above. However, it is also extremely evident when we come to the passage in "The Conservation of Races" where he invokes historical political figures whom he claims represent not themselves individually, but symbolize "striving" social groups and civilizations: "We see the Pharaohs, Caesars, Toussaints and Napoleans of history and forget the vast races of which they were but epitomized expressions" (p. 817).

 Here, then, Du Bois is pointing out that even in the historical scheme of racial matters it was not only "whites" (the "Caesars" and "Napoleans"), but "blacks" (the "Pharaohs" and "Toussaints") as well who used race (or, at the least something with the semblances of race) as a tool for political progress and social survival. Though, we should quickly be clear here, using race as a group organizing concept against racial oppression, and using race to practice and promote racial oppression and racist exclusions—racisms—are two interrelated, but very different things. Take, for example, the "Toussaints" that Du Bois invokes above. Toussaint L'Ouverture, in Du Bois's race thinking here, utilized Haitians' common experience of racial oppression and racist exclusion at the hands of several European colonial powers to forge the first modern black revolution against white supremacy and various forms of racism, such as colonial racism, cultural racism, class or economic racism, deracinative racism, and exterminative racism. In contrast to the "Caesars" and "Napoleans" of history who utilized race as a gateway and bridge to racial and other forms of ethno-cultural oppression and exploitation, here Du Bois is hipping his anti-racist readers to the fact that historically there are precedents for using race to combat racism. Now, I am almost certain that the question that is on the tip of a lot of tongues is: But can we combat racism by utilizing race in a morally mature manner? And, even if we can, are we willing to place our humanity in jeopardy by traveling down the tragic roads and through the tricky back and side streets of the racial state?

The reality of the racial matter is that we are already in the racial state, that we were born into it, born on a racial battlefield, and that whether we consciously or unconsciously contribute to its perpetuation or destruction, we, in so many subtle and not so subtle ways, currently and will continue for the foreseeable future to contribute either to its recreation and reconstruction or to its downfall and ultimate destruction (see Goldberg, 2001; Omi and Winant, 1994; Winant, 2001). It is a frightening thought, but one that must be critically thought out and ethically acted on. Therefore, as a hotly contested concept, race harbors a certain malleability and instrumentality which no group, or elite or aristocracy within a group, has a monopoly on. Race is not a set of singular tried and true transhistorical and transcultural meanings and expressions, but continuously transforms itself and breaks with its former definitions and redefinitions, extending and expanding its range and reach in light of rapidly changing social situations and cultural contexts. Theoretically then, race, as a socio-political concept, could technically and pragmatically be utilized by the racially oppressed to combat racism, an oppressive socio-political condition. This will be the recurring theme and primary point of departure of the subsequent section.

DU BOIS'S CRITIQUE(S) OF RACISM

Du Bois did not have any deep love of race as a concept. In fact, Lott (2001) observes in "The Conservation of Races," Du Bois "seems to have meant to undermine the whole business of constructing racial categories" (p. 69). What excited Du Bois about, and attracted him to, the concept of race were the radical political possibilities it offered for Africana social survival and future flourishing. He argued in "The Conservation of Races," that just as other races had utilized race as an "instrument of progress," so too would continental and diasporan Africans have to use race to forge what was surely a new idea in 1897, "the van of Pan-Negroism" (1986a, pp. 817, 820). However, Du Bois was well aware that because Africana peoples' only exposure to race was the wicked ways in which Europeans used it as an instrument of oppression and intense exploitation, blacks developed a tendency to "deprecate and minimize race distinctions" (p. 815). The young Du Bois, perhaps paradoxically, believed that race could be put to anti-racist purposes, and especially in anti-African, racially segregated, multi-racial and multicultural societies. He counseled the American Negro Academy to reconsider the possible uses and historic abuses of race, stating:

> We are apt to think in our American impatience, that while it may have been true in the past that closed race groups made history, that here in conglomerate America *nous avons changer tout cela*—we have changed all that, and have no need of this ancient instrument of progress. This assumption of which the Negro people are especially fond, can not be established by a careful consideration of history. (p. 817)

For Du Bois, "the Historian and Sociologist" (and, we might add, "Political Economist"), a reconstructed concept of race could be used by continental and diasporan Africans as an "instrument of progress" and a weapon against racial oppression. Race, like so many European inventions and European-derived devices, can be adopted and adapted for Africana interests.

Think for a moment on the ways in which Africana peoples have historically employed non-African technological advances, such as, say, cars and computers, or telephones and televisions? Think about Africana appropriations of various non-African religious traditions, and not simply European but Asian religious traditions? What is more, think about what you are reading and who it has been researched and written by? That is, think about how I—perhaps not "purely," but surely a person of African descent—am using a European language, English, in the interest of the Africana struggle for human rights and racial justice.

People of African descent have a long history of Africanizing non-African concepts, tools, and technologies. Continental and diasporan Africans often use these, among other thought-complexes and instruments, in ways inconsistent with their inventors' intentions, but in ways that speak volumes about Africana culture and conceptions of the world. A concept, tool, or type of technology need not be created by a specific human group in order for that group to utilize it. Culture quickly comes into play here. And it is culture that determines how a concept, tool, or type of technology is viewed, valued, and put to use. Race concepts, though by no means open-ended and/or value-free, can be constructed and contracted by the racially oppressed in the interest of human liberation and social transformation. In *Racist Culture*, David Theo Goldberg (1993) makes an interesting point concerning race in this regard:

> A person need not be a racist, then, merely by use of some version of the concept "race." So it cannot be mere use of race which is objectionable. . . . This prevailing historical legacy of thinking racially does not necessitate that any conceptual use of or appeal to race to characterize social circumstance is inherently unjustifiable. What renders an appeal to racial categorization racist is not that it need be arbitrary. Rather, its racism turns on whether the categorization is constitutive and promotive in the case at hand of racialized exclusions. In other words, what distinguishes a racist from a nonracist appeal to the category of race is the *use* into which the categorization enters, the exclusions it sustains, prompts, promotes, and extends. Foucault argues instructively that no technology, technique, or architecture necessarily restricts freedom or is naturally liberative. In the final analysis, the only and necessarily contingent guarantee of freedom is the practice of freedom itself, is freely living out the conditions of expressive space. Analogously, I want to suggest that though race has tended historically to define conditions of oppression, it could, under a culturalist interpretation—and under some conditions must—be the site of a counterassault, a ground or field for launching liberatory projects or from which to expand freedom(s) and open up emancipatory spaces. (pp. 125, 211, emphasis in original)

Race concepts, then, can be utilized by the racially oppressed to combat their oppression and objectification. The racially oppressed approach and employ race differently, one is tempted to say even diametrically, than their racial oppressors because their socio-political agendas are different and diametric: The latter has an agenda of domination, while the former has an agenda of liberation. Concepts of race, as with racial identities, have historically been and continue currently to be constructed in contexts of racial domination and discrimination. This means, then, that the ruling racial group's view of, and ideological stance toward, race (when and where it is acknowledged) has been and remains one where it is understood to be direly divisive and utterly oppressive. All of this makes pure and perfect sense in the logic of the racial rulers because their entire history of, and relationship to, race has been, to put it plainly, a history of racial oppression and racist exclusion. The ruling race cannot conceive of the racially ruled using race in good conscience because they, the ruling race, have never used race with any ethical or emancipatory intent.

For the racial rulers it is not a question that race can be used in any other way than they have used it. From their point of view, race-consciousness logically leads to racism, to racial domination and racist exclusions. However, for the racially dominated, race is malleable and motive, and neither the racially privileged at present nor even the historic inventors of race have exclusive control over the idea and concept.[2] Du Bois was an early advocate of "race action," "race responsibility," and "race enterprise" in the interest of the racially oppressed, but he advocated all of this with an eye toward and an emphasis on social ethics. In "The Conservation of Races" he stated:

> [I]t is our duty to conserve our physical powers, our intellectual endowments, our spiritual ideals; as a race we must strive by race organization, by race solidarity, by race unity to the realization of that broader humanity which freely recognizes differences in men, but sternly deprecates inequality in the opportunities of development. (1986a, pp. 821–22)

In Du Bois's philosophy of race, race was about anti-racist social transformation as opposed to racist (white supremacist) social domination. Race was (or, could be) liberative, as opposed to oppressive. For Du Bois, the world simply did not have to be the way the white supremacists and racist social (and other) scientists said it was or had to be.

In embracing race as an emancipatory socio-political tool, Du Bois was criticized by whites and shunned by many blacks. With regard to whites' reactions to his embrace of race, he recollected in *Dusk of Dawn*: "'Chauvinism!' they said, when I urged Pan-African solidarity for the accomplishment of universal democracy. 'Race prejudice,' they intimated, was just as reprehensible when shown by black toward white as when shown by white toward black" (p. 781).[3] Moreover, much to his mortification, many persons of

African descent resented his embrace of race as well. From his point of view, they seemed not to have understood what he had characterized over forty years earlier in "The Conservation of Races" as "the central thought of all human history": "the race idea." Writing revealingly of blacks' reactions to his embrace of race in *Dusk of Dawn*, Du Bois remarked, "there were plenty of my colored friends who resented my ultra 'race' loyalty and ridiculed it" (p. 628). Undeterred, Du Bois continued his ruminations on race, placing a greater emphasis on the ethical responsibilities of both the racially oppressed and racially oppressing groups. Race, then, is a chameleonic and controversial concept whose uses and abuses neither the ruling race nor the racially ruled have come to intraracial consensus or definite conclusions concerning. It is also, and perhaps more importantly in Du Bois's philosophy of race, an idea and concept which must be approached morally, with every effort being made to maintain the dignity and inherent value of each and every human group and person.

I am not arguing here that Du Bois understood race to be neutral or non-political, but that he, like Goldberg above, understood race's almost inherent instrumentality to the racially dominated. Looking at race from the eyes of the racially oppressed, Du Bois argued that though "the master's tools will not dismantle the master's house," as Audre Lorde (1984) would have it, if put to proper anti-racist purposes the racially enslaved certainly could make it very hard for the racial masters to live in and enjoy their racial mansions and plantations. And it is the master's discomfort in his once cozy colonial abode that anti-racist radicals bank on when and where they employ race in the interest of anti-racist struggle.

However, all involved in the struggle against racial oppression are not open to using race to combat racism. For some, it is quite simply erroneous and absurd, and symbolizes anti-racists' lowering themselves and their ideals to the level of racists (Appiah, 1990, 1994, 1997; Gilroy, 1993a, 2000; Zack, 1993, 1996, 1998). It is as simple, they say, as the age-old contradiction of "an eye for an eye" and "fight fire with fire." What will be the outcome? What lessons will humanity have learned? Will the world be a better place? Some even go so far as to ask, will we (the well-meaning and morally conscious of the world) still be human after behaving so inhumanely? For others, it is a temporal and extremely time-sensitive tactic, one that must be employed morally and sparingly because using race to combat racial oppression more often than not does not remove racism as much as it temporarily relieves racial tension by rewriting and reinscribing, countering and contradicting dominant racial concepts and codes. In other words, I am saying that race-based anti-racism may at best be a momentary strategy that is applicable at specific socio-historic and politico-economic intervals, but that it should not now nor ever become the most privileged and primary liberatory tool or tactic the racially oppressed utilize in their quest for racial justice. Race-based anti-racism will ultimately reify, that is, move from the level of an idea or abstraction to the level of the concrete and material to inevitable inertia, because the historical horizon and cultural context in which it is undertaken will not last indefinitely. Race-based anti-racism, if endeavored on a mass movement scale, will rapidly alter racial attitudes, thus requiring new (perhaps non-racial) replacement views and values. And this is one of the major issues that many anti-racist advocates of raced-based politics often overlook.

As Goldberg (2001) points out in *The Racial State*, "race can be mobilized to anti-racist purposes at best only as a short term and contingent strategy." Why? Because "racial invocation likely reinscribes elements of the very presumptions promoting racist exclusions it is committed to ending" (pp. 113–14). This is something that Du Bois's philosophy of race anticipated, and that is why he was careful to emphasize that the struggle against racial oppression must never degenerate into any morally reprehensible ideas or acts. Racial justice seekers must morally and cautiously use race as an organizing instrument. In *Dusk of Dawn*, Du Bois (1986a) offered this advice:

> So long as we [are] fighting a color line, we must strive by color organization. We have no choice. If in time, the fight for Negro equality degenerates into organized murder for the suppression of whites, then our last case is no better than our first; but this need not be, if we are level-headed and clear-sighted, and work for the emancipation of all men from caste through the organization and determination of the present victims of caste. (p. 781)

Du Bois's concepts of race and racial struggle, then, were almost utterly the antithesis of white supremacist scientists' conceptions of race. In conceiving of race from an Africana perspective, that is, from the perspective of one thoroughly racially dominated in the (post)modern moment, Du Bois sought to redefine and reconceptualize race. In so doing he offered a race-based anti-racist alternative that destabilized and deconstructed the established imperial order's concepts of race.

As discussed above, historically racial classifications and ethno-cultural categorizations have been invented and assigned primarily by scientists and bureaucrats belonging to racially dominant groups. These agents of the established order usually understand themselves to be racially superior to persons of African origin and descent, and other people of color. Consequently, the racially dominated have imposed on them, and often internalize, white supremacist racial schema. These schema quickly rub the racially dominated wrong, and at such time one of two things takes place: The racially dominated either accept and sometimes subtly embrace white supremacist views and values, or they reject and resist them. In the latter case, the experience of racism and the forging of a distinct racial identity provide the fertile soil in which the seeds of anti-racist thought and praxis are planted.

As the racially oppressed begin to use race for their own anti-racist purposes they must beware of what Cornel West (1993b) has called "the pitfalls of racial reasoning." Race-based anti-racism, as stated above, is only a short-term tactic that must be employed morally and sparingly. Increasingly, emphasis should be placed on social ethics and not purely race-based anti-racist identity politics and struggles. A new politics, perhaps, based more on shared cultural crises, educational issues, and threatening social situations, should be developed and ultimately replace race-based anti-racist organization. Prolonged political mobilization centered on race will eventually weaken the struggle for racial justice because race offers a preexisting and historically problematic identity that was prefabricated and prefashioned by racists, and specifically white supremacists. There simply is no substitute for the racially oppressed forming their own social organizations, political movements, and cultural or ethnic identities, independent of racism. At this point, identity will be formed in the face of shared socio-historic and politico-economic issues and common experiences, as opposed to solely being based on reactions to racial oppression, which could potentially lead the racially oppressed right back down the road to racial essentialism and racial exclusionism. The new politics, then, will be based on new ethical identities as opposed to purely racial or primarily race-based identities and issues.[4]

This brings us full circle, back to the fact that Du Bois developed a discourse on race only insofar as he sought to critique racism and provide a philosophical foundation for anti-racist struggle. He deepened and developed his discourse on race and critique of racism by critiquing the specific race and type of racism that plagued the colonized and colored, and especially blacks: whites and white supremacy. Perhaps the first philosopher of race to systematically explore the imperial international, national, regional, and local dimensions of white supremacy, Du Bois can be said to contribute to what many contemporary race theorists are calling critical white studies.

DU BOIS'S CRITIQUE OF WHITE SUPREMACY, "THE SOULS OF WHITE FOLKS," AND CONTRIBUTIONS TO CRITICAL WHITE STUDIES

Traditionally "white supremacy" has been treated in race and racism discourse as *white domination of and white discrimination against non-whites,* and especially blacks. It is a term that often carries a primarily legal and po-

litical connotation, which has been claimed time and time again to be best exemplified by the historic events and contemporary effects of African holocaust, enslavement, and colonization; the "failure" of reconstruction, the ritual of lynching and the rise of Jim Crow segregation in the United States; and
white colonial and racial rule throughout Africa, and especially apartheid in
South Africa (Cell, 1982; Fredrickson, 1981; Marx, 1998; Shapiro, 1988).
Considering the fact that state-sanctioned segregation and black political disenfranchisement have seemed to come to an end, "white supremacy" is now
seen as classical nomenclature which no longer refers to contemporary racial
and social conditions. However, instead of being a relic of the past that refers
to an odd or embarrassing moment in the United States and South Africa's
(among many other racist nations and empires') march toward transethnic
and multicultural democracy, it remains one of the most appropriate ways to
characterize current racial national and international conditions (Dobratz and
Shanks-Melie, 1997; Kaplan and Bjorgo, 1998; Massey and Denton, 1993;
Nesbitt, 2004; Novick, 1995). Which, in other words, is to say that white supremacy has been and remains central to modernity (and "postmodernity")
because, as I argued above, "modernity" (especially in the sense that this term
is being used in European and American academic and aesthetic discourse)
reeks of racial domination and discrimination. It is an epoch (or aggregate of
eras) which symbolizes not simply the invention of race, but the perfection of
a particular species of *global* racism: white supremacy. Hence, modernity is
not merely the moment of the invention of race, but more, as Theodore Allen
(1994, 1997) argues in *The Invention of the White Race*, it served as an incu-
bator for the invention of the white race and a peculiar pan-European imperialism predicated on the racial ruling, economic exploitation, cultural degradation, and, at times, physical decimation of the life-worlds of non-whites.

In "The Souls of White Folk," which was initially published in the *Independent* in 1910, then substantially revised and published in *Darkwater*
(1920), Du Bois (1995a) stated, "Everything considered, the title to the universe claimed by White Folk is faulty" (p. 454). Long before the recent discourse on critical race theory and critical white studies, Du Bois called into
question white superiority and white privilege, and the possibility of white
racelessness and/or white racial neutrality and white universality. He was one
of the first theorists to chart the changes in race relations from *de jure* to *de
facto* forms of white supremacy, referring to it, as early as 1910, as "the new
religion of whiteness" (p. 454).[5]

White supremacy had not ended and would not end unless and until the
values and views endemic to it and associated with it were or are rejected and
replaced by radical anti-racist, critical multicultural, and uncompromising
ethical views and values. The rejection of white supremacy and the replace-

ment of white supremacist views and values involves not only blacks and
other people of color, but whites as well. As the examples of the Emancipation Proclamation, Reconstruction, and the Civil Rights movement indicate,
changes in the law and its interpretation and application do not always translate into racial justice and social transformation (Berry, 1994; Higginbotham,
1978, 1996; D. King, 1995). White supremacist social views and values
linger long after amendments have been made and laws changed. Therefore,
law-focused critical white studies, and critical race theory, as will be discussed below, provide at best only part of the picture (Bonilla-Silva, 2001;
Delgado, 1995; Delgado and Stefancic, 1997).

The conception and critique of white supremacy that I develop here does
not seek to sidestep socio-legal race discourse as much as it intends to supplement it with Du Bois and others' work in radical politics and critical social
theory. One of the main reasons this supplemental approach to critical white
studies (and critical race theory, as we will see in the subsequent section) is
important is because typically legal studies of race confine theorists to particular national social and political arenas, which is problematic considering
the fact that white supremacy is a global racist system (J. Daniels, 1997;
C. W. Mills, 1999). Du Bois (1995a) declared, "whiteness is the ownership of
the earth forever and ever, Amen!" (p. 454). Here he is sardonically hinting
at the cardinal difference between white supremacy and most other forms of
racism: its worldwide or global historical, cultural, social, political, legal, and
economic influence and impact. White supremacy serves as the glue that connects and combines racism to colonialism, and racism to capitalism. It has
also been illustrated that it exacerbates sexism by sexing racism and racing
sexism, to put it unpretentiously. Thus, white supremacy as a global racism
intersects and interconnects with sexism, and particularly patriarchy as a
global system that oppresses and denies women's human dignity and right to
be humanly different from men, the ruling gender (A. Y. Davis 1981, 1989;
hooks, 1981, 1984, 1995, 2004a, 2004b; J. A. James, 1996a, 1999).

With regard to Du Bois's critique of white supremacy, it is not simply a
global and social phenomenon, but a personal and political one as well. That
is to say that for Du Bois white supremacy is simultaneously systemic and
systematic, and also a matter of racist cultural mores and manners, which
teeter-totter between idealist, materialist, and constructionist accounts of
race. An idealist account of race says simply (or, not so simply) that white
racism against non-whites, and especially blacks, is not so much a matter of
race as it is of culture. Racial idealists argue that European culture and its pre-
colonial history of color-symbolism and religious views—such as, Europeans' conceptions of themselves as "civilized" whites and non-whites as
"wild," "savage," "heathen" or "ethnic" Others; the positive and negative as-

sociations regarding the colors white and black; and the ways in which their racist cultural interpretations of Christianity support not only the white/black color valuations and devaluations but the "civilize and Christianize" missions of European colonialism and imperialism—set the stage for what would later become racism and white supremacy (Fredrickson, 1987; Hornsman, 1986; Jordan, 1977).

Materialist accounts of race, which are primarily inspired by Marxist theory, maintain that racism does not have to do with culture as much as it does political economy. Europeans needed a cheap labor force to extra-exploit and work their newly and imperially acquired continents, countries, colonial settlements, and plantations. For the racial materialists it was not about religion or civilization or science, but an economics and politics reduced to its lowest and most racist level (Cox, 1959, 1987; Genovese, 1965, 1969, 1974, 1979; C. L. R. James, 1963, 1995, 1996; E. Williams, 1966). Finally, racial constructionists contend that *race* is an outgrowth of human beings' inherent ethnocentrism, but that *racism* is a result of Europe's push for global dominance and white world supremacy. In this view, no matter who invented race, its reasons for origination, and whether it is scientifically sound, it is an historical artifact that most modern (and "postmodern") human beings use, either consciously or unconsciously, to make interpersonal, socio-cultural and politico-economic decisions. "Whites" and "non-whites" do not exist prior to the imperial expansion that helped to birth, raise, and rear European modernity. But this is all beside the point to the constructionists. What is relevant is the invention of whiteness and its classical and contemporary uses and abuses, and the ways it has evolved over several centuries, transitioning from *de jure* to *de facto* form, and transforming the racial rules and ethnic ethics of who counts as "white" and "non-white" (T. W. Allen, 1994, 1997; Goldberg, 1997; Harris, 1999b; Lopez, 1995; Omi and Winant, 1994; Roediger, 1994, 1999, 2002).

Du Bois's writings on race do not fit nicely or neatly into any of the aforementioned accounts of race. As even a cursory review of his concepts of race and critiques of racism reveal, at different intervals throughout his long life and career he harbored what would currently be considered aspects of each of the three accounts of race discussed above. For Du Bois, as I intimated earlier, white supremacy was not simply a global and social phenomenon, but a personal and political one as well. Hence, his assertion, in "The Souls of White Folk": "The discovery of personal whiteness among the world's peoples is a very modern thing" (1995a, p. 453). Take special note of the connection Du Bois makes between "personal whiteness" and "modernity," to use the latter term loosely. His dialectical approach to white supremacy accents its interconnections with other systems of oppression because in his critical socio-theoretical framework racism is one of several "very modern" intersecting hegemonic variables. But it is white supremacy's *globality*, the fact that it is a racist global system or "racial polity," as Charles Mills (1999) maintains, that marks it for much-needed critical theoretical consideration.

In his critique of the global aspects of white supremacy, Du Bois critically engaged its origins and evolution, locating its genesis, uniqueness, and ubiquitousness in European imperial global expansion, domination, and colonization. What distinguished white supremacy from local, national, and regional racisms, such as those that exist between certain non-white groups, is its international imperial nature and modern world-historic influence and effects. At the heart of the history of white supremacy, as quiet as it is kept, is a prolonged practice and promotion of an extremely acute form of *cultural racism* and *cultural theft*. For Du Bois (1995a), whites were "super-men" and "world-mastering demi-gods" with "feet of clay" (p. 456). By which he meant, whites, with all their claims of superiority and "super-humanity," were or appeared super-strong because they built their empire(s) on the inventions and innovations, and on the cultures and contributions of the hyperraced and transethnic others, the people of color they colonized (p. 457). But, as the "super-men" with "feet of clay" comment reveals, the colored and colonized were well aware of whites' weakness(es), of their Achilles' heel(s): Their imperial push for global domination, that is, their centuries-spanning project(s) of setting up systems of oppression unwittingly and ironically created intra-imperial cultural tensions, racist sibling rivalries amongst whites themselves, and also created the context and laid the foundation for the very anti-imperial colored/colonized hammer that would smash the imperial white "super-men's" "feet of clay." In "The Souls of White Folk," Du Bois audaciously asserted:

> The greatness of Europe has lain in the width of the stage on which she has played her part, the strength of the foundations on which she has builded, and a natural, human ability no whit greater (if as great) than that of other days and races. In other words, the deeper reasons for the triumph of European civilization lie quite outside and beyond Europe—back in the universal struggles of all mankind.
>
> Why, then, is Europe great? Because of the foundations which the mighty past have furnished her to build upon: the iron trade of ancient, black Africa, the religion and empire-building of yellow Asia, the art and sciences of the "dago" Mediterranean shore, east, south, and west, as well as north. And, where she had builded securely upon this great past and learned from it she has gone forward to greater and more splendid human triumph; but where she has ignored this past and forgotten and sneered at it, she has shown the cloven hoof of poor, crucified humanity—she has played, like other empires gone, the world fool!
>
> If, then, European triumphs in culture have been greater, so, too, may her failures have been greater. (p. 459)

Here Du Bois notes major "gifts" or contributions to culture and civilization that various people of color have made throughout human history, many of them in their pre-colonial (or, rather pre-*European* colonial) periods.[6] He does not diminish or attempt to downplay the "greatness of Europe," but observes that "the triumph of European civilization lies quite outside and beyond Europe." From Du Bois's (1986a) racial frame of reference, each ethnocultural group or, rather, each "race" has a "great message . . . for humanity" (p. 820). He was extremely confident in the greatness of Africana peoples' past and present gift(s) *and* spirit of giving, even in the face of and often, it seemed, in spite of their endurance and experience of holocaust, enslavement, colonization, segregation, and so forth.

One of the main reasons Du Bois believed Africana peoples were uniquely "gifted," and their "gifts" were especially valuable with regard to world culture and civilization was because their anti-racist (and anti-colonial) struggle strategies and tactics had historically and consistently been different from those of any other human group. This is so, in Du Bois's cultural gift theory, on account of the fact that in white supremacist social hierarchy Africans are the antithesis of Europeans, or blacks are the subhuman opposite of white humans. Again, it is a cultural as opposed to biological conception of race that Du Bois opts for to critique and combat white supremacy and advocate Africana unity and black liberation. In *The Education of Black People* (1973), he stated: "Biologically we are mingled of all conceivable elements, but race is psychology, not biology; and psychologically we are a unified race with one history, one red memory, and one revolt" (p. 100).

His "gift theory," like his overall philosophy of race, hinged on a conception of culture that was increasingly informed by continental and diasporan African history, radical politics, and social theory. Just as he rhetorically asked and answered the question, "What, then, is a race?," in "The Conservation of Races," Du Bois's burgeoning anti-biological and pro-socio-cultural conception of race critically queried culture. If race is not biological and it is indeed cultural, as Du Bois came to claim, then one of the first things we need to find out is how he conceived of culture. I will leave it to Du Bois to elaborate his philosophy of culture and its connection(s) to his philosophy of race. In *The Education of Black People*, he rhetorically queried, "What is a culture?" Then he contended:

It is a careful Knowledge of the Past out of which the group as such has emerged: in our case a knowledge of African history and social development—one of the richest and most intriguing which the world has known. Our history in America, north, south and Caribbean, has been an extraordinary one which we must know to understand ourselves and our world. The experience through which our ancestors have gone for four hundred years is part of our bone and sinew whether we know it or not. The method which we evolved for opposing slavery and fighting prejudice are not to be forgotten, but learned for our own and others' instruction. We must understand the differences in social problems between Africa, the West Indies, South and Central America, not only among the Negroes but those affecting Indians and other minority groups. Plans for the future of our group must be built on a base of our problems, our dreams and frustrations; they cannot stem from empty air or successfully be based on the experiences of others alone. (pp. 143–44)

Beginning with "a careful Knowledge of the Past," both continental and diasporan, Du Bois's definition of culture takes a hard turn toward "experience" and he states that the lived-experiences of "our ancestors" are "part of our bone and sinew whether we know it or not." In fact, "we must know" "[o]ur history" in Africa, the Americas—for Du Bois, "the Americas" were not only the United States north and south, but intellectually, politically, and culturally included Central and South America as well—and the Caribbean, in order to "understand ourselves and our world." So, besides being grounded historically in continental and diasporan African lived-experiences, Du Bois's concept of culture gravitates and grows toward an experiential and existential exploration and explanation of Africana life-worlds, of Africana actualities, past and present. In other words, if indeed culture has to do with "a careful Knowledge of the Past out of which the group as such has emerged," the "Past" in Du Bois's thinking was much more than historical, it was also cultural.

Culture, contends Maulana Karenga (1997) is "the totality of thought and practice by which a people creates itself, celebrates, sustains and develops itself and introduces itself to history and humanity" (p. 163). Culture, then, is the thought-, belief-, and value-systems and traditions that people create, extend, and expand to not only make sense of the world, but also to alter it in their own and others' best interests. That is why Du Bois asserted above: "The method which we evolved for opposing slavery and fighting prejudice are not to be forgotten, but learned for our own and others' instruction." Here he is suggesting that classical Africana anti-racist and anti-colonial liberation thought and practice in the fight against white supremacy ("slavery" and "prejudice") could and should be instructional for contemporary Africana and other oppressed people. In Du Bois's gift theory, this is one of Africana peoples' greatest gifts and/or cultural contributions: their spirit of struggle, sacrifice, and service in the interest of revolutionary social transformation and human liberation.

In "The Conservation of Races," Du Bois (1986a) declared: "We believe that the Negro people, as a race, have a contribution to make to civilization and humanity, which no other race can make" (p. 825). He held this belief primarily for two reasons. First, it was based on Africa's past, "one of the richest and most intriguing which the world has known." Most race and/or racist scientists at the turn of the twentieth century either had no knowledge of Africa's past, or they were aware of it and developed their racist theories to counter claims of the greatness of African antiquity. As Du Bois put it in "The Superior Race" (1923): "Lions have no historians" (1995a, p. 474). By which he wished to imply that even though the lion is universally revered as the "king of the jungle," it is nonetheless an animal and, therefore, has no history and, thus, no need of historians. It is only human beings who can make history and create culture, and in a white supremacist world blacks are not human, but subhuman. Therefore, the history and culture that Africans did in fact produce in ancient epochs, or in the pre-colonial period, is viewed as either influenced by or derivative of European culture, or a "primitive" attempt to imitate and emulate European culture, usually Greco-Roman culture. Du Bois's critique of and counter to these claims can be found in his watershed works in the areas of African historiography and African cultural anthropology; for example, works such as *The Negro* (1915), *Africa, Its Geography, People and Products* (1930), *Africa—Its Place in Modern History* (1930), *Black Folk, Then and Now: An Essay on the History and Sociology of the Negro Race* (1939), *Color and Democracy: Colonies and Peace* (1945), *The World and Africa* (1947), and *Africa: An Essay Toward a History of the Continent of Africa and Its Inhabitants* (1961).

The second reason Du Bois (1986a) believed that Africana peoples had a significant contribution to make to culture and civilization was because of their endurance and experiences of holocaust, enslavement, colonization, segregation, and so on, had "gifted" them with "second-sight," as he put it in *The Souls of Black Folk* (p. 364). This "second-sight" enabled black folk to see things that others could not on account of the specificities of their historicity. That is to say, Du Bois believed that blacks' contemporary "gift" to culture and civilization had to do with their particular and peculiar position in and struggle(s) against one of the major systems of oppression plaguing people in the modern moment: white supremacy. Du Bois's belief that Africana people have a "great message . . . for humanity" led him to a life-long critique of white supremacy that is best exemplified by works such as "Race Friction Between Black and White" (1908), "The Souls of White Folk" (1910), "Of The Culture of White Folk" (1917), "White Co-Workers" (1920), "The Souls of White Folk" (1920), "The Superior Race" (1923), "The White Worker" (1935), "The White Proletariat in Alabama, Georgia, and Florida" (1935), "The White World" (1940), and "The White Folk Have a Right to Be Ashamed" (1949). Of these works, "The Souls of White Folk," published in *Darkwater: Voices Within the Veil* (1920), and which recasts and combines Du Bois's 1910 essay by that name and his freshly penned piece, "Of the Cul-

ture of White Folk" (1917), offers his most sustained and sophisticated statement against white supremacy, as it not only critiques white supremacy, but
represents and registers as one of the first attempts to expose white supremacy's influences on and interconnections with other systems of oppression, such as colonialism and capitalism.

As his philosophy of race and critique of white supremacy evolved, so too
did Du Bois's gift theory. It began innocently enough as a claim that Africana
people, "as a race, have a contribution to make to civilization and humanity,
which no other race can make" (1986a, 825). Then, it grew gradually into a
charge to contemporary Africana people to emulate and audaciously endeavor
to surpass their ancestors' contributions to culture and civilization. In "The
Conservation of Races," Du Bois (1986a) declared:

> Manifestly some of the great races of today—particularly the Negro race—have
> not as yet given to civilization the full spiritual message which they are capable
> of giving. I will not say that the Negro race has as yet given no message to the
> world, for it is still a mooted question among scientists as to just how far Egypt
> ian civilization was Negro in its origin; if it was not wholly Negro, it was cer
> tainly very closely allied. Be that as it may, however, the fact still remains that
> the full, complete Negro message of the whole Negro race has not as yet been
> given to the world. (pp. 819–20)

From Du Bois's optic, blacks had been unable to give "civilization the
full spiritual message which they are capable of giving" primarily because
of white supremacy and its enormous and unfathomable effects on Africana
life-worlds and lived-experiences. His early uncertainty regarding the
African origins of ancient Egyptian civilization was laid to rest as a result
of the research of Franz Boas, Leo Frobenius, and Harry Johnston, among
others.[7] If Egypt, undoubtedly one of the greatest classical civilizations,
was African or, at the least, initiated by Africans—as Du Bois documented
in *The Negro, Black Folk, Then and Now,* and *The World and Africa*—then
it would be a great disservice to modern Africana people to argue that they
have "given no message to the world." As he studied and learned more of
Africa's ancient and pre-colonial past, Du Bois's gift theory shifted its emphasis from Africana people giving "the full, complete Negro message . . .
to the world," to accenting and highlighting classical African contributions
to culture and civilization with an eye toward first, confronting and combating the white supremacist theses of, of course, white superiority and
black inferiority and, also, blacks' purported lack of history and culture;
second, providing contemporary Africana people with classical Africana
cultural paradigms and traditional motifs; and, finally, offering a caveat to
continental and diasporan Africans that their task is not so much to give the

definitive Africana message to the world (something, on second thought, that may never really be possible), but to contribute to and continue the Africana struggle for freedom and justice in their age and leave a legacy for succeeding generations.

Generic racism, if there is such a thing, essentially entails racial domination and discrimination. White supremacy does not simply racially oppress, as Du Bois asserts above. Being the fraternal twin (or, at the least, a sibling of some sort) of capitalism it racially oppresses in the interest of nonpareil racialized economic exploitation. It symbolizes the intensification of economic exploitation by adding a racist dimension to capitalist greed and colonial gain. Hinging on a diabolical dialectic that sees whites as superior and non-whites as inferior, white supremacy consumes the world of color and claims non-whites' contributions to human culture and civilization as European or white contributions to culture and civilization. This is so because from the white supremacist point of view, non-whites have never possessed and do not now possess culture and civilization and, therefore, could not possibly contribute to the up-building of something they have never possessed and do not now possess. Further, white supremacy enables and utterly encourages whites to theoretically and culturally loot the knowledge banks and cultural treasure troves of the colored world, similar to the way they did when they established *racial colonialism* and *colonial capitalism*, because it is a global system that rewards based on the embrace of white hegemonic views and values, white conquest, and racialized colonization.

Moving beyond a strictly materialist (politico-economic and/or class-centered) account of race and racism, and hitting at the heart of white supremacy, Du Bois, in "The Souls of White Folk," queried the "colored world" and those whites who would open themselves to moral and materialist questions: "How many of us today fully realize the current theory of colonial expansion, of the relation of Europe which is white, to the world which is black and brown and yellow? Bluntly put, that theory is this: It is the duty of white Europe to divide up the darker world and administer it for Europe's good" (1995a, p. 459). Part of Du Bois's critique of white supremacy reveals his reliance on racial materialist arguments, where the other portion of his critique revolves around his own homegrown cultural nationalism, which was more often later in his life, what I will term, a *cultural internationalism* that sought to accent and highlight commonalities and kinships amongst people of color based on their endurances and experiences of, and struggles against, European imperial expansion and all-out white (cultural, social, political, legal, educational, religious, aesthetic, and economic) domination and discrimination. Du Bois's critical comments in "The Souls of White Folk" deserve quotation at length, as his argument is elaborated throughout several carefully constructed paragraphs that poignantly capture the crux of his critique of white supremacy:

> The European world is using black and brown men for all the uses which men know. Slowly but surely white culture is evolving the theory that "darkies" are born beasts of burden for white folk. It were silly to think otherwise, cries the cultured world, with stronger and shriller accord. The supporting arguments grow and twist themselves in the mouths of merchant, scientist, soldier, traveler, writer, and missionary: Darker peoples are dark in mind as well as in body; of dark, uncertain, and imperfect descent; of frailer, cheaper stuff; they are cowards in the face of mausers and maxims; they have no feelings, aspirations, and loves; they are fools, illogical idiots — "half-devil and half-child."
>
> Such as they are civilization must, naturally, raise them, but soberly and in limited ways. They are not simply dark white men. They are not "men" in the sense that Europeans are men. To the very limited extent of their shallow capacities lift them to be useful to whites, to raise cotton, gather rubber, fetch ivory, dig diamonds — and let them be paid what men think they are worth — white men who know them to be well-nigh worthless.
>
> Such degrading of men by men is as old as mankind and the invention of no one race or people. Ever have men striven to conceive of their victims as different from the victors, endlessly different, in soul and blood, strength and cunning, race and lineage. It has been left, however, to Europe and to modern days to discover the eternal world-wide mark of meanness — color!
>
> Such is the silent revolution that has gripped modern European culture in the later nineteenth and twentieth centuries. Its zenith came in Boxer times: White supremacy was all but world-wide, Africa was dead, India conquered, Japan isolated, and China prostrate, while white America whetted her sword for mongrel Mexico and mulatto South America, lynching her own Negroes the while. (p. 460)

The "civilized" (read: whites) are simultaneously a race in a socio-cultural and politico-economic sense, though they do not think of themselves in racial terms, and they throw temper tantrums when they are thought of in racial terms or as being racialized or raced. They can steal and kill the "uncivilized" (read: non-whites) without regard to rank or reason, and they can at any moment change the rules of the racial hierarchy and racial history because they alone are decidedly and definitively the authors of human culture and civilization, and most certainly the architects of science and technology. As Du Bois demonstrates above, white supremacy is not simply about racial domination and discrimination. Which is to say, white supremacy cannot quickly be reduced to racism, and especially as it is understood in contemporary racial discourse. Much more, white supremacy robs the raced or people of color of their right to be human, of their right to self-definition and self-determination. It reduces human beings to the status of things, which is one of the reasons, as Fanon observed in *The Wretched of the Earth*, when they are discussed by the white world, non-whites (or people of color) are referred to in "zoological terms," in the terms in which animals are discussed and dissected. Fanon (1968) fumed:

> In fact, the terms the [white colonial] settler uses when he mentions the native [the raced, or the colored] are zoological terms. He speaks of the yellow man's reptilian motions, of the stink of the native quarter, of breeding swarms, of foulness, of spawn, of gesticulations. When the settler seeks to describe the native fully in exact terms he constantly refers to the bestiary. (p. 42)

Du Bois's critique of white supremacy also hits head-on the issue of white personhood and black (or non-white) subpersonhood. He asserted: "They [the colored and colonized] are not simply dark white men. They are not 'men' in the sense that Europeans are men." Whiteness and maleness are prerequisites for personhood in the world that modernity made (Bederman, 1995; Ferber, 1998; Spickard and Daniel, 2004; Wolff, 2005). A person, in this world, is one who is rational, self-directing, and morally and legally equal with a white male. Since white males created the laws of this world, none but white males are equal and given moral, legal, and extralegal consideration. Therefore, as the *Dred Scott* decision demonstrates, "a black man has no rights which a white man is legally bound to respect" (see *Dred Scott*, 1857, pp. 403–407). White rights are intimately intertwined with the denial of black rights. Or, to put it another way, white personhood is inextricable from black subpersonhood. In *The Racial Contract*, Charles Mills (1997) contends:

> Whiteness is defined in part in respect to an oppositional darkness, so that white self-conceptions of identity, personhood, and self-respect are then intimately tied up with repudiation of the black Other. No matter how poor one was, one was still able to affirm the whiteness that distinguished one from the subpersons on the other side of the color line. (pp. 58–59; see also Yancy, 2004)

And who or what are these "human things," to borrow a phrase from Du Bois's (1995a) discourse, on the "other side of the color line" (p. 456)? Mills (1997) maintains:

> Subpersons are humanoid entities who because of racial phenotype/genealogy/culture, are not fully human and therefore have a different and inferior schedule of rights and liberties applying to them. In other words, it is possible to get away with doing things to subpersons that one could not do to persons, because they do not have the same rights as persons. (p. 56)

Even in its mildest and most unconscious forms, white supremacy is one of the extremest and most vicious human rights violations in history because it plants false seeds of white superiority and black inferiority in the fertile ground of the future. It takes human beings and turns them into the subhuman things, making them colored means to a white imperial end. Du Bois's critique of white supremacy registers, then, as not only a radical criticism of an increasingly illusive and nebulous racism, but an affirmation of black humanity and an epoch-spanning assertion of Africana and other oppressed peoples' inherent right to human and civil rights. A discussion of Du Bois's discourse on human and civil rights will be better served by examining some of the ways his work connects with and contributes to contemporary critical race theory, which, in some of its articulations, takes as one of its major tasks the critique and confrontation of white supremacy.

DU BOIS'S "THE COMET" AND CONTRIBUTIONS TO CRITICAL RACE THEORY

No longer considered the exclusive domain of legal studies scholars and radical civil rights lawyers and law professors, critical race theory has blossomed and currently encompasses and includes a wide range of theory and theorists from diverse academic disciplines. Its most prominent practitioners, initially law professors and "left scholars, most of them scholars of color," borrowed from many of the political and theoretical breakthroughs of black nationalism, radical feminism, poststructuralism, and postmodernism. They also employed and experimented with new cutting-edge literary techniques and social science methodologies that shaped and shaded their work and burgeoning socio-legal discourse, ultimately giving it a fierceness and flair unheard of in the history of legal studies. Early critical race theorists' work acutely accented "the vexed bond between law and racial power" (Crenshaw, Gotanda, Peller and Thomas, 1995, p. xiii). The emphasis on race and power quickly led them to the critique of "white supremacy and the subordination of people of color," not simply in the legal system, but in society as a whole (p. xiii).

Most notably, critical race theory essentially entails a claim that race and racism are central to European modernity; an insistence that European modernity spawned a homogenizing social, political, legal, and medical system that glosses over the heterogeneity of non-Europeans; a declaration that racism interlocks with sexism and capitalism to form an overarching system of oppression that thrice threatens modern movements for multicultural, transethnic and transgender democracy; a critique of the established orders' claims of colorblindness and racially-neutral rule; a critique of whiteness and white supremacy; a call for racial justice; and a controversial claim that the raced (i.e., non-Europeans) may have to employ race and their experiences of racism as a rallying point to mobilize an anti-racist movement (Crenshaw et al., 1995;

Delgado, 1995; Delgado and Stefancic, 2001; Essed and Goldberg, 2001; Goldberg, Musheno and Bower, 2001; Goldberg and Solomos, 2002). Du Bois's philosophy of race, as we have witnessed throughout this chapter, in many senses foreshadows contemporary critical race theory and, therefore, contributes several paradigms and theoretic points of departure. However, as with so many other aspects of his thought, Du Bois's writings on race and racism have been relegated to the realm, at best, of sociology, which downplays and diminishes their interdisciplinarity and significance for contemporary critical social theory and radical politics. Therefore, his writings on race have been virtually overlooked and/or rendered intellectually invisible by contemporary critical race theorists. With what follows I endeavor to fill this void in contemporary critical race scholarship by analyzing Du Bois's writings on race and racism as contributions to (the reconceptualization and reconstruction of) critical race theory.[8]

In *Critical Race Theory*, Richard Delgado (1995) states that though it began organizing as a "self-conscious entity" in 1989, critical race theory's "intellectual origins go back much further": "The movement has predecessors — Critical Legal Studies, to which it owes a great debt, feminism, and Continental social and political philosophy. It [also] derives its inspiration from the American civil rights tradition, including Martin Luther King, W. E. B. Du Bois, Rosa Parks, and Cesar Chavez, and from nationalist movements, including Malcolm X and the Panthers" (p. xiv). What I wish to highlight here is, first, though it generously draws from European and white American thought-traditions, African American social and political thought and movements have been at the heart of and enormously influential on critical race theory's discourse and debates. This is an important point to make since there has been a relative silence regarding critical race theory in African American Studies in specific, and Africana Studies more generally. If in fact African American radical intellectuals, social critics, and political activists have been at the heart of this discourse, central to its formation, and many of its major advocates and practitioners, then, African American Studies scholars and students would be remiss to continue to allow critical race theory to go unengaged.[9]

A second issue I wish to emphasize here involves Du Bois's place in critical race scholarship. Many, if not all, of the key concerns of contemporary critical race theory are prefigured in Du Bois's discourse on race and racism in ways that makes one wonder whether contemporary critical race theory is simply a continuation, or a contemporary version of Du Bois's classical critical theory of race circulating under a new name. As illustrated above, Du Bois's critique of modernity, albeit often masked and muted, found it, modernity, morally weak and wanting because each of its inventions and innovations were accompanied by unprecedented human and environmental destruction and domination. Which is to say that when and where whites broke new ground, in whatever technical capacity and whichever area of existence, they did so on the graves of non-whites, imperially embalming the earth and making the life-worlds, countries, and continents of non-whites a massive mortuary. No amount of racial naïveté could save non-whites. They therefore had no other recourse but to argue, as Du Bois did time and time again throughout his long career, *race-consciousness*, as will be discussed in greater detail below. At certain intervals in Du Bois's discourse this impulse registered as separatism, at others nationalism, and still others the *cultural internationalism* I observed above. But no matter which position Du Bois embraced and argued, an *anti-racist social ethics* was ever at work and at the heart of his agenda and ultimate objectives (Edelin, 1981). Again, the emphasis on ethics made many of his positions—including and extending beyond his anti-racism—temporal tactics that were extremely time and space sensitive.

One of the most intriguing issues that Du Bois's discourse on race and racism brings to the fore is the often-overlooked fact that it is possible to reject biology-based concepts of race and any and all forms of racism without denying the socio-historic and politico-economic reality of race and racism. The so-called "anti-race" theorists who argue that race and race-consciousness are the cause of racism and racial oppression, are quite simply thinking wrong about race and have not done their homework on the origins and evolution(s), and the historic socio-political uses and abuses of race. Racism, as the critical race theorists never weary of reminding us, is "systematic" and, at this point, deeply "ingrained" in social, political, and cultural consciousness (Crenshaw et al., 1995, p. xiv). It is an invisible invader and often-illusive intruder that has impacted and affected, perhaps, almost every life-experience human beings have had in the modern (and postmodern) moment. Even if utter abandonment of race concepts and race-consciousness were possible, the material and morphological, religious and rancorous, public and private consequences of the last five hundred years of hyper-racialized human existence—that is, rote racialization and racial injustice and the socio-cultural memories associated with these phenomena—would remain. This is part of the point of Du Bois's short story "The Comet" (1920), which dramatizes the persistent racial power relations between a black male "messenger"—or "courier" in contemporary jargon—named Jim Davis, and a young wealthy white woman named Julia, after a comet has unleashed "deadly gases" that claim the lives of everyone in New York City (1996a, p. 613). Jim, of course, represents African American or black thought and traditions, where Julia symbolizes European American or white thought and traditions.[10]

Even more than representing pre-apocalyptic black and white, hence, *racial* thought and traditions, Jim and Julia's journey, that is, their actual lived-experiences in a world where everyone else is dead, symbolizes an often uneasy transgression and transformation of previous (white supremacist and/or anti-black) racial thought and practices, that is, former racial views and values. An alternate interpretation of Jim and Julia as archetypal characters could also read them in a "religious" vein, as a post-apocalyptic Adam and Eve. Instead of a beautiful and peaceful "Garden of Eden," Du Bois places them in a world of death and ugliness, a world which metaphorically mirrors the one white folk imperially invented and orchestrated, especially considering the then-recent bloodbath of World War I. However, Du Bois is quick to reveal, it is not a world of utter desolation and asphyxiation, so long as they free themselves from the vices and vulgarities of the former white supremacist world. This, of course, represents religious persons' life-long struggle to come to terms with the theodic thread that ironically undergirds and connects the religious traditions and expressions of those who worship and serve—to shamelessly steal a favorite phrase from black liberation theologian James Cone's (1975) critical language—the "God of the oppressed," and those who exalt and obey the "God of the oppressor." In this vein, Jim and Julia's entire journey throughout, and experiences in, this world of death and disaster roughly boils down to a choice (the ultimate choice in the realm of religion) between God and the Devil, and/or good and evil. The "religious" interpretation of "The Comet" is given greater credence when we bear in mind Herbert Aptheker's (1985) assertion:

> In all of his writings, the ready use of Biblical language [and symbolism] reflects that he was deeply read in both Testaments. However, Du Bois was not religious in a conventional sense, and he disliked organized religion. He was, however, deeply religious [read: spiritual] in that he believed in a kind of ultimate mystery in life, guided by some Creative Force; he also believed in a form of immortality. (p. xii)

Though extremely intriguing, I will leave the "religious" interpretation of "The Comet" to critics better versed in the analysis of secular texts from a sacred frame of reference; hence, a certain sort of hermeneutics. My interpretation here, as I have intimated, will be almost utterly instrumental. I am interested specifically in the ways this short story foreshadows many of the motifs of contemporary critical race theory, and contributes to its reconceptualization and reconstruction by opening up a dialogue between critical race and radical Africana theorists. Thus, this interpretation, like the story itself, is interdisciplinary, as it draws from African American literary, social, and cultural criticism, and also semiotic, feminist, postmodern, and postcolonial theory. The primary purpose here is to produce an accessible analysis of Du Bois's contributions to the discourse and development of critical race theory, and, in turn, critical race theory's contributions to the discourse and development of Africana critical theory.

"The Comet" offers us an ideal opportunity to observe Du Bois's contributions to critical race theory as it not only prefigures many of the themes taken up by contemporary critical race theorists, but it also pre-indicates some of the literary style(s) of current critical race theory. In *Darkwater* (1920), the volume which houses "The Comet," Du Bois employs a mixture of literary mediums, creating a textual collage that would have made (or, indeed, maybe did make) the African American visual artist and collagist Romare Bearden grin from ear to ear. In a much more pronounced manner than in *The Souls of Black Folk*, Du Bois's writing in *Darkwater* was poignant and polyvocal, shifting back and forth between pungent politico-economic analysis and socio-cultural criticism to pure poetry and lyrical literary experimentation (the latter, à la Jean Toomer's 1923 classic *Cane*, though Du Bois's creative writing had a firmer foundation in the former, social science, and was, therefore, often cerebral and overly sentimental [see Gibson, 1977; Gipson, 1971; Kostelanetz, 1985; Staton, 2001]). Where *The Souls of Black Folk* was a literary look backward at the impact and effects of the African holocaust, enslavement, and Jim Crow segregation on the human pride and passions of African Americans, *Darkwater* was a literary look forward, a "vision of the liberated future" that Larry Neal (1989) and his Black Arts associates were soon to sing of. It was an extremely innovative and thoroughly cosmopolitan text, perhaps one of the first and most widely read to combine literary experimentation and sociological analysis with continental and diasporan African calls for racial justice. It was, amazingly for its time, simultaneously anti-racist, anti-sexist, anti-colonial, and anti-capitalist, devoting at least one chapter to each of the aforementioned issues and/or ideologies. It was, in the end, early Africana *guerrilla wordfare*, to coin a phrase—that is, radical writing as a form of freedom fighting—in the sense that Du Bois employed every major modern style of writing to critique and combat the various types of domination and discrimination in his time and, sad to say, yet in ours. Let us now engage the story.

When the comet came, Jim, the messenger, was down in the Wall Street company's "lower vaults," "in the bowels of the earth, under the world," a place "too dangerous for more valuable men," his now-deceased narrow-minded boss had told him. As a consequence of his being "down there," hard at work in the "dark basement beneath," he was spared the toxic smell of the comet's tail (Du Bois, 1996a, p. 611). Julia, the young wealthy white woman, had been developing film in her plush, private darkroom, and was likewise spared. Jim bewilderingly discovered the death spell that had conquered New York City and immediately headed home to Harlem to check the life status of his family. On his way he encountered Julia. Julia beckoned to Jim from a great distance and, therefore, did not know that he was an African American — which seems beside the point since they are the only known survivors that each other are aware of in the whole of New York City, perhaps in the whole world. But racism is dogged and rears its ugly head (and horns!), even during times of great duress and crisis, as Du Bois demonstrates, perhaps drawing directly from African Americans' recent experiences during and after World War I. Du Bois's depiction of Julia's reaction to being "saved" by a black man helps to highlight the continuing influence and effects of racism, however subtle, even in the event of the sudden absence of "races" and, more tellingly, white male racial rulers.

In some senses Du Bois can be seen as saying that Western European and white American culture are so thoroughly shot through with racism and the thousands of injustices, oppressions, and exclusions that accompany it, that it cannot quickly be unlearned even at the moment of crisis. White males do not have a monopoly on racist thought and behavior, though in white supremacist patriarchal polities they may be its most vocal and vicious proponents. This means, as Du Bois's short story suggests, in the absence of the white male racial ruler, the white woman (who is second to the white male in white supremacist social hierarchy and chain of command) shifts from being the eternal runner-up racial ruler to the head honcho racial ruler. Now turning to the text, the pertinent passage reads:

> He came back on Fifth Avenue at 57th and flew past the Plaza and by the park with its hushed babies and silent throng, until he was rushing past 72nd Street he heard a sharp cry, and saw a living form leaning wildly out an upper window. He gasped. The human voice sounded in his ears like the voice of God. . . .
>
> He wheeled the car in a sudden circle, running over the still body of a child and leaping on the curb. Then he rushed up the steps and tried the door and rang violently. There was a long pause, but at last the heavy door swung back. They stared a moment in silence. She had not noticed before that he was a Negro. He had not thought of her as white. She was a woman of perhaps twenty-five — rarely beautiful and richly gowned, with darkly-golden hair, and jewels. Yesterday, he thought with bitterness, she would scarcely have looked at him twice. He would have been dirt beneath her silken feet. She stared at him. Of all the sorts of men she had pictured as coming to her rescue she had not dreamed of one like him. Not that he was not human, but he dwelt in a world so far from hers, so infinitely far, that he seldom even entered her thought. (p. 614)

To Jim, Julia's voice, the only other "human voice" he had heard in a world where everyone was dead, "sounded in his ears like the voice of God."

Revealing just how temporal and tactical African American race-consciousness can be, Du Bois put Africana humanism on display, with Jim's initial
thoughts of Julia being not that she was "white" or a "woman," but that she
was human and in need of help. Jim's first impulse was to help the human
being "leaning wildly" and hollering out of an upstairs window in the distance. That is the reason that Du Bois, a decidedly detailed and careful creative writer, did not write that Jim initially heard a "woman's voice," but a
"human voice" that "sounded in his ears like the voice of God." In saying
that the "human voice sounded in his ears like the voice of God," Du Bois is
also associating this anonymous (raceless, genderless, and classless) human
being that Jim is hearing and blurrily seeing in the distance, with God, with
that which deserves and demands the utmost reverence in Africana spiritual
traditions and worldviews.[11]

Julia's reaction to Jim is almost the antithesis of Jim's reaction to Julia. The
very first thing that Julia notices is that Jim is a "Negro." Then, writes Du
Bois, "She *stared* at him" (my emphasis). She may have stared at him in the
irksome manner in which Du Bois (1986a) writes that white people "eye[d]"
or stared at him at the opening of *The Souls of Black Folk*:

> Between me and the other world there is ever an unasked question: unasked by
> some through feelings of delicacy; by others through the difficulty of rightly
> framing it. All, nevertheless, flirt round it. They approach me in a half-hesitant
> sort of way, eye me curiously or compassionately, and then, instead of saying di-
> rectly, How does it feel to be a problem? they say, I know an excellent colored
> man in my town; or, I fought at Mechanicsville; or, Do not these Southern out-
> rages make your blood boil? At these I smile, or am interested, or reduce the
> boiling to a simmer, as the occasion may require. To the real question, How does
> it feel to be a problem? I answer seldom a word. (p. 363)

Du Bois makes his readers aware of the fact that Julia's stare, the way she
"eyed [Jim] curiously or compassionately," with that white—"How does it
feel to be a problem?" look, unnerved him. Du Bois shares an irked Jim's inner monologue: "Yesterday, he thought with bitterness, she would scarcely
have looked at him twice. He would have been dirt beneath her silken feet."
It is only after Julia racializes the situation that Jim thinks, not of being racial-
ist in retaliation, but of guarding himself against her highly probable racist or,
at the least, *racial* reaction to seeing a black male rescuer at her front door.
For Julia, "Of all the sorts of men she had pictured as coming to her rescue
she had not dreamed of one like him." Why? Because, as Du Bois declared
above, "They are not simply dark white men. They are not 'men' in the sense
that Europeans are men." Julia had been taught this, and a million other minor things similar to this, all her life. Possibly unbeknownst to her, she had

been taught to fear and hate black men, and black people more generally. Black people were only welcomed and wanted in the fallen, former white supremacist world when they were serving whites in whatever (usually docile and/or severely subordinate) capacity. Blacks were "good" when they did what whites wanted them to do. And, of course, blacks were "bad" when they had the audacity and unmitigated gall to pursue their very human passions for freedom and justice. In the black existential world that Du Bois created in "The Comet," Jim was an unchecked black man, a seemingly rare being in the world of white supremacy, which is one of the reasons Julia's fear of both his blackness and maleness is heightened and increases as the story unfolds.

In spite of the eerie moment of racialization that pulled him back into the world of racial social conventions and interpersonal politics, Jim treated Julia with the utmost care and human consideration, so much so that after being in his presence for a short time she "looked at him now with strength and confidence": "He did not look like men, as she had always pictured men; but he acted like one and she was content" (Du Bois, 1996a, p. 616). Here Du Bois is highlighting and hinting at a couple of things; first, the fact that though Jim did not look like the men or human beings that Julia was accustomed to, he nevertheless carried himself in humble dignity and treated her in a humane and moral manner. That is to say, though Julia unfairly initially judged and devalued Jim based on his biology, he, in the words of Fanon (1967) in *Black Skin, White Masks*, refused to be "the slave of the past" (p. 225). With each of his words and actions, Jim seemed to be saying:

> Like it or not, the past can in no way guide me in the present moment. . . .
>
> I will not make myself the man of any past. I do not want to exalt the past at the expense of my present and of my future. . . .
>
> I can recapture my past, validate it, or condemn it through my successive choices. . . .
>
> I do not have a duty to be this or that. . . .
>
> If the white man challenges my humanity, I will impose my whole weight as a man on his life and show him that I am not that "sho' good eatin'" that he persists in imagining.
>
> I find myself suddenly in the world and I recognize that I have one right alone: That of demanding human behavior from the other.
>
> One duty alone: That of not renouncing my freedom through my choices. (pp. 225–29)

Jim chose to suspend and/or sidestep the social conventions of the white supremacist past in an effort to create a moral and multicultural present and future. He was, or, at the least, he quickly became the antithetical living embodiment of what Julia had learned about African American men, and African

Americans more generally. But, regrettably, none of this dissipated Julia's
deep-seated fear and hatred of blacks. At the first opportunity, she ran away
from the only living soul in New York City, simply because that soul was
housed in a black body.

It was too mighty—too terrible! She turned toward the door with a new fear in
her heart. For the first time she seemed to realize that she was alone in the world
with a stranger, with something more than a stranger,—with a man alien in blood
and culture—unknown, perhaps unknowable. It was awful! She must escape—
she must fly; he must not see her again. Who knew what awful thoughts. . . .

She gathered her silken skirts deftly about her young, smooth limbs—listened,
and glided into a side-hall. A moment she shrank back: the hall lay filled with
dead women; then she leaped to the door and tore at it, with bleeding fingers, until it swung wide. She looked out. He was standing at the top of the alley,—
silhouetted, tall and black, motionless. Was he looking at her or away? She did
not know—she did not care. She simply leaped and ran—ran until she found herself alone amid the dead and the tall ramparts of towering buildings.

She stopped. She was alone. Alone! Alone on the streets—alone in the city—
perhaps alone in the world! There crept in upon her the sense of deception—of
creeping hands behind her back—of silent, moving things she could not see,—
of voices hushed in fearsome conspiracy. She looked behind and sideways,
stared at strange sounds and heard still stranger, until every nerve within her
stood sharp and quivering, stretched to scream at the barest touch. She whirled
and flew back, whimpering like a child, until she found that narrow alley again
and the dark silent figure silhouetted at the top. She stopped and rested; then she
walked silently toward him, looked at him timidly; but he said nothing as he
handed her into the car. (Du Bois, 1996a, p. 617)

Why would Julia run away from Jim, literally, the only living person in the
whole of New York City, perhaps even the world? Why is it that even though
she knows Jim (who has treated her with the utmost respect) is there with her,
she feels "Alone! Alone on the streets—alone in the city—perhaps alone in
the world!"? Because, as Fanon—echoing Du Bois—perceptively pointed out
in *Black Skin, White Masks*, the black man is not a man, but a "nigger." You
see, "A man was expected to behave like a man. I was expected to behave like
a black man—or at least like a nigger," and "The Negro is an animal, the Negro is bad, the Negro is mean, the Negro is ugly" (Fanon, 1967, p. 114). Julia leads us to conclude this with her "Who knew what awful thoughts—[he
may have had or, worst, be having?!]" statement. Which, of course, is a reference to the myth of the black rapist that was then circulating and extremely
popular as a result of Thomas Dixon's best-selling novel, *The Clansman*
(1905), and the movie it spawned, D. W. Griffith's *Birth of a Nation* (1915)
(Gillespie and Hall, 2006; R. M. Henderson, 1972; Schickel, 1983; Slide,

2004). What is amazing and ironic, though, is that Julia thought all of this after Jim forgave her initial racist predilections and treated her as a sister in the house of humanity.

Julia judged Jim not as an individual, but based on her white supremacist prejudgments and prefabrications of the black race. To her, Jim was not a black man, but a black beast that her white father and fiancé had been burdened with, "half-devil and half-child," as Du Bois prickly put it above. Jim was, in the words of Fanon (1967), "over-determined from without" (p. 116). Julia, the default racial ruler in the absence of the white patriarch(s), would not allow Jim and his "tom-toms, cannibalism, intellectual deficiency, fetishism, racial defects, slave-ships, and above all else, above all: "Sho' good eatin'," to be or become human (p. 112). He would be held down, as he always had been, "kept in his place," as it were, just as the physically absent though ideologically present white father and fiancé would have it. She, and precisely she alone, would uphold the ways of the white supremacist (and patriarchal!) world, even if that meant, literally, running from life to death. This, of course, symbolizes Julia's second breach of Jim's efforts to bring into being a new moral and multicultural world. However, when Julia's white supremacist paroxysm subsides, and she returns to the apocalyptic present reality without races, Jim—*not* in the fashion of the good and faithful "darkie," but in the morally firm and forward-thinking spirit of, say, Frederick Douglass and Frances Harper—forgives her her racist prepossessions and proclivities a second time. He soberly suggests that they continue their search for other survivors, which intimates two things.

First, it accents black resilience and spirituality in the face of human misery and senseless suffering. In other words, Jim's decision to move on speaks to Africana peoples' impulse to go on no matter what the odds, circumstance, or situation. Thus, this connects *Darkwater* (the book which houses "The Comet") with *The Souls of Black Folk*, and particularly its opening chapter, "Of Our Spiritual Strivings," which prosaically documents and details black folks' use of their spirituality and quickly (re)forming culture to overcome, perhaps, the greatest collective adversities in Africana history: the African holocaust, colonization, enslavement, and subsequent segregation. Second, and closely connected to the first point, Jim's rectitude and unreluctant willingness to continue the search for survivors symbolizes the Africana emphasis on ethics when reasoning racially. Like many of his enslaved ancestors and political progeny in the soon-coming Civil Rights movement, he would not lower himself to a racial reactionary and/or "reverse-racist" level. He knew, as Audre Lorde (1984) asserted in *Sister Outsider*, "it is the responsibility of the oppressed to teach the oppressors their mistakes" (p. 114). He knew, again as Lorde laid bare, "Once you live any piece of your vision it opens you to constant onslaught" (p. 107). Jim withstood Julia's brutal racial blows and, with reconciliatory tears in her eyes and his hurt heart covered and chin up, they continued the search. But not without Julia soon thereafter having an incredible racial revelation as a consequence of Jim's anti-racist ethics.

Jim's anti-racist ethics in this instance would have made Martin Luther King Jr. marvel because it cut to the core of Julia's *racist consciousness* and made her reconsider her racial reasoning and Jim's (and his peoples') humble humanity. Even in the face of a second racial betrayal Jim was merciful and "made her comfortable," finding them safe carnageless shelter and preparing food—though, I revel in reporting, not in the Fanonian "sho' good eatin'!" fashion. In addition—and this is a turning point—he "timidly . . . took a shawl and wound her in it, touching her reverently, yet tenderly" (Du Bois, 1996a, p. 619). Now as "[h]e watched the city. She watched him. He seemed very human,—very near now." The dye was cast, and Jim and Julia spoke as if it were their first time speaking, reflecting on the world as it was, and as it was to be:

> "Have you had to work hard?" she asked softly.
> "Always," he said.
> "I have always been idle," she said. "I was rich."
> "I was poor," he almost echoed.
> "The rich and the poor are met together," she began, and he finished:
> "The Lord is the Maker of them all."
> "Yes," she said slowly; "and how foolish our human distinctions seem—now," looking down to the great dead city stretched below, swimming in unlighted shadows.
> "Yes—I was not—human, yesterday," he said.
> She looked at him. "And your people were not my people," she said; "but today—" She paused. (p. 619)

Moving many of the more familiar social markers and social barriers, Du Bois presents a dialogue that is a simultaneously simple and complex study in racial, sexual, and class differences. He begins with class differences, emphasizing that where the black has always worked, the white has "always been idle," figuratively speaking. Death and disaster brought "the world of poverty and work" and "the world of wealth and prosperity" together (p. 617). As in so many Africana spiritual and religious traditions, death is not simply an end, but also a beginning. Du Bois, waxing utopian here, demonstrates the awesome and ironic power of death to give new life when he has the characters refer to their class positions in the past tense. Julia says, "I *was* rich," and Jim remarks, "I *was* poor" (my emphasis). Does this mean, then, that Julia *was* "white," and Jim *was* "black"? The text suggests as much when

Julia, the former racial ruler, says, "how foolish our human distinctions seem—now." Jim unapologetically answers, "Yes—I was not—human, yesterday." A new day has dawned, and Julia and Jim may very well be the forerunners to the "new men" and "new humanity" that Fanon (1968) wrote about in *The Wretched of the Earth* (p. 36).

It is also interesting to observe that Jim had been subtly and sincerely trying to share his (and his peoples') vision of a "new humanity" with Julia their entire journey. But, blinded by the white supremacist views and values of yesterday, Julia could not see. It took Jim unerringly practicing anti-racist ethics to open her eyes. And now what does Julia see? "He was a man,—no more; but he was in some larger sense a gentleman,—sensitive, kindly, chivalrous, everything save his hands and—his face" (Du Bois 1996a, p. 619). As a result of his strict adherence to his (and his peoples') anti-racist ethics, in Julia's eyes Jim went from subhuman to human to, virtually, superhuman—his hands and face withstanding.

Why, we are quick to query, his hands and face withstanding? Because Du Bois wanted to preserve the mark of difference. Even in Utopia blacks can never forget the lived-experiences and life-lessons of the former anti-black world, which is one of the reasons Jim's hands will continue to be rough, as a reminder of yesterday's years and years of hard work and harsh labor conditions. His face would remain distinct because the black face and head have ever been one of the most contested sites and sources of cultural valuation and degradation, and also one of the greatest markers of Africana identity (dare I say "ancestry"). In the final analysis, Jim's journey to Utopia had been, in several senses, the antithesis of Julia's, and his hands and face would continue to tell the tale.

Just as Fanon would explain it forty years later in *The Wretched of the Earth*, Jim's anti-racist ethics transformed both the colonized and the colonizer, or rather, in this instance, the raced and the racial ruler. In Fanon's (1968) words, "the 'thing' which has been colonized becomes [hu]man during the same process by which it frees itself" (p. 37). At the beginning of "The Comet" Du Bois revealed regarding Jim, his social status, and sense of self-worth: "Few noticed him. Few ever noticed him save in a way that stung. He was outside the world—'nothing!' as he said bitterly" (Du Bois, 1996a, p. 611). Now Jim was at the center of the world, and regarded by the only other surviving soul as human, not simply because he was the only other human being left alive but because of his anti-racist ethics. This had a profound impact on Jim, who once thought of himself as "outside of the world—nothing!" Now,

Memories of memories stirred to life in the dead recesses of his mind. The shackles seemed to rattle and fall from his soul. Up from the crass and crushing

and cringing of his caste leaped the lone majesty of kings long dead. He arose
within the shadow, tall, straight, and stern, with power in his eyes and ghostly
scepters hovering to his grasp. It was as though some mighty Pharaoh lived
again, or curled Assyrian lord. (p. 620)

In a sense, Jim freed himself *and* Julia from the vices and vulgarities of
white supremacy, and in the end he was reconnected with the very past which
white supremacy had long attempted to culturally thieve and hide from him
and his people.[12] The "shackles" and chains, symbolizing he and his peoples'
enslavement (both *de jure* and *de facto*), fell "from his soul." He held "the
lone majesty of kings long dead," "[i]t was as though some mighty Pharaoh
lived again, or curled Assyrian lord." Jim was royal, and entered the spiritual
court of kings and queens predicated not on any authoritarianism or elitism (à
la Du Bois's early articulation of the "Talented Tenth"), but based on his public and personal ethics.

However, and not to sound cynical, his heaven on earth was short-lived.
Just as he and Julia were both contemplating their *post-racial* revelations
and the future, they heard the honk of a car horn. Immediately, she "covered
her eyes with her hands, and her shoulders heaved. He dropped and bowed,
groped blindly on his knees about the floor" (p. 620). The white father and
fiancé soon thereafter burst into the room. The world was not lost, "[o]nly
New York" (p. 621). After tending to the white damsel in distress, the father
and fiancé took note of Jim. The fiancé was, of course, perplexed: "Suddenly
he stiffened and his hand flew to his hip. 'Why!' he snarled. 'It's—a—
nigger—Julia! Has he—has he dared—'" (p. 621). Julia informed them that,
"'He has dared—all, to rescue me,' she said quietly, 'and I—thank him—
much.' But she did not look at him again" (p. 621). Jim was back in the
world of white supremacy. He was *negro persona non grata* again. He was
black, and she was white, and no matter what racial transgressions and transformations they experienced, these breakthroughs would not be translated to
the wider (or, rather, racially ruling white) world without both of them ar-
dently espousing and sharing their new anti-racist knowledge. In this context
(that of the return of white supremacist patriarchy) Julia had to take the
moral lead, as Jim had previously in the world without white supremacist patriarchy, but she did not and the all too familiar racial regression that is characteristic of black/white interpersonal interactions in white supremacist society resumed its reign.

Julia "did not look at him again," because he did not register as human any-
more. He was "black" (or, worst, a "nigger") and, therefore—to resonate with
Ralph Ellison –invisible. Where Jim once, however recent and momentarily,
felt like a king, hearing the car horn reversed his feelings and flung him back

into the world of white supremacy, which is one of the reasons Du Bois tells us at hearing the car horn he "dropped and bowed, groped blindly on his knees about the floor." Jim prostrated himself as though he were in the presence of a princess. It is almost as if he knew Julia would morally and *racially* betray him a third time, and this is where the story ends. Barely getting out of the presence of the white supremacist patriarchs without being lynched, as it was suggested several times by on looking white supremacist patriarchs, Jim is reunited with his wife and is told of the death of their child. The black child's death symbolizes the bleakness of black folks' future, the continued denial of black humanity and dignity, and blacks' ultimate non-existence in the future white supremacist world.

What does all (or any) of this have to do with critical race theory? Quickly and in conclusion, there are several critical race themes strewn throughout the story. Du Bois twists and turns many of the motifs in ways that are at once interesting and invigorating. First, consider Du Bois's emphasis on and critique of the racial (and racist) dimensions of class. Critical race theorists argue that racism exacerbates class and creates the very chasm (or "veil" in Du Bois's discourse) between whites and non-whites that Du Bois detailed in his story (Delgado and Stefancic, 2001; Ford, 1995). Hence, Julia stated that Jim "dwelt in a world so far from hers, so infinitely far, that he seldom even entered her thought." White supremacy, and all of the racial exclusions that accompany it, place non-whites well beyond the pale of human consideration because it is only whites who are and can be considered "human" and register as such on the social barometer of a white supremacist world. Class struggle in a white supremacist world, then, cannot help but to take on a racial character because race in a race supremacist context is never neutral, but always and ever political and deeply connected to economic power and privileges or economic disadvantages and disenfranchisements.

Second, Du Bois's short story suggests that more radical measures than mere piecemeal socio-political reform and reluctant gradualism are needed to make the system an authentic transethnic and multicultural democracy, as opposed to what Charles Mills (1998) has termed a "*Herrenvolk*" or ruling race democracy (pp. 139-66). There is a sense in which "The Comet" can be read as a racially oppressed and poverty-stricken person's dream come true, not in any racially malicious sense but in a Fanonian sense, in terms of the oppressed desperately desiring to see their oppressors and the oppressive system they imperially invented toppled. The story is also Fanonian in the sense that there is room for racial reconciliation and redemption if—and this is an extremely important "if" that cannot be over-emphasized—*if* they both free themselves from the social conventions, vices, and vulgarities of the former white supremacist world.

More than once Jim, symbolic of the oppressed race-class, demonstrates his rectitude regarding race and, by the end of the story, Julia, symbolic of the oppressing race-class, learned a lesson in anti-racist social ethics from him (or did she?). This connects with the discourse of critical race theory when we bear in mind that part of its criticism is directed at the established order's claims of colorblindness and racially neutral rule (Bell, 1995; Gotanda, 1995; Lee, 1995; Lopez, 1995, 1996). Jim did not politely tip-toe around race and racism. He knew he was not considered human by white supremacist social standards and, therefore, based on her initial *racial* reaction, was not regarded as a human being by Julia. Here he follows Fanon and nods to the critical race theorists, as he refuses to allow a racist system and/or a racist individual associated with that system to question and/or deny his humanity and dignity. He did precisely what Fanon suggested above, he brought his "whole weight" as a human being to bear on Julia and showed her that he was "not that 'sho' good eatin' that [s]he persist[ed] in imagining." In other words, and in critical race lingo, Jim spoke anti-racist truth to racist power. He was not put off by Julia's age or gender, and he realized early on that white men have no monopoly on racist thought and behavior: white supremacy has infected, so it seems, the whole of the white race (Delgado and Stefancic, 1997; Harris, 1995).

Finally, Julia's decision to racially regress at the end of the story by rendering the previously visible Jim an invisible black, or "nigger," as her fiancé would have it, symbolizes not simply the return of white supremacist patriarchy, but it also represents one of the main reasons critical race theorists endorse race-consciousness as a counter to white racism (Guiner, 1995; Peller, 1995). Kimberlé Crenshaw and company claim: "With its explicit embrace of race-consciousness, Critical Race Theory aims to reexamine the terms by which race and racism have been negotiated in American consciousness, and to recover and revitalize the radical tradition of race-consciousness among African Americans and other peoples of color—a tradition that was discarded when integration, assimilation and the ideal of color-blindness became the official norms of racial enlightenment" (Crenshaw et al., 1995, p. xiv). Along these lines, "The Comet" illustrates critical race theorists' key claim regarding race-consciousness: that it will never be enough for the racially oppressed to repudiate racism. As I have stated throughout this chapter, though anti-racism has always emenated and more than likely will always primarily emanate from the realm of the racially oppressed, for it to be most effective *both* the racially ruled and the racial rulers must mutually repudiate racism. Du Bois demonstrated what will happen if all of the onus is placed on the racially ruled: they will end up, literally, parodying and prostrating themselves each time they are in the hallowed presence of whiteness. Unless and until the racial rulers relinquish race and rid themselves of racism, the racially ruled have no other recourse (at this point) but to employ race as a socio-political vehicle to counter racism and create anti-racist theory and praxis.

A large part of the racially ruled's anti-racist theory and praxis has been preoccupied with colonialism and the prospects of decolonization—issues which remarkably have yet to resonate or register as central concerns in the discourse of contemporary critical race theory. This is extremely curious considering the fact that many of the earliest expressions of radicalism amongst the racially oppressed were aimed at critiquing various forms and forces of *colonial racism* and/or *racial colonialism*. Du Bois was one of the major doyens of this discourse and, by most accounts, is considered to have made his most lasting contributions as a pioneer Pan-Africanist and anti-colonialist. As a consequence, chapter 3 will analyze Du Bois's anti-colonial and Pan-African theory and praxis for its contribution to contemporary anti-colonial discourse, and particularly "postcolonial" theory.

NOTES

1. With regard to Anthony Appiah's assault on Du Bois's philosophy of race, his "The Uncompleted Argument: Du Bois and the Illusion of Race," originally published in *Critical Inquiry* in 1985, was revised, re-titled, and reprinted as "Illusions of Race," in his *In My Father's House: Africa in the Philosophy of Culture* (Appiah, 1992, pp. 28–46). In "Race, Culture, Identity: Misunderstood Connections" (1996), Appiah amends some his argument(s) against Du Bois's so-called "socio-historical" conception of race, and claims that Du Bois was up to much more than he, Appiah, had initially realized. For hard-hitting critiques of Appiah's criticisms of Du Bois's concepts of race and critiques of racism, see Patrick Goodin's "Du Bois and Appiah: The Politics of Race and Racial Identity" (2002), Paul Taylor's "Appiah's Uncompleted Argument: W. E. B. Du Bois and the Reality of Race" (2000), and Lucius Outlaw's legendary and heatedly debated "defense" of Du Bois, "'Conserve' Races?: In Defense of W. E. B. Du Bois" (1996b). Further, for a vociferous yet not vicious critique of Du Bois, Appiah and Outlaw's discourse and debates on Du Bois, race, culture and identity, see Robert Gooding-Williams's "Outlaw, Appiah, and Du Bois's 'The Conservation of Races'"(1996). Concerning the claim that Du Bois may very well be "just another over-engaged 'race man' posthumously positioned as a radical theorist," see chapter 5 of the present study where I discuss the disingenuousness and difficulties of reading a multidimensional theorist such as Du Bois from a one-dimensional frame of reference.

2. I am well aware of the fact that part of my interpretation here sounds a little "postmodern," especially with my claims concerning race's malleability and fluidity. However, the reality of the racial matter is that there is a stream of the black radical thought tradition that is, to put it plainly, *anti-European modernity*. If Euro-modernity

is predicated on the exploitation, death, and destruction of Africana peoples and cultures, then it seems logical that an Africana "anti-modern," as opposed to "postmodern" tradition would arise. Indeed it did, and one of the primary tasks of Africana critical theory has been and remains to document and develop this discourse (see Rabaka, 2003a, 2003c, 2005a, 2006a, 2006b). What modernity means in the African world is very different from that of the European world, and we could aver the Asian world as well. The African philosopher Kwame Gyekye has eloquently argued, in *An Essay on African Philosophical Thought* (1995) and *Tradition and Modernity: Philosophical Reflections of the African Experience* (1997), that where Europeans may have been trying to free themselves from many of their more oppressive traditions during their "Enlightenment" (all the while colonizing and enslaving "Others"!), Africans have spent most of European modernity asserting their humanity and attempting to modernize what they can from their past. It is not as though Africana peoples are inherently against modernity or modernization, but the Europeanization (and/or imperialization) of their modernity. For further discussion of Africana anti-modernism, and Du Bois's anti-modernism in specific, see Wilson Jeremiah Moses's *Afrotopia* (1998), and especially the chapter "W. E. B. Du Bois and Anti-modernism." And for a discussion of black borrowings from and critical contributions to postmodernism, see Gordon (1997b), hooks (1990, 1991, 1994), and West (1988, 1989, 1993c, 1993d).

3. White criticism of black race-consciousness is a theme that runs throughout Du Bois's discourse. Whatever he felt about it at any given historical interval, it made no matter to him when examined in light of an Africana history-, culture-, and philosophy-informed socio-political perspective. Du Bois, a doyen in Africana historical discourse, consistently counseled blacks, as well as whites, to study continental and diasporan African history and culture. With no knowledge of Africana history, even well-meaning (white and/or black) interpreters were doomed to misinterpret Africana life-worlds and lived-experiences. Regarding the white criticism of the black race-consciousness theme that runs throughout Du Bois's discourse, see not only *Dusk of Dawn*, as quoted in the text, but also his *John Brown* (1909), *Color and Democracy: Colonies and Peace* (1945), *The Autobiography of W. E. B. Du Bois* (1968), and *Against Racism* (1985), among other pieces published in periodicals (see Du Bois, 1980b, 1982a, 1982b, 1982c, 1982d, 1983a, 1983b, 1985c, 1986c, 1986d).

4. My interpretation of Du Bois's social ethics, as well as my general argument throughout the preceding paragraphs has been deeply influenced by Ramona Edelin's doctoral dissertation, "The Philosophical Foundations and Implications of William Edward Burghardt Du Bois's Social Ethic" (1981), which carefully and critically elaborates Du Bois's life-long preoccupation with and predilection for social ethics.

5. Two classic works in Du Bois Studies have influenced and informed my interpretation of Du Bois's critique of white supremacy and contributions to critical white studies. Ironically, both were published at the twilight of the turbulent Black Power Period (1965–1975). The first is Diorita Fletcher's "W. E. B. Du Bois's Arraignment and Indictment of White Civilization" (1973), and the second is William Tuttle's "W. E. B. Du Bois's Confrontation with White Liberalism During the Progressive Era" (1974). Since the mid-1970s there has been scant attention given to interpreting Du

Bois's scholarship as a critique of white supremacy. It is hoped that the work here will fill this gaping intellectual omission.

6. Here, I am hinting at the fact that people of color have a long history of colonizing one another, albeit never in the world-imperial and white supremacist fashion of European imperialism and global domination. This, of course, is a fact that the recondite historical researcher, Du Bois, did not allow to fall through the cracks in his more mature historical writing. For, perhaps, the best examples from his oeuvre, see *The Negro* (1915), *Black Folk Then and Now* (1939), and *The World and Africa* (1947).

7. Of the three figures named, Boas, Frobenius, and Johnston, Boas's research had the most profound impact on Du Bois's thinking concerning the African origins of Egyptian civilization and African antiquity in general. On Du Bois and Boas's intellectual relationship and reciprocal influence on each other, see Werner Lange's "W. E. B. Du Bois, Franz Boas and the Rise of Antiracism in American Anthropology" (1982) and Julia Liss's "Diasporic Identities: The Science and Politics of Race in the Work of Franz Boas and W. E. B. Du Bois, 1894–1919" (1998).

8. For a few examples of works that offer interdisciplinary interpretations of Du Bois, and which treat his critical social and radical political thought, see Cain (1993), Coates, Browning and Beenah (1996), Dennis (1997), Drake (1985), Horne (1986), Marable (1986), Nonini (1992), Owen (1973), Rabaka (2003d, 2006b), Richards (1970), Robinson (2000), Vivian (1997), Wright (1985), and Yuan (1998). Also, as may be extremely evident at this point, the present study in its entirety can be read as one long interdisciplinary (re)interpretation of Du Bois's discourse that brings it into dialogue with contemporary discursive formations and practices: from critical race and postcolonial theory to postmodern/post-Marxist and radical feminist/womanist theory.

9. There have, of course, been exceptions, more or less intellectual flirtations between critical race and Africana theorists, for instance, works such as Collins (2002), Gordon (1999), and Outlaw (1990). However, these works are more in the realm of intellectual history, sort of documenting the often-omitted Africana dimension of critical race theory. What I propose to do here is to use Du Bois as a theoretic point of departure to highlight and accent the major themes of critical race theory as it is currently practiced. In addition, my work here also endeavors to place new issues on critical race theory's agenda, issues that will continue to be downplayed and diminished until Du Bois's anti-racist discoveries (among other Africana intellectual-activists') are critically engaged for their contribution to contemporary race and racism discourse.

10. In his creative writings, Du Bois often used characters in an archetypal and/or symbolic sense, as representing not so much their own individual impulses, but the ideals and aspirations of their people, cultures, countries, and communities. This, of course, often overly racialized and bogged his characters down with what could be termed "idealism," usually giving them utopian (and frequently Left) leanings. But this archetypal idealization and racialization of his characters also gave them a startling realism that is as telling about Du Bois's racial and cultural thought as it is about the times in which he was writing. Needless to say, Du Bois's creative writings always

retained a level of scholasticism that made them fiction in form, nonfiction in subject matter, and often experimental and innovative in style (see Du Bois, 1985b). For further discussion of Du Bois as a littérateur, see Andrews (1985), Aptheker (1989), Byerman (1994), Phillips (1995), and, of course, Rampersad (1990).

11. This interpretation of God, God's relationship with human beings, and human beings' reverence for God (and the deities associated with God) in Africana spiritual traditions has been informed by Blakely, van Beek and Thomson (1994), Fulop and Raboteau (1996), Gyekye (1995, 1996), Idowu (1975), Mbiti (1975, 1989), Ray (2000), Wilmore (1989), and Zahan (1979).

12. The "hidden history" theme runs throughout Du Bois's corpus and informs his historical writing, fiction, gift theory, and socio-political thought, among other aspects of his philosophy and intellectual framework. Needless to say, none of the aforementioned carries the critical weight and gravity of history. History had a special place in Du Bois's social and political theory, as it provided human beings with a map of the past social world and markers that might be useful in efforts to chart the present social world. This made history especially important to continental and diasporan Africans because white supremacy and other forms of anti-African racism were predicated on false claims that Africans had no history, and, therefore, had not made any contributions to human culture and civilization. In a high-handed sense, history documents and details human triumphs and tragedies. Therefore, if and when Africans did register in historical records, it was only in the latter tragic sense, which ultimately gave way to the black pathology discussions of Eurocentric historical discourse. For more detailed discussions of Du Bois as historian and his philosophy of history, see Blight (1994), Byerman (1994), Gooding-Williams (1987), Gregg (1998), Guzman (1961), Lash (1957), Moses (1978, 1998), Rabaka (2003a), Richards (1970), Robinson (2000), Stewart (1996), Stuckey (1987, 1994), Walden (1963b), Walker (1975), and Wesley (1965).

Chapter Three

Du Bois and the Politics and Problematics of Postcolonialism

"So long as the colonial system persists and expands, theories of race inferiority will help to continue it. Right here lies the great danger of the future. One of the vast paradoxes of human nature is that no matter how degraded people become, it is impossible to keep them down on a large scale and forever. Rebellion will certainly ensue. If this is true of Europe, it is just as true and just as significant for Asia and Africa. The continents which have withstood the European exploitation of the nineteenth century are for that very reason not going to remain quiescent under a new order—unless that new order has a distinct place for them which allows their progress, development, and self-determination."—Du Bois, 1945, p. 97

"All the elements of a solution to the great problems of humanity have, at different times, existed in European thought. But the action of European men has not carried out the mission which fell to them, and which consisted of bringing their whole weight violently to bear upon these elements, of modifying their arrangement and their nature, of changing them and finally of bringing the problem of mankind to an infinitely higher plane."—Fanon, 1968, p. 314

"Always bear in mind that the people are not fighting for ideas, for the things in anyone's head. They are fighting to win material benefits, to live better and in peace, to see their lives go forward, to guarantee the future of their children. . . . [W]e do not fall back on clichés or merely harp on the struggle against imperialism and colonialism in theoretical terms, but rather we point out concrete things."—Cabral, 1972, pp. 86, 145

"He [Du Bois] recognized the importance of the bonds between American Negroes and the land of their ancestors and he extended his activities to African affairs. After World War I he called Pan-African Congresses in

1919, 1921 and 1923, alarming imperialists in all countries and discon-
certing Negro moderates in America who were afraid of this restless, militant, black genius. Returning to the United States from abroad he found
his pioneering agitation for Negro studies was bearing fruit and a beginning was made to broaden Negro higher education. He threw himself into
the task of raising the intellectual level of this work."—M. L. King Jr.,
1970, pp. 22–23

INTRODUCTION: DU BOISIAN CONTRIBUTIONS TO
AND CRITICISMS OF POSTCOLONIALISM

According to leading postcolonial studies scholars Ashcroft, Griffiths and
Tiffin (1998), "postcolonialism"—the term "signifying" the discourse(s) of
postcolonial theorists—has been used widely "to signify the political, linguistic and cultural experiences of societies that were former European
colonies" (p. 186).[1] It attempts to critically and dialectically engage the effects of the various processes of European conquest and colonization on the
histories, cultures, societies and self-conceptions of both "the colonized" *and*
"the colonizers," to use Césaire and Fanon's phrasing. For some postcolonial
critics and theorists the term "post-colonialism" is misleading—as is purported to be the case with the term "postmodernism"—because many have interpreted the "post" in "postcolonialism" to mean, literally, "after-colonialism" or "after-independence" (Ashcroft, Griffiths and Tiffin, 1995, p. 2).[2] The
postmodern critics Steven Best and Douglas Kellner (1991) relate that "[t]he
prefix 'post' . . . signifies an active rupture (*coupure*) with what preceded it"
(p. 29). Ania Loomba (1998), however, contends that "the prefix 'post,'"
when affixed to the term *colonialism*, "complicates matters because it implies
an 'aftermath' in two senses—temporal, as in coming after, and ideological,
as in supplanting" (p. 7).

Ashcroft, Griffiths and Tiffin (1998) have stated that "[t]he prefix 'post' in
the term [post-colonialism] also continues to be a source of vigorous debate
amongst critics" (p. 187). They have admonished postcolonial theorists to
consider the "full implications" of using the term "postcolonial" to mean "after-colonialism" or "after-Independence":

> The term "post-colonial" is resonant with all the ambiguity and complexity of
> the many different cultural experiences it implicates, and . . . it addresses all as-
> pects of the colonial process from the beginning of colonial contact. Post-colo-
> nial critics and theorists should consider the full implications of restricting the
> meaning of the term to "after-colonialism" or after-Independence. All post-colo-
> nial societies are still subject in one way or another to overt or subtle forms of

neo-colonial domination, and independence has not solved this problem. The development of new elites within independent societies, often buttressed by neo-colonial institutions; the development of internal divisions based on racial, linguistic or religious discriminations; the continuing unequal treatment of indigenous peoples in settler/invader societies—all these testify to the fact that post-colonialism is a continuing process of resistance and reconstruction. This does not imply that post-colonial practices are seamless and homogeneous but indicates the impossibility of dealing with any part of the colonial process without considering its antecedents and consequences. (1995, p. 2)

When Ashcroft and his colleagues advance that "[a]ll post-colonial societies are still subject in one way or another to overt or subtle forms of neo-colonial domination" and that "independence has not solved this problem," they seem, in several ways, to be echoing many of the positions taken by Aimé Césaire in *Discourse on Colonialism*, Frantz Fanon in *The Wretched of the Earth* and *Toward the African Revolution*, Kwame Nkrumah in *Neo-Colonialism*, and Amilcar Cabral in *Revolution in Guinea* and *Return to the Source*. However, and as I shall argue in this chapter, there is another, shall we say "proto-postcolonial" theorist—to sort of coin a cumbersome phrase—whose life-work and critical contributions to postcolonial discourse and theory have often gone overlooked and unengaged by contemporary colonial and postcolonial theorists. I am, of course, referring to Du Bois and his place in the discourse on decolonization.[3]

This chapter's thesis is easily explained as follows: Du Bois offers contemporary colonial and postcolonial theorists a critical conception of colonialism in several ways. First, by analyzing colonialism's fundamental features (which will be outlined below), and, second, by focusing his readers' attention on the world-historic fluctuations and mutations of (neo)colonialism, Du Bois highlights—as Tejumola Olaniyan (2000) recently noted—the varied nature of colonialism, not simply in topographical terms, but also in so far as the particularities of the colonized peoples' pre-existing or "pre-colonial" cultures are concerned. This is an extremely important point to make because many postcolonial theorists have a tendency to gloss over the specificities and the different degrees to which various peoples were historically and currently continue to be colonized (see Chambers and Curti, 1996; Chatterjee, 1993; Moore-Gilbert, 1997; Schwarz and Ray, 2000). Finally, by linking colonialism with capitalism, and by refusing to isolate economic exploitation from racial domination and gender discrimination, Du Bois's conception of colonialism prefigures and provides a paradigm for and a critique of contemporary postcolonial discourse.

By "deliberately using the word 'colonial' in a much broader sense than is usually given it," and in asserting that "there are manifestly groups of people, countries and nations, which while not colonies in the strict sense of the word, yet so approach the colonial system as to merit the designation *semicolonial*," Du Bois (1985a) not only anticipates, but contributes the concept of "semi-colonialism" to postcolonial discourse (pp. 229, 236, my emphasis). It is this concept of "semi-" or "quasi-" colonialism that distinguishes Du Bois's conception of colonialism from Césaire (1972), Fanon (1965, 1967, 1968, 1969), Nkrumah (1964, 1965, 1970b, 1973a), Cabral (1972, 1973, 1979), and a whole host of classical anti- and de-colonial theorists. Moreover, it is this same theory of "semi-colonialism" that enables me to assert that, on the one hand, Africana Studies scholars, and Du Bois scholars in specific, may find much of interest in postcolonial theory. We need mince no words in laying bare the fact that both Africana and postcolonial theorists are involved in similar (and, I would aver often identical) projects of radical critique. For Africana theorists, to speak generally, great and grave issues emanate from the socio-historical realities of not simply anti-African racism and racial colonialism, but sexism and capitalism as well. For postcolonial theorists, again generally speaking, criticisms have been leveled against each of the aforementioned and, in specific, the ways in which past and present forms of colonialism exacerbate and perpetuate racism, sexism, and capitalism. Indeed, a burgeoning philosophical framework that brings diverse discourse on colonialism, anti-colonialism, and the coming *post*-colonial world into dialogue is on the rise.

On the other hand, it should be stated outright, Du Bois—an intellectual-activist who critiqued colonialism throughout his eighty-year publishing career—has been relegated to the periphery of postcolonial discourse. As a result, as I argue throughout this chapter, postcolonial theorists in many senses undermine and do themselves a disastrous disservice because they ignore and/or erase a wealth of critical concepts and categories, such as "semi-colonialism," that could very well aid them in their efforts to theorize and bring into being a truly *post*-colonial world. This chapter, then, will be devoted to exploring Du Bois as both progenitor of, and contributor to, postcolonial discourse. It engages the politics and problematics of post-colonialism from the aforementioned Africana critical-theoretical perspective, and a Du Boisian perspective in particular.

DU BOIS'S CONCEPT(S) OF COLONIALISM

In arguing that there are partially colonized peoples and countries, Du Bois offers postcolonial theorists a concept that helps to highlight the continuation of colonialism in our (post)modern moment. If "[a] colony, strictly speaking, is a country which belongs to another country, forms part of the mother country's industrial organization, and exercises such powers of government, and such civic and cultural freedom, as the dominant country allows," then there exists today, even *after* independence, in Africa, in the Americas and the Caribbean, in Asia and in Australia, colonies—albeit "quasi-" or "semi-" colonies, but colonies nonetheless (Du Bois, 1985a, p. 229). Du Bois's concept of colonialism is predicated on what he understands to be universal or common characteristics, "certain characteristics of colonial peoples, which are so common and obvious that we seldom discuss them and often actually forget them." These characteristics, which remain part and parcel of the life-worlds and lived-experiences of the wretched of the earth, essentially entail the following: (1) physical and/or psychological violence, domination, and discrimination; (2) economic exploitation; (3) poverty; (4) illiteracy; (5) lawlessness, stealing, and crime; (6) starvation; (7) death; (8) disaster; (9) disease; (10) disenfranchisement; (11) the denial of "cultural equality;" and, (12) the denial of participation in political processes (pp. 229–36).[4]

Moving beyond the "narrower definition" and "the strict sense of the word" colony—and, I would like to suggest, "colonialism"—Du Bois's conceptualization of colonialism challenges postcolonial theorists to be cognizant of the fact that the prefix "post" in "postcolonialism," on the one hand, may very well signify a rupture with that which preceded it. But, on the other hand, the "post" in postcolonialism can also be said to signify a dependence on, a continuity with, and a filial connection to, that which follows it. Which, of course, has led some critics to argue that what is currently being called the "postcolonial" is actually a covert intensification of the colonial. Hence, from the critics of postcolonialism's perspective, it is nothing other than contemporary *neocolonialism* clandestinely creeping around the many remaining wretched parts of the earth with a new academy-friendly name and a long-overdue face-lift to hide its hideous face and horrid fangs.[5]

The Nigerian philosopher Emmanuel Eze (1997b) has argued that "post" should be employed as a prefix in so far as colonialism is concerned, "only as far as the lived-actuality of the peoples and the lands formerly occupied by European imperial powers can suggest, or confirm, in some meaningful ways, the sense of that word, the 'post' of the (post)colonial" (p. 341). Ashcroft and associates (1989, p. 2) assert that there is "a continuity of preoccupations throughout the historical process initiated by European imperial aggression," so much so that "all the culture affected by the imperial process from the moment of colonization to the present day" must, to paraphrase Fanon (1968, p. 37), be called into question. And Anthony Appiah (1992) avers, "[t]o theorize certain central features of contemporary culture as *post* anything, is, of course, inevitably to invoke a narrative, and from the Enlightenment on, in

Europe and in European-derived [and dominated] cultures, that 'after' has also meant 'above and beyond'" (pp. 140–41).[6] Now the critical questions confronting us are: Have we really reached the *post-* (as in, *after*) colonial period? How can we be in the period *after* colonialism when most of the fundamental features of colonialism continue to plague "three-quarters of the people living in the world today"? Is it possible that we have gotten "above and beyond" colonialism when it is understood that even with "political independence" the impact and influence of European imperial powers continue to "displace" pre-colonial philosophical, spiritual, and axiological systems and traditions (Ashcroft, Griffiths and Tiffin, 1989, pp. 1, 8-10)?[7]

Here it will be helpful to compare Du Bois's concept of colonialism with that of other leading anti-colonial theorists. According to Amilcar Cabral (1979) there have historically been two major forms of imperialist domination that have affected Africana people:

1. Direct domination: by means of a political power made up of agents foreign to the dominated people (armed forces, police, administrative agents and settlers)—which is conventionally called *classical colonialism* or *colonialism*.
2. Indirect domination: by means of a political power made up mainly or completely of native [African] agents—which is conventionally called *neocolonialism*. (p. 128, emphasis in orignal)

Cabral's concept and categories of colonialism, especially when compared with Du Bois's, accent and enable us to conceive of colonialism not so much as an historical and cultural coordinate of the past, but as one of the present. For Cabral, colonialism (whether direct or indirect) has the same basic objective and effect: the "denial of the historical process of the dominated people, by means of violent usurpation of the freedom of the process of development of the national productive forces" (pp. 129–30).[8] And those forces that are most productive to a people struggling for national liberation are the ones that help them create thought and practices that not only confront and contradict the established imperial order, but also bring into being the "new humanity" and "new society" that Du Bois, Fanon, Che Guevara, and Herbert Marcuse, among others, wrote and spoke so passionately about.[9] Coupling Du Bois's conception of colonialism with Cabral's, we see then that it is possible for "classical colonialism," as "direct domination," to come to an end without neocolonialism—and the "indirect domination" it entails—being exhausted and extinguished.

In fact, Kwame Nkrumah (1965) contended that most African nations were "nominally independent"—that is, independent only in name, not in fact—because even after "independence" their economic systems and, therefore, social and political policies were directed by, and dictated from, non-African or foreign forces (p. ix). More credence is given to this line of thinking when it is understood that neocolonialism, like the form(s) of classical colonialism that preceded it, is predicated upon the paralysis and retardation of the historical process or "historicity" of Africana and other colonized peoples. "The reality of colonialism," suggests the Eritrean philosopher Tsenay Serequeberhan (1994), is "the violent superimposition of European historicity on African historicity" (p. 111). In other words, classical and neo-colonialism, and all the dogma and domination they necessitate, represent, and register as "the negation of the cultural difference and specificity that constitutes the historicity and thus humanity of the non-European world" (p. 58). These conclusions bring us to a discussion of the period between colonialism and postcolonialism.

BETWEEN COLONIALISM AND POSTCOLONIALISM: THE TRANSITIONAL STAGE/STATE THESIS

Postcolonial theory, literature, culture, and the like, denotes the intellectual productions of formerly colonized peoples *after* colonization. Considering the fact that "[h]istorical epochs do not rise and fall in neat patterns or at precise chronological moments," and considering the fact that the culture of the colonizing country continues to affect the culture of the colonized even *after* "independence," much of the discourse of postcolonialism is extremely misleading (Best and Kellner, 1997, p. 31; Loomba, 1998, pp. 10-12). Based on Du Bois's conceptualization of colonialism, it seems safe to say that we are not in a *post*colonial period, but in a transitional stage/state between a now-aging colonial era and an emerging postcolonial era that remains to be adequately conceptualized, charted, and mapped. Transition from one era to the next, we are told, is always "protracted, contradictory, and usually painful" (Best and Kellner, 1997, p. 31). But the task for contemporary critical theorists is not to jump on the (extremely "premature") postcolonial bandwagon (Loomba, 1998, p. 7). On the contrary, our task is to attempt to explore this transitional moment, to grasp the connections between "classical colonialism" and "neocolonialism," and to project present and future postcolonial possibilities. Hence, one of the most important tasks of a critical anti-colonial theory of contemporary society is to capture and critique both the continuities and discontinuities of the colonial and neocolonial in order to make sense of our currently quite colonized life- and language-worlds.

Although it is prudent to be skeptical and critical of certain segments of postcolonial discourse, and especially the extreme forms of this discourse which attempt to render the assumptions and assertions of anti-colonialists and decolonialists of the past obsolete, it must be admitted that significant changes have taken and are taking place, and that many of the classical anti- and de-colonial theories and practices no longer adequately describe or explain contemporary (neo)colonialism. Whereas the "classical colonial" period, as Cabral (1979) pointed out, was distinguished by "direct domination," since the gaining of "independence" African and other colonized people, neo-colonized people, if you will, have experienced "indirect domination," which is still, I should add, a form of domination nonetheless (p. 128).

Africana critical thought at its best has consistently been anti-colonial, and this is especially evident when we turn to the treasure trove of theoretical and practical insights of the Pan-African tradition.[10] Keeping a keen and critical eye on Du Bois's concept of "semi-colonialism," it must be borne in mind that colonial status has consistently been extended and expanded to encompass and include the lived-experiences and life-worlds of the Africans of the diaspora.[11] Further, following Du Bois's line of thinking, and as asserted above, the nature, processes, and effects of colonization have changed, and colonialism in its new forms—just as Du Bois pointed out with the "classical," direct domination forms of colonialism—is not something that can be confined simply to "people of color" in "third world" and/or "underdeveloped" countries. If we dare attempt to fully grasp and grapple with this expanded Du Boisian definition of colonialism, then, one of the most daunting questions besetting and bombarding contemporary Africana and other radical anti-colonial theorists is: If the injustices and other inequities of racial colonial rule have not, in fact, been eradicated, and if colonialism continues, albeit in another indirect and/or covert form, how then can we combat colonialism in the (post)modern moment? It is here, I think, that we can come to appreciate several aspects of classical anti-colonial and contemporary postcolonial discourse.

SOME OF THE POSITIVES OF POSTCOLONIAL DISCOURSE

Loomba (1998) stated, "the grand narrative of decolonization has, for the moment, been adequately told and widely accepted. Smaller narratives are now needed, with attention paid to local topography, so that maps can become fuller" (p. 252). Many postcolonial theorists are involved in projects of constructing regional or national narratives and, similar to some postmodernists, are excited by the "multiplicity of histories" that challenge political and cultural "monocentricism," and especially Eurocentrism and other linear conceptions of history.[12] Postcolonial discourse has also often provided (neo)colonized, anti- and de-colonial theorists with a much-needed network and discursive arena in which to compare, contrast, and create coalitions based upon common historical experiences and endurances.

However, I would be the first to say that contemporary anti-colonial theorists should be suspicious of extreme or "strong" postcolonialism, and especially those versions which assert that the "post" in "postcolonialism" literally means "after," as in "after-colonialism." For some postcolonial theorists, the extremists, colonialism is a thing of the past and we have already entered into the postcolonial period. Without understanding the reconfiguring nature of colonialism, some postcolonial theorists have conflated changes in the character of colonialism with the "death," demise and/or destruction of colonialism—this is, again, precisely why I assert that Du Bois's concepts of colonialism and semi-colonialism are so important for contemporary anti-, de-, and post-colonial theory and praxis.

Loomba (1998) claims, "colonialism was challenged from a variety of perspectives by people who were not all oppressed in the same way or to the same extent" (p. 8). This statement helps to highlight the heterogeneous nature of both classical and neo-colonialism. Colonialism took, and is taking place in the lives and on the lands of various peoples who have had comparably different historical and cultural experiences. This means, then, that it is important not to gloss over the precolonial, colonial, and possible postcolonial life- and language-worlds of historically and currently colonized people. In our attempts to engage "the colonial problem" and put forward postcolonial solutions, we should keep in mind that, "[o]pposition to colonial rule was spearheaded by forms of national struggle which cannot offer a blueprint for dealing with inequities of the contemporary world order" (p. 14). Why? Because the "contemporary world" is not the world of classical colonialism, and as Arif Dirlik (1994) and Crystal Bartolovich (2000) have pointed out, the connections and power relations between neo-colonialism and global (multi-national and corporate) capitalism have intensified and are often obscured by the poststructuralist and/or postmodernist conceptually incarcerating jargon of postcolonial theorists. In Dirlik's (1994) words:

> Postcolonial critics have . . . had little to say about contemporary figurations.
> . . . They have rendered into problems of subjectivity and epistemology concrete
> and material problems of the everyday world. While capital in its motions con
> tinues to structure the world, refusing it foundational status renders impossible
> the cognitive mapping that must be the point of departure for any practice of re
> sistance. . . . (pp. 352–53)

DU BOIS AND/AS AFRICANA ANTI-COLONIAL THEORY

Though the "contemporary world" is not the classical colonial world, there is much in classical anti- and de-colonial theory that could contribute to contemporary anti-colonial theory and praxis. Classical anti- and de-colonial theorists—W. E. B. Du Bois, C. L. R. James, Aimé Césaire, Frantz Fanon, Kwame Nkrumah, and Amilcar Cabral, among others—offer insights concerning colonialism that enable contemporary anti-colonial theorists to explore and critically examine the ways that colonialism has continued by comparing and contrasting our present so-called "postcolonial" condition(s) with past "classical," "direct domination" colonial conditions. Reflecting on the passage cited above, it seems safe to say that had Dirlik read Du Bois (I have in mind here *Darkwater*, *Color and Democracy*, and *The World and Africa*), for example, he would not only have been able to advance a *critique* of, but also an *alternative* to postcolonial theorists' inattention to the connections between neocolonialism and contemporary capitalism. For instance, Du Bois, in an early draft of a chapter from *Color and Democracy* (1945), thundered:

> [L]et me sum up . . . the colonial problem: the depressed peoples and classes of the world form the vast majority of mankind today in the era of the highest civilization the world has known. The majority of human beings do not today have enough to eat and wear or sufficient shelter for decent existence; the majority of the world's peoples do not understand what the world is, what it has been and what the laws of its growth and development are; and they are unable to read the record of this history. Most human beings suffer and die years before this is necessary and most babies die before they ever really live. And the human mind with all its visions and possibilities is today deliberately distorted and denied freedom of development by people who actually imagine that such freedom would endanger civilization. Most of these disinherited folk are colored, not because there is any essential significance in skin color, but because most people in the world are colored. What now can be done about this, in this day of crisis, when with the end of a horrible and disgraceful war in sight, we contemplate Peace and Democracy? What has Democracy to do with Colonies and what has skin-color to do with Peace? (1985a, p. 236)

Du Bois was apparently "postcolonial" long before contemporary postcolonial discourse; a curious thing when one considers that his work has routinely been omitted from this discourse. He engaged colonialism and "the colonial problem" from his 1895 doctoral dissertation, *The Suppression of the African Slave Trade*, through to his final pieces of radical journalism in *The National Guardian*.[13] For Dirlik, capitalism—albeit "global," "multi-national" and/or "corporate" capitalism—continues to structure the world. For Du Bois, writing fifty years prior to Dirlik, it was not simply capitalism connecting with colonialism that was structuring the world. And neither capitalism nor colonialism were "the" most decisive and distinguishing factors, or "the" fundamental features of modern human existence and experience. Du Bois's (1985a) "cognitive mapping" project took into consideration not only the interlocking and intersecting nature of neocolonialism and, as he put it, "the new capitalism," but also racism and sexism (pp. 232, 239).[14] There is, to my mind, no better example of Du Bois's critical engagement of the dialectics of colonialism and capitalism right along with racism and sexism, and the interlocking, intersecting, and interconnecting nature of each of the aforementioned, than his 1920 monumental pièce de résistance, *Darkwater: Voices from Within the Veil.*[15]

By placing colonialism within the structuring rubric of capitalism, and by arguing that capitalism is "the" central structuring and organizing institution in our (post)modern moment, Dirlik in some senses reproduces the very reductive arguments that caused so many anti-colonial and radical theorists of color to move away from "orthodox" Marxist interpretations of the world.[16] Du Bois consistently "displaced" Eurocentric (or "monocentric") meta-narratives emanating from the European "mother countries" and metropolises by accenting and engaging the life-worlds and lived-experiences of non-European, poor, poverty-stricken people, and often women of color, in three significant ways.[17] First, and as will be discussed in greater detail in chapter 5 and as Joy James (1996b) has correctly observed, Du Bois practiced a "pro-feminist politics" that, though complicated and contradictory, stands in stark relief when compared to the ethereal posturings of many self-described "male-feminists" of the present era. In essays such as "Woman Suffrage," "The Damnation of Women," and "Sex and Racism," to give but a few examples, Du Bois, as Cheryl Gilkes-Townsend (1996) pointed out, not only placed "black folk" at the center of his analysis, he placed black women at center, and they in a certain sense consistently served as a litmus test for Africana and, more generally, human liberation (see Du Bois, 1995a, pp. 291–318).

Secondly, Du Bois also critically engaged the treatment of children in the modern world. By devoting one issue of the *Crisis* each year to children, editing the *Brownies' Book*, and writing essays such as, "Of the Passing of the First-Born," "Of Children" and "The Immortal Child," Du Bois turned his readers' attention to the colonization of children's life-worlds and lived-experiences, and the need for people in positions of power to think of succeeding generations, not simply in human terms, but also in so far as environmental issues were concerned.[18] And finally, Du Bois's concepts of colonialism, while deeply rooted in continental and diasporan African history and culture, consistently exhibited a dialectical radical humanism that took into consideration the life-struggles of both African and non-African colonized people. For instance, in "Japanese Colonialism," "Japan, Color, and Afro-Americans," "China and Africa," "Colonialism, Democracy, and Peace after the War" and *Color and Democracy*, Du Bois often made concrete connections between colonialism in continental and diasporan Africa and colonialism and colonization processes impacting and affecting the indigenous populations and traditional cultures of the Americas, Asia, Australia, and the Caribbean (Du Bois, 1945, 1965, 1985a, 1995a, 2005a; see also Horne, 1986; Juguo, 2001; Marable, 1986).

CONCLUSION: DU BOIS, DECOLONIZATION, AND ANTI-COLONIAL THEORY

Du Bois serves as a critic and critique of postcolonialism in so far as his discourse demystifies and destabilizes several of the main tenets of postcolonialism. Where it is argued that postcolonialism represents a specific species of thought that theorizes the world "after" colonialism, Du Bois puts forward the principal features of colonialism, which in turn helps to highlight the fact that although we are not enduring "classical colonialism," we are, as Cabral and Nkrumah asserted, experiencing "neocolonialism." Du Bois can also be seen as a critic and critique of postcolonialism when it is understood that he refused to reduce colonialism to direct domination or strictly economic exploitation.

For Du Bois (1985a) capitalism and colonialism, as they emanate from European "mother countries" and metropolises, represent "two of the most destructive [forces] in human history" and are "today threatening further human death and disaster" (p. 233). We then, as critical and radical anti-colonial theorists, have a solemn duty to develop theory and praxis that counters and combats not only capitalism and colonialism, but also any and all forms of imperialism. We must consistently build bridges between classical and contemporary anti-colonial thought and practices. Additionally, as Du Bois's discourse accents, there is a real need to critically engage Pan-African and Africana anti-colonial thought-traditions, as these traditions may offer much of interest and much that can be instructive in our current struggle(s) against the ever-present (neo)colonialism in most of our lives. Du Bois (1971b) reminds us once again that the anti-colonial struggle has consistently had as its aim "intellectual understanding and cooperation" among all colonized peoples "in order to bring about at the earliest possible time . . . industrial and spiritual emancipation" (p. 208). Finally, we must not be fooled into believing that either colonialism or capitalism, or racial domination and discrimination are things of the past so long as they determine, define, and deform our present. We must consistently fight for freedom, keeping Cabral's (1972) caveat in mind:

> [L]et us go forward, weapons in hand . . . let us prepare ourselves . . . each day, and be vigilant, so as not to allow a new form of colonialism to be established in our countries, so as not to allow in our countries any form of imperialism, so as not to allow neocolonialism, already a cancerous growth in certain parts of Africa and of the world, to reach our own countries. (p. 85)

Du Bois's engagement of colonialism soon gave way to a more serious critique of capitalism. As a system of oppression, colonialism has historically been primarily predicated on robbing people of color of their resources, land, and labor—in a word (or in a couple of words), colonialism loots their very lives and livelihood. Capitalism, on the other hand, has never conceded to the conventions of the color-line. It economically exploits and underdevelops poor whites as well as blacks and other people of color. However, when and where capitalism connects with colonialism, which is almost everywhere considering the historical fact that the rise of capitalism coincides with European imperial expansion around the globe, it exploits people of color in ways in which it does not white workers because workers of color under a white supremacist capitalist system not only lose their labor, but their sense of self and their kinship with their history and culture.

For Du Bois, colonialism and capitalism are two very different oppressive systems that, especially considering their racial (or racist) character, intersect in the lives of people of color, and twice (or thrice) threaten their humanity and ability to contribute to human culture and civilization. The racial political economic aspects of colonialism and capitalism have historically made them inextricable; where one was found, the other was always there somewhere, in some way as well. This being the case, Du Bois developed what was conceivably the first critical *race* theory of capitalism. However, he observed at the outset of this venture that one of the major differences involved in the critique of colonialism and the critique of capitalism was the fact that capitalism's economic exploitation extended well beyond the world of color and workers of color.

White workers had long leveled serious criticisms of capitalism, and undeniably during the late nineteenth and early twentieth centuries their best work in this vein was embodied in Marxism. Yet, Du Bois pointed out, white Marxists omitted the racist dimensions of capitalism from their discourse, or diminished and downplayed these dimensions when black Marxists were brave enough to bring these issues to the fore. It was with this in mind that Du Bois developed not only a critical race theory of capitalism, but a critical race theory of the Eurocentricism and white supremacism of Marxism as well. His relationship with Marxian theory (and dogma) was long, varied, and intricate, and often obfuscated by both black and white Marxists wishing to claim him for their respective "radical" camps. In the next chapter I discuss Du Bois's critiques of capitalism and Marxism, as well as his development of a conception of democratic socialism that sought an alternative egalitarian society free from the machinations of racism, colonialism, and capitalism.

NOTES

1. For further discussion and examples of other works that have influenced my conception(s) of postcolonialism, see Ashcroft, Griffiths and Tiffin (1989, 1995), Castle (2001), Chambers and Curti (1996), Childs and Williams (1997), Chrisman (2003), Gandhi (1998), Gilroy (2005), Goldberg and Quayson (1999), Gruesser (2005), Juan (2000), Lazarus (2004), Loomba (1998, 2005), A. J. Lopez (2005), Mardorossian (2005), Moore-Gilbert (1997), Parry (2004), Puri (2004), Quayson (2000a, 2003), Serrano (2005), Singh and Schimdt (2000), Venn (2006), Werbner (2002), Williams and Chrisman (1994), and Young (1999, 2003).

2. For further discussion, see McClintock (1994) and Rattansi (1997). In terms of the problematics and some of the positives of postmodernism, see Antonio and Kellner (1994), Best and Kellner (1991, 1997, 2001), Dickens and Fontana (1994),During (1987), Graff (1973), Harvey (1989), Hassan (1987), Hutcheon (1990), Jameson (1991), Lyotard (1984), Rosenau (1992), Seidman (1994), Seidman and Wagner (1992), and Smart (1992, 1993).

3. For analyses of Du Bois's anti-colonial and (proto) post-colonial thought, see Mostern (2000), Berman (2000), Blau and Brown (2001), Contee (1969a, 1969b), Horne (1986), Ijere (1974), Magubane (1987), Marable (1983/84), Martin and Yeakey (1982), Rabaka (2005a), Rogers (1955), and Romero (1976). And, on the theory of decolonization and its discourse, I am primarily referring to what Fanon (1968), in *The Wretched of the Earth*, described as "the veritable creation of new men" and the "program of complete disorder" that they usher into existence "to change the order of the world," "from the bottom up" (pp. 35–36). As a cultural and political program, one of the central objectives of decolonization is to initiate the protracted process of "the colonized" resisting and deracinating (literally, ripping out by the roots) the imperial culture and thought of "the colonizers." However, Fanon was quick to point out that by decolonization he was not suggesting that "the colonized" return to a pristine precolonial past. For him, no such a state ever existed and therefore cannot be recreated or recaptured. Colonized people in the process of decolonizing themselves and liberating their countries must focus first and foremost, Fanon admonished, on those aspects of their traditional culture that will aid them in their fight to regain their long-denied humanity. In line with this, it should be observed that Cabral contributed to and continued the discourse on decolonization by arguing that "the colonized" should "return to the source" of their history and culture, but should be careful not to deem

everything associated with "the colonizer's" culture with imperialism. He asserted: "A people who free themselves from foreign domination will not be culturally free unless, without underestimating the importance of the positive contributions from the oppressor's culture and other cultures, they return to the upwards paths of their own culture" (1979, 143; see also Cabral, 1973). Decolonization, then, is a complex and continuing process that demands a critical engagement of the colonized's precolonial, colonial, and current history and culture rather than something that is automatically achieved with a blare of trumpets and a blaze of fireworks at the moment of independence. For more on decolonization, see Castle (2001), Goldberg and Quayson (1999), Ngũgĩ (1972, 1983, 1986, 1993, 1997), and Werbner (2002).

4. For further discussion of Du Bois's concept(s) of colonialism's "common characteristics," see Du Bois (1930a, 1930b, 1945, 1958, 1961a, 1965, 1968b, 1970a).

5. In light of the fact that many, if not most, of the formerly colonized countries remain under some mutated and/or (post)modern form of colonialism, Amilcar Cabral's assertions concerning *classical colonialism* as "direct domination," and *neocolonialism* as "indirect domination" help to highlight and accent a bitter and brutal truth: We—meaning formerly and currently colonized peoples—are not in a *post*colonial period, which is to say that we are not in a period *after* colonialism when and where we understand colonialism as Cabral (1979) did: as interlocking systems of racial and gender domination and discrimination *and* economic exploitation (p. 128). In fact, at this point it seems safe to say that we are actually in a transitional stage/state between a now-aging colonial era and an emerging postcolonial era that remains to be adequately conceptualized, charted, and mapped. This point will be discussed in greater detail in the subsequent section. For other examples of works which question and confront the "post" in "postcolonial," see Appiah (1992), During (1987), Loomba (1998), McClintock (1992, 1995), Mishra and Hodge (1991), Olaniyan (1992, 2000), Parry (1987), Rattansi (1997), Sadar (1998), and Shobat (1993).

6. Tejumola Olaniyan also eloquently addresses this issue in "Narrativizing Postcoloniality" (1992).

7. For a fuller discussion and other corroborating claims, see Prakash (1995) and Rajan and Mohanran (1995).

8. As with Fanon in *The Wretched of the Earth* (see chapter 1, "Concerning Violence"), Cabral's concept of violence extends well beyond the realm of physical violation and encompasses those psychological factors and forces that inhibit human wholeness, critical self-consciousness, and free and full development. Which, in other words, is to say that the ethical and justificatory hub and hinge of Cabral's concept of violence is a struggling peoples' right to self-definition and self-determination. For further discussion, see Bienen (1977), Blackey (1974), Chabal (1981a, 1983), Chilcote (1968, 1991), McCollester (1973), McCulloch (1983), Serequeberhan (1994), and Táíwò (1999a, 1999b).

9. See, for instance, Du Bois (1945, 1968b, 1999), Fanon (1967, 1968), Guevara (1968), and Marcuse (1969, 1972a). On national liberation, see Fanon, "The Pitfalls of National Consciousness" and "On National Culture," both in *The Wretched of the Earth* (1968); Fanon, "Decolonization and Independence" and "Unity and Effective Solidarity are the Conditions for African Liberation," both in *Toward the African*

Revolution (1969); Nkrumah, *Towards Colonial Freedom* (1962), *Consciencism: Philosophy and Ideology for Decolonization* (1964), *Neo-Colonialism: The Last Stage of Imperialism* (1965), *Africa Must Unite* (1970a), *Class Struggle in Africa* (1970b), *Revolutionary Path* (1973a), and *The Struggle Continues* (1973b); Cabral, "National Liberation and Peace: Cornerstones of Non-Alignment," "The National Movements of the Portuguese Colonies," and "The Development of the Struggle," all in *Revolution in Guinea* (1972); Cabral, "National Liberation and Culture" and "Identity and Dignity in the Context of National Liberation Struggle," both in *Return to the Source* (1973); Cabral, "Presuppositions and Objectives of National Liberation in Relation to Social Structure," in *Unity and Struggle* (1979); and Chabal, "National Liberation in Portuguese Guinea, 1956–1974" (1981b).

10. For critical discussions of Pan-African theory and praxis, see Axelsen (1984), English and Kalumba (1996), Esedebe (1994), Geiss (1974), Langley (1973, 1979), Serequeberhan (1994), Thompson (1969), and Walters (1993). And for discussions of Pan-Africanism that details Du Bois's position as doyen of this discourse, see Contee (1969a, 1969b, 1971, 1972), Efrat (1967), Gbadegesin (1996), Gershoni (1995), Martin and Yeakey (1982), Moore (1970), Recht (1971), Reed (1975, 1997), Rogers (1955), and Romero (1976).

11. See Du Bois (1945, 1958, 1965), Ashcroft, Griffiths and Tiffin (1989, 2), Loomba (1998, 12), Cook and Henderson (1969), Drachler (1975), Harris (1993), Lemelle and Kelley (1994), Thompson (1987), Von Eschen (1997), and Walters (1993).

12. For a discussion, see Alva (1995) and Ashcroft, Griffiths and Tiffin (1989, pp. 11–12). On postmodern conceptions of history and the history of ideas, see Appleby, Covington, Hoyt, Latham and Snieder (1996). And for strong critiques of Eurocentricism and other linear conceptions of human history, see Chatterjee (1993), Blaut (1993), and Keita (2000).

13. With regard to the primary sources, see Du Bois (1971a, 1971b, 1986a, 1995a, 1996a).

14. On the concept of "cognitive mapping," see Jameson (1988). For discussions of some of the ways in which race, gender, class, and sexuality interlock and intersect, see Hull, Scott and Smith (1982), Smith (1983), Guy-Sheftall (1995), James and Sharpley-Whiting (2000), and Zack, Shrage and Sartwell (1998).

15. For those with specific interests in other representative works by Du Bois that more or less simultaneously engage racism, sexism, colonialism, and capitalism, see his often overlooked *Africa in Battle Against Colonialism, Racism, and Imperialism*, and his novels, *The Quest of the Silver Fleece*, *Dark Princess*, and *The Black Flame Trilogy:* Book One, *The Ordeal of Mansart*; Book Two, *Mansart Builds a School*; and Book Three, *Worlds of Color* (Du Bois 1911, 1928, 1957, 1959, 1960c, 1961b). Du Bois's histories are also helpful, especially his later historical writings that accentuate and place the agency of women of African descent on par with that of men of African descent. See *The Negro*, *The Gift of Black Folk: Negroes in the Making of America*, *Black Folk, Then and Now: An Essay in the History and Sociology of the Negro Race*, and *The World and Africa* (Du Bois 1939, 1965, 1970a, 1970b).

16. This is a theme that many theorists of color have consistently confronted, see, for example, A. Y. Davis (1998), C. L. R. James (1994, 1996, 1999), Marable (1983, 1996), Robinson (2000), Rodney (1972, 1981, 1990), and West (1988b). I explore this issue in greater detail in the subsequent chapter using Du Bois's radical theoretical trajectory as a point of departure.

17. For a further discussion of Du Bois's theoretical practice(s) of "displacement," see Adell (1994) and Byerman (1994).

18. For Du Bois's discourse on children and ecological issues, see Du Bois (1969c, 1972a, 1983a, 1983b, 1997a, 1999). Also resourceful in this regard, see Johnson-Feelings (1996). And for a sampling of some of the better secondary sources, see Diggs (1976) and Lee (2000).

Chapter Four

Du Bois's Critique of Capitalism, Critical Marxism, and Discourse on Democratic Socialism

"Argument concerning whether 'Marxist' influences on Du Bois's thought were dominant, or whether Pan-Africanism or non-Marxist socialism constituted the central orienting principle of his ideas, is beside the point."—A. L. Reed, 1997, p. 84

"We cannot talk of Dr. Du Bois without recognizing that he was a radical all his life. Some people would like to ignore the fact that he was a Communist in his later years. . . . It is time to cease muting the fact that Dr. Du Bois was a genius and chose to be a Communist. Our irrational obsessive anticommunism has led us into too many quagmires to be retained as if it were a mode of scientific thinking."—M. L. King, 1970, pp. 26–27

"Du Bois committed himself to the development of a theory of history, which by its emphasis on mass action was both a critique of the ideologies of American socialist movements and a revision of Marx's theory of revolution and class struggle. . . . [A]s a critic of Marx, Du Bois had possessed no obligations to Marxist or Leninist dogma, nor to the vagaries of historical analysis and interpretation that characterized American Communist thought."—C. J. Robinson, 2000, pp. 196, 228

"So while Du Bois formally embraced orthodox Marxism in the last years of his life, he conducted a political practice that critically engaged Marxist theory. It is a misnomer to call the most radical aspects of his oeuvre simply black Marxism." —Bouges, 2003, p. 89

"I am certainly not a conservative. I should call myself a Socialist, although that isn't a very definite term."—Du Bois, 1971b, p. 701

INTRODUCTION:
DU BOIS'S RACE-CENTERED AND RACISM-CONSCIOUS
CRITIQUE OF CAPITALISM AND MARXISM

As intimated in the previous chapter, Du Bois's critique of colonialism is in-extricable from his critique of capitalism. In some senses it could be averred that as he developed his simultaneously socio-historic and politico-economic analyses, beginning with race and racism and quickly connecting them to colonialism (as we have seen in chapters 2 and 3), Du Bois eventually added capitalism to his anti-imperialist agenda as a major target of oppression and exploitation to be eliminated. On the one hand, one of many things that dis-tinguish his criticisms of capitalism from colonialism involves the fact that from his optic capitalism and colonialism are two very different—albeit in-timately interrelated—oppressive and exploitive systems that must be ap-proached in a manner that speaks to their specificities. On the other hand, an-other contributing defining and distinguishing marker of Du Bois's critique of capitalism is linked to the fact that some whites, that is, some members of the ruling race, also understood capitalism to be an oppressive and exploitive system and had developed critical theory and radical political praxis tradi-tions that could be loosely drawn from and put to use in the Africana fight for freedom and justice. Though, as Du Bois observed early, most white crit-ics of capitalism focused almost exclusively on capitalism's economic ex-ploitative aspects without so much as mentioning how it intersected with and exacerbated racial oppression. This led Du Bois at the outset of his critique of capitalism to simultaneously critique capitalism *and* the white critics of capitalism.

The white critics of capitalism were critical of it for very different reasons than those of their colored "comrades." And Du Bois was one of the first rad-ical theorists of color, and perhaps, without a doubt the first Africana theorist, to register this difference. As several interpreters of Du Bois have observed, he had a critical and dialectical relationship with the white critics of capital-ism, especially Marxist socialist and communist thought and practice. Ac-cording to Adolph Reed (1997), in *W. E. B. Du Bois and American Political Thought*, "everyone agrees that Du Bois died a socialist, but few agree on when he became one or on what kind of socialist he was" (p. 83).

In *W. E. B. Du Bois: Negro Leader in a Time of Crisis*, the brutally polem-ical Francis Broderick (1959) explains that Du Bois's thought may be diffi-cult to periodize in the manner that many intellectual historians are accus-tomed to on account of the fact that "[h]is ideas changed constantly, but the major changes came gradually, with a considerable overlap" (p. 124). This is an important point, especially considering the present examination of Du

Bois as a critical theorist, because it speaks to the systematic, multidimensional, and interdisciplinary quality and character of his thought. Broderick's comments in this regard deserve further quotation:

> Writing month after month on current events, he [Du Bois] did not, of course, abruptly end one period of intellectual change and begin another. He might drop a hint, then wait twenty years before picking it up for further development. His praise of self-sufficient, segregated Negro communities came at the flood tide of the Niagara Movement. He was making advances to socialism in 1907, although in early 1908 he affirmed his attachment to the principles of the Republican party. Africa had an almost mystical fascination for him even on his twenty-fifth birthday, but thirty years elapsed before the fascination produced a program of action. Even as the hope for alliance with workers and colored men dominated his thought in the 1930s, a minor theme, self-sufficiency for the Negro community, was rising in a crescendo which by the early 1930s would make it dominant. Conversely, as new ideas came to prominence after the World War, the old ones did not disappear: the essence of his lecture "Race Relations in the United States," for the American Academy of Political and Social Science in 1928 could have been written twenty-five years before. His ideas changed constantly, but the major changes came gradually, with considerable overlap. (pp. 123–24; see also Du Bois, 1982b, pp. 139–43, pp. 303–8)

Du Bois's "socialism," to use this term loosely, may have never been as scientific, dogmatic, and/or orthodox Marxist as many intellectual historians have claimed, or would like to claim. As he matured, both personally and professionally, his thought took on a chameleonic character, crisscrossing back and forth between the chasms of race and class. His thought often exhibited internal tensions, sometimes appearing race-centered, and at other times seeming overly concerned with class, labor, and economic justice issues. In addition, the complexity and multidimensionality of his thought gave it a contradictory and often confusing character, which, as we will soon see in the subsequent chapter, was exacerbated by the fact that sexism was also a major item on his anti-imperial agenda right alongside racism, colonialism, and capitalism. Du Bois's criticisms of capitalism, then, are distinguished from those of the white critics of capitalism, especially the Marxists, because his criticisms harbored an acute sensitivity to and critical employment of subjugated knowledge regarding the ways in which capitalist oppression intersects and interconnects with racial and sexual domination and discrimination.[1]

Du Bois, indeed, was a "socialist," and he openly admitted as much. But, as many black and white Marxist theorists have pointed out, what it meant to be a Marxist or socialist prior to the Russian Revolution of 1917 was very different than claiming to be one after this historic event (Kolakowski, 1978b, 1978c). Prior to the Russian Revolution, socialism generally entailed a belief in non-violent social revolution or, rather, social reform, trade and industrial unionism, public ownership of utilities and properties, municipal improvement, corporate regulation, and a wide range of other economic and public policies. After the Russian Revolution, socialism became the bane of many social circles in capitalist countries because it was purported to be the transitional state between capitalism and communism, as claimed by Karl Marx and his disciples in their (critical) theorizations. The Russian Revolution was not the prim and proper, prudent non-violent textbook revolution that so many French, English, and white American socialists had hoped for and long dreamed about (Carr, 1966; Fitzpatrick, 1982). In fact, according to Roger Gottlieb (1992), in *Marxism 1844–1990,* though the Russian communists took state power in the spirit of the ideas of Marx and Engels, their interpretation and practice of communism "had virtually nothing in common with Marx's vision of socialism" (p. 77; see also C. L. R. James, 1993; Marcuse, 1958). None of this, of course, stopped the Russian communists' actions and interpretations from staining Marxism and socialism in the American social imagination, as the hysteria of the House Committee on Un-American Activities under the auspices of Senator Joseph McCarthy clearly illustrated (Doherty, 2003; Schrecker, 1998). In the final analysis, similar to the term *race* (and the terms of racism), as discussed in chapter 2, at the turn of and throughout the twentieth century *socialism* had a mercurial and malleable meaning, or set of meanings.[2]

Du Bois critically engaged various versions of socialism (or, more generally, Marxism) for many of the same reasons that the Trinidadian triumvirate of C. L. R. James, Oliver C. Cox, and Eric Williams did: because it offered an array of criticisms of capitalism that cut to its core and made visible its obstinately invisible imperial machinations. However, it must be borne in mind that each of the aforementioned continuously criticized Marxism for its neglect of the racist aspects of capitalist culture and political economy. They were never Marxist in any orthodox or doctrinaire sense because, as Du Bois and James's radical thought regularly reminds us, blacks and other people of color were often seen as threats to white workers, white trade unions, and white labor movements' strides toward economic justice. White supremacy shaped and shaded the white critics of capitalism's theorizations and politics, especially in the Socialist and Communist parties. This had the effect of placing Du Bois and the other black critics of capitalism outside of the orthodox Marxist orbit. In a sense, this forced them to develop their own race-centered and racism-conscious critiques of capitalism; something most white Marxists had never even dared dream of doing. It also led the black radicals to a critical and, at times, volatile relationship with the white critics of capitalism, Marxism, and Marxist party politics.[3]

Just as he had pioneered as an anti-racist, Pan-Africanist and anti-colonial theorist, Du Bois recusantly reinterpreted and critically engaged Marxism from perspectives that previously had not been considered by either Marxist or non-Marxist theorists. That is to say that when he critically questioned Marxian theory from an Africana historical, cultural, social, and political frame of reference, and/or from the position of hyper-raced, "colored" and colonized people generally, he identified several of its theoretic inadequacies. It is the identification of these inadequacies and his development of a distinctly black (read: race-centered and racism-conscious) critique of capitalism that makes Du Bois stand out among black radical theorists.[4]

Whether they agreed or disagreed with him, few could escape Du Bois's enormous and almost unfathomable influence on black radicalism during his day. For instance, take perhaps the most noted of the Trinidadian triumvirate, C. L. R. James, who is by many accounts one of the greatest intellectuals the Caribbean has produced. In *C. L. R. James and Revolutionary Marxism*, Scott McLemee (1994) argues that though James was highly critical of Du Bois, Du Bois did indeed "deeply influence him" (p. 225). In an often-overlooked 1965 tribute to the recently deceased Du Bois, James wrote:

> There is no need to subscribe to all that Dr. Du Bois has said and done. . . . Only the future can tell to what degree the historical audacities of Du Bois are viable. . . . Dr. Du Bois has always been put forward as one of the great black men and one of the great leaders of the black people. But, I have said that he is one of the great intellectuals—American intellectuals—of the twentieth century, and today and in years to come his work will continue to expand in importance while the work of others declines. (C. L. R. James, 1977, pp. 202, 211)

Du Bois's thought appealed to James and others of his ilk because it was culturally grounded, critical, and dialectical. In his approach to Marxism, Du Bois consistently demonstrated his ability to distinguish between its progressive and retrogressive elements. One of the many areas that Du Bois—among many other black radical theorists—found Marxism wanting was in its neglect to theorize the life-worlds and lived-experiences of the racially oppressed (his beloved black folk and other people of color).

As early as his 1907 essay, "The Negro and Socialism," Du Bois detected and detailed deficiencies in the Marxist tradition which included, among other things, a silence on and/or an inattention to race, racism, and anti-racist struggle; colonialism and anti-colonial struggle; and the ways in which *both* capitalism and colonialism exacerbate not simply the economic exploitation of non-Europeans, but continues (both physical and psychological) colonization beyond the realm of political economy. Du Bois, therefore, laboring long and critically with Marxian theory and methodology, deconstructed it and developed his own original radical democratic socialist theory that: simultaneously built on his pioneering work as a critical race theorist and radical anti-colonialist; called for the radical transformation of U.S. society and the power relations of the world; was deeply concerned about and committed to world peace and demanded disarmament; and advocated the liberation of all colonized, politically oppressed, and economically exploited persons.

Du Bois was well aware of the fact that anyone in the citadel of super-capitalism, the United States, who openly embraced socialism or Marxism in any of its manifestations would quickly become a social and political pariah. But against a barrage of black bourgeois and white conservative criticism he sought socialism and a methodical and meticulous understanding of Marxism. As discussed in greater detail below, Du Bois did not believe that the Russian communists had a monopoly on Marxism any more than he believed that the Marxists put a patent on the critique of capitalism. Marxism was merely one of many tools in Du Bois's ever-evolving critical socio-theoretical framework, and just as the meaning of socialism and Marxism changed as a result of revolutionary praxis and retheorization, so too did Du Bois's relationship with and critical appreciation and/or race(ism)-conscious rejection of certain aspects of Marxism change.

The succeeding sections of this chapter, consequently, will be devoted to reconstructing and, in many senses, (re)*developing* Du Bois's democratic socialist theory. The primary objectives here are to identify and analyze those aspects of his democratic socialism that continue to be relevant with regard to contemporary critical social theory and radical politics, and isolate those aspects of his socialist theory that are now obsolete or in need of revision and further development due to the new social and political problems of the present age. In line with the general theme of the present study, to explore Du Bois's work for its import to critical social theory, this chapter aims to interrogate Du Bois as a critic of both capitalism *and* Marxism.

As it would be almost impossible to understand his critique of capitalism without first understanding his critical relationship with Marxism, I will begin by briefly explaining Du Bois's critical appreciation and/or rejection of specific tenets of Marxism. Although he was critical of capitalism prior to his embrace of certain elements of Marxism, Marxism did indeed provide him with many much-needed tools to develop a deeper understanding of and more sophisticated critique of capitalism. Next, I shall quickly treat his deconstruction of Marxian methodology and creation of race/class categories of analysis before concentrating on his critique of capitalism. And finally, I will critically analyze Du Bois's discourse on democratic socialism and explore its relevance for contemporary critical social theory and radical politics. We begin with a discussion of Du Bois's critical appreciation of and/or rejection of certain aspects of Marxism.

DU BOIS'S CRITIQUE OF MARXISM

In his classic study *The Golden Age of Black Nationalism, 1850–1925*, Wilson Moses (1978) correctly contends, "Du Bois was an anticapitalist long before he was a socialist" (p. 138). In 1903, the year he published his watershed work, *The Souls of Black Folk*, Du Bois wanted nothing whatsoever to do with what he called "a cheap and dangerous socialism" (cited in Moses, 1978, p. 138). There has long been a tendency in Du Bois studies, and especially among those working on his critical race and radical thought, to either exclusively engage his work prior to and including *The Souls of Black Folk*, or to disavow his early articulations and emphasize the radicalism of his later years. But this is intellectually disingenuous and, it would seem, a great disservice to Du Bois, who spoke and wrote endlessly of our ethical obligation to constantly search for both scientific and social truth. In addition, this elision creates an arbitrary and artificial dichotomy in Du Bois's oeuvre that robs contemporary radicals of a paradigm and an opportunity to chart the political growth and development of a classical radical theorist and critic.

Traditionally when Du Bois's radical thought and relationship to socialism has been engaged, three themes dominate the discourse. First, Du Bois is argued to have rashly turned to radicalism, embracing a brand of socialism based on the articulations of white critics of capitalism (this includes Marxists, anti-Marxists, and non-Marxists). Second, the Russian Revolution is reported to have convinced him once and for all of the sanctity of socialism and Marxism. And third—and the most common claim—his magisterial Marxian text, *Black Reconstruction of Democracy in America* (1935), is asserted to represent the completion of his conversion to Marxism. However, Du Bois's texts tell a different tale, and it is to these neglected narratives that I now intend to turn. I will briefly treat each of the three themes before discussing his distinct and constantly developing conception of socialism.

With regard to the first theme, Moses (1978) maintains, "Du Bois is remembered as one of the great socialists of the twentieth century and it is easy to forget the conservatism of his intellectual origins" (p. 138). However, we should mince no words and make no mistakes about it, though Du Bois ultimately arrived at socialism, he only "became a socialist by gradual stages" (p. 138). His embrace of socialism did not entail the type of religious "leap of faith" or rituals of religious conversion that have historically been associated with some theorists' turn to Marxism. The careful and critical Du Bois came to socialism only after years of studying its theories and observing its practices, and, even after he came to it, it is difficult to say with any accuracy what type of socialism he initially or ultimately embraced.[5]

Though much has been made of Du Bois's 1907 essays, "Socialist of the Path" and "The Negro and Socialism," which, of course, reveal his turn to "radical thought" and socialism, few have commented on the fact that even after his supposed "socialist turn," Du Bois continued to carry out one of the most thorough criticisms of Marxian theory in radical intellectual history. Many Du Bois scholars have observed his historic 1907 turn to socialism, but they do not provide an archaeology of the crucial *why* and *how* he decided to embrace socialism as a political theory and praxis. Further, most Du Bois scholars pass over roughly thirty years of his critical writings on socialism and Marxism to quickly get to the tried and true example of his employment of Marxian methodology and major contribution to what is currently called "black Marxism." I am, of course, referring to Du Bois's 1935 classic *Black Reconstruction of Democracy in America*.[6]

Du Bois was a consistent critic of Marxism, and not an uncritical and impetuous demagogue and disciple of the white critics of capitalism and their theories. In 1911 he officially joined the Socialist Party. Ironically, in that same year he delivered an address in New York entitled, "Socialism Is Too Narrow for Negroes" (1911), before an audience of one thousand socialists. In his speech he told his "comrades":

> You come to us, and with all the faith that your idea, the idea of Socialism inspires you, and you tell the Negro race to join the Socialist movement, which aims at the abolition of all ills and inequalities. You will find, however, that the Negro race will look upon you, upon the Socialists, with the same suspicion that it looks upon all white men. It will regard you as enemies just as it has been taught to regard all white men. (Du Bois, 1982b, p. 40)

Why, we are all asking? Because,

> the Socialist movement really does not offer such a remedy for the race problem as Socialists generally think. The Socialist movement, like a great many reform movements in religion, in humanitarian and social relations of men, in the labor movement, have been movements which have concerned themselves with the European civilization, with the white races. So long as the Socialist movement can put a ban upon any race because of its color, whether that color be yellow or black, the Negro will not feel at home in it. (p. 40)

In so many words, Du Bois was calling his socialist comrades white supremacists and Eurocentricists (to their faces!) because their brand of socialism was racially exclusive, focusing narrowly on "the European civilization" and "the white races." Surely this type of intra-party criticism (Du Bois was a member of the party at this point) was unprecedented in socialist circles at the time. But because most Du Bois scholars rush to *Black Reconstruction*, they miss many of his seminal criticisms of socialism that led him to develop the distinct black Marxist method of their most beloved book. Now, one may also be wondering: well, why did Du Bois join the Socialist Party if he knew it was racist? He quickly and coolly answered: the Socialists were "the only party which openly recognizes Negro manhood." According to Manning Marable (1986), in *W. E. B. Du Bois: Black Radical Democrat*, Du Bois's motivations for joining the Socialist Party also grew out of his associations with several of the white socialists who helped him found the National Association for the Advancement of Colored People (NAACP) and his "overriding commitment to racial and economic justice" (p. 90). Soon, says Marable, "Socialism was integrated into his [Du Bois's] larger struggle against racial inequality" (p. 90).[7]

Du Bois's tenure in the Socialist Party was very brief, only lasting one year, from 1911 to 1912. As he revealed in *Darkwater* (1920), he simply could not stomach the fact that his so-called socialist "comrades," and a political organization that he was a member of, "openly excluded Negroes and Asiatics" (Du Bois, 1996a, p. 552). Du Bois's prompt departure from the party was precipitated by what he perceived to be its timidity toward concrete criticisms of, as opposed to radical rhetoric against, racial discrimination and racist exclusions within its own ranks. Soon after joining the party he began a campaign to recruit and elect African American officers. But the white socialists would not budge. Marable (1986) makes the point that though Du Bois "may have resigned from the Socialist Party, . . . he remained a Socialist" (p. 90).

The second recurring theme that dominates the discourse on Du Bois's radical thought involves his impression of and interpretation of the Russian Revolution and its impact on his outlook. Clearly the Soviet experiment with communism had a deep and profound impact on Du Bois. But again, his interest in the Russian Revolution has often been interpreted as an unequivocal and unflinching acceptance of everything that it entailed. However, and in the fashion of his foray into socialism, and Marxism in general, Du Bois continued to critically question Russian communism. In fact, he exhibited such an uncharacteristic reticence regarding the Russian Revolution and its immediate aftermath that he was harshly criticized by the Jamaican poet laureate and black radical Claude McKay.

From McKay's optic, Du Bois had written critically of the Russian Revolution and was therefore a traitor to the working classes and black masses because, as McKay fumed, "the Negro in politics and social life is ostracized

only technically by the distinction of color; in reality the Negro is discriminated against because he is the lowest type of worker" (McKay quoted in Du
Bois, 1995a, p. 531). Now, it is Du Bois's rejoinder to McKay that sheds light
on his position on the Russian Revolution and possibly lays to rest incredulous claims regarding his early, extremely critical interpretation of it. Du
Bois's blazing response to McKay was entitled, "The Negro and Radical
Thought" (1921). In the essay he takes "Mr. McKay" to task for privileging
class over race (something several of Du Bois's critics would argue that he
did in his later work) and making the erroneous assumption that he "sneered"
at the Russian Revolution. Du Bois (1995a) declared:

> [W]e have one chief cause—the emancipation of the Negro, and to this all else
> must be subordinated—not because other questions are not important but be
> cause to our mind the most important social question today is recognition of the
> darker races.
>
>   Turning now to that marvelous set of phenomena known as the Russian Rev
> olution, Mr. McKay is wrong in thinking that we have ever intentionally sneered
> at it. On the contrary, time may prove, as he believes, that the Russian Revolu
> tion is the greatest event of the nineteenth and twentieth centuries, and its lead
> ers the most unselfish prophets. At the same time *The Crisis* does not know this
> to be true. Russia is incredibly vast, and the happenings there in the last five
> years have been intricate to a degree that must make any student pause. We sit,
> therefore, with waiting hands and listening ears, seeing some splendid results
> from Russia . . . and hearing other things which frighten us. (p. 532).

At first issue is Du Bois's unapologetic display of black nationalism. In his
words, "we have one chief cause . . . the emancipation of the Negro." In addition, and this should be underscored, it must be borne in mind that he made
this statement well-nigh fifteen years after his supposed socialist turn in 1907.
Again, I refute the claim that he was a Marxist-socialist in any orthodox or
doctrinaire sense. In fact, what we see here is Du Bois being highly critical of
a radical of African descent—the fact that he was a "Negro poet of distinction"
notwithstanding—who had accepted the orthodox Marxist obsession with economics and emphasis on class struggle (p. 531). And finally, Du Bois's comments on the Russian Revolution reveal that five years after "that marvelous
set of phenomena" he was still not convinced of or committed to the Russian
version of communism. However, and in characteristic fashion, he did remind
his radical "Negro" readers that "the immediate work for the American Negro
lies in America and not in Russia" (pp. 532–33). He also counseled black radicals to continue to question socialism and communism, all the while he was
extending and expanding his critique of Marxism. Du Bois rhetorically questioned and answered:

What is today the right program of socialism? The editor of *The Crisis* considers himself a Socialist but he does not believe that German State Socialism or the dictatorship of the proletariat are perfect panaceas. He believes with most thinking men that the present method of creating, controlling and distributing wealth is desperately wrong; that there must come and is coming a social control of wealth; but he does not know just what form that control is going to take, and he is not prepared to dogmatize with Marx or Lenin. Further than that, and more fundamental to the duty and outlook of *The Crisis*, is this question: How far can the colored people of the world, and particularly the Negroes of the United States, trust the working classes?

Many honest thinking Negroes assume, and Mr. McKay seems to be one of these, that we have only to embrace the working class program to have the working class embrace ours; that we have only to join Trade Unionism and Socialism or even Communism, as they are today expounded, to have Union Labor and Socialists and Communists believe and act on the equality of mankind and the abolition of the color line. *The Crisis* wishes that this were true, but it is forced to the conclusion that it is not. (p. 533)

Fifteen years after his supposed socialist turn, and five years after the Russian Revolution, Du Bois considered himself a socialist but was "not prepared to dogmatize with Marx or Lenin." This may seem curious to many contemporary readers but, again, Du Bois did not think that the Marxists had a monopoly on socialism. In 1921 he continued to carry out his critique of Marxism, calling into question its usefulness to the racially oppressed, and particularly people of African origin and descent.

It was racial discrimination and racist exclusionism, not only by white capitalists but also by white workers that distinguished the plight of the black worker. Black workers were *black* before they were workers, which in many white supremacist capitalists, unionists, labor organizers, and workers' minds precluded blacks from ever being workers in either a Marxian or non-Marxian sense. This is to say that black workers were never thought of in the raceless terms in which white workers were thought of when white Marxists, economists, labor scholars, political scientists, and sociologists, among many others, theorized "the working class" (Kelley, 1994, 1997a). Black workers were always and ever *raced first*, to shamelessly appropriate Marcus Garvey's famous phrase for my own critical theoretical purposes. The bottom line, and the main point Du Bois wanted to make in the passage above, was that white workers undeniably suffer severely within a capitalist system. But, he emphatically emphasized, being a white worker within a white supremacist capitalist system is not nearly as tragic and traumatic as being black *and* a worker in a white supremacist capitalist system (Marable, 1983, 1993, 1995, 1996, 1997, 2002).

Fifteen years after "The Negro and Radical Thought" (1921), Du Bois produced what many critics have long hailed as his definitive statement on the differences between the white worker and the black worker, his 1935 masterpiece *Black Reconstruction of Democracy in America*. This, of course, brings us to the third and final theme that dominates the discourse on Du Bois's radicalism. With the publication of *Black Reconstruction*, Du Bois is purported to have finally shown his hand and crossed over completely to Marxism. Critics have taken great pleasure in pointing out this or that Marxian element or influence in his later radical writings, especially in *Black Reconstruction*. But the truth of the matter is one-dimensional, narrow-minded, and Eurocentric interpretations of Du Bois do his legacy a great disservice and rob contemporary critical theorists of an opportunity to explore the richness and wide range and reach of his radical thought.

Indeed, *Black Reconstruction* is one of many watershed works in Du Bois's corpus, and my critical remarks here should not be confused with criticisms of the book (which incidentally will not be directly engaged in this instance), but more criticisms of the book's reception. *Black Reconstruction*'s reception — and we could say contemporary reception of classical reception of this text — is important here in terms of developing Africana critical theory because if this important work in black radicalism is interpreted as a work wholly within the Marxian tradition, then Du Bois quickly and logically (from a Marxist and Eurocentricist frame of reference) becomes a disciple, or worst an ideologue in a tradition in which he actually innovated, created, and contributed new concepts and categories of analysis. My efforts here are primarily geared toward exposing the fact that even after he wrote *Black Reconstruction*, Du Bois did not uncritically accept Marxism, but continued to draw from those aspects of the theory which he understood to offer the greatest contribution to his "one chief cause—the emancipation of the Negro." Moreover, let us bear in mind that for Du Bois "all else must be subordinated" to the "one chief cause," "not because other questions are not important but because to our mind the most important social question today is recognition of the darker races."

I utterly agree with the two-time Pulitzer Prize-winning Du Bois biographer David Levering Lewis (2000) in *W. E. B. Du Bois: The Fight for Equality and the American Century, 1919–1963*, when he noted: "The book [*Black Reconstruction*] represented one of those genuine paradigm shifts periodically experienced in a field of knowledge, one that sunders regnant interpretations into the before-and-after of its sudden, disorienting emergence. Had he ventured to paraphrase Marx, who both inspires and deforms the book, Du Bois might well have observed that he had set reconstruction historiography upright after finding it standing on its head" (p. 367). *Black Reconstruction* represents and registers as a "genuine paradigm shift" because it recasts both Reconstruction historiography and Marxian historical materialism from "the black point of view," a cool-penned Lewis quipped regarding the methodological orientation of Du Bois's Reconstruction research, from his 1910 bombshell "Reconstruction and Its Benefits" through to his 1935 blazon *Black Reconstruction* (p. 351).

Du Bois maintained a critical relationship with Marxism from the time of his supposed socialist turn in 1907 and up to and after the publication of *Black Reconstruction* in 1935. In 1936, ironically a year after *Black Reconstruction* had a ripple effect on Reconstruction historiography and supposedly made him the black Marxist *par excellence*, Du Bois continued to carry out his criticism of socialism and communism in an obscure and often overlooked *Journal of Negro Education* essay entitled, "Social Planning for the Negro, Past and Present." The essay is essentially a history of African American's social and political thought and movements, from enslavement to the present, circa 1936. After accenting the rebellions of Denmark Vesey and Nat Turner; noting Harriet Tubman and the Underground Railroad; highlighting Paul Cuffe's emigration plan; praising John Brown and Frederick Douglass for their courageous abolitionism; and, writing almost objectively of Booker T. Washington and his program, the essay gives way to its concluding section, which Du Bois dubbed "The Present Dilemma."

Emphasis should be placed on the last section of Du Bois's essay because it represents one of the first times he discussed African Americans and their then-current conditions after the publication of *Black Reconstruction*. *Black Reconstruction* was a critical look at African Americans' past from "the black point of view" (à la Lewis), where "Social Planning for the Negro: Past and Present," as the title suggests, was an examination of African Americans' classical and contemporary conditions from "the black point of view." In addition, the final section of Du Bois's essay is a clarion example of his continued critical relationship with Marxism after the publication of *Black Reconstruction*.

Du Bois (1982c) begins the section by putting forward his long-held contention that "the problem of race discrimination always cuts across and hinders the settlement of other problems" (p. 36). The problem he is hinting at here has to do with both race and class, actually racial oppression and economic exploitation in the forms of racism and capitalism. Faced with the reality of the economic depression in the U.S. at that time, Du Bois argued that African Americans had three options available to them: "(1) a movement toward invoking the protection of restored capitalism, (2) a movement toward alliance with organized labor, and (3) a movement toward socialism" (p. 36). With regard to the first and second options, Du Bois succinctly stated:

> There is only one haven of refuge for the American Negro. He must recognize that his attempt to enter the ranks of capital as an exploiter came too late, if it

were ever a worthy ideal for a group of workers. He is now forever excluded by the extraordinary monopoly which white capital and credit have upon the machines and materials of the world. Moreover, that solution after all was possible only for the few. The great mass of Negroes belong to the laboring class. (pp. 37–38)

African Americans simply could not join with the capitalists because they had no capital, and even if and when they did produce or procure capital, racism still reared its ugly head (and horns!). Besides, Du Bois questions, is it a "worthy ideal," economically exploiting others? And, considering African Americans' historical experiences at the hands (and under the boots) of white supremacist capitalists: aren't or shouldn't blacks almost inherently be anti-capitalist? Keep in mind, "The great mass of Negroes belong to the laboring class" and have historically ever since Africans first came to the Americas in shackles and chains at the dawn of the sixteenth century. The first option was, therefore, quickly dispelled.

As far as the second option of African Americans joining the unions, racism again proved a decisive factor. The unionists, as Du Bois discussed in "The American Federation of Labor and the Negro" (1929), were white racists who saw blacks as job-stealers and would not allow them to join the unions. There went the second option, dismissed with a quick-witted and uncomplicated brevity. This left, then, the third and final option, socialism. Du Bois (1982c) mused:

Suppose, now, that the Negro turns to the promise of socialism whither I have long looked for salvation. I was once a member of the celebrated Local No. 1 in New York. I am convinced of the essential truth of the Marxian philosophy and believe that eventually land, machines and materials must belong to the state; that private profit must be abolished; that the system of exploiting labor must disappear; that people who work must have essentially equal income; and that in their hands the political rulership of the state must eventually rest.

Notwithstanding the fact that I believe this is the truth and that this truth is being gradually exemplified by the Russian experiment, I must nevertheless ask myself seriously; how far can American Negroes forward this eventual end? What part can they expect to have in a socialistic state and what can they do now to bring about this realization? And my answer to this has long been clear. There is no automatic power in socialism to override and suppress race prejudice. This has been proven in America, it was true in Germany before Hitler and the analogy of the Jews in Russia is for our case entirely false and misleading. One of the worst things that Negroes could do today would be to join the American Communist Party or any of its many branches. The Communists of America have become dogmatic exponents of the inspired word of Karl Marx as they read it. They believe, apparently in immediate, violent and bloody revolution, and they are willing to try any and all means of raising hell anywhere and under any circumstances. This is a silly program even for white men. For American colored men, it is suicide. In the first place, its logical basis is by no means sound. The great and fundamental change in the organization of industry which Karl Marx with his splendid mind and untiring sacrifice visualized must, to be sure, be brought about by revolution, but whether in all times and places and under all circumstances that revolution is going to involve war and bloodshed, is a question which every sincere follower of Marx has a right to doubt. (p. 38)

Du Bois began on a sincere and somber note, revealing his belief in "the promise of socialism" and "the essential truth of the Marxian philosophy." Next, he outlines socialism and sings some of its praises, laying bare its emphasis on utilizing natural, technological, and human resources in the best interest of the most needy among the masses, the laboring classes, and future generations. Socialism had a certain longstanding appeal for Du Bois (1986c) not simply because he believed that it was "the end to economic reform" (pp. 49–53). But it also appealed to him because it was a system of social organization that resembled ancient African communalism, where "crops are divided, not necessarily according to the amount of work that the man does or the efficiency of it, but according to the needs of the members of the tribe" (Du Bois, 1971c, p. 165). This last point is one that often goes overlooked by students of Du Bois's radical writings, but it is extremely important nevertheless.[8]

Now, back to the previous passage, we come to the crux of his criticisms of Marxist socialism and communism: "There is no automatic power in socialism [or communism] to override and suppress race prejudice." Du Bois had read those well-worn famous first few pages of the *Communist Manifesto*, where Karl Marx and Friedrich Engels wrote with great glee of the global triumph of the white bourgeoisie over the colored world's cultural and historical formations. In an almost knee-jerk reaction, which has since become an unspoken rite of passage among black radicals, he critically queried: what happens when socialists or communists are white supremacists and Eurocentricists? This is a question that Karl Marx and many of his communist comrades never considered, because they suffered from white supremacism and looked on European imperial expansion as a "necessary evil" that "opened up fresh ground for the rising bourgeoisie" that would ultimately forge "weapons that bring death to itself" (Marx and Engels, 1978, pp. 474, 478; see also Marx and Engels, 1972; C. W. Mills, 2003; Serequeberhan, 1994). Du Bois pleaded with African Americans and other "colored men" not to join the Communist or Socialist Party, as he had done, but to organize among themselves, study socialism and communism from their own frames of reference, and develop race-centered and racism-conscious critiques of capitalism.[9]

It was not simply the racism and Eurocentrism of the white socialists and communists that Du Bois took issue with. He also felt that their emphasis on "immediate, violent and bloody revolution" was not feasible for African Americans who at the time constituted less than 10 percent of the U.S. population. White communists and socialists could advocate "immediate, violent and bloody revolution" to the white working class because they were the majority of the U.S. population and, thus, stood a greater chance of destabilizing the imperial economic order. However, for black folk to take this position, from Du Bois's optic, was not only untenable but quite simply "suicide." In an extremely unorthodox and heretic manner, Du Bois (1982c) was searching for an alternative to violent social revolution, but he never ruled out self-defensive violence as a last resort, stating: "We abhor violence and bloodshed; we will join no movement that advocates a program of violence, except as the last defense against aggression" (p. 39).[10]

Du Bois was acutely aware of blacks' social status and political position in the white supremacist world (see chapter 2). By this time, circa 1936, he had undertaken several studies of lynching and mob violence and, as a result, was painfully cognizant of the fact that white supremacists had no regard whatsoever for black life.[11] His criticisms of Marxism here were groundbreaking in the sense that he exposed the nexus between white conservatives, white liberals, and white radicals: their whiteness and (conscious and unconscious) adherence to white supremacy. Du Bois may have been duped when he joined the Socialist Party in 1911, but now he knew that the white socialists and communists could be just as white supremacist as the white capitalists. The white communists and socialists had volumes of radical rhetoric regarding the "brotherhood of mankind" and the equality and inherent rights of all workers, when in all actuality they meant *white* workers and even more, as we will see in the next chapter, they meant white *male* workers.

Each time Du Bois criticized the white socialists or communists it forced him to dig deeper and develop his own version of socialism, one distinctly race-centered and racism-conscious. It was premature to spend too much time theorizing communism since, along orthodox Marxist lines, Du Bois believed that socialism must precede communism. As he asserted in "The Negro and Socialism" (1958), "the salvation" of persons of color, and people of African descent in particular, "lies in socialism" (Du Bois, 2000a, p. 418). However, he was extremely adamant in stating that continental and diasporan Africans should not graft Eurocentric (Marxist-Leninist) and/or Asiocentric (Maoist) communism or socialism onto Africana life-worlds, but that they should "study socialism, its rise in Europe and Asia, and its peculiar suitability for the emancipation of Africa" and her peoples (p. 416). Du Bois maintained that the "question of the method by which the socialist state can be achieved must be worked out by experiment and reason and not by dogma. Whether or not methods which were right and clear in Russia and China fit our circumstances is for our intelligence to decide" (p. 418).

In its broadest sense "socialism," according to Du Bois in "Socialism and the American Negro" (1960), means "the ownership of capital by the state; the regulation of all industry in the interests of citizens and not for private profit of the few; and the building of a welfare state where all men work according to ability and share income according to need" (1985a, p. 295). However, he is quick to point out that "[t]he complete socialism called communism has been reached by no nation," and he included the politico-economic experiments of the Soviet Union (Russia) and China in his analysis (p. 295). In attempting to understand Du Bois's connections and contributions to contemporary critical theory, it is important to point out—as Cedric Robinson (2000) has in *Black Marxism*—that, "Du Bois was one of the first American theorists to sympathetically confront Marxist thought in critical and independent terms" (p. 207). Because of the brevity of his tenure in the Socialist Party, which he felt betrayed African Americans on account of its internal racial hierarchy (which replicated U.S. society and the European imperial impulse) and the Socialists' non-existent external critique and confrontation of racism, and considering his longstanding distrust of the Communist Party, the Party which drove him to unflinchingly state: "American Negroes do not propose to be the shock troops of the Communist Revolution, driven out in front to death, cruelty and humiliation in order to win victories for white workers"—it is not hard to understand *how* or *why* I, following Robinson, read Du Bois as more of a critic of Marxism than a Marxist in any dogmatic or orthodox sense (Du Bois, 1995a, p. 591; Robinson, 2000, p. 228).

Du Bois is easily understood to be a contributor to critical social theory when and where the critique of *both* capitalism and Marxism are acknowledged as basic characteristics of critical theory (Agger, 1992; Kellner, 1989, 1995; Wilkerson and Paris, 2001). And when his critiques of capitalism and Marxism are coupled with his pioneering work as an anti-racist and anti-colonial theorist, Du Bois immediately emerges as an innovator in the critical theory tradition. An innovator who broadened critical theory's base by using Africana liberation thought and practices as his foundation and grounding point of departure. As I have discussed Du Bois's anti-racism and anti-colonialism in relation to contemporary critical theory in chapters 2 and 3, I will forgo a recollection of it here and very briefly delineate some of the central ideas involved in his critique of capitalism before concluding with a discussion of his development of democratic socialism.

DU BOIS'S CRITIQUE OF CAPITALISM

Du Bois's critique of capitalism was not clear-cut or laid out in an easily accessible manner, but rather interspersed throughout his oeuvre and surfaced as a result of his critiques of racism and colonialism, which ultimately spawned his discourse on democratic socialism. As early as 1901, six years prior to his so-called "socialist turn" and sixteen years before the Russian Revolution, he argued that the ideal of modern society was embodied in the maxim, "from each according to his ability—to each according to his needs" (Du Bois, 1986b, p. 25). His primary problem with capitalism stemmed from what he understood to be its emphasis on individual gain and personal greed—in a word, private profit at any cost. As an economic system, capitalism privileged the wants and whims of the rich minority over the authentic human needs of the poor majority. The situation became much more complex and was compounded when the political economy of race and racism were taken into consideration.

Du Bois's initial criticisms of capitalism were not radical, but rather reformist. His concept of socialism could be characterized as evolutionary as opposed to revolutionary, which made it a major point of contention between him and young "New Negro" radicals. For instance, in "The Class Struggle" (1921), he stated:

> The N.A.A.C.P. has been accused of not being a "revolutionary" body. This is quite true. We do not believe in revolution. We expect revolutionary changes in many parts of this life and this world, but we expect these changes to come mainly through reason, human sympathy and the education of children, and not by murder. We know that there have been times when organized murder seemed the only way out of wrong, but we believe those times have been very few, the cost of the remedy excessive, the results as terrible as beneficent, and we gravely doubt if in the future there will be any real recurrent necessity for such upheaval. (1995a, p. 555)

According to the editors of the black socialist magazine the *Messenger*, A. Philip Randolph and Chandler Owen (1971), Du Bois's "anti-revolutionary" socialist thought was that of "the Old Crowd Negro," and it revealed "Du Bois's ignorance of [Marxian] theory and his inability to advise the Negro in the most critical period of the world's history" (pp. 95, 93). Randolph and Owen, representing themselves as "New Negro" radicals, mercilessly criticized Du Bois's early socialism for its emphasis on moderate and moralistic gradual social reform as opposed to all-out social revolution. In "Du Bois on Revolution: A Reply" (1921), they argued that Du Bois misunderstood revolution because he appeared to almost utterly associate it with violence, or "organized murder," as he put it above. Revolutions need not entail violence, the *Messenger* mused, as the examples of the Copernican revolution and the revolutions in economic and sociological thought of the nineteenth century (à la John Stuart Mill, Adam Smith, Herbert Spencer, August Comte, and Richard Ely) demonstrate. Du Bois, from the *Messenger* editors' point of view, simply did not take seriously the fact that "every notable and worth-while advance in human history has been achieved by revolution, either intellectual, political or economic" (Randolph and Owen, 1971, p. 94).

There was much truth to many of Randolph and Owen's criticisms of Du Bois's early socialism. However, because of the longevity of his "unhappy marriage" with Marxism, the *Messenger*'s criticisms are time-sensitive and should not be applied to the whole of Du Bois's work geared toward critiquing capitalism and developing democratic socialism. Marable (1986) points out that though Randolph and Owen eventually began to be regarded as the "Lenin and Trotsky" of Harlem, their revolutionary socialism was short-lived (p. 109). Owen, Marable reports, "became embittered by the racism in the Socialist party and in 1923 withdrew from radical politics" (p. 110). Randolph continued to edit the *Messenger*, though it took a decidedly "more moderate political tone" (p. 110). He, of course, went on to become one of the most acclaimed civil rights leaders in U.S. history, leading and organizing the March on Washington with one of the unsung heroes of Civil Rights movement, Bayard Rustin (see Anderson, 1973, 1997). One of Randolph's more noted biographers, Paula Pfeffer (1990), in *A. Philip Randolph: Pioneer of the Civil Rights Movement*, remarked rather earnestly: "Randolph had begun his career as a radical by denouncing Du Bois's conservativism, but by the time of his death, Du Bois had become far more radical than Randolph" (p. 256).

Randolph and Owen's criticisms of Du Bois's socialism help to highlight the important but long-ignored fact that his conception of socialism changed just as twentieth-century capitalism and his relationship with Marxism changed. As Marable (1986) pointed out, even when Du Bois joined the Socialist Party in 1911 it "did not mark any significant turn to radicalism" (p. 90). Moses (1978) goes further to argue that his "early years with *The Crisis* fall into the period when Du Bois toyed with the idea of non-revolutionary white-collar socialism of the American domestic variety. . . . Even as late as 1912, at the age of forty-four, Du Bois had not become a committed radical, but was still an optimist Progressive" (p. 139). Marable, Moses, and Reed each note that Du Bois's conception of socialism for a protracted period of time was in line with that of the reformist British Labor Party, which he applauded time and again throughout the pages of the *Crisis* (Marable, 1986, pp. 109, 112; Moses, 1978, p. 140; A. L. Reed, 1997, pp. 83–89).

In *W. E. B. Du Bois: The Quest for the Abolition of the Color-line*, Zhang Juguo (2001) observes that it was Du Bois's four visits to the Soviet Union in 1926, 1936, 1949, and 1958 and his visits to other socialist countries, such as Czechoslovakia, East Germany, and China that quickened, broadened, and "deepened his understanding of socialism" (p. 137). After his 1926 visit to the Soviet Union, Du Bois clearly took a greater interest in the more radical aspects of socialism, though he repeatedly asserted that the Russian Revolution was not the rule. However, he was convinced that Russia "had chosen the only way open to her at the time" (Du Bois, 1995a, p. 632). He realized early on that there was no blueprint for bringing socialism into being, and that what might work in one country may not work in another.

Partly as a result of the nationwide economic depression of the 1930s, and in some degree owing to African Americans' incessant political disenfranchisement and economic exploitation, Du Bois began to seriously engage socialism on his own terms; that is, from a Pan-African or, what we might term today, *Africana* frame of reference. As a result, he developed one of the first race-based and racism-conscious critiques of capitalism employing a Marxist methodological orientation. In his burgeoning anti-bourgeois and anti-racist view, capitalism was not simply (as many of the white Marxists would have it) a system of economic exploitation, but also a "racial polity"; that is, a system of racial domination and discrimination (C. W. Mills, 1998, 1999). Race *and* class struggle combined to create the phenomenological dimensions characteristic of black existence in a white supremacist social world (Gordon, 1995a, 1997a). Moreover, because he found Marxism inadequate for the tasks of theorizing race and racism in both capitalist and colonial systems, Du Bois created his own—and some of the first—race/class concepts and categories of analysis.

Where the imperial aspects of colonialism were undeniable from Du Bois's optic—perhaps, ironically, because of his meanderings in Marxism—he believed that capitalism had certain beneficial elements. However, because of the racialized nature of capital in the white supremacist world system, capitalism was utilized greatly and inordinately for the benefit of whites. Du Bois (1985a) asserted:

> Capitalism was a great and beneficent method of satisfying human wants, without which the world would have lingered on the edge of starvation. But like all invention, the results depend upon how it is used and for whose benefit. Capitalism has benefited mankind, but not in equal proportions. It has enormously raised the standard of living in Europe and even more in North America. But in the parts of the world where human toil and natural resources have made the greatest contribution to the accumulation of wealth, such parts of the earth, curiously enough, have benefited least from the new commerce and industry. This

is shown by the plight of Africa and India today. To be sure Africans and Indians have benefited from modern capital. In education, limited though it be; in curbing of disease, slow and incomplete as it is; in the beginning of the use of machines and labor technique; and in the spread of law and order, both Negroes and Hindus have greatly benefited; but as compared with what might have been done; and what in justice and right should have been accomplished, the result is not only pitiful, but so wrong and dangerous as already to have helped cause two of the most destructive wars in human history, and is today threatening further human death and disaster. (pp. 232–33)

Du Bois's critique of capitalism moved well beyond the Marxists' two-class critique and class struggle thesis. In his socio-theoretical framework there were not only classes but also races, and the white race was the ultra-"ruling class"—were we to refer back to Marx's class theory—*and* the ruling race (Marx and Engels, 1978, p. 489). For Du Bois, it was not as simple as the bourgeoisie and the proletariat fighting it out until the finish. There was also the obdurate fact of race and racism, and even more, as his comments above accent, *racial* colonialism and *racial* capitalism.

Marx and Engels asserted in *The Communist Manifesto*, "The ruling ideas of each age have ever been the ideas of its ruling class" (p. 489). Du Bois continually questioned: So, what happens when the "ruling class" is racist? And what happens when the proletariat is composed of more than merely white workers? With many orthodox Marxists, Du Bois believed that capitalism had helped to modernize and rationalize the economy. However, in contrast to the Marxists, he asserted that there was a racist dimension to the modernization and rationalization associated with capitalism. In addition, and as will be discussed in the next chapter, he also came to understand capitalist modernization and rationalization to have a sexist (and particularly a patriarchal) dimension.

As Du Bois saw it, capitalism was inextricable from the rise of racism. Therefore, a Marxist or class analysis engaged only part of the race/class problem. What he and countless others in the Africana tradition of critical theory sought by coupling anti-racism or critical race theory with Marxism was to comprehensively understand and develop solutions to both sides of the race/class equation, to the problems of racism and capitalism. Perhaps Cornel West's (1993a) contentions in *Keeping Faith: Philosophy and Race in America* best capture the position of black Marxists and/or race/class theorists: "I hold that Marxist theory as a methodological orientation remains indispensable   —
although ultimately inadequate—in grasping distinctive features of African American oppression. . . . Marxist theory still may provide the best explanatory account for certain phenomena, but it also may remain inadequate for other

phenomena—notably here, the complex of racism in the modern West" (pp. 258, 267). West's view has consistently been echoed throughout the history of Africana theory, though not without reservation and serious criticism.

Here it should be earnestly asserted that black nationalism, Pan-African-ism, and other race-centered black schools of thought have their theoretic weaknesses as well: biological determinism, racial essentialism, ahistoricism, and mysticism, to name only a few of the fallacies (Gilroy, 1993a, 1993b; Gordon and Gordon, 2006a, 2006b; Moses, 1998). The narrow focus on race in many instances reifies the thought of race theorists, turning what would be, or what would have been, race theory into racial ideology. What Africana crit-ical theory proposes is a synthesis of the best (meaning, the most emancipa-tory elements) of both the "race" and "class" schools. Marxism may be "in-dispensable" when it comes to the critique of capitalism but, as West (1996) testifies in "Black Strivings in a Twilight Civilization":

> For those of us interested in the relation of white supremacy to modernity (African slavery in the New World and European imperial domination of most of the rest of the world) or the consequences of the construct of "race" during the Age of Europe (1492–1945), the scholarly and literary works of Du Bois are *indispensable*. For those of us obsessed with alleviating black social misery, the political texts of Du Bois are insightful and inspiring. In this sense, Du Bois is the brook of fire through which we all must pass in order to gain access to the intellectual and political weaponry needed to sustain the radical democratic tra-dition in our time. (p. 55, my emphasis)

According to West, Marx is "indispensable" for class analysis, where Du Bois is "indispensable" for racism criticism—but, truth be told, as West (1989) tells it in *The American Evasion of Philosophy*, Du Bois is also an in-novator in the Marxist tradition (pp. 145–50). He was not only a pioneer race theorist, but also a pioneer class theorist. His work prefigured and proposed issues that remain on the radical political and critical theoretical agenda. He challenged white Marxists to take seriously the centrality of race and racism to capitalism and European imperial expansion. The white Marxists shot back that race consciousness is "false consciousness" and a capitalist or bourgeois invention created to divide the workers. Divide the workers? How curious, thought Du Bois. He questioned: When have white and black workers ever been united, ever really and truly worked *unified* in the history of capitalism and since the emergence of global white supremacy?

Part of the problem with Du Bois's critique of capitalism involves his con-tention that capitalism was inequitably creating an enormous amount of wealth and power that was being unjustly distributed on a roughly "whites only" basis. This was compounded by his search for a solution to both the race and class aspects of this issue. The white Marxists, focusing almost exclusively on the class dimension of the problem, found their solution in the proletariat, that is, the white working class. Du Bois (1995a) dismissed the white proletariat, querying: "Why should we assume on the part of unlettered and suppressed masses of white workers, a clearness of thought, a sense of human brotherhood, that is sadly lacking in the most educated [white] classes?" (p. 533). Recollecting the fact that Du Bois is considered one of the great democratic socialists of the twentieth-century, it is amazing that he never adequately addressed the question of *who* the revolutionary social agents would be that would crush capitalism and usher in democratic socialism. Also, and of the utmost importance here, is the question of *how* the transition from capitalism to democratic socialism would take place. The aforementioned are two major deficiencies of Du Bois's social theory (and classical critical theory discourse in general) that should be addressed by contemporary critical theorists.[12]

It could be that there are no ideal agents of revolutionary social change. Considering the vicissitudes of capitalism one of the things that anti-capitalist agents and theoreticians have to bear in mind is that a social faction that may have revolutionary potential in one era, may not in the next. This means, then, that as capitalism grows and changes, so too must anti-capitalist theory—hence, as noted above, Du Bois's evolving critical relationship with Marxist theory. He not only criticized Marxism, but also revised and reconstructed the Marxian tradition by providing new theories, concepts, and categories of analysis—such as race, racism, and anti-racist theory, and colonialism and anti-colonial theory—that extend and expand Marxism's original intellectual arena and political program. Robinson's (2000) remarks in this regard are extremely insightful: "Du Bois committed himself to the development of a theory of history, which by its emphasis on mass action was both a critique of the ideologies of American socialist movements and a revision of Marx's theory of revolution and class struggle" (p. 196). Further, he "possessed no obligation to Marxist or Leninist dogma, nor to the vagaries of historical analysis and interpretation that characterized American communist thought" (p. 228).

This means, then, that when Du Bois advanced democratic socialism, or communism as he did at the end of his life, he did so from a position independent of mainstream Marxism and Marxist party politics, and often from an optic that stands outside the Marxist tradition all together. It is in this sense that Moses (1978) maintains, "[e]ven when he urged Communism, the aging Du Bois did so on black nationalistic rather than on Marxist grounds" (p. 140). Du Bois's concept of democratic socialism highlights and accents several aspects of classical and contemporary social reality which Marx, his disciples, and the members of the Frankfurt School/Institute of Social Research neglected or downplayed in their discourse. These assertions are given greater weight and gravity when we turn to Du Bois's discourse on democratic socialism.

DU BOIS'S DISCOURSE ON DEMOCRATIC SOCIALISM

In one of his later essays on socialism, "The Negro and Socialism" (1958), Du Bois argued that a socialist society is a society where there exists "the central idea that men must work for a living, but that the result of their work must not mainly be to support privileged persons," persons who as a result of the labor and economic exploitation of the "colored" masses and working classes have an exponential amount of power and privilege (2000a, p. 410). It is a society where "the welfare of the mass of people should be the main object of government," a society where the government is "controlled by the governed," which is to say it is a democratic society (p. 410). In such a society, Du Bois declared, "the mass of people, increasing in intelligence, with incomes sufficient to live a good and healthy life, should control all government, and . . . they would be able to do this by the spread of science and scientific technique, access to truth, the use of reason, and freedom of thought and of creative impulse in art and literature" (p. 410).

Calculating "seventy-five to ninety percent" of the earth's population to be people of color and living in what he called "the colonies proper: America, Africa, and Asia," Du Bois (1985a) was critically conscious of the fact that if indeed socialism purported to be concerned principally with "the mass" of "the governed" having a crucial and critical voice in their government, then people of color should have prominent positions in national and international affairs and policy-making (p. 230). It could be no other way, he asserted, or else people of color ultimately would be lead to "the last red alternative of revolt, revenge and war" (Du Bois, 1995a, p. 80). Where revolution was something he once shied away from, and where war was something that he utterly despised, Du Bois now openly considered both as options for bringing democratic socialism into being. Gone was the talk of a gradual transition from capitalism to socialism, and here we as well see a significant change in Du Bois's conception of socialism and his strategies and tactics to realize a socialist society.

For centuries capitalism has had people of color in its clutches, therefore, the colored and colonized were justified in their fight against it. Their fight would not only free people of color, it would also free white workers as well. Du Bois (2000a) reasoned: "The footsteps of the long oppressed and staggering masses are not always straight and sure, but their mistakes can never cause the misery and distress which the factory system caused in Europe, colonial imperialism caused in Asia and Africa, and which slavery, lynching, disenfranchisement, and Jim Crow legislation have caused in the United States" (p. 414). In order to fully realize socialism, Du Bois (1995a) stated that there must be "Freedom." By "Freedom" he meant *"full economic, political and social equality"* of all people *"in thought, expression and action, with no discrimination based on race or color"* (p. 614, emphasis in original). "Freedom" is fundamental to socialism, and without the "full economic, political and social equality" of all citizens within a particular public sphere, socialism remains an unrealized project of historical, cultural, socio-political, and economic change.

African Americans "were not" and have never been socialists, contended Du Bois (1985a), "nor did they know what communism was or was doing. But they knew that Negro education must be better; that Negroes must have better opportunity to work and receive a wage which would let them enjoy a decent standard of life" (p. 304). For this reason, socialism, being a "democratic program," could not "contemplate the complete subordination of one race to another" (p. 218). It was to be a "program" or "project" of radical social and historical transformation that sought ultimately to establish "world democracy" so that there might be "world peace" (pp. 209, 184). Du Bois queried: "without democracy, what hope is there of Peace?" (p. 237).[13]

The "essence of democracy," for Du Bois, "demands freedom for personal tastes and preferences so long as no social injury results" (p. 215). This is important to point out because in Du Bois's conception of democracy it was not merely a political project, but a cultural one as well (p. 231). He explains:

> the vaster possibility and the real promise of democracy is adding to human capacities and culture from hitherto untapped sources of cultural variety and power. Democracy is tapping the great possibilities of mankind from unused and unsuspected reservoirs of human greatness. Instead of envying and seeking desperately outer and foreign sources of civilization . . . in these magnificent mountains a genius and variety of human culture, which once released from poverty, ignorance and disease, will help guide the world. Once the human soul is thus freed, then and only then is peace possible. There will be no need to fight for food, for healthy homes, for free speech; for these will not depend on force, but on increasingly on knowledge, reason and art. (pp. 242–43)

As long as "the human soul" remained in bondage, so long would the world exist on the brink of "war after war" (p. 184). Under capitalism and colonialism the vast majority of human beings have "for the most part no voice in government" (p. 230). Under these systems it is only "the blood-sucking whites" who "rule and receive large income while others," mostly the "dark" or "native" proletariat, "work and live in poverty" (Du Bois 2000a, p. 417; 1995a, p. 616; 1985a, p. 216). Moreover, capitalism and colonialism, interpreted as two sides of the same coin and two of the greatest impediments to "world democracy," had to be eradicated on the grounds that since their inception they have consistently caused the great mass of human beings, who are (it should be reiterated) "colored," to exist in various states and stages of "slavery, cultural disintegration, disease, death, and war" (Du Bois, 1985a, p. 196). Moreover, democracy, which for Du Bois was fundamentally predicated upon "free discussion," required at minimum the "equal treatment [of] the colored races of the world" (pp. 303, 218).

As stated above, a prerequisite for Du Boisian democracy is "freedom," and "the real freedom toward which the soul of man has always striven" is, of course, "the right to be different, to be individual and pursue personal aims and ideals" (Du Bois, 1995a, p. 617). Long before postmodernist discourse and debate on the politics of difference, Du Bois asserted, "the richness of a culture . . . lies in differentiation" (p. 617). He contended that "Difference" did not necessarily equal "Dangerous," and that once the bare necessities of "food, shelter, and . . . security" were met, then "human friendship and intermingling . . . based on broad and catholic reasoning" could lead to "happier . . . individual and . . . richer . . . social" lives (p. 617). He continues:

> Once the problem of subsistence is met and order is secured, there comes the great moment of civilization: the development of individual personality; the right of variation; the richness of a culture that lies in differentiation. In the activities of such a world, men are not compelled to be white in order to be free: they can be black, yellow or red; they can mingle or stay separate. The free mind, the untrammeled taste can revel. In only a section and a small section of the total life is discrimination inadmissible and that is where my freedom stops yours and your taste hurts me. Gradually such a free world will learn that not in exclusiveness and isolation lies inspiration and joy, but that the very variety is the reservoir of invaluable experience and emotion. This crowning of equalitarian democracy in artistic freedom of difference is the real next step of culture.
>
> The hope of civilization lies not in exclusion, but in inclusion of all human elements; we find the richness of humanity not in the Social Register, but in the City Directory; not in great aristocracies, chosen people and superior races, but in the throngs of disinherited and underfed men. Not the lifting of the lowly, but the unchaining of the unawakened mighty, will reveal the possibilities of genius, gift and miracle, in mountainous treasure-trove, which hitherto civilization has scarcely touched; and yet boasted blatantly and even answer to every meticulous taste and rare personality. (p. 617)

Du Bois's radical democratic theory eschews the elitism of his "Talented Tenth" thesis, what Moses (1978) calls "the conservatism of his intellectual origins," and is predicated upon "the inclusion of all human elements," "the richness of humanity," "not the great aristocracies, chosen people and superior races," but on "the throngs of disinherited and underfed men" (p. 138).[14] Du Bois, as radical democratic theorist, looks not to the elite, as he once did, but to "disinherited" and "underfed" human beings to bring about the radical socialist transformation of society. In his view, a capitalist society, a so-called "developed society," is to a certain extent a colonized society because it is a society where life and language are directed, defined and deformed to suit the wants and desires of the ruling race, gender, and/or class(es) (see Habermas, 1984, pp. 374–75). Always and everywhere colonization, like Pandora's box once opened, seeps into every sphere of the life- and language-worlds of both the colonized and the colonizer. It is precisely as Du Bois (1985a) said it would be, a world of "race war," "racial friction," and "disastrous contradiction" (pp. 183, 181, 206). Only in "a free world" where "the problem of subsistence is met and order secured" can human beings arrive at "the great moment of civilization." This "moment," representing perhaps *the* high point in human history in Du Bois's thought, would foster "the development of individual personality," and these "new" individuals, free from the constant pursuit of their basic needs and capitalist greed—similar to Fanon's (1968, p. 36) "new men" who speak a "new language" to express their "new humanity"—would pride themselves on "the right of variation." In such a world, human beings "are not compelled to be white in order to be free: they can be black, yellow or red; they can mingle or stay separate." The "free world" Du Bois envisioned is a world that puts the premium on the potentialities of humble, hard working, ordinary people.

Du Bois's concept of democracy, perpetually engaging "power relations," understood, as Michel Foucault (1997) did, that "in human relationships, whether they involve verbal communication . . . or amorous, institutional, or economic relationships, power is always present" (p. 292). It exists on "different levels" and in "different forms," but being a relationship where "one person tries to control the conduct of the other" (p. 292). "[P]ower relations are mobile," meaning "they can be modified" because "they are not fixed once and for all" (p. 292). Power, being omnipresent, mutates, shifts and changes as human beings and their reality changes, and this makes human beings' relationships to power "mobile, reversible, and unstable" (p. 292).

In fact, Foucault relates that the very notion of a "power relation" is "possible only insofar as the subjects are free" (p. 292). In power relations "there is necessarily the possibility of resistance because if there were no possibility of resistance (of violent resistance, flight, deception, strategies capable of reversing the situation), there would be no power relations at all" (p. 292). In any power relation there exists the possibility of liberation, and "liberation and the struggle for liberation are indispensable for the practice of freedom" (p. 284).

Conquered, colonized, colored people must be willing to struggle for liberation and higher levels of human life, and if they are not, they will never know, or have the possibility of "the practice of freedom," which for Du Bois rested on radical democracy and/or democratic socialism. Du Bois (1995a) cautiously offered a caveat: "No group of privileged slave-owners is easily and willingly going to recognize their former slaves as men" (p. 616). This means, then, that "former slaves" have as one of their life-tasks the reclamation and rehabilitation of their denied humanity. Whether they regain their denied humanity, as Foucault suggests, through "violent resistance, flight, deception, [or any other] strategies capable of reversing the situation," is totally up to them and their specific time and circumstances.

As "the majority of men do not usually act in accord with reason, but follow social pressures, inherited customs and long-established, often subconscious, patterns of action," Du Bois (1995a) believed that "race prejudice . . . will linger long and may even increase" (p. 618). He charged people of color, and "the black race" in particular, with a special duty, *not*—as Fanon (1968, p. 315) said—to imitate European civilization and culture in "obscene caricature." On the contrary, Du Bois (1995a) believed that "[i]t is the duty of the black race to maintain its cultural advance, not for itself alone, but for the emancipation of mankind, the realization of democracy and the progress of civilization" (p. 618). Civilization is to progress, and democracy is to be realized, only insofar as "the masses" of human beings gain "the social control" of "the methods of producing goods and of distributing wealth and services. And, the freedom which this abolition of poverty will involve, will be freedom of thought and not freedom for private profit-making" (Du Bois, 1985a, pp. 197–98).

Du Bois's democratic socialism, perhaps above all else, is distinguished by its anti-racist social ethics. It was not simply capitalism and class struggle that impeded socialism, but equally racial domination and discrimination. Where he began his adventure in socialism toying with its most conservative, reformist, and gradualist strains, historical happenings on the world scene and the acute and increasing economic exploitation of blacks in white supremacist societies led him to couple his critical race and anti-colonial theory with class theory. As a consequence, Du Bois developed some of the first race/class theory and criticisms of Marxism from an Africana frame of reference. However, race and class were not the only issues Du Bois believed were deterring a democratic socialist society. There was also the problem of gender domination and discrimination, something the prophet of problems wrote extensively about, but an issue that most Du Bois scholars have buried beneath a barrage of criticism regarding his race manhood, black radicalness, and lack of skills as a littérateur. The next chapter, then, will be devoted to the often-overlooked anti-sexist and male-feminist dimensions of Du Bois's discourse.

NOTES

1. My interpretation of (white) Marxism here and throughout this chapter has been primarily drawn from several "Hegelian" or "Western" Marxist works, as well as a few of the more philosophy-focused texts in Marxist studies, see Anderson (1976), Arnold (1990), Aronson (1995), Buhle (1991), Callari, Cullenberg and Biewener (1995), Castoriadis (1991, 1997), Gottlieb (1989, 1992), Gouldner (1980), Hindess (1993), Howard (1972, 1988), Howard and Klare (1972), Jacoby (1981), Jameson (1971, 1975, 1979, 1990), Jay (1984), Kellner (1995), Kelly (1982), Kolakowski (1978a, 1978b, 1978c), Leonhard (1971), Lichtheim (1965, 1966), Marcuse (1960, 1967, 1970b), Nelson and Grossberg (1988), and Therborn (1996).

2. For a discussion of socialism's fluidity and malleability throughout the twentieth century, and especially at the century's end, see Aronson (1995), Callari, Cullenberg and Biewener (1995), Castoriadis (1988a, 1998b, 1993), Cole (1950–1965), Ferguson (1998), Laclau and Mouffe (1985, 1987), Magnus and Cullenberg (1995), Marcuse (1965a, 1965b), Nelson and Grossberg (1988), and Self (1993).

3. For further discussion of black Marxism and black Marxists' relationship with the white critics of capitalism and white Marxism, see Bouges (1983), Cox (1948, 1959, 1962, 1964, 1976, 1987), Cruse (1967, 2002), A. Y. Davis (1998), C. L. R. James (1992, 1994, 1996), Kelley (1990, 1994, 2002), Marable (1985a, 1987, 1996), C. W. Mills (2003), Outlaw (1983a, 1983b, 1987), C. J. Robinson (2000), Serequeberhan (1990), and West (1988b, 1993a, 1999). And for analyses of the Trinidadian triumvirate, among other African Caribbean intellectuals' communion with Marxism, see Bouges (2003), Hennessey (1992), Henry (2000), and W. James (1998).

4. According to Anthony Bouges (2003), in *Black Heretics, Black Prophets: Radical Political Intellectuals*, "in radical historical studies, when one excavates a different archive, alternative categories are opened up" (p. 86). To be sure, black radical theorists, such as Du Bois and C. L. R. James, "deployed Marxism, but in [their] hands the categories used to describe historical processes were wrought into something else" (p. 81). That "something else" which Marxian categories were shaped and molded into by these theorists was based on their understanding of what Fanon (2001) referred to as "the lived experience of the black." Africana history and culture are the "different archives" that black radicals work with and operate from. These archives are not only in many senses distinctly different from the archives of white Marxists, but embedded in them are recurring racial motifs that shade and color Africana critical theory and radical political praxis. White Marxists' efforts to diminish and downplay racial domination and discrimination have made black radicals' marriage to Marxism a turbulent and very unhappy one. For example, in *From Class to Race: Essays in White Marxism and Black Radicalism*, Charles Mills (2003) maintains:

> Throughout the twentieth century, many people of color were attracted to Marxism because of its far-ranging historical perspective, its theoretical centering of oppression, and

its promise of liberation. But many of these recruits would later become disillusioned, both with Marxist theory and the practice of actual (white) Marxist parties. The historical vision turned out to be Eurocentric; the specificities of their racial oppression were often not recognized but were dissolved into supposedly all encompassing class categories; and the liberation envisaged did not include as a necessary goal the dismantling of white supremacy in all its aspects. Cedric Robinson's pioneering *Black Marxism* (2000), first published in 1983, recounts the long-troubled history of left-wing black diasporic intellectuals (W. E. B. Du Bois, C. L. R. James, George Padmore, Richard Wright, Aimé Césaire) with "white Marxism," and it argues for the existence of a distinct "black radical political tradition" whose historic foci and concerns cannot be simply assimilated to mainstream white Marxist theory. So even if the origin of white supremacy is most plausibly explained within a historical materialist framework that locates it in imperialist European expansionism—as the product, ultimately, of class forces and bourgeois class interests—race as an international global structure then achieves an intersubjective reality whose dialectic cannot simply be reduced to a class dynamic. (p. xvi)

In other words, black radicals' issues with white Marxism often stem from the fact that they understand racism to be both economic *and* experiential. Racial oppression has more than merely an economic exploitative or class dimension that can coolly and calmly be conjectured by well-meaning white Marxist social scientists. As I discussed in detail in chapter 2, racism is motive, and white Marxists' attempts to reduce it to an outgrowth or offshoot of class struggle, or something internal to class conflict robs the racially oppressed of an opportunity to critically theorize their lived-reality and a major determinant of their social identities.

5. My claims here, and much of my interpretation of Du Bois's socialism and relationship to Marxism has been critically culled from two excellent, though ultimately flawed, unpublished doctoral dissertations, among several other sources cited in the text. See William Wright's "The Socialist Analysis of W. E. B. Du Bois" (1985) and Ji Yuan's "W. E. B. Du Bois and His Socialist Thought" (1998). Because these works are extended studies that focus exclusively on Du Bois's socialist thought they offer students of Du Bois's socialism some of the best criticisms available of his ever-increasing radicalism, and a long overdue look at the myriad meanings of Marxism, socialism, and communism in twentieth-century black radical discourse.

6. With regard to the "roughly thirty years" of Du Bois's critical writings on socialism, Marxism, and radical thought (including his labor studies) that many Du Bois scholars have had a tendency to pass over in order to get to *Black Reconstruction*, see, for instance: "Socialist of the Path" (1907), "The Negro and Socialism" (1907), "The Economic Aspects of Race Prejudice" (1910), "The Economics of Negro Emancipation in the United States" (1911), "Socialism Is Too Narrow for Negroes" (1911), "A Field for Socialists" (1913), "Socialism and the Negro Problem" (1913), "The Problem of Problems" (1917), "Brothers, Come North" (1920), "Of Work and Wealth" (1920), "Of the Ruling of Men" (1920), "The Social Equality of Blacks and Whites" (1920), "Socialism and the Negro" (1921), "The Negro and Radical Thought" (1921), "Class Struggle" (1921), "Communists Boring into Negro Labor" (1926), "Russia, 1926" (1926), "The Denial of Economic Justice to Negroes" (1929), "The American Federation of Labor and the Negro" (1929), "The Negro and Communism" (1931),

"Communists and the Color Line" (1931), "Socialism in England" (1932), "Karl Marx and the Negro" (1933), "Marxism and the Negro Problem" (1933), "The U.S. Will Come to Communism" (1933), "Where Do We Go from Here?: An Essay on the Negroes' Economic Plight" (1933), "The Present Economic Problem of the American Negro" (1935), and "A Negro Nation Within the Nation" (1935). My interpretation and reconstruction of Du Bois's concept of socialism and critique of capitalism and Marxism, as well as my general argument here, derives in part from careful and critical investigation of these articles and essays (see Du Bois, 1965, 1970c, 1970d, 1971a, 1971b, 1985a, 1986a, 1995a, 1996a).

7. Similar to Moses (1978, p. 138), who contends that Du Bois "became a socialist by gradual stages," Marable (1986) argues:

> Du Bois's introduction to Marxism and socialism was extremely fragmentary. At Harvard, Marx's work was briefly discussed, "but only incidentally and as one whose doubtful theories had long since been refuted," Du Bois wrote later. "Socialism as dream of philanthropy or as will-o'-wisp of hotheads was dismissed as unimportant." At [the University of] Berlin, "Karl Marx was mentioned, only to point out how thoroughly his theses had been disproven; of his theory itself almost nothing was said." Only at Atlanta University did Du Bois begin to acquaint himself with writings by socialists and radical liberals. . . . In the second issue of the *Horizon*, in February 1908 [sic], Du Bois stated that he considered himself a "Socialist-of-the-Path." Du Bois had certain misgivings about the Socialist party, but still believed that "the socialist trend" represented the "one great hope of the Negro American." As the Socialist party acquired a mass following, Du Bois monitored its progress as an ally to the democratic struggles of blacks. In February 1908, Du Bois advised readers of the *Horizon* that "the only party today which treats Negroes as men, North and South, are the Socialists." (p. 89; see also Du Bois, 1985c, p. 6)

From the foregoing it seems clear that even Du Bois's early relationship with Marxism was critical, complex, and extremely complicated. Similar to the thought of many black radicals, Du Bois's radical ruminations cannot easily and one-dimensionally be characterized as Marxist or "black Marxist" because, as we will soon see, his thought routinely re-theorized Marxist class theory by combining it with a critical race component, and by emphasizing racial strife within the working class. At times in Du Bois's later discourse race simply was not as central as many black nationalist and other race-centered theorists would like. But it would be difficult for these theorists to argue that race occupies a secondary or tertiary position in his critical socio-theoretical framework. Race and racism were consistent foci of his discourse, but as his thinking evolved, and he identified capitalism and sexism as oppressive systems that interlock with racism, each system was often simultaneously engaged. It is the simultaneity (and, I should add, the interdisciplinary nature) of Du Bois's engagement of these interlocking oppressive systems that misleads many Du Bois scholars into arguing that in his later years he privileged class over race. This issue does not arise as much where Du Bois's discourse on colonialism is concerned because of the overt racially oppressive character of colonialism (hence, *racial colonialism*) in continental and diasporan African modernity.

8. In *Black Folk, Then and Now* (1939) and *The World and Africa* (1947), Du Bois made a few cursory remarks concerning "cooperative movements in Africa" and "West African collectivism" that emphasized communist and socialist sentiments in

ancient and pre-colonial Africa (i.e., before Karl Marx was born and Europe made colonial contact). He believed that contemporary communist and socialist societies could learn many valuable lessons from classical African social organization, politics, and economics because in ancient Africa each of these systems was interrelated and stressed collectivism over individualism. The contention that Africa's past possibly offers us useful paradigms to improve our *Africana* present has been echoed recently by the Ghanian philosopher Kwasi Wiredu (1991), who asserted, "the philosophical thought of a traditional (i.e., preliterate and nonindustrialized) society may hold some lessons of moral significance for a more industrialized society" (p. 98). However, Du Bois was not all nostalgic about ancient Africa and proved to be a harsh critic where ruling classes privileged their personal or familial wants and whims over the vital needs of the masses. For further discussion, see Du Bois (1939, pp. 296-99, 1965, pp. 160–61). Considered "the father of Pan-Africanism," Du Bois's accent on ancient African communist and socialist sentiment was extremely influential on several of the mid-twentieth century pioneer Pan-Africanists; particularly Kwame Nkrumah, who, along with Julius Nyerere, went the farthest (theoretically and practically) in terms of developing a distinctly African version of socialism that purported to be loosely based on classical African social organization customs. An astute statesman and theoretician, Nyerere went so far to dub his "definition of socialism in Tanzanian terms," *Ujamaa*, which essentially means "familyhood," to emphasize Africans' filiation to each other and all humanity. On Nkrumah and Nyerere's Pan-African socialism, see Nkrumah (1970a, 1970b, 1973a) and Nyerere (1966, 1968, 1973).

9. For a discussion, see Du Bois's post-*Black Reconstruction* radical writings: "Lifting from the Bottom" (1937), "A Social Program for Black and White Americans" (1943), "A Program of Organization for Realizing Democracy in the United States by Securing to Americans of Negro Descent the Full Rights of Citizens" (1944), "My Evolving Program for Negro Freedom" (1944), "The Negro and Imperialism" (1944), "Behold the Land" (1947), "Socialism" (1948), "A Petition to the Human Rights Commission of the Social and Economic Council of the United Nations; and to the General Assembly of the United Nations; and to Several Delegations of the Member States of the United Nations" (1949), "There Must Come a Vast Social Change in the United States" (1951), "Address at the American Labor Party Election" (1952), "Negroes and the Crisis of Capitalism in the United States" (1953), "Colonialism and the Russian Revolution" (1956), "Ethiopia: State Socialism under an Emperor" (1955), "The Stalin Era" (1956), "Socialism and Democracy" (1957), "Negroes and Socialism" (1957), "A Future for Pan-Africa: Freedom, Peace, Socialism" (1957), "The Future of All Africa Lies in Socialism" (1958), "The Negro and Socialism" (1958), "The Dream of Socialism" (1959), "The Vast Miracle of China Today" (1959), "Socialism and the American Negro" (1960), *Socialism Today* (1960), "Whither Now and Why" (1960), and "Application for Membership in the Communist Party of the United States of America" (1961). See Du Bois (1965, 1970c, 1970d, 1971a, 1971b, 1985a, 1986a, 1995a, 1996a). One of the best studies of Du Bois's later years, particularly the period after the second European world war (i.e., "World War II"), is Gerald Horne's *Black and Red: W. E. B. Du Bois and the Afro-American Response to the Cold War, 1944–1963*, which I have relied on heavily here to develop

my argument.

10. One of Du Bois's best statements on black self-defense against white supremacist violence is his classic September 1919 *Crisis* essay, "Let Us Reason Together." In the essay he exploded in moral outrage in the aftermath of a heated six-month period of violent racial conflict, which James Weldon Johnson famously referred to as the "Red Summer of 1919." During this nadir in U.S. race relations more than twenty-five cities and small towns erupted in anti-black violence. Black blood flowed in the streets, not simply in Southern cities, but also in Chicago and Washington D.C., the nation's capital! Where Claude McKay captured the wrathful and resilient mood of the masses of black folk in his protest poem, "If We Must Die," similarly Du Bois (1971b) decidedly summoned blacks to defend themselves, thundering:

> Brothers, we are on the Great Deep. We have cast off on the vast voyage which will lead to Freedom or Death. For three centuries we have suffered and cowered. No race ever gave Passive Resistance and Submission to Evil longer, more piteous trial. Today we raise the terrible weapon of Self-Defense. When the murderer comes, he shall no longer strike us in the back. When the armed lynchers gather, we too must gather armed. When the mob moves, we propose to meet it with bricks and clubs and guns. But we must tread here with solemn caution. We must never let justifiable self-defense against individuals become blind and lawless offense against all white folk. We must not seek reform by violence. We must not seek vengeance. "Vengeance is Mine," saith the Lord; or to put it otherwise, only Infinite Justice and Knowledge can assign blame in this poor world, and we ourselves are sinful men, struggling desperately with our homes, our wives and children against the lawless stint or hesitation; but we must carefully and scrupulously avoid on our own part bitter and unjustifiable aggression against anybody. (pp. 14–15)

Here, Du Bois not only foreshadows and lays a foundation for many of the central themes of the Civil Rights and Black Power movements, but he displays an ability to articulate black anger and outrage in a rational and morally mature manner. Both Martin Luther King Jr. and Malcolm X would later echo aspects of the argument Du Bois laid out above, each taking elements of the ideas in their own distinct direction. The main point that I want to place emphasis on here has to do with Du Bois's advocacy of black self-defense and the fact that more like Malcolm X (especially in his later years), and unlike King or Bayard Rustin, Du Bois was not unerringly wedded to any specific social strategy or political tactic (e.g., passive resistance and/or non-violence). He was consistently open to using what he understood to be the best plans of defense and social survival thought and practices available to blacks in white supremacist capitalist society. An additional issue that distinguishes Du Bois's social theorizing stems from his constant coupling of diverse and disparate (Africana *and*, much to the chagrin of many black nationalists, European) radical thought-traditions: from Pan-Africanism to Pragmatism, Marxism to Feminism, and Black Nationalism to German Romanticism (see Anderson and Zuberi, 2000; Aptheker, 1989; Beck, 1996; Bell, Grosholz and Stewart, 1996; Berman, 1997; Boxill, 1996; Broderick, 1958b, 1959, 1974; Cain, 1993; Clarke et al., 1970; Drake, 1985; Gilroy, 1993a; J. A. James, 1996b; Meier, 1959, 1963; Moses, 1975, 1978, 1998; Rampersad, 1990; A. L. Reed, 1997; Rudwick, 1960, 1968, 1982; Sundquist, 1993; West, 1989, 1996; Zamir, 1994, 1995).

11. Du Bois's most noteworthy studies of lynching and mob violence are: "Race Friction Between Black and White" (1908), "The Litany of Atlanta" (1906), "Agitation" (1910), "Does Race Antagonism Serve Any Good Purpose?" (1914), "Lynching" (1914), "The Lynching Industry" (1915), "Houston" (1917), "The Massacre of East St. Louis" (1917), "Rape" (1919), "Let Us Reason Together" (1919), "Jim Crow" (1919), "The Technique of Race Prejudice" (1923), "The Tragedy of Jim Crow" (1923), "A University Course in Lynching" (1923), "Lynchings" (1927), "Mob Tactics" (1927), "Lynchings" (1932), "Violence" (1934), and "Prospects of a World Without Race Conflict" (1944). See Du Bois (1970c, 1971b, 1983a, 1983b, 1986a). On the U.S. legacy of lynching and anti-black violence and, more generally, Du Bois's place in this discourse, see Herbert Shapiro's *White Violence and Black Response: From Reconstruction to Montgomery* (1988).

12. Herbert Marcuse's critical social theory suffered from a similar deficiency, according to Douglas Kellner (1984). In perhaps his most popular work, *One-Dimensional Man* (1964), Marcuse pessimistically mused that capitalism had contained the forces of revolutionary social change, which could be loosely interpreted as "the white workers." However, in his next three books, *An Essay on Liberation* (1969), *Five Lectures: Psychoanalysis, Politics, and Utopia* (1970), and *Counter-Revolution and Revolt* (1972), he identified various groups ("outsiders," "outcasts," and "exiles," which included women and "minorities") that could potentially initiate social transformation. Ultimately, Marcuse embarked upon a search for a revolutionary subject for social change that continues to baffle and elude critical theorists to this day. This, then, is not a deficiency that is particular to Du Bois's discourse, but one that is endemic to critical theory in general (see also Abromeit and Cobb, 2004; Kellner, 1989; Marcuse, 1997a, 2001, 2004; Wilkerson and Paris, 2001).

13. Du Bois stated in 1947, just after the second European world war (i.e., "World War II"), "I am a pacifist." He more or less meant that he was against war, because he never really ruled out self-defensive violence as an end-game option (as we have seen in our discussions of "Let Us Reason Together" and "Social Planning for the Negro: Past and Present"). He certainly was no pacifist in the sense that Bayard Rustin was a pacifist (see Anderson, 1997; D'Emilio, 2003; Rustin, 1971, 2003). All that said, Du Bois was actually one of the most noted anti-war activists of mid-century America. His discourse on war and peace (and pacifism) was initiated in his "Credo," in 1904, and was deepened and developed over the succeeding sixty years of his life. He penned many important and influential essays on peace that have yet to be taken seriously by his interpreters and critics. In fact, part of my argument here involves a calm contention that his homespun democratic socialism is almost incomprehensible without an acute understanding of his work as an anti-war activist and peace advocate. His most noteworthy anti-war essays include: *Color and Democracy: Peace and the Colonies* (1945), "Peace: Freedom's Road for Oppressed Peoples" (1949), "Colonial Peoples and the Fight for Peace" (1949), "No One Who Saw Paris Will Ever Forget" (1949), "Moscow Peace Congress" (1949), *I Speak for Peace* (1950), "No Progress Without Peace" (1950), "The Right to Advocate Peace" (1951), *Peace Is Dangerous* (1951), "America and World Peace" (1952), *In Battle for Peace* (1952), "Insist on Peace: Now and Forever" (1953), "A Decent World for All" (1954), "For-

mosa and Peace" (1955), "The World Peace Movement" (1955), "Gandhi and the American Negroes" (1957), "Crusader Without Violence" (1959), "Africa and World Peace" (1960) and *The Peoples of Africa and World Peace* (1960). See Du Bois (1970c, 1970d, 1971a, 1971b, 1985a, 1986a, 1995a, 1996a).

14. Du Bois developed and, in a sense, democratized his Talented Tenth theory. Compare "The Talented Tenth" (1903) with "The Talented Tenth Memorial Address" (1948). In 1903 he was without a doubt staunchly black bourgeois with, at best, a brewing sense of social reform. By 1948 he was a world-worn Civil Rights leader and recognized radical who refused to be silenced by McCarthyism, white supremacism, and/or black conservatism. His shift away from elitism coincided with his turn to socialism, which, we will recall, was embraced only after years of careful and critical consideration (see Du Bois, 1986a, 1996c). On the origins of the theory of "the Talented Tenth" and Du Bois's essay by that name, see Higginbotham (1993) and Lewis (1993). And for critiques of Du Bois's use of the concept and his essay, see Broderick (1959), Bulmer (1995), Cain (1993), Carter (1998), DeMarco (1983), Dennis (1977, 1996a), Drake (1985), Drummer (1995), Gates and West (1996), Gatewood (1994), Green (1977), J. A. James (1997, 2000), Killian (1999), Kilson (2000b), Marable (1986), Meier (1959, 1963), Rabaka (2003a, forthcoming), Reed (1997), Rudwick (1956, 1960, 1968, 1982), Smith (1975), Travis (1996), Tyner (1997), and Zamir (1994, 1995).

Chapter Five

Du Bois and "The Damnation of Women": Critical Social Theory and the Souls of Black Female Folk

"The meaning of the twentieth century is the freeing of the individual soul; the soul longest in slavery and still in the most disgusting and indefensible slavery is the soul of womanhood."—Du Bois, 1995a, p. 298

"The uplift of women is, next to the problem of the color line and the peace movement, our greatest modern cause."—Du Bois, 1969a, p. 181

"I am not free while any woman is unfree, even when her shackles are very different from my own. And I am not free as long as one person of color remains chained. Nor is any one of you."—Lorde, 1984, p. 133

"Separatist ideology encourages us to believe that women alone can make feminist revolution—we cannot. Since men are the primary agents maintaining and supporting sexism and sexist oppression, they can only be successfully eradicated if men are compelled to assume responsibility for transforming their consciousness and the consciousness of society as a whole. After hundreds of years of anti-racist struggle, more than ever before non-white people are currently calling attention to the primary role white people must play in the anti-racist struggle. The same is true of the struggle to eradicate sexism—men have a primary role to play. This does not mean that they are better equipped to lead feminist movement; it does mean that they should share equally in resistance. In particular, men have a tremendous contribution to make to feminist struggle in the area of exposing, confronting, opposing, and transforming the sexism of their male peers. When men show a willingness to assume equal responsibility in feminist struggle, performing whatever tasks are necessary, women should affirm their revolutionary work by acknowledging them as comrades in struggle."—hooks, 1984, p. 81

INTRODUCTION: DU BOIS'S ANTI-SEXIST SOCIAL
THOUGHT AND RADICAL GENDER POLITICS

Du Bois's contributions to critical theory, and Africana critical theory in specific, are perhaps ultimately most distinguished by his passionate pro-women politics or what Michael Awkward (2000) dubbed Du Bois's "male-feminism," which amazingly integrates each of the aforementioned areas of critical inquiry—racism (Chapter 2), colonialism (Chapter 3), and capitalism (Chapter 4)—into a full-fledged critical, socio-theoretical framework. Du Bois (1898) claimed in his classic essay "The Study of Negro Problems," that the omission of persons of African descent from the realm of social scientific study, and their relegation and reduction to paradigms of pathology when they are studied, robs all "true lovers of humanity" who "hold higher the pure ideals of science" of the rigorous and robust practice of human science (p. 23). In this same vein, he also argued that there could be no authentic human science unless and until the contradictions and conundrums of women's *sociality*—that is, women's socio-political lived-experiences, their social life-realities in this "man-ruled world," and their relations among themselves and with men—were critically reflected in social scientific and other humanistic studies of the social world (Du Bois, 1995a, p. 297). Du Bois was neither the first nor the last black man to think along these lines.[1]

There have been several men of African descent, and African American males in specific, who have spoken and written critically about sexism and the social subordination of persons on account of their gender (Adu-Poku, 2001; Awkward, 2000; Byrd and Guy-Sheftall, 2001; Carbado, 1999; Digby, 1998; Gordon, 1997b; Lemons, 1997, 2001). Immediately the often-noted name of Frederick Douglass (1992) comes rushing to the fore, and further research reveals that Douglass, as he on occasion observed, was deeply influenced by the progressive gender politics of Charles Lenox Remond, after whom he, Douglass, named one of his sons (Douglass, 1994; Foner, 1964, 1992; McFeely, 1991; Quarles, 1997). Both Douglass and Remond were active African American male abolitionists who were also avid and uncompromising women's rights and women's suffrage advocates. It was Remond who helped to spearhead the American Anti-Slavery Society (AASS); became its first full-time African American lecturer; and initially, along with his sister, Sarah Parker Remond, broached the subject of women's rights and women's suffrage within that organization. At the World's Anti-Slavery Convention, held in London in 1840, he sent shockwaves through the proceedings by openly condemning the convention's sexist policy, which denied women's right to participate, and abruptly left the meeting (Appiah and Gates, 1999, p. 1611; see also Quarles, 1991; D. P. Wesley, 1993).

According to Philip Foner (1992), in his introduction to *Frederick Douglass on Women's Rights*, Douglass was influenced by both Charles and Sarah Remond: where Charles played a pivotal role in the AASS, being "the best known black abolitionist until Douglass appeared on the scene," Sarah was active in the Female Anti-Slavery Society (FASS), quickly becoming one of its most popular and persuasive speakers (p. 12). She, along with her brother and Frederick Douglass, toured the anti-slavery lecture circuit (D. P. Wesley, 1993). Douglass was so deeply influenced by the Remonds, and other innumerable experiences in his fight for African American freedom and women's liberation, that throughout his *oeuvre* anti-racist and anti-sexist arguments seem to dovetail incessantly, giving his speeches and writings a rare radical humanistic tone and timbre (Douglass, 1950–1975). His remarkable radical humanism, as several of his biographers and interpreters have observed, was garnered, forged, and refined within the mercurial context of his life-long liberation thought and practices (Lawson and Kirkland, 1999; Martin, 1984, 1990; Quarles, 1966; Sundquist, 1990). Initially those thoughts and practices were geared toward Douglass securing his own liberty and, then, the liberation of his enslaved kith and kin. Once he emancipated himself, Douglass not only blossomed into one of the most radical abolitionists, but also, as is often overlooked, one of the most radical and outspoken "women's rights men" of the nineteenth century (Douglass, 1992; Martin, 1984). After Abraham Lincoln issued the Emancipation Proclamation, and some of the most severe aspects of African American enslavement were outlawed, Douglass never tired of reminding his listeners and readers that "in some respects the woman suffrage movement is but a continuance of the old anti-slavery movement" (cited in Foner, 1992, p. 42).

However, as the life and legacy of Sojourner Truth and the Black Women's Club movement attest, the nineteenth century—similar to the twentieth century—women's liberation movement was not without its own homespun "feminist" racism (Caraway, 1991; Cash, 1986; A. Y. Davis, 1981; E. L. Davis, 1996; Dill, 1979; hooks, 1981; Painter, 1993, 1996). Douglass, throughout his women's liberation speeches and writings, therefore, consistently turned his critical attention to the life-worlds and lived-experiences of black women, who along with pro-women's rights black men were frequently barred from ("mainstream" and/or white women-dominated) women's suffrage movement meetings and publications. From his optic, African Americans, as a socio-historical group, had to grapple with white supremacy and the continuing contemporary effects of enslavement. And women (and "radical women's rights men"), according to Douglass, also had to confront and combat male supremacy. Therefore, those persons who were black *and* women had the onerous task of eradicating both white and male supremacist social ideology and practices, or what we might presently call "racist" and "sexist" thought and practices (Douglass, 1950–1975, 1992; hooks, 1984, 1989, 1990, 1991). Critically speaking directly to this issue, in *Douglass' Monthly* in 1859, Douglass declared: "Other women suffer certain wrongs, but the wrongs peculiar to woman out of slavery, great and terrible as they are, are endured as well by the slave woman, who has also to bear the ten thousand wrongs of slavery in addition to the common wrongs of woman."

It was with arguments such as these, arguments in which Douglass developed a simultaneous critique of racism and sexism, that he made his greatest contribution to what we variously call in our modern and/or "postmodern" moment: "black feminism," "African feminism," "womanism," and/or "Africana womanism." And it is also through these same simultaneously anti-racist and anti-sexist arguments that Douglass's life and legacy provided a paradigm and point of departure for the twentieth century's most noted African American male women's liberation theorist: W. E. B. Du Bois. In works such as "Douglass as Statesman" (1895), "Frederick Douglass" (1943), and "A People's Leader: A Review of *The Life and Writings of Frederick Douglass* edited by P. S. Foner" (1950), Du Bois (re)introduced and radically (re)interpreted Douglass, highlighting and accenting his abolitionism, unceasing humanism, and advocacy of women's equality.

Although Douglass's women's rights work stands in need of additional radical reinterpretation, I will forgo further detailed discussion of it here and focus instead on Du Bois's anti-sexist critical social theory. One reason for forgoing Douglass's womanist work is because he, more than any other male of African descent (and, perhaps more than any other male in general), has consistently received much-deserved high honors and critical acclaim—from both black and white, male and female women's liberation activists and academics—as a model male anti-sexist (Foner, 1964, 1992; Byrd and Guy-Sheftall, 2001; Martin, 1984; Quarles, 1991, 1997; Sundquist, 1990). A second reason for side-stepping Douglass and going directly to Du Bois's anti-sexist social thought is because there is a great need now for a more *modern* antisexist male model, one who offers ethical and historical alternatives not only to racism and sexism, but also to our more-than-modern (some say "postmodern") forms of capitalism and colonialism. Du Bois's thought and texts, in several senses, can be said to offer us radical alternatives to our present social and political problems revolving around racism, sexism, capitalism, and colonialism.[2]

Though many read him as an archetypal "race man," according to Joy James (1997) in *Transcending the Talented Tenth*, Du Bois actually practiced "a politics remarkably progressive for his time and ours" (p. 36).[3] James notes, "Du Bois confronted race, class, and gender oppression while maintaining conceptual and political linkages between the struggles to end racism, sexism, and war" (p. 36–37). His socio-theoretical framework was dynamic and constantly integrated diverse components of African American liberation theory; Pan-Africanism and anticolonial theory; women's liberation theory; peace and international politics theory; and Marxist and non-Marxist class theory, among others.

In "The Souls of Black Women Folk in the Writings of W. E. B. Du Bois," Nellie McKay (1990) contends: "At a time when black male writers concentrated their efforts on the social, economic, and educational advancement of black men as the 'leaders' of the race, Du Bois is something of an anomaly in his recognition that black women were equal partners in the struggle to claim the human dignity all black people were seeking" (p. 236). Moreover, in *Daughters of Sorrow: Attitudes Toward Black Women, 1880–1920,* Beverly Guy-Sheftall (1990) maintains that Du Bois was not only one of "the most passionate defenders of black women," but also one of the "most outspoken [male-] feminists" in African American history and, more generally, American history (p. 13). In fact, in Guy-Sheftall's opinion, Du Bois "devote[d] his life's work to the emancipation of blacks *and* women" (p. 161, emphasis in original).[4]

In *W. E. B. Du Bois: Black Radical Democrat,* Manning Marable (1986) echoes Guy-Sheftall's observations, declaring, "[l]ike Douglass, Du Bois was probably the most advanced male leader of his era on the question of gender inequality" and woman suffrage, though he was deeply "troubled by the racism within the white women's movement" (p. 85). Particularly perplexing for Du Bois was the white women's movement's inattention to and perpetuation of racism. For instance, Du Bois was bothered by the racial politics of the National American Woman Suffrage Association, whose president, Carrie Chapman Catt, asserted that democratic rights had been granted to African American men "with possibly ill-advised haste," producing "[p]erilous conditions" in U.S. society as it introduced "into the body politic vast numbers of irresponsible citizens." Belle Kearney, the Mississippi suffragist leader, practiced an even more overtly racist politics by advocating that white women's enfranchisement would guarantee, among other things, an "immediate and [more] durable white supremacy" (cited in Marable, 1986, p. 85; see also Blee, 1991, 2002; Caraway, 1991; Ferber, 2004; Newman, 1999; Twine and Blee, 2001; Ware, 1992). Du Bois (1995a), in characteristic fashion, shot back: "Every argument for Negro suffrage is an argument for woman's suffrage; every argument for woman's suffrage is an argument for Negro suffrage; both are great movements in democracy" (p. 298).

In terms of developing Africana critical theory of contemporary society, what I am most interested in here is how Du Bois maintained, as James put it above, "conceptual and political linkages" between various antiracist, anti-sexist, anticolonial, and anticapitalist thought-traditions and socio-political movements. Unlike most of the critics in the Frankfurt School tradition of critical theory, Du Bois did not downplay gender domination and discrimination. On the contrary, he placed the critique of sexism and racism right alongside the critique of capitalism, class analysis, and class conflict theory. In tune with the thinking of many Marxist feminists and socialist feminists, Du Bois was critical of both capitalism and patriarchy (Eisenstein, 1979; Sargent, 1981; Weinbaum, 1978). He understood women, in general, to have great potential as agents of social transformation because of their simultaneous experience of capitalist and sexist oppression. However, similar to contemporary Africana anti-sexist social theorists, both black feminists and Africana womanists, Du Bois understood women of African descent, in particular, to have even greater potential as agents of radical social change on account of their simultaneous experience of racism, sexism, and economic exploitation, whether under capitalism or colonialism (Guy-Sheftall, 1995; hooks, 1981, 1984, 1995; Hudson-Weems, 1995, 1997; James and Sharpley-Whiting, 2000; Nnaemeka, 1998). Du Bois's socio-theoretical framework, therefore, has immense import for the discussion at hand so far as it provides Africana critical theory with a paradigm and point of departure for developing a multi-perspectival social theory that is simultaneously critical of racism, sexism, capitalism, and colonialism.

Though there is much in Du Bois's women's rights and women's suffrage work that warrants our attention, this chapter will focus on those aspects of his women's liberation thought that register as seminal and significant contributions to the development of black radical politics and critical social theory. For the purpose of coherence, the chapter is divided into five sections, each of which corresponds with one of Du Bois's major anti-sexist contributions to Africana critical theory of contemporary society. The first section, "Frankfurt School Critical Theory, Feminist Theory, and the Racial Politics of Contemporary Social Theory," critically analyzes the subtle racial politics of Frankfurt School-based feminist theory. It helps to highlight how Frankfurt School-styled feminist critical theorists have neglected race and racism in their discourse and the need for critical theories of contemporary "postmodern" and/or "postcolonial" societies to not only take gender domination and discrimination much more seriously, but critical race theory, philosophy of race, and the history of racism as well.

The second section, "Du Bois's Development of and Contributions to an Anti-Racist, Anti-Sexist, Anti-Colonial, and Anti-Capitalist Critical Theory of Contemporary Society," brings Du Bois's anti-sexist social thought into dialogue with several seminal turn-of-the-twentieth-century Africana women's liberation theorists: specifically Frances Harper and Anna Julia Cooper. It begins by contextualizing Du Bois's anti-sexist social thought within the world and thought-tradition(s) of Africana women's liberation theory; something that has heretofore rarely, if ever, been endeavored. Classical and contemporary (re)constructions and (re)inscriptions of Du Bois solely as a "race man" are explored and exploded throughout the section. Such interpretations, it is argued, are not only intellectually disingenuous to Du Bois's life and legacy, but also the very type of "one-dimensional" thought that critical theorists seek to challenge, change, and offer viable alternatives to—and especially those critical theorists with concrete commitments to constantly broadening the base of critical theory.

The third section, "Du Bois and the Mythic Idealization of Black Womanhood and Black Motherhood," acutely explores Du Bois's (re)presentation and (re)positioning of black women and black mothers. It accents his efforts to counter both white and male supremacists' contentions concerning black women, and illustrates the ongoing importance of ideological struggle and ideology critique where Africana philosophy, radical politics, and critical social theory are concerned. The fourth section, "The Black Women's Club Movement, Josephine St. Pierre Ruffin, and the Roots of Du Bois's Anti-Sexist Radicalism," performs an archaeology of Du Bois's early life and thought and identifies the black women's club movement, and Josephine Ruffin's radicalism in particular, as a central site and source of his paradigm(s) for social organization, political education, black feminism/womanism, and radical journalism. The final section, "'The Damnation of Women': Du Bois's Male Anti-Sexist Manifesto," focuses on Du Bois's classic male anti-sexist manifesto, "The Damnation of Women." It brings together the insights from the previous sections and seeks to provide a radical reinterpretation of Du Bois's womanist work—an Africana critical theoretical interpretation that points contemporary political activists and social theorists not only in new directions in critical social theory, but along alternative paths toward a new humanity and new society.[5]

To begin, let us critically review some of the major movements in contemporary feminist philosophy and, particularly, cutting-edge work on the anti-sexist, radical socio-political scene. This will aid us in our endeavor to distinguish Du Bois's contributions and place as a paradigmatic figure in the Africana tradition of critical theory, from the insights and advances of feminists working in the Frankfurt School tradition of critical theory. A brief but critical examination of Frankfurt School-based feminism will also provide us with an opportunity to take a serious look at one of the most provocative theoretical productions in recent radical thought history: Nancy Fraser's (1989) articulation of a "feminist critical theory" of contemporary society.

FRANKFURT SCHOOL CRITICAL THEORY, FEMINIST THEORY, AND THE RACIAL POLITICS OF CONTEMPORARY SOCIAL THEORY

In "What's Critical about Critical Theory?: The Case of Habermas and Gender," Nancy Fraser (1991) asserts that "a critical social theory of capitalist societies needs gender-sensitive categories," which is to say that critical theory should move away from the "usual androcentric understanding" and ordering of things commonplace in orthodox Marxian theory (p. 371). It should, contrary to the critical theories of many members of the Frankfurt School, seriously engage the particularities of, and differences between, female and male domination and discrimination. For instance, as Jürgen Habermas says "virtually nothing about gender" in *Theory of Communicative Action*, his much-touted magnum opus, Fraser finds his critical theory seriously deficient (p. 358). By conducting a "gender-sensitive reading" of his social theory, Fraser reveals that "there are some major lacunae in Habermas's otherwise powerful and sophisticated model of the relations between public and private institutions in classical capitalism" (p. 370). For Fraser, when Habermas writes of the worker-citizen-soldier in his critique of the public and private spheres under capitalism, he lays bare some of the major weaknesses of his—and, in my opinion, many of the other members of the Frankfurt School's—critical theory: his failure to come to critical terms with "the gender subtext of the relations and arrangements he describes," and the fact that "feminine and masculine identity run like pink and blue threads through the areas of paid work, state administration and citizenship as well as through the domain of familial and sexual relations. This is to say that gender identity is lived out in all arenas of life" (pp. 367, 370).[6]

In agreement with Fraser, I believe that "gender-sensitive readings" of, and radical changes in, "the very concepts of citizenship, childrearing and unpaid work," as well as "changes in the relationships among the domestic, official-economic, state and political-public spheres" are necessary (p. 371). However, my conception of critical theory also takes into consideration the *racial subtext* and argues for *race-sensitive readings* of power relations in the modern and "postmodern" moments. I am very excited about the prospects of developing "feminist," "gender sensitive" and/or, as I prefer, *critical women's liberation theory*. Which, in other words, is to say that I am deeply devoted to developing critical social theory and cultural analysis that acknowledges, in Fraser's words, that: "We are, therefore, struggling for women's autonomy in the following special sense: a measure of collective control over the means of interpretation and communication sufficient to permit us to participate on par with men in all types of social interaction, including political deliberation and decision-making" (p. 378).

What bothers me about Fraser's articulation of a feminist critical theory, however, is the limited scope of her social-theoretical framework. While she correctly takes Habermas—and, in many senses, the whole of the ╷Frankfurt School tradition of critical theory—to task for the "gender-blindness" or, what I am wont to call, the *gender insensitivity* of his social-theoretical framework, like Habermas, Fraser fails to theorize some of the ways racism adds a different, perhaps deeper dimension to domination and discrimination in contemporary society. Put another way, I am highly perplexed by the *racial myopia*, that is, the racial blindness of a sophisticated feminist social theorist such as Fraser who, perhaps utilizing the Frankfurt School critical-theoretical framework and philosophically following many of its male members, treats race, racism, anti-racist struggle, and critical race theory as incidental and, more to the point, tertiary to the critique of sexism (and particularly patriarchy) and capitalism. ╷

Many theorists have explored sexism, and many theorists have explored racism, and a multitude of theorists (especially Marxists!) have critiqued capitalism. But racism *and* sexism *and* capitalism (*and* colonialism, I might add), treated in a critical conjunctive manner—perhaps of the sort advocated by the "black lesbian feminist socialist mother of two, including one boy," Audre Lorde (1984, p. 114), and the kind of analysis that the black feminist sociologist Deborah King (1995) writes of in her classic essay, "Multiple Jeopardy, Multiple Consciousness: The Context of Black Feminist Ideology"—calls for a critical engagement of Du Bois as it does for no other.

What do we find when we turn to Du Bois's thought and texts?

In Du Bois's corpus we are undoubtedly, and perhaps unexpectedly for some, exposed to an arsenal of criticisms which challenge and seek to provide solutions to several of the major social and political problems of the nineteenth, twentieth, and, I should like to be one of the first to add, twenty-first centuries. Though his thought covers a wide range of intellectual terrain and ducks and dips into and out of various academic disciplines (history, sociology, philosophy, political science, economics, religion, education, and literature, among others), Du Bois, it can be said at this point with little or no fanfare, laid a foundation and provides a critical-theoretical framework for the systematic study of the four key forms of domination and discrimination that have shaped the modern world for several centuries: racism, sexism, colonialism, and capitalism. All of his work, whether we turn to his novels, volumes of poetry, plays, autobiographies, cultural criticisms, histories, social studies, political treatises or economic analyses, emanate from the four aforementioned forms of oppression.

Returning to Fraser and feminist critical theory, again I feel compelled to reiterate that I utterly agree with her project when and where she argues that

the worker-citizen-soldier in classical and contemporary Marxian traditions
(of which Frankfurt School critical theory is a provocative and extremely important twentieth-century strand) is not androgynous or gender neutral but, in
fact, dreadfully gendered, and thoroughly male-centered at that. Fraser's radical socialist-feminist theory resonates deeply with my articulation of an
Africana critical theory of contemporary society when she accents some of
the ways in which basic Marxian categories, such as "worker," "wage," "consumer," and "citizen,"—in her own words:

> are not, in fact, strictly economic concepts. Rather, they have an implicit gender
> subtext and thus are "gender-economic" concepts. Likewise, the relevant con-
> cept of citizenship is not strictly a political concept; it has an implicit gender
> subtext and so, rather, is a "gender-political" concept. Thus, this analysis reveals
> the inadequacy of those critical theories that treat gender as incidental to poli-
> tics and political economy. It highlights the need for a critical-theoretical cate-
> gorical framework in which gender, politics and political economy are internally
> integrated. (1991, p. 371)

For Fraser, there are few, if any, gender-neutral concepts in Marxian theory. In fact, much of Marxism, as she avers above, is rather gender-specific
and often only speaks to male struggles against economic exploitation; which
is to say that Marxism, as it was originally conceived and propagated from
Karl Marx through to Herbert Marcuse and the Western or Hegelian Marxist
tradition, is one long theorization of working-class men's experience of, and
class struggles against, the evils of capitalism (Anderson, 1976; Gottlieb,
1992; Kolakowski, 1978a, 1978b, 1978c; Jay, 1984). The trick, though, and
one that has not gone unnoticed by Marxist feminists and socialist feminists,
is that for a very long time many Marxists (many female Marxists notwithstanding) did not realize or critically take into consideration the simple fact
when they wrote or spoke of "workers," "wages," "citizens," and the like,
their ideas and arguments were premised on a false gender neutrality that
more often than not signified males and their gender-specific sociopolitical
wishes and whims (see Barrett, 1980; Eisenstein, 1979; Guettel, 1974; and
Sargent, 1981).

In a patriarchal society, it is "normal," utterly "universal" for theorizing
men to exclude the plight of women from their so-called "radical social theory," "theories of social change," and/or their dialectical discourses on domination and liberation (see Benhabib and Cornell, 1987). For male theorists
to identify themselves and their discourses as patriarchal, male-supremacist
or masculinist, or to make mention of gender at all, is—from their vantage
point—superfluous because of the super-structural and supra-structural dynamics of patriarchy and the ways it plays itself out in the said society.

Fraser is, indeed, on point when she suggests that what is needed is a closer, more critical "gender-sensitive reading" of classical and contemporary radical thought and praxis in order to develop a critical theory of contemporary society.

Africana critical theory of contemporary society, however, parts company with Fraser's feminist critical theory when it calls for "a critical-theoretical categorical framework in which gender, politics, and political economy are internally integrated" without so much as mentioning, let alone seriously engaging, the socio-historical fact that race and racism as well have shaped the modern world and, therefore, should be included in any authentic critical theory of *contemporary* society. Contemporary society, as several self-described "feminists" and "womanists" of African descent have argued, is simultaneously sexist, racist, and economically exploitive—one need not think long about the various vicissitudes of contemporary capitalism and colonialism (see Guy-Sheftall, 1995; James and Sharpley-Whiting, 2000; Nnaemeka, 1998). The task, then, of contemporary critical theory is to seek solutions to these four fundamental social and political problems, among others as they arise.

In the classical Marxist tradition, and in most of the contemporary Marxist tradition, when Marxists theorize the plight of the "worker," they are not only writing about gender-specific workers, *male workers*, but also, as demonstrated in the previous chapter, racially specific workers, *white workers*. The terms that the Marxists use are neither gender- nor race-neutral terms. For instance, just as males are normative in a patriarchal society, so too are whites in a socio-historically white supremacist society. Again, it is superfluous to make mention of such matters as race and gender in a white and male supremacist society, because the white male worldview is always and ever thought and taught to be "neutral" and "universal." To put it plainly: In a white *and* male supremacist society, all are indoctrinated with the dominant ideology, which is inherently a hegemonic white male worldview. Moreover, the appeal of purportedly gender- and race-neutral terms—such as, *worker*, *consumer*, and *citizen*—is that they often silently signify white males without actually overtly saying so. What this means, then, is that there are actually invisible pre-reflexive parenthetical adjectives clandestinely attached to these supposedly gender- and race-neutral terms: (white male) *worker*, (white male) *consumer*, and (white male) *citizen*.

Hence, had Fraser turned to Du Bois's discourse, she would have found not only a critical and analytical engagement of capitalism and sexism, but also one of the most sustained and sophisticated theorizations of race and racism, perhaps, in recent human history. She would, further, have been able to observe not simply the gendered subtext of the Marxian tradition, but also its racial (and racist) subtext, positing, as I intend to, the need for Marxists to critically note that their basic concepts and categories are race and gender specific (and supremacist), as well as political and economic. In other words, I am arguing, following the Eritrean philosopher Tsenay Serequeberhan (1994), that "political 'neutrality' in philosophy, as in most other things, is at best a 'harmless' naïveté, and at worst a pernicious subterfuge for hidden agendas" (p. 4). It is not enough, from the Africana critical theoretical perspective, for Fraser to highlight gender's import for radical political and economic analysis without, in the spirit of Du Bois and countless colored and colonized "others," stretching it to encompass the study of race, racism, critical race theory, and contemporary antiracist struggle. Finally, in Du Bois's corpus, had Fraser turned to his thought, she would have also found an anticolonial theory and discourse on decolonization that could have possibly helped her extend and expand her concept of the "inner colonization of the life-world," which she borrowed from Habermas, and "decolonization," which she—similar to almost the entire Frankfurt School tradition of critical theory—limits to life-worlds and lived-experiences in capitalist countries (Fraser, 1989, pp. 129–43, 161–87).

Capitalism, it should be stated outright, does marginalize, exploit, and oppress women in ways markedly different from men, and especially in patriarchal capitalist societies. However, and equally important, capitalism also perpetuates and exacerbates racial domination and discrimination. This is a socio-historical fact that many Marxist feminists and socialist feminists have long neglected, and also a fact to which Du Bois and a host of Africana women's liberation theorists have devoted a great deal of time and intellectual energy. Though there is much more in Fraser's theory and the feminist critiques of Frankfurt School critical theory that I find philosophically fascinating, for the purposes of the discussion at hand I have accentuated those aspects of Fraser's arguments that help to highlight the distinctive features of Du Bois's anti-sexist discourse and my articulation of an Africana critical theory of contemporary society. It is with the foregoing in mind that I now turn to what could be termed Du Bois's development of and contributions to an anti-racist, anti-sexist, anti-colonial, and anti-capitalist critical theory of contemporary society.

DU BOIS'S DEVELOPMENT OF AND CONTRIBUTIONS TO AN ANTI-RACIST, ANTI-SEXIST, ANTI-COLONIAL, AND ANTI-CAPITALIST CRITICAL THEORY OF CONTEMPORARY SOCIETY

Du Bois developed theory that was simultaneously critical of racism, colonialism, capitalism, and traditional Marxism. In what follows I will bring this thought into dialogue with his women's liberation work. Similar to Frederick Douglass (1992), Du Bois demanded that women's human and civil rights be respected and protected. But, beyond Douglass, Du Bois thoroughly theorized and "strategized woman suffrage and female equality," argues Gary Lemons (2001) and Nellie McKay (1985, 1990), "from a standpoint grounded in the lived experiences" and literature of black women (Lemons, 2001, p. 74). Bringing his critique of capitalism and careful study of modern political economy to bear on "this man-ruled world" and its absurd "sex conditions," Du Bois—again, following Frederick Douglass—advocated that women have "equal pay for equal work," stating: "We cannot abolish the new economic freedom of women. We cannot imprison women again in a home or require them all on pain of death to be nurses and housekeepers" (Du Bois, 1995a, pp. 289, 297, 309; see also Douglass, 1992, pp. 63–65).[7]

Many Du Bois scholars have pointed out that Du Bois prophesied that "the problem of the twentieth century" would be "the problem of the color line" (see Anderson and Zuberi, 2000; Andrews, 1985; Bell, Grosholz and Stewart, 1996; Clarke, Jackson, Kaiser and O'Dell, 1970; Fontenot, 2001). However, what many of these scholars have failed to mention is the fact that Du Bois made this statement in 1900 (in "To the Nations of the World"), and that he augmented and revised this thesis several times within the remaining sixty-three years of his life (see Du Bois, 1995a, pp. 639–41). In fact, by the time he published *Darkwater* in 1920, Du Bois (1995a) stressed not only the "sex conditions," "sex equality," and "sex freedom" of women, but he also asserted that "women are passing through, not only a moral, but an economic revolution" (pp. 308, 311). Further, forty-three years before his death, Du Bois—seemingly unbeknownst to the great majority of past and present Du Bois scholars—stated: "The uplift of women is, next to the problem of the color line and the peace movement, our greatest modern cause" (p. 309).[8]

Du Bois developed a "critical sociology," according to Cheryl Townsend Gilkes (1996), which "emphasized that gender, race, and class intersected in the lives of black women to foster an important critical perspective or standpoint" (pp. 117, 112; see also Lucal, 1996). "Standpoint" is a term currently employed in black feminist discourse, and feminist discourse in general, to denote, as Patricia Hill Collins (1996) points out, the fact that:

First, Black women's political and economic status provides them with a distinctive set of experiences that offers a different view of material reality than that available to other groups. The unpaid and paid work that Black women perform, the types of communities in which they live, and the kinds of relationships they have with others suggest that African American women, as a group, experience a different world than those who are not Black and female. Second, these experiences stimulate a distinctive Black feminist consciousness concerning that material reality. In brief, a subordinate group not only experiences a different reality than a group that rules, but a subordinate group may interpret that reality differently than a dominant group. (p. 223)[9]

Du Bois believed that women, and women of African descent in particular, were (within white and male supremacist societies) a "subordinate group" who by dint of hard labor and harsh living conditions had developed a distinct gender, racial, and class consciousness.[10] With "[a]ll the virtues of her sex . . . utterly ignored," "the primal black All-Mother of men," "the African mother" endured, on Du Bois's (1995a) account, "[t]he crushing weight of slavery" only to be re-subjugated in a world that claimed to "worship both virgins and mothers," but "in the end despises motherhood and despoils virgins" (pp. 304, 300, 301, 300). African American women, in the period after *de jure* "American slavery," were flung into a world where they were dominated and discriminated against simultaneously on account of their race and gender. Their subordination, then, was inherent—though implicit on many accounts—in the evolving social ontology of white and male supremacist U.S. society.[11] The chronic experience and effects of the interlocking and intersecting nature of race, gender, class, and as late, sexuality, have led many Africana women's liberation theorists to posit that women of African descent experience a reality that is distinctly different from the lived-experiences of those persons who are not black *and* female. Theories of "double," "triple," and "multiple" jeopardy abound but, curiously, rarely if ever has Du Bois's women's liberation work figured prominently in this discourse.[12]

Du Bois spent the great bulk of his life and intellectual energy wrestling with different forms of domination and discrimination, and though he often missed the mark in his personal life (I am tempted to say, in his personal "affairs") with women, specifically with his wife and daughter, there remains much that can be salvaged from his anti-sexist social thought. To leave Du Bois to the traditional "race man" line is, to my logic, to throw the baby out with the bath water. The more radical and critical thing to do is to search for and salvage what we can from Du Bois's life-work that will aid us in our endeavors to develop an Africana critical theory of contemporary society, which includes a definite and distinctive anti-sexist dimension alongside its anti-racism, anti-colonialism, and anti-capitalism. This, then, is an effort to build on and go beyond Du Bois; it is aimed at bringing his anti-sexist social thought into dialogue with past and present Africana women's liberation theorists.

As with any thought-system or philosophical method there are things that are positive and others that are negative in Du Bois's discourse, which, of course, brings us to the question of dialectics. A dialectical approach to Du Bois enables us to simultaneously acknowledge the sexism he practiced at specific intervals in his private life, while focusing on his production and pro-motion of anti-sexist positions and policies in his public life. This approach also opens objective interpreters of Du Bois to the fact that he—as is common with many men struggling against their sexist socialization and internaliza-tion of sexism—may very well have had instances of sexist thought and be-havior in both his public and private life-worlds.

Were we to highlight Du Bois's sexism without accenting his anti-sexism (or vice versa) we would be producing and practicing the very type of one-di-mensional interpretation and thought that critical theory purports to be com-bating and offering ethical and radical alternatives. Because he has long been cast in the "race man" cloak, it is difficult for many Du Bois scholars (and others) to look at his life and work from multidimensional theoretical optics. What I wish to accent here, above all else, are those aspects of Du Bois's life-work that contribute to the development of Africana critical theory, which means that I am primarily concerned with those aspects of his discourse that critique domination and provide the promise of liberation. The Du Bois that I am interested in did not shy away from the forms of domination that women, and particularly women of African descent, experienced as a result of white and male supremacy. Surely his essays such as "The Work of Negro Women in Society" (1902), "The Black Mother" (1912), "Hail Columbia!" (1913), "Woman Suffrage" (1915), "The Damnation of Women" (1920), and "Sex and Racism" (1957), to name only a few, are sincere testimonies and somber testaments that affirm his claim in the last paragraph of "The Damnation of Women": "I honor the women of my race" (Du Bois, 1995a, p. 311).[13]

Divulging the fact that "women of African descent have struggled with the multiple realities of gender, racial, and economic or caste oppression," Joy James, similar to Cheryl Townsend Gilkes, contends that black women have "created . . . space for a more viable democracy" (James and Sharpley-Whiting, 2000, p. 1; see also Gilkes, 1996, pp. 114, 116–17). Democracy, one of the most prevalent and pervasive themes in Du Bois's discourse, has not existed and will never exist so long as any human group, no matter how small or so-called "mi-nority," is excluded from the civic decision making-processes of their national communities and the international community. Du Bois included women when he spoke of "peasants," "laborers," and "socially damned" persons who must always be considered if the United States, or any nation for that matter, is to achieve anything remotely close to democracy. For instance, in *Darkwater*, in the chapter entitled "Of the Ruling of Men," Du Bois (1969a) asserted:

> Today we are gradually coming to realize that government by temporary coali-tion of small and diverse groups may easily become the most efficient method of expressing the will of man and of setting the human soul free.

. . . [N]o nation, race, or sex, has a monopoly of ability or ideas . . . no human group is so small as to deserve to be ignored as a part, and as an integral and re- spected part, of the mass of men . . . above all, no group of twelve million black folk, even though they are at the physical mercy of a hundred million white ma- jority, can be deprived of a voice in government and of the right to self-devel- opment without a blow at the very foundations of all democracy and all human uplift. . . . [N]o modern nation can shut the gates of opportunity in the face of its women, its peasants, its laborers, or its socially damned. How astounded the future world-citizen will be to know that as late as 1918 great and civilized na- tions were making desperate endeavors to confine the development of ability and individuality to one sex—that is, to one-half of the nation; and he will prob- ably learn that a similar effort to confine humanity to one race lasted a hundred years longer. (pp. 153–54)

Du Bois directed his intellectual attention to the plight of black women, and they were so far as he was concerned, "an integral and respected part" of his beloved black folk. In fact, the black woman, "the primal black All-Mother of men," could not and would not be held in check, neither by white nor male supremacy. Why? Because she was leading both a "moral" and an "economic" revolution (Du Bois, 1995a, pp. 300, 308). Gilkes (1996) con- tends that "for Du Bois, black women represent a unique force for progres- sive change in the United States" because of the degree(s) to which they ex- perience and endure various forms of racial and gender oppression and economic exploitation (p. 113).

Where most of the male social theorists of his age placed a greater empha- sis on class theory, class formation, class consciousness and the impact of po- litical economy on culture and society, Du Bois engaged the intersections of race, class, *and* gender utilizing Africana lived-experiences and liberation thought and practices as a model for his theories of social change and concept of an ever-expanding, all-inclusive democracy. Gilkes notes, "Du Bois's vi- sion pointed to a society that could confront, respect, and embrace the gifts of all" (p. 133). His was a sociological imagination that did not limit itself to the issues of the white male working-class(es), as was the custom in his day, but sought to develop "a broad theory of history that concerned itself with the de- velopment of democracy and of American culture" (p. 114). Going against the socio-theoretical grain of his times, as Gilkes observes, Du Bois staunchly opposed the "subordination of the problems of gender and race in the devel- opment of sociological theory" (p. 117). Hence, here again, Du Bois's critical socio-theoretical framework is distinguished from that of classical Western European and Frankfurt School social theorists, who by most accounts rele- gated race and gender, and racism and sexism, not merely to the margin, but to oblivion. When race and gender did or does register in classical and contemporary Eurocentric social and "critical" discourse they are seen as social negatives that somehow fell from the sky, as though Europeans were not the architects of the concept of race and racism, and as though men were not the masterminds behind gender domination and discrimination against women and other men who embrace and endorse what bell hooks (1991) calls, "alternative masculinities" (see also hooks, 2004a, 2004b).

It was precisely "the problems of gender and race" which Karl Marx, Emile Durkheim, and Max Weber, the "three names [that] rank above all others," according to Anthony Giddens (1971, p. vii), downplayed in their "development of sociological theory." Du Bois's socio-theoretical framework is distinguished by the fact that it sought solutions to the problems of racism, sexism, and colonialism, while keeping a keen and critical eye on the ways that capitalism defines, deforms, and destroys an ever-expanding, all-inclusive democracy. On the prevalence of "the problem of class" in early modern social theory, Gilkes (1996) observes:

> Although issues of class, race, and gender ought to be addressed, most early social theory only focused on class and not on gender or race. In spite of its prominence in American society, the problem of race relations was not accorded the same theoretical importance as were issues centered on class, change, and social structure. Critical theories that assumed the primacy of human action and enterprise in the process of social change often dismissed the issues of race and gender as subordinate to or derived from the problem of class. The result . . . has been a neglect of gender and of racial-ethnic oppressions. (p. 113)

Because of the socio-historical fact of their suffering, what black feminist sociologist Deborah King (1995) calls the "multiple jeopardy" of being black, female, poor, and perpetually hyper-sexualized—which, in other words is to say that black women to varying degrees simultaneously experience and endure racism, sexism, and the ravaging effects of economic exploitation, whether under capitalism or colonialism, among other existential issues—Du Bois understood women of African descent to be the almost ideal agents of radical social change. In black women and their lived-experiences, in their lived-actualities, Du Bois found radical subjects for social change and the spreading of radical democratic thought and practice. Though rarely referred to, Du Bois's "perspectives on African American women," asserts Gilkes (1996), "anticipated and influenced concepts and ideas we currently use to examine the intersection of gender, race, and class with reference to African American women" (p. 132). She continues, "his work is the earliest self-consciously sociological interpretation of the role of African American women as agents of social change," and therefore offers modern radical theorists and activists a multi-perspectival model on which to build an anti-racist, anti-sexist, anti-colonial and anti-capitalist critical theory of contemporary society (p. 134).

Gilkes reminds us that African American women were an integral part of all three of the "great revolutions" Du Bois prophesied in *Darkwater* which must take place if America (and the wider world) was to truly achieve democracy: the revolution against racism or the color line; the revolution against sexism, and specifically the subordination of women; and the revolution against economic exploitation, which included both capitalism and colonialism. Here we see most clearly how Du Bois went about confronting and contesting the major and most daunting existential issues of his epoch (and ours): racism, sexism, capitalism, and colonialism. Of the "great revolutions," first, there was the revolt of the masses of colored folk against colonialism and the color line. This, of course, translated itself in Du Bois's discourse into his anti-colonial and anti-racist writings in *The Moon*, *The Horizon*, *The Crisis*, *Phylon*, and *The National Guardian*, amongst other publications, public intellectualism and political activism. Women of African descent were cast in a "messianic" or "prophetic" role in the revolution against racial domination and discrimination, because Du Bois believed their sufferings "provided them with a legitimate voice of challenge" (Gilkes, 1996, p. 120). Who knew then, and who would know now, perhaps more so than many other classes of citizens, the deficiencies of U.S. democracy than those persons experiencing white and male supremacy and economic super-exploitation? Prefiguring Patricia Collins's notion of "subjugated knowledge," Du Bois attempted to accent and highlight the "hidden" and/or "suppressed" knowledge produced by black women as they confronted, combated, and often contradicted both white and male supremacy (see P. H. Collins, 1990, pp. 3–40, 201–38; 1998, 95–123; 2000, 51–90).

The second "great revolution" that black women were to participate in, according to Du Bois, was the revolution of womanhood. He contended that it was the "new revolutionary ideals" of women, and especially women of African descent, "which must in time have vast influence on the thought and action of this land [the United States of America]" (Du Bois, 1995a, p. 311). Here he is clearly drawing from the social theory of several Africana women's liberation theorists of his era: Anna Julia Cooper, Ida B. Wells, Josephine St. Pierre Ruffin, Frances Ellen Watkins Harper, and Maria Stewart among them. Ever the serious student of African American socio-political thought and culture in its totality, Du Bois was keenly conscious of African American women's liberation thought-traditions: from the anti-sexist abolitionism of Maria Stewart, Sojurner Truth, and Frances Harper, to the black women's club and civil rights activism of Anna Julia Cooper, Ida. B. Wells, and Mary Church Terrell.

Frances Harper in particular was distinguished and deserved recognition, according to Du Bois (1911b), on account of her incessant efforts "to forward literature among colored people" (p. 20). Harper, Du Bois epitaphically intoned, was "a worthy member of that dynasty, beginning with the dark Phyllis [Wheatley] in 1773 and coming on down to Dunbar, Chesnutt and Braithwaite of our day" (p. 21). It is highly plausible that Harper's women's liberation theory, and especially her classic 1893 essay, "Woman's Political Future," had an impact on the development of Du Bois's women's rights consciousness when we consider the fact that Harper was a major force in both the black women's club movement and the then-burgeoning black literary tradition (see Harper, 1988, 1990).[14] It is hard to overlook the similarities in Harper and Du Bois's women's liberation theory, both of which highlight and hinge upon women's character and their distinct moral mission nationally and internationally. Take the following passage from Harper's (1995) essay, "Woman's Political Future," as an initial example:

Today there are red-handed men in our republic, who walk unwhipped of justice, who richly deserve to exchange the ballot of the freeman for the wristlets of the felon; brutal and cowardly men, who torture, burn, and lynch their fellowmen, men whose defenselessness should be their best defense and their weakness an ensign of protection. More than the changing of institutions we need the development of a national conscience, and the upbuilding of national character. Men may boast of the aristocracy of blood, may glory in the aristocracy of talent, and be proud of the aristocracy of wealth, but there is one aristocracy which must ever outrank them all, and that is the aristocracy of character; and it is the women of a country who help to mold its character, and to influence if not determine its destiny; and in the political future of our nation woman will not have done what she could if she does not endeavor to have our republic stand foremost among the nations of the earth, wearing sobriety as a crown and righteousness as a garment and a girdle. In coming into her political estate woman will find a mass if illiteracy to be dispelled. If knowledge is power, ignorance is also power. The power that educates wickedness may manipulate and dash against the pillars of any state when they are undermined and honeycombed by injustice. (p. 41)

Harper's words help to drive home the point that women, and women of African descent in particular, were believed by many—again, Du Bois among them—to be destined to make great contributions to the deconstruction and radical reconstruction of (American) democracy. Similar to Maria Stewart—who in 1832 queried, "How long shall the fair daughters of Africa be compelled to bury their minds and talents beneath a load of iron pots and kettles?" (Stewart, 1987, p. 38)—Harper held fast to the notion that though women were relegated to the home and housework, there would come a time, in a not too distant future, when the ruling race/gender/class would have to come to terms with women's growing socio-political power. That power, unlike men's power, would not rest on the "might-makes-right" theses of the Western European social contract tradition (e.g., Jean-Jacques Rousseau, *Discourse on the Origins and Foundations of Inequality*; Thomas Hobbes, *Leviathan*; John Locke, *Two Treatises of Government*; and Immanuel Kant, *The Metaphysics of Morals*), but would revolve around women's contributions to "the development of a national conscience, and the upbuilding of national character."[15] Harper (1995) continues in this vein:

> Political life in our country has plowed in muddy channels, and needs the infusion of clearer and cleaner waters. I am not sure that women are naturally so much better than men that they will clear the stream by the virtue of their womanhood; it is not through sex but through character that the best influence of women upon the life of the nation must be exerted.
>
> . . . O women of America! into your hands God has pressed one of the sublimest opportunities that ever came into the hands of the women of any race or people. It is yours to create a healthy public sentiment; to demand justice, simple justice, as the right of every race; to brand with everlasting infamy the lawless and brutal cowardice that lynches, burns, and tortures your own countrymen. (p. 42)

Also a dominant theme in Du Bois's women's rights discourse, as we shall soon see, "character" was the cornerstone of Harper's conception of womanhood and it lay at the heart of her women's liberation theory as well. Women would "mold" the country's character, help to "determine its destiny," and "create a healthy public sentiment," not by mimicking the ruling race/gender/class—who socio-historically have been simultaneously racist, sexist, and classist—but by "demand[ing] justice, simple justice, as the right of every race."

In *A Voice from the South: By a Black Woman of the South*, published in 1892, the noted Africana women's liberation theorist, Anna Julia Cooper (1998), echoes Harper's contentions of black women's social, political, and cultural contributions through their special character by asserting that: "The colored woman of today occupies, one may say, a unique position in this country" (p. 112). She continues, "[i]n a period of itself transitional and unsettled, her status seems one of the least ascertainable and definitive of all the forces which make for our civilization." Where white men in mobs, as Harper alludes to above, had historically "lynch[ed], burn[ed], and torture[d]" their black fellow "countrymen," and where white women and black men had long been vying with one another—in light of the white and male supremacy of the U.S. government—for the right to vote, Cooper maintained that each of the aforementioned ("all of the forces which make for our civilization") could learn many lessons from black women's lived-experiences and liberation thought and practices. Why, we feel compelled to query? Because the black woman "is confronted by both a woman question and a race problem, and is as yet an unknown or a unacknowledged factor in both" (p. 112–13).[16]

Harper charged women in general with the task of "demand[ing] justice, simple justice, as the right of every race." Cooper, however, took this claim a step further and focused in no uncertain terms on "the BLACK WOMAN," her plight and sociopolitical position (p. 63, capitalization in original). For Cooper, what distinguished the black (or "colored") woman's standpoint from that of white men, white women, and even that of black men, was the sociohistorical fact that she "is confronted by both a woman question and a race problem." In critically engaging racism and sexism, the black woman, the "unknown" and "unacknowledged factor in both," had developed a "unique position," a "peculiar coign of vantage" which enabled her to "weigh and judge and advise" (p. 114). So, where Harper charged women in general with the task of "demand[ing] justice, simple justice, as the right of every race," Cooper, we could say, charged black women with the task of *demanding justice, simple justice, as the right of every race and both sexes*. On the unique vocation of black women, Cooper wrote:

> What a responsibility then to have the sole management of the primal lights and shadows! Such is the colored woman's office. She must stamp weal or woe on the coming history of this people. May she see her opportunity and vindicate her high prerogative. (p. 117)

The majority of black women had long been "thoughtful spectators," standing "aloof from the heated scramble . . . above the turmoil and din of corruption and selfishness." This helped to foster their "unique position," their "peculiar coign of vantage" which enabled them to critically look at and carefully listen for "the teachings of eternal truth and righteousness" rising out of the furious fight for the soul, not simply of America, but of humanity. Cooper continues:

> One needs occasionally to stand aside from the hum and rush of human interests and passions to hear the voices of God. And it not infrequently happens that the All-loving gives a great push to certain souls to thrust them out, as it were, from the distracting current for a while to promote their discipline and growth, or to enrich them by communion and reflection. And similarly it may be woman's privilege from her peculiar coign of vantage as a quiet observer, to whisper just the needed suggestion or the almost forgotten truth. The colored woman, then, should not be ignored because her bark is resting in the silent waters of the sheltered

cove. She is watching the movements of the contestants none the less and is all the better qualified, perhaps, to weigh and judge and advise because not herself in the excitement of the race. Her voice, too, has always been heard in clear, unfaltering tones, ringing the changes on those deeper interests which make for permanent good. She is always sound and orthodox on questions affecting the wellbeing of her race. (p. 114)

For Cooper, it was not simply black women's character, but also their "unique [socio-historical] position" that fostered their moral mission and enabled them to speak their special moral message. This is a point that was not lost on Du Bois, who put his own special spin on this thesis in his classic essay "The Damnation of Women." Du Bois, as Eric Sundquist (1993) observed, "appears to have absorbed a good deal from others without leaving the fullest accounts of his tutelage" (p. 552). Surely this was the case when it came to Africana women's liberation theory, and Cooper's contributions in specific. For instance, both Joy James (1997) and Charles Lemert (1998) have noted that Cooper and Du Bois met at and participated in the 1900 Pan-African Congress in London and "over the years, had corresponded . . . over several notable race matters" (Lemert, 1998, p. 12; see also Cooper, 1998, p. 336).

Cooper's woman-centered socio-political concepts increasingly crept their way into Du Bois's discourse as he continued to develop his critical theory of contemporary society. In his most sustained effort in the area of Africana women's liberation theory, "The Damnation of Women," Du Bois (1995a) quoted Cooper's famous "when and where I enter" sentence, but failed to mention Cooper by name or to cite the source of the sentence:

> As one of our women writes: "Only the black women can say 'when and where I enter, in the quiet, undisputed dignity of my womanhood, without violence and without suing or special patronage, then and there the whole Negro race enters with me.'" (pp. 304–305)

The unnamed woman writer, and the unacknowledged source of the sentence, in a sense, "allows Cooper to disappear as her words appear," Joy James (1997) argues (pp. 42–46). This, in turn, renders Cooper anonymous and robs Du Bois's readers of an opportunity not simply to engage Cooper's woman-centered cultural criticism, but also to compare Cooper and Du Bois's women's rights work and social philosophy. Cooper's anonymity enables Du Bois and his Africana women's liberation theory to appear as an androgynous or "transgender representative for the entire vilified and oppressed race" (p. 45). This, to put it plainly, is not only problematic, but helps to demonstrate an instance were Du Bois was intellectually dishonest and, in a way, embraced his "race man" intellectual reputation. He should have given Cooper credit for her ideas and acknowledged her work as his point of departure for this section of his essay. Instead, he did the intellectually (and ethically) inexcusable: He rendered Cooper intellectually invisible and anonymous, and placed himself in the traditional "race man" or black patriarchal position of omniscient intellectual leader and "protector and provider" of black women, those dark damsels in distress, if you will. Indeed, Du Bois did, as Sundquist asserted above, gather "a good deal from others without leaving the fullest accounts of his tutelage." This scenario may actually be even more pronounced when his women's rights work is further critically approached and thoroughly analyzed.

Recall earlier I observed that Du Bois stated, "women of Negro descent . . . are passing through, not only a moral, but an economic revolution." Here Du Bois is, perhaps, following Frances Harper and surely Anna Julia Cooper with his emphasis on black women's special moral message and ethical obligation to black liberation. For Du Bois, as it was for Harper and Cooper, it was character that rested at the heart of the moral revolution that women of African descent were bringing into being. Character was one of the many great contributions Africana women were counted on to make to the development and dissemination of democracy in the modern moment. In *Darkwater*, which was written almost a quarter of a century after Harper delivered "Woman's Political Future" and Cooper published *A Voice from the South*, Du Bois (1995a) commented on the character of black women, stating:

> So some few women are born free, and some amid insult and scarlet letters achieve freedom; but our women in black had freedom thrust contemptuously upon them. With that freedom they are buying an untrammeled independence and dear as is the price they pay for it, it will in the end be worth every taunt and groan. Today the dreams of the mothers are coming true. We still have our poverty and degradation, our lewdness and our cruel toil; but we have, too, a vast group of women of Negro blood who for strength of character, cleanness of soul, and unselfish devotion of purpose, is today easily the peer of any group of women in the civilized world. (p. 311)

Here Du Bois defies white and male supremacist notions of womanhood, and constructs what could be termed a part Pan-African, part black nationalist-feminist/womanist version of womanhood. He encouraged "our women in black" to struggle for liberation in both the public and private spheres (pp. 309–11). Moreover, Du Bois—in the fashion of Cooper's woman-centered socio-cultural criticism—thought it important to point out that women of African descent were attempting to grasp and grapple with distinctly different social and political issues than their white counterparts, though both groups of women were discriminated against on account of their gender. Race, racism, and anti-racist struggle made and continues to make distinct differences in the lived-experiences, life-worlds, and liberation theory and praxis of women of African descent, and this is especially true when coupled with their simultaneous struggles for gender justice and an end to economic exploitation. To put it another way, gender *and* racial domination and discrimination, and the theory and praxis developed to combat these oppressions, have served and continue to serve as central determining factors in Africana women's lived-experiences and life-worlds, and it is this stubborn socio-historical fact, combined with the contradictions of capitalism and/or colonialism, that have routinely put many Africana women's liberation theorists at loggerheads with the inexcusable racial lethargy and lacunae of ruling race/class feminists and feminism.

DU BOIS AND THE MYTHIC IDEALIZATION OF BLACK WOMANHOOD AND BLACK MOTHERHOOD

Certainly some of Du Bois's women-focused work, and specifically his thoughts on motherhood, borders on a mythic idealization of the maternal. He invokes "Neith, the primal mother of all," as a universal symbol of maternalism. She is "the primal black All-Mother of men . . . whose feet rest on hell, and whose almighty hands uphold the heavens; all religions, from beauty to beast, lie on her eager breasts; her body bears the stars, while her shoulders are necklaced by the dragon . . . " (Du Bois, 1995a, p. 300). Neith's spirit, classically embodied in Ethiopian queens, those "dusky Cleopatras, dark Candaces, and the darker, fiercer Zinghas," has made its way down to "our own day and our own land—in gentle Phillis [Wheatley]; Harriet [Tubman], the crude Moses; the sibyl Sojourner Truth; and the martyr, Louise De Mortie" (p. 301).

Out of Africa came many contributions to human culture and civilization, but none, according to Du Bois, greater than Africa's "peculiar emphasis" on "the mother-idea." Where the "father and his worship is Asia" and "Europe is the precocious, self-centered, forward-striving child . . . the land of the mother is and was Africa" (p. 301). Though Du Bois is certainly to be commended for his efforts to accent and highlight Africana women's experiences in "this man-ruled world"—as he sternly stated in "Woman Suffrage"—there may also be a sense in which he overstates his case and, consequently, unwittingly aids in the reification and perpetuation of what Michele Wallace (1990a) terms, "the myth of the superwoman," and/or what Patricia Hill Collins (2000, pp. 174–75) more recently referred to as, "mother glorification" and the myth of "the superstrong Black mother."

It was Du Bois (1995a) himself who stated: "They [black women] existed not for themselves, but for men . . . " (p. 299). He paints a portrait of black women as strong, self-sacrificing, and long-suffering, but does not detail how these, among other, quintessentially womanist character traits can be and historically have been abused, and not only by white men and women, but by black men as well (see duCille, 1994; Griffin, 2000; Guy-Sheftall, 1990; hooks, 1981). On this point Du Bois's analysis does not take into consideration the concrete issues involved in many black mothers' lived-actuality; issues which demand that we acknowledge black mothers' strengths, but also their weaknesses and limitations. That is to say, for example, that we should keep cognizant of the fact that black mothers simply cannot do it all, and the fact that though some may very well be "superstrong," no human being, male or female, can be "superstrong" at every interval in human experience.

Du Bois wrote affectionately of "a vast group of women of Negro blood who for strength of character, cleanness of soul, and unselfish devotion of purpose, is today easily the peer of any group of women in the civilized world." Here he is attributing to black mothers many characteristics associated with archetypal motherhood (Cahill, 1982; Rich, 1976; Trebilcot, 1984). In doing this he was attempting to construct what he believed to be a positive image for Africana women in general, and black mothers in particular. However, Du Bois failed to see that he was constructing what Patricia Hill Collins (2000), in "Mammies, Matriarchs, and Other Controlling Images," calls a "controlling image" of Africana women, which praises black mothers' resilience in a white and male supremacist society that has historically labeled them as not only bad mothers, but matriarchs, "bitches," and whores (pp. 69–96; see also duCille, 1994; hooks, 1989, 1990, 1991). In his subtle gender-blindness, Du Bois did not see that in order for them to remain on their pedestal, black mothers had to continue to be superstrong, self-sacrificing, and long-suffering, and especially with regard to the men in their lives, whether father, brother, son, husband, lover, or traditional black church pastor.

What is more, by viewing black women primarily as mothers or essentially in their maternal mode, Du Bois also limits black women to a biological function or "sex role" and, in a sense, quarantines them to the domestic domain or private sphere. This is not only problematic, but seems contradictory considering his assertion: "The future woman must have life work and economic independence. She must have knowledge. She must have the right of motherhood at her own discretion" (Du Bois, 1995a, p. 300).[17] How will women, and Africana women in specific, ever achieve "economic independence" and/or pursue their "life work" if: (1) they are to be "good mothers" on the terms which Du Bois outlined above (self-sacrificing and long-suffering, among several others), and (2) men (and men of African descent notwithstanding) are not taken to task for their faulting with regard to fathering and fatherhood?

By placing such a strong emphasis on black women's experience as mothers, Du Bois, inadvertently I think, downplays the multidimensionality, the very variegations of Africana women's lived-experiences and life-worlds. It is not that Du Bois did not advocate that women be more than mothers and have the right to be more than mothers, but that he did not develop this aspect of his Africana women's liberation theory to the depth and detail that he did his concept of motherhood. In addition, it could also be averred that Du Bois's over-emphasis on motherhood, his mother glorification, also led him to level several lopsided interpretations of women that speak volumes about how "sex roles" discourse often provides a subtle subtext for many male articulations of and approaches to women's liberation theory. For example, when Du Bois writes of Toussaint L'Overture, Frederick Douglass, and Alexander Crummell in *Darkwater*—the text which houses his most sustained treatment of "the woman question" and motherhood, "The Damnation of Women"—there is no talk of fatherhood or fathering. Which is to say that Du Bois did not see noted black men simply as fathers, but in multidimensional terms, as revolutionists, political radicals, great writers, orators, and the like. The "sex roles" subtext was indeed at work in this instance, and it informed Du Bois's, albeit problematic, *pro*-women politics.

There is, however, also another way that we could analyze this. Could it be that Du Bois understood black women to be so "socially damned" that he felt that the only way to get his readers of 1920 (both black and white) to sympathize with his subject, the black woman, was to situate her lived-experience and life-world in an area of the human experience which many regard as universally respected: motherhood? Think about it. At the turn of the twentieth century and up to the 1920s—which is to say, from the height of the New Negro movement to the Harlem Renaissance—who chronicled the experiences of black women besides black women? Certainly not prominent black male intellectuals and leaders. Ask yourself: Where is Booker T. Washington's work on women's rights? What was Marcus Garvey's position on the role of women in the black revolution? We are left wondering what Alain Locke, or James Weldon Johnson, or any number of black male intellectuals and leaders at the turn of the twentieth century through to the 1920s thought of the struggle for women's rights.

Now, as I see it, there are several ways we could approach this, but keeping the overall objective of the Africana critical theory project in mind, I am not so interested in pointing out what this or that thinker did not theorize, as I am with providing a paradigm for a critical theory of contemporary society that soberly and seriously critiques racism, sexism, and colonialism, just as intensely as it does capitalism. With that being said, I feel compelled to state outright: Du Bois was doing a little literary double-dealing here, and in some ways it works, but in other respects it does not and, consequently, it reveals some of the lacunae and serious limitations of his womanist work. I want to suggest that Du Bois perhaps could have side-stepped some of the seeming contradictions of his construction of a "primal black All-Mother of men" myth had he emphasized and passionately advocated the very real need for men (and, again, men of African descent notwithstanding) to take fatherhood as sincerely and seriously as many women take motherhood. This would have opened his argument up for critical discussions of female/male complementarity, socio-political co-creation, community caretaking and cultural working—which in my thinking remains important whether one is heterosexual or homosexual, because racism continues to bind black men to black women, and vice versa, as it is a form of domination and discrimination that affects persons of African descent across the wide spectrum of the various ways of being African-in-the-world (Byrd and Guy-Sheftall, 2001; Carbado, 1999; Guy-Sheftall, 1995).

A second way of engaging some of the stereotypes in Du Bois's womanist work is to open ourselves to the idea that it is highly plausible that he purposely constructed a "super black woman," a "primal black All-Mother of men," in an attempt to counter claims of white women's superiority and black women's inferiority. Du Bois wanted to offset the racist images of black womanhood and black motherhood, so he advanced almost the exact antithesis of those images. In *To Wake the Nations: Race in the Making of American Literature*, Eric Sundquist (1993) observes that though Du Bois's views on women and sexuality were "sometimes prudish," they "were hardly unbending. . . . Rather, they were frequently strategic and in any event must be judged in the context of his reaction to white racist attacks on African American [women,] sexuality and family morality" (pp. 586). Du Bois, Sundquist continues, understood himself to be "countering the contemporary archetype of the Negro as licentious or race-mixing 'beast,'" by highlighting African American women's history and reconstructing an image of black women, black mothers, and the black family; therefore, rescuing and reclaiming for them the "moral integrity that had been undermined by the social effects of slavery and by racist theory" (p. 584).[18]

In his efforts to counter the racist myths about black womanhood and black motherhood, Du Bois in his classic 1912 essay, "The Black Mother," challenged "the master class['s]" conception of "the black mammy" in no uncertain terms (Du Bois, 1995a, p. 294). For those of "the master class," such as Thomas Nelson Page, who "after—with wet eyelids—recounting the virtues of his mammy, declares petulantly that she did not care for her own children," Du Bois reminds them that "the black mammy" is a perpetual "perversion of motherhood" (p. 294). Why? Because "the black mammy" always and ever "existed under a false social system," one that "deprived her of [both] husband and child," not to mention her right to *self-determination* and *self-definition*—two cornerstone characteristics of the conceptual universes of both black feminism and womanism (Du Bois, 1995a, p. 294; see also P. H. Collins, 1993, 1998, 2000; Guy-Sheftall, 1995; hooks, 1981, 1984; Hudson-Weems, 1998a, 1998b, 1998c).

The "master class"—following the fashion of white supremacist patriarchy— only appreciated black women and black motherhood when they could dominate and control black women's lived-experiences and life-worlds. But they had little or no respect for the black mother "in her own home, attending to her own babies." In fact, "as the colored mother . . . retreated to her own home, the master class . . . cried out against her. 'She is thriftless and stupid'" (Du Bois, 1995a, p. 294).

It is in the context of these racist assaults, both physically and psychologically, on black women that Du Bois developed his Africana culture-based anti-sexist counterclaims. These claims were both grounded in and grew out of his knowledge of Africana women's lived-experiences and their socio-political theory and praxis. As much is evinced when we turn to his work with the black women's club movement, which will be discussed in the subsequent section. Against theorists and critics who customarily read Du Bois primarily and one-dimensionally as a "race man," I think that it is extremely important at this point to observe along with Gary Lemons (2001) that, "not only was his [Du Bois's] conception of anti-racist resistance feminist-inspired, his worldview was profoundly influenced by black women" (p. 73).

In fact, few scholars, black feminists and womanists notwithstanding, have pointed out that in many instances in his writings, pro-women's rights or otherwise, Du Bois placed black women's socio-political theory and praxis on par and, at certain intervals, *over* that of black men. A prime example is the following passage:

> As I look about me today in this veiled world of mine, despite the noise and more spectacular advance of my brothers, I instinctively feel and know that it is the five million women of my race who really count. Black women (and women whose grandmothers were black) are today furnishing our teachers; they are the main pillars of those social settlements which we call churches; and they have with small doubt raised three-fourths of our church property. If we have today, as seems likely, over a billion dollars of accumulated goods, who shall say how much of it has been wrung from the hearts of servant girls and washerwomen and women toilers in the fields? As makers of two million homes these women are today seeking marvelous ways to show forth our strength and beauty and our conception of truth. (Du Bois, 1995a, p. 308)

Here, Du Bois is making a veiled reference to the black women's club movement, which coincidentally just so happens to be the very movement that fueled and provided a foundation for his burgeoning pro-women politics and a paradigm for his, literally, life-long social and political activism. The black women's club movement, moreover, introduced and exposed Du Bois, not simply to the womanist social theory and praxis of Frances Harper, Anna Julia Cooper, Josephine Ruffin, Ida B. Wells, and Mary Church Terrell—all major foundational figures in the black women's club movement—but it also introduced him to "the first truly national black organization that functioned with strength and unity": the National Association of Colored Women (Hine and Thompson, 1998, p. 180).

It was one of the great tragedies of Du Bois's personal history that his mother, Mary Silvina Burghardt Du Bois, died on March 23, 1885, approximately one month after her son's sixteenth birthday. In *W. E. B. Du Bois: Biography of a Race, 1868–1919*, the first volume of his monumental two-volume Pulitzer Prize-winning biography, David Levering Lewis (1993) paints a picture of the relationship between the "crippled" single-mother and precocious son as being "laconic" and financially troubled, but extremely caring and close: "They were a regular feature of town life, occasioning well-intentioned remarks about their mutual devotion. Willie was always 'a little surprised because people said how nice I was to my mother.' 'I just grew up that way. We were companions,' he said, pure and simple" (p. 30). Some time before her death, Mary Silvina suffered a paralytic stroke that "impaired her left leg or arm, or both," but even with her disabilities she "invested what was left of herself in Willie" (pp. 29–30). She continued to work, and with the help of her brother and some of Great Barrington's prominent citizens, she cared for her son until he graduated from high school, in 1884.

As Arnold Rampersad (1990) pointed out, in *The Art and Imagination of W. E. B. Du Bois*, "There can be little doubt that Du Bois's remarkable regard for women, especially black women, had its roots in his deep regard for his mother" (p. 4). With the death of his mother, Du Bois began to deepen his burgeoning womanist consciousness by becoming more involved in black women's social uplift efforts, and specifically the black women's club movement. The women of the black women's club movement became, in many senses, surrogate mothers for the now motherless and fatherless Du Bois. As a result, early in his long life he became keenly aware of the sacrifices and compromises that many black women made for black men, black children, and the overall Africana liberation struggle. Du Bois felt compelled to not only acknowledge the sacrifices and compromises that black women made for Africana freedom, but he was also motivated to expand his own and others' understanding of these sacrifices and compromises. One of the ways Du

Bois did this was by documenting and developing Africana women's social theory and political activism.

There is a subtle pro-womanist subtext that shades and colors Du Bois's social theory. It runs through his thought like a river cutting through the earth on its way to the ocean. Though his thought gives way at times to both the mythical and the mystical, and especially where black women are concerned, it can be said with no hyperbole and high-sounding words that the philosophical foundation of Du Bois's male-feminism/womanism was the black women's club movement. In fact, I would go so far to say that Du Bois's theories at many intervals are incomprehensible without serious consideration being given to the impact and influence of several of the central theorists of the black women's club movement on his thought throughout his long life. Secondly, and continuing this line of thinking, I would also suggest that the black women's club movement provided Du Bois with concrete and culturally grounded points of departure and paradigms for social organization, social and political activism, inter-organizational cooperation, radical journalism, critical education for Africana liberation, black womanhood, black motherhood, and the black family. Let us take a look, then, at what we could call the "roots" of Du Bois's anti-sexist radicalism.

THE BLACK WOMEN'S CLUB MOVEMENT, JOSEPHINE ST. PIERRE RUFFIN, AND THE ROOTS OF DU BOIS'S ANTI-SEXIST RADICALISM

Du Bois's pro-women politics neither begins nor ends with his 1920 publication, *Darkwater*. On the contrary, Cheryl Townsend Gilkes (1996) has asserted that as far back as his 1883 to 1885 articles for the *New York Globe*, Du Bois displayed "a sensitivity to the contributions of black women to community life" (p. 118). He advocated women's equality and engaged "women's issues" in the *Fisk Herald* in 1885, responding to an article on women's liberation by observing, "The column on woman's work is interesting, and a first rate woman's rights argument" (Du Bois, 1973, p. 5). After becoming the editor-in-chief of the *Fisk Herald* in 1887, Du Bois published a semi-autobiographical novella, *Tom Brown at Fisk*, which featured a female schoolteacher protagonist who exclaimed in the opening paragraph of the piece: "It's hard to be a woman, but a black one—!" (p. 6).

By 1892 he was publishing his "Harvard Daily Themes" in the *Courant*, "a weekly newspaper of women's rights, civil rights, and informed opinion," which was edited by the noted African American "militant suffragette," Josephine St. Pierre Ruffin (Lewis, 1993, p. 105; see also Arroyo, 1993; Fay,

1999). Ruffin would go on to found the Women's Era Club in 1893, and edit its newspaper, the *Women's Era* (Gunning, 1997; Perkins, 1997). She also co-organized a national convention of black women's clubs that would lead to the formation of the National Federation of Afro-American Women and, ultimately, the National Association of Colored Women.[19]

Although David Levering Lewis (1993) argues, "Nowhere does Du Bois suggest that Mrs. Ruffin's feminist politics influenced his own precocious views about the rights of women. Mary Silvina's son had already arrived at them independently by then, yet the distinguished personalities and articulate opinions he met in Charles Street [i.e., in Ruffin's house] may well have quickened and sharpened the positive views he had come to hold" (p. 105). Gilkes makes a strong counterclaim concerning the editorial relationship between Ruffin and the young Du Bois. According to Gilkes (1996), their editorial relationship "was highly significant," because it was Ruffin who introduced the young Du Bois to the world of the black women's club movement and to Ida B. Wells, another co-founder of the Woman's Era Club, and "a prime mover in the black women's club movement" (p. 118). In dialoguing with Ruffin and Wells, among other "clubbers," Du Bois observed firsthand African American social organization, political activism and, most importantly with regard to the present discussion: Africana women's liberation thought. Consequently, he developed an unusual sensitivity to African American women's sufferings and their contributions to American history, culture, and society in general, and African American history, culture, and community in specific (B. Aptheker, 1975; Griffin, 2000; Lemons, 2001; Lucal, 1996; McKay, 1985, 1990; Pauley, 2000; Yellin, 1973).

In fact, the influence of Ruffin in particular on Du Bois's thought should not be downplayed because, as Gilkes (1996) contends, "[i]t was Ruffin who provided the classic definition of a woman's movement from an African American perspective: she defined the black women's movement as a movement for the benefit of women and men, and she invited men to join women's work and struggles" (p. 118). In her address to the First National Conference of Colored Women, convened under her leadership and held in Boston, in 1895, Ruffin hit at the heart of the black women's club movement. Her remarks set the parameters and in several senses served as moral and sociopolitical guides for black women's club activities and social uplift efforts: from the National Association of Colored Women through to the National Council of Negro Women (Collier-Thomas, 1980, 1993; Salem, 1990, 1993; C. H. Wesley, 1984). Ruffin (1895) stated, in part:

> Our woman's movement is a woman's movement in that it is led and directed by women for the good of women and men, for the benefit of *all* humanity,

which is more than any one branch or section of it. We want, [and] we ask the active interest of our men, and, too, we are not drawing the color line; we are women, American women, as intensely interested in all that pertains to us as such as all other American women; we are not alienating or withdrawing, we are only coming to the front, willing to join any others in the same work and cordially inviting and welcoming any others to join us. (p. 14, emphasis in original)

Ruffin helped the young Du Bois understand the importance of not simply getting more men involved in the black women's club movement, but also of black men developing more critical, self-reflexive stances toward patriarchy and both white and black bourgeois thought and practices. Of all the things Du Bois learned from and admired about the black women of the club movement and some of their progressive white counterparts, it was, according to Gilkes (1996), "their ability to work together across class and color lines in spite of their disagreements" (p. 130). Clearly Ruffin intimates as much with her above contention, "we are not drawing the color line," and her assertion, "we are women, American women, as intensely interested in all that pertains to us as such as all other American women." A more socially and politically mature Du Bois would later employ many of the strategies and tactics, and also many of the members of the black women's club movement to build the Niagara Movement and, ultimately, the National Association for the Advancement of Colored People (NAACP).

It is far from a coincidence that two of the foundational figures of the black women's club movement contributed to the founding and initial formation of the NAACP: Mary Church Terrell and Ida B. Wells (Lewis, 1993, p. 391).[20] Further, Ruffin, politically active until the end of her life and always keeping a keen and critical eye on her surrogate son, Du Bois, helped to found the Boston branch of the NAACP (Arroyo, 1993). In fact, so enduring was Ruffin's influence on Du Bois (1968a) that half a century after their initial encounter he, in his last autobiography, *The Autobiography of W. E. B. Du Bois*, recalled:

Mrs. Ruffin of Charles Street, Boston . . . was a widow of the first colored judge appointed in Massachusetts, an aristocratic lady. . . . She began a national organization of colored women and published the *Courant*, a type of small colored weekly paper which was spreading over the nation. In this I published many of my Harvard daily themes. (p. 137)

Du Bois's commitment to women's rights, though full of contradictions, was consistent throughout his career. What many Du Bois scholars have overlooked is the simple, though central, fact that for Du Bois, women—and women of African descent in particular—were integral to democracy because, "Du Bois's vision" was one that "pointed to" and attempted to produce "a society that could confront, respect, and embrace the gifts of all" (Gilkes, 1996, p. 133). Observe how similarly Du Bois's radical democratic theory sounds against the backdrop of Ruffin's radical womanist dictum: "Our woman's movement is a woman's movement in that it is led and directed by women for the good of women and men, for the benefit of *all* humanity, which is more than any one branch or section of it." Du Bois's radical democratic theory has a deep, though sometimes subtle womanist dimension to it. A dimension that helps to highlight both its roots in the radical politics of the black women's club movement and also its relevance for developing a critical theory of contemporary society that is simultaneously anti-sexist and anti-racist, and utterly against the new forms of capitalism and colonialism.

Of the "three great revolutions" that Du Bois maintained that black women were to play a pivotal part in, in *Darkwater* the last "great" revolution was to be against economic exploitation—i.e., the new forms of capitalism and colonialism (Du Bois, 1969a). Du Bois (1995a) believed that "[t]he emancipation of man is the emancipation of labor and the emancipation of labor is the freeing of that basic majority of workers who are yellow, brown, and black" (p. 606). In "slavery," in "concubinage," as cooks, nurses, and washerwomen, Du Bois (1970b) recognized the significance of black women's work, stating: "economic independence is . . . the central fact in the struggle of women for equality" (p. 142). In fact, "the usual sentimental arguments against women at work were not brought forward in the case of Negro womanhood." This helps to highlight how black women's lived-experiences, their lived-actualities challenge not only patriarchal notions of "a woman's place," but more specifically black male and many non-African women's misconceptions about "a woman's place" (p. 142).

In brief, Du Bois's discourse, on deep and diverse levels, prefigures and provides a paradigm for the development of a radical anti-sexist dimension of Africana critical theory because it simultaneously sought black liberation *and* gender equality *and* the "economic emancipation" and "democratization of modern society" (Du Bois, 1985a, p. 181, 1995a, p. 615). Du Bois's women's liberation theory, inextricable from his critiques of racism, colonialism, capitalism, and Marxism, took into consideration the "subjugated" and/or "suppressed" knowledge of a particular social, historical, and cultural group or class, Africana women, and attempted to apply it toward the goal of human emancipation (see P. H. Collins, 1990, pp. 221–38). Nowhere is this more evident in Du Bois's anti-sexist social thought, and specifically with regard to black women in the U.S., than in his classic male anti-sexist manifesto, "The Damnation of Women."

"THE DAMNATION OF WOMEN":
DU BOIS'S MALE ANTI-SEXIST MANIFESTO

In his essay "The Damnation of Women," Du Bois (1995a) states that there are three "great causes" in the modern world to which every human being should devote special concern and careful consideration: "the problem of the color line," "the uplift of women," and "the peace movement" (p. 309). Black women, Du Bois sardonically remarked, "existed not for themselves, but for men," "[t]hey were not beings, they were relations and these relations were enfilmed [sic] with mystery and secrecy" (p. 299). Where the majority of his black male contemporaries conceded, "a woman's place is in the home," Du Bois did not associate femininity with fragility or domesticity. He was a consistent defender of black womanhood, criticizing both white supremacist and black masculinist myths and stereotypes where women of African descent were concerned. As discussed above, in his 1912 essay, "The Black Mother," Du Bois defended black women, and black motherhood in particular, against the race supremacist assaults and assumptions of both white men and white women. Three years later, a galled Du Bois called black men's open and uncritical acceptance of male supremacy into question. His brothers in black were thinking and doing the unpardonable: disenfranchising their sisters in black in much the same manner that whites were blacks, and the rich were the poor. Even if it meant becoming the laughingstock of the land, Du Bois (1995a) would, in the spirit of Frederick Douglass and Charles Lenox Remond, be disloyal to the patriarchal privileges and practices of "this man-ruled world" (p. 297).

In his classic 1915 *Crisis* essay, "Woman Suffrage," which is a defense of women's right to vote and pursue political office, Du Bois (1995a) took Howard University dean Kelly Miller to task for comments he made against woman suffrage and womanist political practice (pp. 297–98). Du Bois, an ardent advocate of women's rights and women's suffrage, stated that dean Miller and men of his ilk who argue that "the bearing and rearing of the young is a function which makes it practically impossible for women to take any large part in general, industrial and public affairs; that women are weaker than men; that women are adequately protected under man's suffrage; that no adequate results have appeared from woman suffrage and that office-holding by women is 'risky,'" are not only aping the assertions of white masculinists and supremacists, but also putting forward "ancient" arguments. From Du Bois's radical democratic woman-centered perspective, "The actual work of the world today depends more largely upon women than upon men" (p. 297).

Just as Du Bois, in *The Philadelphia Negro*, argued that "[t]he world was thinking wrong about race," in "Woman Suffrage" he intended to show Kelly

Miller and his colleagues that they were thinking wrong about gender ("the problem of gender"), and "the woman question" in particular (Du Bois, 1968a, p. 197; see also Du Bois, 1996b; Bay, 1998). He chided with his unique male-womanist wisdom: "The statement that woman is weaker than man is sheer rot: It is the same sort of thing that we hear about 'darker races' and 'lower classes.' Difference, either physical or spiritual, does not argue weakness or inferiority" (Du Bois, 1995a, p. 297). Here, by comparing masculinist sentiment with white supremacist and bourgeois ideology, Du Bois accentuates the interconnections between sexism, racism, and classism. Black men, then, who argue women's inferiority, wish to dominate and discriminate against women based on their differences from men. This, to Du Bois, is no different than the white racist theorist who theorizes black inferiority and subhumanity; and no different than the bourgeois thinker who theorizes the vices and vulgarities of urban underclass(es), and especially inner city youth.

The connection that Du Bois makes between sexism, racism, and classism also indicates that he was, to a certain extent, not only conscious but critical of the supposed gender neutrality and universality of men's patriarchal thought and practice. What is more, Du Bois's womanist thought in this instance demonstrates that he was aware that the black men who argue women's inferiority wish to dominate and discriminate against women based on their differences *not* from "men"—in some supposed general, neutral, or universal sense—but from *white* and *wealthy* men. "Men," as with "women," only exist in archetypal form, as pure classless and raceless entities, in the heads of established order intellectuals and in the one-dimensional, whitewashed books that they write.

Du Bois's womanist critical thought points to a set of subtle pre-reflective parenthetical signifiers (adjectives), which are subtextual markers included along with the purportedly neutral and universal terms (i.e., "man," "woman," "boy," and "girl"). So, in all actuality when Kelly Miller and other pro-patriarchal men argue against women's equality based on their perceived differences—read: deficiencies and deviations—from the supposed male norm, they are arguing against women's equality based on the *white* male as the archetype. Moreover, Miller and men of his ilk do not simply take the *white* male as the means by which to measure women's humanity (or lack thereof), but they also use the *wealthy* white male as the model male, as the universal embodiment of humanity.

The foregoing analysis reveals two things. First, that most men's worldview in white and male supremacist capitalist societies is simultaneously race-, gender-, and class-specific and hegemonic. And, secondly, the aforementioned helps to highlight the fact that though many black men may be deeply devoted to the struggle against white supremacy and for black liberation, without serious, sustained, and simultaneous struggle against racism *and* sexism *and* capitalism, black liberation will be nothing more than, as Fanon (1968) put it in *The Wretched of the Earth*, "a fancy-dress parade and the blare of the trumpets" (p. 147). The domination and discrimination would still be with us, part and parcel of our lived-experiences, and nothing will have changed except for the color (and class in some respects) of the oppressors. In Fanon's words: "There's nothing save a minimum of readaptation, a few reforms at the top, a flag waving: and down there at the bottom an undivided mass [of women], still living in the middle ages, endlessly marking time" (p. 147).

In "The Damnation of Women," as he invoked the names of the Haitian revolutionists Toussaint L'Ouverture and Jean Jacques Dessalines, Du Bois also called on Harriet Tubman, Sojourner Truth, and Mary Ann Shadd; quoted anonymously his contemporary Anna Julia Cooper; and made reference to Ida B. Wells (Du Bois, 1995a, pp. 306–7; see also Griffin, 2000; James, 1996b, 1997). Further, in an audacious turn of phrase, Du Bois placed the resistance activities of black women on par with those of black men, going so far as to recall Sojourner Truth's classic query to Frederick Douglass, "Frederick, *is God dead?*," when the male-womanist abolitionist, in a moment of desperation, declared that African Americans would have to fight for their freedom by force of arms. Douglass is reported to have stated: "It must come to blood; they [enslaved Africans] must fight for themselves, and redeem themselves, or it would never be done." Truth was apparently troubled, according to Harriet Beecher Stowe and a host of white writers, by Douglass's radical tenor and questioned his faith in God, who—as Stowe's recounting of the story goes—would guide African Americans to an imminent victory over slavery and white supremacy (Douglass, 1994, p. 719; Painter, 1996, pp. 160–163).

In recounting black history, Du Bois cast black women in revolutionary roles. The struggle against slavery and white supremacy was not simply waged by black men, but by black men *and* black women for all people of African descent and humanity as a whole. Du Bois (1995a) reminded his readers that although black women, those "long-suffering victims" and "burdened sisters," were "sweetly feminine," "unswervingly loyal," "desperately earnest" and "instinctively pure in body and soul," they were yet and still an "army" leading "not only a moral, but an economic revolution" (pp. 298, 308). Attempting to emphasize the strength and resilience of black women, Du Bois retorted:

No other women on earth could have emerged from the hell of force and temptation which once engulfed and still surrounds black women in America with half the modesty and womanliness that they retain. I have always felt like bowing myself before them in all abasement, searching to bring some tribute to these long-suffering victims, these burdened sisters of mine, whom the world, the wise, white world, loves to affront and ridicule and wantonly to insult. I have known the women of many lands and nations—I have known and seen and lived beside them, but none have I known more sweetly feminine, more unswervingly loyal, more desperately earnest, and more instinctively pure in body and in soul than the daughters of my black mothers. (pp. 311–12)

Keeping in mind our above discussion of Du Bois's efforts to counter racist claims concerning black womanhood, note here how he highlights "the wise, white world['s]" *black misogyny*. The "wise, white world" includes white men *and* white women. So, to speak of "the wise, white world['s]" *black misogyny* is to speak of both white men and white women's hatred and domination of, and discrimination against black women. In this instance, Du Bois's pro-womanist politics points to the ways in which race is gendered and gender is raced. Which, in plainer English and in other words, is to say that his black woman-centered social thought keeps a keen eye on the ways that the combination of white *and* male supremacy targets persons who are black *and* female in a manner and to a degree much different than it does those persons who are white and female or black and male. To be black in a white supremacist society, as Du Bois argued in *The Souls of Black Folk*, is indeed to be seen and approached more as a problem than a person. Further, to be black in such a society is to be perpetually plagued by that ever unasked question that is seemingly on the tip of every tongue at every turn: "How does it feel to be a problem?" (Du Bois, 1986a, p. 363).

To be a woman in a male supremacist society, as Carole Pateman (1988) put it in *The Sexual Contract,* is to be seen and treated as a semi-citizen, if women are seen and treated as sometime-citizens at all. It is an experience that affords few luxuries and little or no illusions about ones' socially supposed place and sex role, about men's power to discipline and punish women with impunity. However, to be a black woman in a white *and* male supremacist society, as Audre Lorde (1984) asserted in *Sister Outsider*, is to be seen and ever approached, not as one who is humanly different, but as one who is subhuman, who is humanly deviant and deficient. Black women in white and male supremacist societies experience different, perhaps deeper forms of racist and sexist domination and discrimination because they register as the antithesis, as the combined embodiment of the negation of both whiteness and maleness.[21] To acknowledge *black misogyny*, then, is to simply say as Lorde (1984) did, "Some problems we share as women, some we do not" (p. 119). It is to talk of that long taboo topic in feminist and womanist theory and praxis revolving around the difference(s) that race, racism, and anti-racist struggle historically have made and continue currently to make in the lived-experiences and life-worlds of women of color, and women of African descent in particular.

Du Bois's women's liberation theory is further distinguished by its emphasis on the political economy of racism and sexism in white and male supremacist capitalist societies. Early in his career, Du Bois noted the connections between capitalism, racism, and sexism (Gilkes, 1996; Lucal, 1996, McKay 1985, 1990). This is extremely unique when one considers the rigid racist and sexist socio-theoretical framework that most turn-of-the-twentieth century social theorists (male and female) were operating out of. In "Grounding with My Sisters: Patriarchy and the Exploitation of Black Women," Manning Marable (1983) maintains:

> Black social history, as it has been written to date, has been profoundly patriarchal. The sexist critical framework of American white history has been accepted by black male scholars; the reconstruction of our past, the reclamation of our history from the ruins, has been an enterprise wherein women have been too long segregated. Obligatory references are generally made to those "outstanding sisters" who gave some special contribution to the liberation of the "black man." Even these token footnotes probably do more harm than good, because they reinforce the false belief that the most oppressed victim of white racial tyranny has been *the black man*. . . . From the dawn of the slave trade until today, U.S. capitalism was both racist and sexist. The super-exploitation of black women became a permanent feature in American social and economic life, because sisters were assaulted simultaneously as workers, as blacks, and as women." (p. 70, emphasis in original)

Du Bois's anti-racist and anti-sexist socio-theoretical framework was one of the first to critically engage black women's simultaneous social statuses "as workers, as blacks, and as women." Increasingly he focused on black women's role in the "economic revolution," stating, our "black women toil and toil hard," they "are a group of workers, fighting for their daily bread like men; independent and approaching economic freedom" (Du Bois, 1995a, p. 308). It was not enough for black liberationists to struggle against white supremacy; it was not enough for women liberationists to struggle against male supremacy; and it was not enough for Marxists and other leftists to struggle against capitalist exploitation. What was needed was a critical conjunctive socio-theoretical framework that took into consideration each of the aforementioned forms of domination and discrimination. For Du Bois, a radical social theorist, a real revolutionist has the onerous task of critiquing society as a whole, not simply the parts of it that most inhibit and encumber the theorist's particular race, gender, and/or class. In "The Damnation of Women," Du Bois turned his reader's attention to the plight of black women, thus putting into principled practice his admonition that a radical theorist critique society as a whole, not simply selected parts of it which hinder and harm the theorist and their kin and kith.

CONCLUSION: DU BOIS AND (AFRICANA) CRITICAL WOMEN'S LIBERATION THEORY

Du Bois seems to have possessed the ability to synthesize disparate discourses into his own somewhat sophisticated critical social theory. For instance, it is interesting to point out that though he initially drew from elite black women's work that cast bourgeois black women in leadership roles, work such as that of Anna Julia Cooper and some of the members of the black women's club movement, he continued to deepen and develop his concept(s) of class(ism) and the political economy of race(ism) and sex(ism). Ultimately, Du Bois developed a critical socio-theoretical framework that transcended and transgressed, if you will, the gender (male) and class (bourgeois) elitism of his younger years. Critically comparing Cooper and Du Bois's social theory, Joy James (1997) helps to drive this point home:

> Cooper's gender politics revolved around poor black women's struggles and elite black women's agency. But Du Bois's evolving class politics allowed him to, theoretically, attribute greater agency to *poor* black women workers and laborers. Du Bois's later writings surpass Cooper's 1892 work in democratizing agency. Cooper repudiates masculine elites, or privileged black male intellectuals. However, her repudiations do not extend to feminine elites, or privileged black female intellectuals. Cooper countered the dominance of male elites with that of female elites and remained somewhat oblivious of the limitations of her caste and class-based ideology. Cooper's 1892 book [*A Voice from the South*] failed to argue that the intellectual and leadership abilities of black women laborers equaled those of black women college graduates, whereas Du Bois's later revisions of the Talented Tenth included nonelite black women and men. In this respect, we see that Du Bois's maturing politics were less hampered by the cultural conservatism of bourgeois notions of respectability for (black) women. (p. 45, emphasis in original)

It is not my intention here to (re)interpret and (re)inscribe Du Bois as some sort of super anti-sexist social theorist. I am well aware of the ways that an anti-sexist male perspective in a male supremacist society is not as suspect as an anti-sexist female perspective—though I would concede that an anti-sexist male perspective *is* suspect to a certain degree and that gender progressive males are marginalized and ostracized in such a social world, though they have never been marginalized and ostracized to the extent to which (anti-sexist) women have historically been in the said social world. However, and in all intellectual honesty, an anti-sexist male (with the most minute amount of academic credentials and/or institutional affiliation) can quickly become, in the minds of the ruling race/gender/class and their media machines in a male supremacist social world, an authoritative anti-sexist voice of reason. This, of course, is similar in many senses to the ways that white "race traitors" and white anti-racists are exalted as the definitive voices of anti-racist reason and radical anti-racist political practice in white supremacist society. Du Bois's discourse destabilizes and resists efforts to position him purely (and, disingenuously I think) as "race man," or "male-feminist"/"male-womanist," or "Marxist," or "Pan-Africanist," or "black nationalist," or even "integrationist," because—as I stated above—he continuously deepened and developed the basic concepts and categories of his socio-theoretical framework and synthesized disparate discourses into his own original critical theory of contemporary society.

To read "The Conservation of Races," *The Souls of Black Folk*, *Darkwater*, and *Dusk of Dawn* is to read not merely studies in race, but also studies in class and caste. To read *Black Reconstruction*, *Color and Democracy*, and *The World and Africa* is not simply to read studies in race, caste, and class, but also studies in Pan-Africanism and anti-colonialism. And, finally, when "The Damnation of Women," "The Work of Negro Women in Society," "The Black Mother," "Suffering Suffragettes," "Hail Columbia!," "The Burden of Black Women" and "Sex and Racism" are read, what one is reading are not just studies in race and class theory, but also critical analyses of gender domination and discrimination, and especially as these interlocking systems of oppression affect the life-worlds and lived-experiences of black women. It is the multidimensionality of Du Bois's discourse that makes it difficult for opportunistic interpreters to appropriate and (re)articulate his thought and texts in a monodimensional manner. Moreover, it is this same multidimensionality in Du Bois's discourse that provides paradigmatic examples of some of the ways male anti-sexist social theorists can simultaneously avoid being appropriated as "the" authoritative and most rational voices of gender justice, and connect critiques of sexism with those of racism and classism.

If male anti-sexist social theorists openly and honestly dialogue with, document and disseminate the community and campus work of female anti-sexist social theorists, then it will be very hard for male supremacist media machines to project the gender progressive male voice as the definitive voice of gender justice. Critically engaging women's liberation theory and practice by actively participating in the said theory and practice, male anti-sexist social theorists can and should expand the range and use(s) of women's liberation theory and other anti-sexist social theory to include the work of both women *and* men who sought and are seeking gender justice. Male anti-sexist social theorists must simultaneously (re)claim and (re)construct male anti-sexist gender justice, and women's liberation theory and praxis traditions, and share the knowledge they discover and create with gender justice-seeking women and men. In fact, one of the special tasks of anti-sexist men is to encourage our brother-friends to critically examine ways that they embrace patriarchy and perpetuate and exacerbate sexism and female domination and discrimination. Male anti-sexist social theorists and activists are long overdue in articulating to sexist men the violent psychological and physical consequences of male supremacist thought and behavior, and how, as quiet as it is kept, this thought and behavior not only robs women of their human and civil rights, but also often causes serious life-threatening conflicts and contradictions among men.

What I am calling for here is for anti-sexist men to unflinchingly encourage sexist men to self-consciously confront and correct their sexist socialization and sexist thought and behavior. Anti-sexist men must embrace the revolutionary responsibility of providing new paradigms for modern masculinity. We must show the world, and especially women, our sister-friends, that patriarchal, phallocentric, militaristic and misogynistic masculinity are not definitive practices or modes of masculinity but deformations and destructions of masculinity. Masculinity, henceforth and forevermore, must be predicated on moral practice. What it means to be a "man" must begin to be bound up with males' embrace of the ethical obligation to end female domination and discrimination and their promotion of women's liberation and radical anti-sexist social reorganization.

Africana male anti-sexist social theorists and activists must be bold enough and brave enough to take our cue from our anti-sexist forefathers, men ("father figures") like Charles Lenox Remond, Frederick Douglass, and W. E. B. Du Bois, among others, who—as I have endeavored to illustrate above—possessed problematic but nonetheless progressive stances on gender justice and, specifically, Africana women's liberation. However, and even more than turning to the anti-sexist thought and practice traditions of our forefathers, anti-sexist men of African descent must learn the many lessons our freedom-fighting foremothers' legacies of liberation thought and practice have to teach. This impulse to learn radical life-saving and life-enhancing lessons from our foremothers must also extend to the thought, texts, and practices of anti-sexist Africana women in our present age. A common characteristic of both black feminist and womanist discourse is the notion that theory and practice must simultaneously speak to the special needs of women of African descent and the emancipatory aspirations of African people nationally and internationally. This means, then, that (most) modern black feminists and womanists do not adhere to the constraints of Western European constructions of gender and/or sex roles. The only "role" women and men of African descent have is that of black revolutionaries: radical anti-racist, anti-sexist, and anti-imperialist rebels and renegades.

NOTES

1. For a discussion of Du Bois's philosophy of social science and social scientific methodology, see Du Bois (1978, 1996b), Anderson and Zuberi (2000), Bulmer (1991), Burbridge (1999), Dennis (1975), Edelin (1981), B. S. Edwards (2001), Everage (1979), K .K. Gaines (1996), Gilkes (1996), Gordon (2000b, 2000c), Green (1973), A. Johnson (1949), A. J. Jones (1976), Juguo (2001), Katz and Sugrue (1998), Larue (1971), McDaniel (1998), Neal (1984), Outlaw (2000), A. L. Reed (1997), Rudwick (1969, 1974), C. M. Taylor (1981), E. Wright (2001) and Zamir (1995).

2. In his introduction to *One-Dimensional Man*, Herbert Marcuse (1964) argues that, "[s]ocial theory is concerned with the historical alternatives which haunt the established society as subversive tendencies and forces" (pp. xliii–xliv) Part of the task of a critical theory of contemporary society, then, lies in its ability to critique society "in light of its used and unused or abused capabilities for improving the human condition" (p. xlii). When I write of "ethical," "historical," and/or "radical" alternatives here, I am advocating new modes of human existence and interaction predicated on practices rooted in the realities of our past, present, and hoped-for future. I am following in the footsteps of one of the great impresarios of the Black Arts movement, Larry Neal (1989), who taught us that one of the most urgent tasks of radical artists and intellectuals is to offer "visions of a liberated future." In offering *ethical alternatives* to the established order, critical theorists highlight and accent right and wrong thought and action, perhaps the single most important issue in the field of moral philosophy (Frey and Wellman, 2003; Lafollette, 1999, 2003; Singer, 1993; Sterba, 1998). The critique of racism, sexism, and colonialism register, or rather *should* register right alongside the critique of capitalism in critical theorists' conceptual universe(s), because part of the established order's ideology and, in particular, part of its political and economic agenda involves domination and discrimination based on race, gender, and capitalist and/or colonial class/caste. Anti-racist, anti-sexist, and anti-colonial thought, practices, and social movements help to provide *historical alternatives* that Marx's and Marxists' criticisms of capitalism, to date, have not been able to adequately translate into reality (Aronson, 1995; Best, 1995; Callari, Cullenberg and Biewener, 1995; Gottlieb, 1992; Nelson and Grossberg, 1988; Magnus and Cullenberg, 1995). In fact, many former and neo-Marxists openly acknowledge that "classical" Marxism privileged class and gave special priority to economic issues which enabled it to easily overlook and/or omit the multiple issues arising from the socio-historical realities of racism, sexism, and colonialism in modern history, culture, politics, and society (Agger, 1992, 1998; A. Y. Davis, 1981, 1989, 1998; Dussel, 1985, 1995, 1996; Ingram, 1990, 1995; Kellner, 1989, 1995; Kuhn and Wolpe, 1978; Marsh, 1995, 1999, 2001; Matustik, 1998; C. W. Mills, 1987, 1997, 1998, 2003; Nelson and Grossberg, 1988; Sargent, 1981; Vogel, 1983; Weinbaum, 1978; West, 1988, 1993a). What I am calling for here, though, is not a neglect of class and the role that political economy plays in contemporary culture and society, but rather the placing of critical class theory in dialogue and on equal theoretical terms with critical race theory, women's liberation theory, and postcolonial theory in order to develop a broader-based, polyvocal radical political theory of contemporary society. The sites and

sources of oppression in contemporary culture and society are multiple and do not emerge from the economy and the crises of capitalism alone. New critical theory must take into consideration the long neglected or often overlooked new and novel forces and forms of domination and discrimination. Africana critical theory is an effort aimed at chronicling continental and diasporan African radicals and revolutionaries' contributions to a critical theory of contemporary society.

3. On Du Bois and his "race man" reputation, see Carby (1998).

4. Some may find Guy-Sheftall's (re)construction of Du Bois as a male-"feminist" troubling. However, as Hazel Carby (1998) contends, it should be held in mind that Du Bois means "many things to many people" (p. 14). He is one of the many male and female "rediscovered ancestors" whose thought and texts are currently being engaged by contemporary theorists "in response to the needs of various agendas," academic and otherwise (p. 14). Where Guy-Sheftall (1990) and McKay (1990) read Du Bois as a male-"feminist," Joy James (1996b, 1997) proffered a "pro-feminist" Du Bois. More recently, Gary Lemons (2001) argued that Du Bois's pro-women's rights and women's suffrage work can actually be read as both "black feminist" *and* "womanist." It is not the intention of this chapter to argue whether Du Bois was a "womanist" or a "feminist"—two terms, it should be pointed out, that were not *en vogue* in Africana intellectual arenas until after his death. The primary purpose here is to discover what implications Du Bois's pro-women's rights and women's suffrage work has for the development of an anti-racist, anti-sexist, anti-capitalist, and anti-colonial critical theory of contemporary society. Therefore, this study will draw from the women's liberation theory of a wide range of women *and* men of African descent who self-describe and self-define themselves as "womanists," "Africana womanists," "black feminists," and "African feminists," among other nomenclature (see hooks, 1984, 2000b; Hudson-Weems, 1998b, 1998c, 2001a; Nnaemeka, 1998).

5. My commentary on Du Bois's "male-feminism," "pro-feminist politics" "womanism" and/or, as I prefer, his women's liberation theory or anti-sexist critical social theory, is primarily drawn from "A Woman" (1893), "The Work of Negro Women in Society" (1902), "The Woman" (1911), "The Black Mother" (1912), "Suffering Suffragettes" (1912), "Suffrage Workers" (1912), "Votes for Women" (1912), "Hail Columbia!" (1913), "The Burden of Black Women" (1914), "Woman Suffrage" (1915), "Votes for Women" (1917), "The Damnation of Women" (1920), "The Freedom of Womanhood" (1924), "So the Girl Marries" (1928), "The Vision of Phillis the Blessed: An Allegory of Negro American Literature in the Eighteenth and Nineteenth Centuries" (1941), "Sex and Racism" (1957), and "Greetings to Women" (1959). See Du Bois (1980, 1982a, 1982b, 1983, 1985a, 1986a, 1986c, 1995, 1996a). I have also consulted several secondary sources, among them, B. Aptheker (1975), Diggs (1974), Gilkes (1996), Griffin (2000), J. A. James (1996b, 1997), Lemons (2001), Lucal (1996), McKay (1985, 1990), Pauley (2000), and Yellin (1973).

6. With regard to Frankfurt School critical theory, Erich Fromm and Herbert Marcuse incorporated aspects of what could loosely be termed "feminist theory" into their articulations of a critical theory of contemporary society. However, neither theorist was consistent nor ever fully developed a feminist and/or anti-sexist dimension of their respective theories of social change. Though Fromm's inchoate socialist-feminist

thinking by far surpasses that of Marcuse prior to the 1960s, it is important to observe Marcuse's efforts in the last decade of his life to take a "feminist turn," if you will, and to merge Marxism with feminism, among other elements of 1960s radical social thought and political practice. See, for example, Fromm's "The Theory of Mother Right and Its Relevance for Social Psychology," "Sex and Character," "Man-Woman," and "The Significance of Mother Right for Today," and Marcuse's "Dear Angela," *Counterrevolution and Revolt*, and "Marxism and Feminism" (Fromm, 1947, 1955, 1970; Marcuse, 1971, 1972a, 1974). For critical commentary on these thinkers' pro-feminist thought, see P. Mills (1987), Funk (1982), and Kellner (1984, 1989, 1992). And for further feminist critiques of classical and contemporary Frankfurt School-based critical theory, see Benhabib (1986, 1992), Fraser (1989, 1991), and Meehan (1995). More than any other major Frankfurt School critical theorist—Theodor Adorno, Max Horkheimer, Walter Benjamin, and Jürgen Habermas—my conception of critical theory has been indelibly influenced by Herbert Marcuse, whose critical theory increasingly incorporated and openly exhibited the influence of Africana liberation theory (Martin Luther King Jr., Malcolm X, Frantz Fanon, and the Black Panthers), Latin American liberation theory (Che Guevara and Fidel Castro), and women's liberation theory (Rosa Luxemburg and Angela Davis) (see Marcuse, 1969, pp. 7, 46–47, 79–91; 1970a, pp. 82–108; 1972a). Though Marcuse never dialogued with Africana, Latin American, and women's liberation theory with the depth and detail which he did European and European American (male) theory, and considering the fact that his approach to the life-worlds and lived-experiences of people of color was thoroughly shot through with the accoutrements of Eurocentricism—Marcuse (1972a, pp. 9, 29) employed labels and language such as, "backward capitalist countries" and "barbarian civilization[s]"—there may, yet and still, be much in his social thought that could be of use to Africana and other critical theorists of color (see Marcuse, 1964, 1969, 1970a, 1972a).

7. For treatments of male-feminism, and black male-feminism or womanism in particular, see Adu-Poku (2001), Awkward (2000), Byrd and Guy-Sheftall (2001), Carbado (1999), Digby (1998), Douglass (1992, 1999), Jardine and Smith (1987), Lemons (1997, 2001) and Sterba (2000). And, concerning Du Bois's assertion that women receive "equal pay for equal work," it is interesting to note that this claim lies at the heart of modern Marxist feminist discourse, and especially the "comparable worth" theorists' work. See, for example, Amott and Matthaei (1984), Barrett (1980), Feldberg (1984), Fox (1980), Guettel (1974), Kuhn and Wolpe (1978), Malos (1980), and Mullaney (1983).

8. Nellie McKay, Gary Lemons, and Hazel Carby each bemoan the fact that there is a strong tendency in Du Bois studies to read him primarily as a "race man" and downplay his "feminist" and/or "womanist" discourse. In her essay "The Souls of Black Women Folk in the Writings of W. E. B. Du Bois," McKay (1990) claims that Du Bois was one of very few black men who wrote "feminist autobiography": "More than any other black man in our history, his three autobiographies [*Darkwater*, *Dusk of Dawn*, and *The Autobiography of W. E. B. Du Bois*] demonstrate that black women have been central to the development of his intellectual thought" (pp. 229, 231). McKay, who is a literary theorist and critic, argues that one of the reasons that so

many Du Bois scholars read him as a "race man" is because they often overlook his "more creative, less sociological works, where most of his thoughts on women and his own fundamental spirituality are expressed" (p. 230). "Few people, even those who have spent years reading and studying Du Bois," quips McKay, "know that he wrote five novels and published a volume of poetry" (p. 231). In "'When and Where [We] Enter': In Search of a Feminist Forefather—Reclaiming the Womanist Legacy of W. E. B. Du Bois," Lemons (2001) laments: Du Bois's "womanist activism remains to be fully claimed by contemporary Black men, as he continues to be viewed primarily as a 'race man'" (p. 72). What perplexes Lemons is the fact that the critics who elide and erase Du Bois's women's liberation work do not simply do Du Bois a disservice, but rob contemporary men, and men of African descent in particular, of an Africana male *anti-sexist* role model. According to Lemons, "not only" was Du Bois's "conception of anti-racist resistance feminist-inspired, his worldview was profoundly influenced by Black women" (p. 73). Finally, in the first chapter of her book, *Race Men*, "The Souls of Black Men," Hazel Carby (1998) offers contemporary academics and political activists a deconstruction of Du Bois as "race man" that acknowledges that he "advocated equality for women and consistently supported feminist causes" (p. 12). Carby, who asserts that it is not her intention to claim that Du Bois was "a sexist male individual," is not, however, as concerned with Du Bois's "male-feminist" thought—though she gives it a highly critical treatment—as with many black male intellectuals' erasure and omission of his feminist thought from their discourse on Du Bois and their obsessive concerns with "the reproduction of Race Men" (pp. 12, 25). She states: "If, as intellectuals and as activists, we are committed, like Du Bois, to struggles for liberation and democratic egalitarianism, then surely it is not contradictory also to struggle to be critically aware of the ways in which *ideologies of gender* have undermined our egalitarian visions in the past and continue to do so in the present" (p. 12, my emphasis). Carby's caveat, like the cautions of McKay and Lemons, essentially asks that we be cognizant of not only the "ideologies of gender" in the present, but also the "ideologies of gender" of the past, and how this specific species of ideology may have influenced and/or, more than likely, indeed did influence the ways our intellectual ancestors theorized about this or that issue. In other words, we must make ourselves and others critically conscious of sexist sentiment in both classical and contemporary Africana liberation thought and practices. My work here, then, registers as an effort to simultaneously deepen and develop the anti-sexist aspects of Africana critical theory, and an attempt to move beyond one-dimensional interpretations of Du Bois which downplay the multidimensionality of his thought and texts. It is important here to note that because of the richness and wide range and reach of Du Bois's thought, within Du Bois studies there are various research areas and agendas—for example, history, philosophy, social theory, politics, economics, aesthetics, religion, education, and so forth. Depending on one's intellectual orientation and academic training and discipline, his thought and texts may serve a multiplicity of purposes and may be approached from a wide array of discursive directions. Needless to say, my interpretations of Du Bois have been deeply influenced by my training in and trek through Africana studies, and specifically Africana philosophy, social theory, and radical politics.

9. Collins's contentions here are right in line with the arguments of many of the major feminist standpoint theorists: Nancy Harstock's "The Feminist Standpoint: Developing the Ground for a Specifically Feminist Historical Materialism" and Sara Ruddick's "Maternal Thinking as a Feminist Standpoint," immediately come to mind. However, what distinguishes Collins's standpoint theory from those of Harstock and Ruddick is her emphasis on race and the realities of racism in the life-worlds of women of color, and women of African descent in particular. For further discussion, see P. H. Collins (1998, 2000), Harstock (1995), and Ruddick (1999).

10. For Africana womanist, black feminist, and/or feminist discussions of the intersection and interconnections of race, gender, and class, see Awkward (2000), Bambara (1970), Bobo (2001), Butler and Walter (1991), Busby (1992), Christian (1985, 1989, 1994), P. H. Collins (1993, 1998, 2000), A. Y. Davis (1981, 1989, 1998), Dill (1979, 1983), Dove (1998a, 1998b), Guy-Sheftall (1990, 1995), hooks (1981, 1984, 1989, 1990, 1991, 1995, 2000a), Hudson-Weems (1995, 1997, 1998a, 1998b, 2000), Hull, Scott and Smith (1982), James and Busia (1993), J. A. James (1996a, 1996b, 1997, 1999), James and Sharpley-Whiting (2000), Lorde (1984, 1988), Marsh-Lockett (1997), Nnaemeka (1998), B. Smith (1983, 1998), Terborg-Penn, Harley, and Rushing (1987), Zack (1997, 2000), and Zack, Shrage and Sartwell (1998). Black feminist/womanist historians have also engaged the overlapping nature of race, gender, and class in the lives of women of African descent. A few of the most noteworthy major studies are: Giddings (1984), Hine (1990), Hine, King and Reed (1995), Hine and Thompson (1998), J. Jones (1985), Noble (1978), and D. G. White (1999).

11. For a discussion, consult Angela Davis's (1995) essay, "Reflections on the Black Woman's Role in the Community of Slaves," which remains one of the best introductions to African American women's existential universe during enslavement. In "Sexism and the Black Female Slave Experience," and in *Ain't I a Woman* generally, bell hooks (1981) provides a provocative and penetrating analysis of sexual stereotypes and racial myth making that were/are continually created in white and male supremacist efforts to socio-politically control and "steer" black women away from the sites and sources of power, and also the people in/with power away from black women's lived-experiences and life-worlds (pp. 15–49). Patricia Hill Collins (2000) also comments on sexual stereotypes and racial myth-making, and particularly with regard to "the politics of the maternal" in "Mammies, Matriarchs, and Other Controlling Images" (pp. 69–96). She too is critical of white and male supremacist efforts to socio-politically control and "steer" Africana women and has put forward a blistering critique in "The More Things Change, the More They Stay the Same: African American Women and the New Politics of Containment" (P. H. Collins, 1998, pp. 11–43). In a similar spirit, Hammond (1997) and Towns (1974) offer a couple of the best critical genealogies of the mythologization of black women's sexuality. And finally, Joy James (1999), in "Depoliticizing Representations: Sexual-Racial Stereotypes," critiques some of the ways Africana women's radicalism (during and after enslavement) has been downplayed because of the over-sexualization, "mammification," and "bitchification" of black women in modern mass media and print (pp. 123–50).

12. For a discussion of the "jeopardy" theses, see Frances Beale's (1995) "Double Jeopardy: To Be Black and Female" and Deborah King's (1995) "Multiple Jeopardy, Multiple Consciousness: The Context of Black Feminist Ideology."

13. Each of the aforementioned essays can be found in Du Bois (1995a), with the exception of "The Work of Negro Women in Society," which was originally published in the *Spelman Messenger* in February 1902 and is included in Du Bois (1982a, pp. 139–44). For a more detailed list of Du Bois's work on women, women's rights, and women's suffrage, amongst other black feminist and/or Africana womanist issues, see note #5.

14. For biographical, political, and intellectual explorations of Harper's life and legacy, see Boyd (1994), Carby (1987), Collier-Thomas (1997), Foster (1993), Giddings (1984), Graham (1973, 1986), Greer (1952), Hine and Thompson (1998), and D. G. White (1999). The claim that it is "highly plausible" that Harper influenced, however indirectly, the development of Du Bois's women's liberation theory is based on Jesse Michael Lang's (1992) "Anticipations of the Booker T. Washington–W. E. B. Du Bois Dialectic in the Writings of Frances E. W. Harper, Ida B. Wells, and Anna Julia Cooper."

15. Gatens (1991), Grimshaw (1986), Lloyd (1984), Okin (1992), Pateman (1988, 1989), Nagl-Docekal (1998), and Tuana (1992) provide a few of the more salutary and sustained feminist critiques of the Western social contract tradition, while Boxill (1992), Lawson (1992), Lott (1998), McGary and Lawson (1992), McGary (1999), C. W. Mills (1997, 1998), Outlaw (1983a, 1983b, 1987, 1995, 1996a), and West (1982, 1988a, 1989, 1993a) offer some of the more noteworthy Africana (male) critiques of both contractarianism and Western social and political philosophy in general.

16. For critical engagements of Cooper's intellectual biography, women's liberation theory, and philosophy of education, see Alexander (1995), Baker-Fletcher (1991, 1994), Gabel (1982), Hutchinson (1981, 1993) and K. Johnson (2000). Further, for a fuller discussion of what Harper and I are referring to when we write of the "white men in mobs . . . 'lynch[ing], burn[ing], and tortur[ing]' their black fellow 'countrymen'" (I take her to include black women, their fellow countrywomen, here as well), see: Angela Y. Davis (1998), "Violence Against Women and the Ongoing Challenge to Racism," among her many other writings on "racialized punishment" and the criminalization of people of color, collected in *The Angela Y. Davis Reader*; Joy James (1996a, 1997), "Erasing the Spectacle of Racialized State Violence," in *Resisting State Violence*, and "On Racial Violence and Democracy," in *Transcending the Talented Tenth*; Manning Marable's (1983) classic, "The Meaning of Racist Violence in Late Capitalism," in *How Capitalism Underdeveloped Black America*; and, by far the best study on this subject to date, Herbert Shapiro's (1988) *White Violence and Black Response: From Reconstruction to Montgomery*. Du Bois, of course, wrote a great deal concerning white violence, both physical and psychological, and the need for both black self-defensive violence and non-violence. See, for example: *John Brown* (1909), "The Souls of White Folk" (1910), "Cowardice" (1916), "The Massacre of East St. Louis" (1917), "Let Us Reason Together" (1919), *Darkwater* (1920), "A University Course in Lynching" (1923), "Mob Tactics" (1927), *Black Reconstruction* (1935),

Black Folk Then and Now (1939), *Color and Democracy: Colonies and Peace* (1945), *African in Battle Against Colonialism, Racism, and Imperialism* (1960), and *Against Racism* (1985a). For a further discussion, see Du Bois (1939, 1945, 1960, 1962, 1970c, 1971a, 1972a, 1972b, 1983, 1985a).

17. Here Du Bois is hinting at his long-held position, which Guy-Sheftall (1995) terms a "progressive stance," that maintains that black women should have the right to choose motherhood as opposed to having it forced upon them by white and/or male supremacists' social standards (p. 12). His most developed statement on this issue is "Black Folk and Birth Control" (1932), in which he states that African Americans, with the aid of "the American Birth Control League and other agencies," have a "difficult and insistent problem" before them as to discerning the best method by which to spread "among Negroes an intelligent and clearly recognized concept of proper birth control, so that the young people can marry, have companionship and natural health, and yet not have children until they are able to take care of them" (Du Bois, 1982b, pp. 320–21). Du Bois, like many African Americans during his long lifespan, "want[ed] the black race to survive" (p. 321). However, he was quick to offer a caveat: "[We] must learn that among human races and groups, as among vegetables, quality and not mere quantity really counts" (p. 321). His argument was that during enslavement "every incentive was furnished to raise the largest number of children possible," this, of course, was in the best interest of the white ruling race/class, as they would then have more workers and, thus, more wealth (p. 320). But in the post-emancipation period, Du Bois observed, African Americans had to reclaim and reconstruct family and extended family traditions that were conducive to their new social situations and circumstances. Part of Du Bois's argument was predicated on economic considerations— keep in mind that he was writing during the height of the so-called "Great Depression." But other aspects of Du Bois's argument rest on a radical cultural philosophy that privileged African American social development and cultural survival. According to Du Bois, African Americans must not be fooled by "the fallacy of numbers," they must think practically and take into consideration the historical and cultural context in which their children will be born (p. 321). African American children will perish or prosper based on their parents' preparation and maturation: cultural, social, political, educational, economic, and so forth.

18. For a provocative exploration of the impact of enslavement on black mothers' moral vision, see Cynthia Willet's *Maternal Ethics and Other Slave Moralities* (1995). And for an excellent study that accents some of the issues black women have historically faced and continue currently to face with regard to the exploitation and suppression of their sexuality, see Evelynn Hammond's, "Toward a Genealogy of Black Female Sexuality" (1997). Further, for critical discussions of some of the simultaneously racist and sexist myths and stereotypes about black women that Du Bois was attempting to offset with his womanist work during this period, see perhaps the best book-length sources on the subject: Beverly Guy-Sheftall, *Daughters of Sorrow: Attitudes Toward Black Women, 1880–1920* (1990), Jacqueline Jones, *Labor of Love, Labor of Sorrow: Black Women, Work and the Family from Slavery to the Present* (1985), and Patricia Morton, *Disfigured Images: The Historical Assault on Afro-American Women* (1991).

19. For further discussion of the history and evolution of the black women's club movement, from the National Federation of Afro-American Women to the National Association of Colored Women, see Cash (1986, 2001), E. L. Davis (1996), Dickson (1982), Dublin, Arias and Carreras (2003), Giddings (1984), Hendricks (1998), E. B. Higginbotham (1993), Hine and Thompson (1998), Knupfer (1996), Miller (2001), Perkins (1981, 1997), Salem (1990, 1993), Shaw (1991), C. H. Wesley (1984), and D. G. White (1999).

20. For further discussion of Wells and Terrell, see Hendricks (1993), Holt (1982), B. W. Jones (1990, 1993), McMurry (1998), Peebles-Wilkins and Aracelis (1990), Royster (1997), Schechter (2001), Sterling (1979, 1984), Terrell (1932, 1996), M. I. Thompson (1990), Townes (1989), and Wells (1969, 1970, 1991, 1993, 1995).

21. In "Sex, Race, and the Matrices of Desire in an Anti-Black World," the Caribbean philosopher, Lewis Gordon (1997b), argues that the normative desire in an anti-black world is to avoid "*being* the black and feminized," because "in such a world a rational person wants to be white and masculine" (p. 77, emphasis in original). Why, one may ask? In a word, an "anti-black world is also a misogynist world" but we must bear in mind, "a misogynist world is not necessarily an anti-black one" on account of the mobile, reversible, and unstable nature of intra-racial power relations among white males and females (p. 76). What this means is that an anti-black world is almost inherently an anti-woman world. White and masculine are positive socio-political variables in such a world. When this line of thinking is taken to its extreme white and masculine are combined and inextricable and, for all practical purposes, white *equals* masculine and masculine *equals* white. Therefore, those farthest from *being* white and masculine in a white and male supremacist society—i.e., black women—almost invariably experience and endure deeper and comparably different forms of domination and discrimination than both their black male and white female counterparts.

Chapter Six

Conclusion: Du Bois, the Problems of the Twenty-First Century, and the Reconstruction of Critical Social Theory

"In the folds of this European civilization I was born and shall die, imprisoned, conditioned, depressed, exalted and inspired. Integrally a part of it and yet, much more significant, one of its rejected parts; one who expressed in life and action and made vocal to many, a single whirlpool of social entanglement and inner psychological paradox, which always seem to me more significant for the meaning of the world today than other similar and related problems.

Little indeed did I do, or could I conceivably have done, to make this problem or to loose it. Crucified on the vast wheel of time, I flew round and round with the Zeitgeist, waving my pen and lifting faint voices to explain, expound and exhort; to see, foresee and prophesy, to the few who could or would listen. Thus very evidently to me and to others I did little to create my day or greatly change it; but I did exemplify it and thus for all time my life is significant for all lives of men." —Du Bois, 1986a, p. 555

"Theories of society and social change which imply objective historical tendencies and an objective evaluation of historical alternatives now appear as unrealistic speculation, and commitment to them as a matter of personal (or group) preference." —Marcuse, 2001, p. 39

"Despite ironic cruelties and contradictions, battles for democratic power create moments of beauty and integrity that coincide with the ugliness of struggle." —J. A. James, 1996a, p. 22

THE PROBLEMS OF DU BOIS STUDIES IN
THE TWENTY-FIRST CENTURY

Du Bois's work has previously been engaged and presented in one-dimensional ways that obscure its resilience and relevance for contemporary critique, radical politics, and social movements. One-sided biographical and intellectual historical studies of Du Bois that read and render his thought and texts in arbitrary and artificial terms not only obfuscate Du Bois's intellectual past—and, therefore, much of modern black intellectual history—but these studies also adumbrate (classical and contemporary) Africana Studies' contributions to the quickly emerging interdisciplinary intellectual present. As I have endeavored to illustrate throughout this study, Du Bois was an early interdisciplinarian whose history- and culture-centered theorizings consistently identified key sociopolitical problems and utilized a wide range of work from various disciplines in an effort to produce solutions to those problems. The "problems" that Du Bois's thought sought to grasp and grapple with went well beyond the realm of race and racism, and often encompassed other enigmatic issues, such as sexism, colonialism, capitalism, and American imperialism, which all remain on the radical political agenda.

Though his work is most frequently read for its contributions to the critique of racism, and white supremacy in specific, Du Bois actually understood racism to be one of many interlocking oppressive systems that threaten not only the souls of black folk, but also the heart and soul of humanity. As Du Bois developed his discourse, various themes and theories were either embraced or rejected contingent upon particular historical and cultural conditions, which, reiteratively, helps to highlight the fact that his social and political theory was deeply grounded in history and culture. The deep historical and cultural dimension in Du Bois's thought suggests that he took seriously the role of a critical social theorist as someone who is concerned with crises in human life and who is committed to constantly (re)conceptualizing what is essential to human liberation and creating a new social world. As a critical social theorist, Du Bois's distinction is undoubtedly apparent when we note his ability to synthesize historical studies, cultural criticism, radical political theory, and economic analysis, with social philosophy and public policy in an effort to: (1) discover the fundamental features of contemporary society; (2) identify its most promising potentialities and paths to a liberated future; and, (3) accessibly advance ways that the current society could be transformed to realize these newly identified egalitarian goals.[1]

As far back as his 1898 essay, "The Study of Negro Problems," Du Bois (1978) declared: "Whenever any nation allows impulse, whim or hasty conjecture to usurp the place of conscious, normative, intelligent action, it is in grave danger. The sole aim of any society is to settle its problems in accordance with its highest ideals, and the only rational method of accomplishing this is to study those problems in the light of the best scientific research" (p. 75). Sidestepping the scientism and quest for rationalism in the quote, Du Bois seems to suggest two things. First, just as society changes, so too must the social theory that seeks not simply to chart those changes, but to have an emancipatory influence on them. And, second, social theory must be much more *critical*, meaning it is imperative for it to constantly carry out ideological critique, as there are many imperial and neo-imperial "impulse[s], whim[s]" and "hasty conjecture[s]" that are blocking human beings from realizing their "higher ideals."[2]

Conventionally Du Bois's corpus has been categorized as falling into three distinct stages: first, there is his early elitist ("Talented Tenth"), social scientist, and quasi-cultural nationalist stage from 1896 to 1903; second, his Pan-African socialist or "black Marxist" middle stage from 1904 to 1935; and, third, his radical humanist, internationalist, and peace activist final stage from 1936 to the end of his life in 1963 (see Broderick, 1959; DeMarco, 1983; Moore, 1981; Rudwick, 1968; Wolters, 2001). Many problems, however, arise when Du Bois is periodized and interpreted in this way. At first issue is the simple fact that this scheme shrouds the complexity and interdisciplinarity of the first and second stages and, therefore, does not adequately prepare or equip social theorists of the present age with the intellectual history and conceptual tools necessary to critically interpret and understand Du Bois's later life ("third stage") ruptures with his early elitism and mid-period political radicalism. Throughout this study, I have demonstrated that Du Bois's thought does not fit into the nice and neat conceptual categories of traditional disciplines, but may best be interpreted by examining it as *interdisciplinary theory with emancipatory intent*. What appears to many Du Bois scholars and critics as three distinct stages in his oeuvre is actually a single, protracted, critical, and conjunctive thought process that—on careful and close reading—reveals recurring themes of epistemic openness and radical political receptiveness.

Throughout each of the "three stages," Du Bois's writings return again and again to the critique of domination and discrimination, human liberation, radical democratic political action, and revolutionary social transformation. Though he began with bourgeois (and sometimes even Eurocentric imperial) notions of social uplift, by the so-called "second stage" Du Bois was clearly collapsing conventional social scientific categories and exploring new social identities and programs of political action.[3] He incorporated a wide range of academic theory and grass roots political praxis into his burgeoning critical social theoretical framework, thus his thought displays an unusual openness to and critical engagement of black nationalism, black separatism, Pan-Africanism,

African communalism, Marxism, Leninism, Maoism, German romanticism, German nationalism, British socialism, American pragmatism, Third Worldism, multiculturalism, pacifism, and feminism (and/or womanism), among other thought-traditions.

It would seem that the leitmotifs in Du Bois's thought would make his ideas more accessible and easier to interpret. However, it must be emphasized that though there are many recurring themes in his writings, he consistently revised his social theory and political analysis throughout each of the "three stages." Consequently, there are specific issues—usually race, gender, and class issues—that transgress the traditional "three stages" conceptualization of Du Bois's corpus, and which are persistently and, perhaps, perplexingly present at each stage. I argue, once more, that it is the interdisciplinary nature of his work that makes it so difficult to interpret in a one-dimensional or *monodisciplinary*, as opposed to multidisciplinary, manner. Also, Du Bois's interdisciplinarity, coupled with his accent on political economy and social theory, and his consistent emphasis on race, gender, and class issues, make his work an ideal model for reconceiving and recreating critical theory of contemporary society.

Interpretations of Du Bois based on the tripartite paradigm, then, are extremely problematic and often theoretically myopic, frequently displaying the disciplinary desires of the critic to fashion a Du Bois for their specific (postmodern or postcolonial) purposes.[4] However, Du Bois will not be anyone's theoretical straw man, or "race man" either, if you will. His thought, like that of other provocative thinkers, must be approached from an angle that is sensitive to intellectual, historical, and cultural context in order to be adequately, and one could say *correctly*, interpreted. As discussed in chapter 2, for instance, Du Bois carried out one of the most devastating critiques of white supremacy in the first half of the twentieth century. But one will hardly be able to fully appreciate the originality of his arguments, the radicalism of his political actions, and their relevance to critical theory of contemporary society unless his anti-racism is linked to his anti-colonial, anti-capitalist, and anti-sexist social theorizing.

By taking a conceptual (as opposed to the conventional chronological) approach to Du Bois's writings, I have been able to accent some of the significant developments of his thought that speak to ongoing and important issues revolving around race, gender, class, and the reconstruction of critical social theory. Instead of viewing changes in his thought as signs of confusion, vacillation, or intellectual inertia, I have emphasized the subtle logic of the modifications Du Bois made in his thinking by placing it in the context of continental and diasporan African intellectual history, culture, and struggle, as well as world intellectual history, culture, and struggle. Additionally, engaging Du

Bois's corpus conceptually has also enabled me to stress its strengths and weaknesses as a paradigm and point of departure for a much more multicultural, transethnic, transgender, and sexuality-sensitive critical theory of contemporary society. Similar to several other critical social theorists, Du Bois oriented his political theory toward what he perceived as the most progressive political struggles (or lack thereof) of a particular moment and, thus, articulated possibilities and potentialities specific to *his* contemporary society and social reality, rather than putting forward a blueprint for future social change or an architecture for emancipation in an epoch to come.[5]

This means, then, that "we are on our own"—as the post-Marxists and post-feminists regularly remind us (Aronson, 1995; Gamble, 2002). However, it does not mean that we should abandon those aspects of Du Bois's social thought that may aid us in our endeavors to develop a new, more multicultural, transethnic, transgender, and sexuality-sensitive critical theory of contemporary society. Critical theory seeks to comprehend, critique, and offer alternatives to the contradictions of current culture and society. Therefore, it is always in need of revision and, literally, demands development because its basic concepts and categories are time- and situation-sensitive. In other words, the basic concepts and categories of critical theory are historical; and history, to put it plainly, has never bowed to the wishes and whims of any human being or human group. Hence, history is always unfolding and playing itself out in new and unimagined ways. Critical theory, then, being a form of historical and cultural critique, must remain receptive to the various ways in which the world is changing if it is to truly transform contemporary culture and society (see Pensky, 2005; Rasmussen, 1999; Rasmussen and Swindal, 2004; L. Ray, 1993).

DU BOIS, RACE(ISM), AND THE RECONSTRUCTION OF CRITICAL SOCIAL THEORY

In this study I have endeavored to elucidate ways in which Du Bois contributes to critical theory in general, and a new, broader-based critical theory that seriously engages and takes as its point of departure the social and political thought of black radicals and revolutionaries. Throughout his life, Du Bois's critique of racism was relentless and, however flawed, remains one of his greatest contributions to both classical and contemporary social theory. But, as this study illustrates, Du Bois's much-heralded concepts of race and critiques of racism are virtually incomprehensible and seemingly incoherent without taking into consideration his bravura and often simultaneous critiques of sexism, colonialism, and capitalism. Where most critical theorists, at least in the Frankfurt School and other Western Marxist critical thought traditions, identified capitalism as the primary problem and essential source of human suffering and social misery, Du Bois's critical thought, though it began with a race base, ultimately developed a conjunctive model that did not privilege one social or political problem over another.

This study has also analyzed and explained the many tensions and ambiguities in Du Bois's corpus by demonstrating how his thought and texts are deeply connected to, and, as is usually the case, in dialogue with specific historical happenings, cultural conditions, and political practices. Additionally, dual emphasis was placed on, first, how Frankfurt School and Western Marxist critical theory has long overlooked racism, sexism, and colonialism, thus making it the very "one-dimensional" thought that Marcuse (1964) warned against and, second, how Du Bois's thought relates to the reconstruction of critical theory. Over the last quarter of a century there have been consistent calls within critical theoretical discourse for a "return to Marx" in order to reconstruct critical theory and make it more viable in light of the vicissitudes of contemporary capitalism.[6] However, what many of these otherwise sophisticated critical social theorists fail to perceive is that it was and remains their over-dependency on Marx and Marxism that has made so much of their work theoretically myopic and intellectually insular.

Like a dog chasing its own tail, many of the more Marxist-influenced critical theorists have locked their discourses into a vicious cycle, going round and round, covering a lot of the same theoretical terrain and identifying similar economic issues as the infinite cause of contemporary social suffering without opening their conceptual universes to the world of ideas and the radical thought-traditions of "Others" (or theorists and activists of color). Many of these same critical social theorists bemoan the sorry state of contemporary critical theory but are either too intellectually timid, intellectually elitist, or, dare I say, racially exclusivist to move beyond merely mentioning the fact that critical theory should be antiracist, antisexist, and anticolonial. Mentioning racism, sexism, and/or colonialism in passing, at the end of an article, or at the back of a book, and always in subordination to "the evils of capitalism," does not do the billions of human beings who suffer at the hands of these interlocking oppressive systems a favor.[7]

If, indeed, critical theory is theory critical of domination and discrimination, and a social theory that simultaneously offers accessible and ethical alternatives to the key social and political problems of the present age, then any theory claiming to be a critical theory of contemporary society must thoroughly theorize not only capitalism, but racism, sexism, and colonialism, and how each of the aforementioned interconnects and intersects to deform and destroy life and the ongoing prospects of liberation. Du Bois, thus, emerges from this study as an interdisciplinary, multi-faceted, and philosophically fascinating paradigmatic figure whose work indisputably contributes to contemporary efforts to reconceptualize and reconstruct critical theory. Critical theory cannot and will not be able to revise itself unless and until it seriously considers the contributions of social theorists and activists of color. This generation of critical theorists, then, has a unique and time-sensitive task before it, and, simply said, it is as follows: We must put into principled practice *immediately* what critical theory has so long advanced theoretically. In terms of the Africana tradition of critical theory, that critical theoretical admonition has been captured best by Fanon (1967), in *Black Skin, White Masks*, when he wrote:

> I, the man of color, want only this:
> That the tool never possess the man. That enslavement of man by man cease forever. That is, of one by another. That it be possible for me to discover and to love man, wherever he may be . . .
> It is through the effort to recapture the self and to scrutinize the self, it is through the lasting tension of their freedom that men will be able to create the ideal conditions of existence for a human world.
> Superiority? Inferiority?
> Why not the quite simple attempt to touch the other, to feel the other, to explain the other to myself?
> Was my freedom not given to me then in order to build the world of the *You*?

(pp. 231–32, emphasis in original)

THE CONTINUING CRITICAL IMPORTANCE OF DU BOIS AND HIS DISCOURSE

In summary, it must be openly admitted that the theoretic tensions noted in the previous paragraphs point to and produce an extremely uneasy combination of criticisms and interpretations that defy simple synopsis or conventional conceptual rules. Consequently, most of Du Bois's critics have heretofore downplayed and diminished the real brilliance and brawn of his work by failing to grasp its antinomies and have, therefore, put forward a divided and distorted Du Bois, who is either, for example, a Pan-Africanist *or* Europhile, a black nationalist *or* radical humanist, a social scientist *or* propagandist, a race man *or* radical women's rights man, a bourgeois individualist *or* dogmatic Marxist collectivist. Each of the aforementioned superficial ascriptions falls short of capturing the complex and chameleonic character of Du Bois's discourse and the difficulties involved in interpreting it using one-sided, single-subject theory and/or monodisciplinary devices.

Many dismiss Du Bois and charge his work with being dense because it employs a wide range of theory from several different disciplines. Others, such as myself, are attracted to his work because it is theoretically thick, rich in both radicality and originality, and boldly crosses so many academic and political boundaries. No matter what one's ultimate attitude toward Du Bois, I believe the fact that his thought and texts continue to cause contemporary controversies, and that they have been discussed and debated across the disciplines for over a century, in some degree points to the multidimensionality and interdisciplinarity of his ideas, which offer enigmatic insights for everyone either to embrace enthusiastically or demur definitively. Hence, the dialectic of attraction and repulsion in Du Bois studies can partly be attributed to the ambiguities inherent in his thought and the monodisciplinary anxieties of many of the interpreters of his work. Suffice to say this is the case, then, several previous studies of his thought are seriously flawed because they have sought to grasp and grapple with Du Bois's oeuvre using a monodisciplinary instead of a multidisciplinary model.

Whatever the deficiencies of his thought and the problems with his approach to critical issues confronting Africana and other oppressed people, Du Bois forces his readers to think deeply, to criticize thoroughly, and to move beyond the imperial impulses of the established order. Many critics have made solid criticisms of some aspect of Du Bois's thought but, when analyzed objectively, his life-work and intellectual legacy are impressive and inspiring, as is his loyalty to the most radical thought and practice traditions in Africana and world history. His impact and influence have been widespread, not only cutting across academic disciplines, but setting aglow several social movements and political programs.

Where some theorists dogmatically hold views simply because they are fashionable or politically popular, Du Bois's work draws from a diverse array of often eclectic and enigmatic sources and, therefore, offers no closed system or absolute truths. His thought was constantly open and routinely responsive to changing historical and cultural conditions, both nationally and internationally. There are several sometimes stunning transformations in his theory that are in most instances attempts to answer conundrums created by changing socio-political, historical, and cultural conditions. In conclusion, then, I want to suggest that it is the openness and consistently non-dogmatic radicalism of Du Bois's project, the richness and wide range and reach of his ideas, and the absence of any finished system or body of clearly defined truths that can be accepted or rejected at ease, which constitute both the contemporary philosophical fascination with and continuing critical importance of W. E. B. Du Bois and his discourse.

NOTES

1. With regard to the last three points, which provide a basic outline for my conception of critical theory, I have drawn heavily from the work of Joy James (1996a, 1997, 1999), whose texts have consistently raised the issue of connecting theory to praxis; the realities of the "ugliness" of anti-racist, anti-sexist, and anti-imperial struggle (both inside and outside "radical" thought-traditions and movements); and the need for progressive intellectual-activists to move "beyond literary insurgency or rhetorical resistance to bring the element of the fight into our daily lives with the specificity of political struggles around economic, sexual, and racial violence" (J. A. James, 1996a, p. 23). Here I am also borrowing, however loosely, from the theoretical orientations and methodological work of Marcuse (1969, 1972a, 1997a, 2001), Habermas (1984, 1986a, 1986c, 1987a), and Foucault (1997, 1998, 2000). Foucault's conception of and contributions to critical theory, in particular, helped me to hone a critical methodological perspective that transgresses not only the boundaries of traditional academic disciplines, but also the Frankfurt School critical theorists' obsession with Marx and Marxism as the major theoretical thread that connects one version of critical theory to another. Where Foucault turned to Nietzsche and other pre-Marxian thinkers to develop his critical theoretical discourse, I, of course, have labored with Du Bois, and have plans to call on several other Africana social and political theorists.

2. For a series of critical discussions on the centennial of Du Bois's essay, "The Study of Negro Problems," and its relevance for contemporary Africana and global radical politics, social thought and movements, philosophy, economic analysis, cultural criticism, feminism, and radical humanism, see Anderson and Zuberi (2000). The influence of this essay on my conception of critical theory, Africana critical theory, cannot be over-emphasized.

3. Wilson Moses (1978, 1996, 1998) and Paul Gilroy (1993a) have demonstrated that the "Eurocentric imperial" aspects of Du Bois's early social uplift theory were derived, in part, from his affinity to German nationalism, which he had admired, arguably, since his undergraduate days at Fisk. For further discussion, see also Lewis (1993), A. L. Reed (1997), and Zamir (1995).

4. I have in mind here, particularly, the work of Appiah (1992), Gilroy (1993a), and Posnock (1995, 1997, 1998).

5. In terms of the time-sensitivity and theoretical specificity of critical theory, Marcuse made an excellent statement regarding the critical theorist's primary task of wrestling with the most pressing issues of their epoch, as opposed to pointing to, or pointing out, the future "forces of transformation." In his own words:

> If Marx saw in the proletariat the revolutionary class, he did so also, and maybe even primarily, because the proletariat was free from the repressive needs of capitalist society, because the new needs for freedom could develop in the proletariat and were not suffocated by the old, dominant ones. Today [in 1967] in large parts of the most highly developed capitalist countries that is no longer the case. The working class no longer represents the negation of existing needs. That is one of the most serious facts with which we have to

deal. As far as the forces of transformation themselves are concerned, I grant you without further discussion that today nobody is in a position to give a prescription for them in the sense of being able to point and say, "Here you have your revolutionary forces, this is their strength, this and this must be done." The only thing I can do is point out what forces potentially make for a radical transformation of the system. (Marcuse, 1970a, p. 70)

This means, then, that critical theorists need not feel compelled to accept the call of the prophet. Critical theory is, or at its best should be, deeply rooted in empirical and historical research, and its theoretical positions are linked to concrete social and political struggles. Therefore, though a part of its focus is on the future, critical theory is ultimately a theory of the present whose philosophical foundation rests on and revolves around classical and contemporary radical theory and revolutionary praxis.

6. For instance, see James Marsh's texts (1995, 1998, 1999) and, especially, his groundbreaking essay, "Toward a New Critical Theory," where he forcefully asserts:

I think we need a much fuller appropriation and use of Marx than is going on in either postmodernism or Habermasian critical theory. If capitalism is deeply pathological and unjust, as I think it is and as I have argued in all of my works, then we need the resources of what still remains the deepest and most comprehensive critique of capitalist political economy, that which occurs in the late Marx in the pages of the *Grundrisse, Capital,* and *Theories of Surplus Value,* a total of seven volumes that are more relevant than ever. For these reasons, I draw on Marx's theory of exploited labor in the workplace, his theory of tyranny, in which the economy and money impinge on noneconomic aspects of the lifeworld in a way that is absurd, his theory of a marginalized industrial reserve army, his theory of value and surplus value, and his account of substantive socialism. Capitalist pathology is not just colonization of lifeworld by system, although that is certainly an important part of such pathology, but includes exploitation, tyranny, domination, and marginalization as well. (Marsh, 2001, p. 57)

7. I want to clarify here, so that my critical comments are not confused with being anti-Marxist. I am in complete intellectual and political sympathy with Douglas Kellner (1995), in "The Obsolescence of Marxism?," when he contends:

[W]e need to build on viable political and theoretical perspectives and resources of the past, and I would argue that Marxism continues to provide vital resources for radical theory and politics today. . . . In sum, I believe that we need new theoretical and political syntheses, drawing on the best of classical Enlightenment theory, Marxian theory, feminism, and other progressive theoretical and political currents of the present. Key aspects for such new syntheses, however, are found in the Marxian tradition, and those who prematurely abandon it are turning away from a tradition that has been valuable since Marx's day and will continue to be so in the foreseeable future. Consequently, Marxism is not yet obsolete. Rather, the Marxian theory continues to provide resources and stimulus for critical theory and radical politics in the present age. (pp. 25–26)

Kellner and I, however, part company when and where he gives a detailed discussion of the relevance of European derived and developed theories or, rather, Eurocentric theories—Enlightenment theory, Marxism, and feminism—and only alludes to the work of non-European theorists or, as he put it "*other* progressive theoretical and political currents" for renewing radical politics and critical theory in the present (my emphasis). To his credit Kellner states, "radical politics today should be more multicultural, race and gender focused, and broad-based than the original Marxian theory" (p. 20). But he does not identify or critically engage the "other progressive theoretical and political currents" the way, and to the depths to which, he does a plethora of white male radical thinkers whose thought, he believes, contributes indelibly to the reconstruction of critical theory. How will radical politics and critical theory become "more multicultural and race and gender focused" if it does not turn to the thought and texts of the most progressive race and gender theorists; some of whom happen to be of African origin or descent, and some of whom are, of course, women? My conception of critical theory, Africana critical theory, utterly agrees that Marx and Marxism have long provided the most comprehensive class analysis and critique of capitalist political economy. But it finds Marxism shamefully deficient where the critique of racism, sexism, and colonialism are concerned. For these reasons, Africana critical theory, in addition to Marx and Marxism, draws on black Marxism, philosophy of race, sociology of race, and critical race theory; black feminism, Marxist-feminism, anti-racist feminism, feminist philosophy, male-feminism, and womanism; and, Pan-Africanism, African socialism, Fanonian philosophy, and decolonization theory, among others. Developing this argument any further would constitute the basis of another book, which I intend to write, but for the time being I offer this study on Du Bois's contributions to the reconstruction of critical social theory.

Bibliography

Abromeit, John, and Cobb, W. Mark. (Eds.) (2004). *Herbert Marcuse: A Critical Reader*. New York: Routledge.

Adell, Sandra. (1994). *Double Consciousness/Double Bind: Theoretical Issues in Twentieth-Century Black Literature*. Urbana: University of Illinois Press.

Adorno, Theodor W. (1991). *The Culture Industry: Selected Essays on Mass Culture* (Jay M. Bernstein, Ed.). New York: Routledge.

——. (2000). *The Adorno Reader* (Brain O'Connor, Ed.). Malden, MA: Blackwell.

Adu-Poku, S. (2001). "Envisioning (Black) Male Feminism: A Cross-Cultural Perspective." *Journal of Gender Studies* 10, 157–67.

Agger, Ben. (1992). *The Discourse of Domination: From the Frankfurt School to Postmodernism*. Evanston, IL: Northwestern University Press.

——. (1998). *Critical Social Theory*. Boulder, CO: Westview.

Alcoff, Linda Martin. (1998). "Racism." In Alison M. Jaggar and Iris Marion Young (Eds.), *A Companion to Feminist Philosophy*. (pp. 475–84). Malden, MA: Blackwell.

Aldridge, Delores. (1988). *New Perspectives on Black Studies*. Special Issue, *Phylon* 49, (1).

Aldridge, Delores, and Young, Carlene. (Eds.) (2000). *Out of the Revolution: An Africana Studies Anthology*. Lanham, MD: Lexington.

Alexander, Elizabeth. (1995). "'We Must Be About Our Father's Business: Anna Julia Cooper and the In-Corporation of the Nineteenth Century African American Woman Intellectual." *Signs* 20, (2), 336–56.

Alexander, M. Jacqui, and Mohanty, Chandra Talpade. (Eds.) (1997). *Feminist Genealogies, Colonial Legacies, Democratic Futures*. New York: Routledge.

Allen, Ernest, Jr. (1992). "Ever Feeling One's Twoness: 'Double Ideas' and 'Double Consciousness' in *The Souls of Black Folk*." *Critique of Anthropology* 12 (3) (September), 261–75.

Allen, Robert. (1974). "The Politics of the Attack on Black Studies." *Black Scholar* 6 (1), 1–7.

Allen, Theodore W. (1994). *The Invention of the White Race*, volume 1. New York: Verso.

———. (1997). *The Invention of the White Race*, volume 2. New York: Verso.

Alridge, Derrick P. (1997). "The Social, Economic, and Political Thought of W. E. B. Du Bois During the 1930s: Implications for Contemporary African American Education." Ph. D. dissertation, Pennsylvania State University.

———. (1999). "Conceptualizing a Du Boisian Philosophy of Education: Toward a Model for African American Education." *Education Theory* 49 (3), 359–79.

Alkalimat, Abdul. (1986). *Introduction to Afro-American Studies: A People's College Primer.* Chicago: Twenty-First Century Books and Publications.

———. (Ed.) (1990). *Paradigms in Black Studies: Intellectual History, Cultural Meaning, and Political Ideology.* Chicago: Twenty-First Century Books and Publications.

Alva, J. J. K. de. (1995). "The Postcolonization of the (Latin) American Experience, A Reconsideration of 'Colonialism,' 'Postcolonialism' and 'Mestizaje.'" In Gyan Prakash (Ed.), *After Colonialism: Imperial Histories and Postcolonial Displacements.* (pp. 241–275). Princeton, NJ: Princeton University Press.

Amott, Teresa, and Matthaei, Julie. (1984). "Comparable Worth, Incomparable Pay." *Radical America* 18, (5), 21–28.

Anderson, Elijah, and Zuberi, Tukufu. (Eds.) (2000). *The Study of African American Problems: W. E. B. Du Bois's Agenda, Then and Now.* Thousand Oaks, CA: Sage.

Anderson, Jervis. (1973). *A. Philip Randolph: A Biographical Portrait.* New York: Harcourt Brace Jonanovich.

———. (1997). *Bayard Rustin: Troubles I've Seen, a Biography.* New York: Harper-Collins.

Anderson, Perry. (1976). *Considerations on Western Marxism.* London: New Left Books.

Anderson, Talmadge. (Ed.) (1990). *Black Studies: Theory, Method and Cultural Perspective.* Pullman, WA: Washington State University Press.

Andrews, William L. (Ed.) (1985). *Critical Essays on W. E. B. Du Bois.* Boston: G. K. Hall.

Andrews, William L.; Foster, Frances Smith; and Harris, Trudier. (Eds.) (1997). *The Oxford Companion to African American Literature.* New York: Oxford University Press.

Anthias, Floya, and Yuval-Davis, Nira. (1992). *Racialized Boundaries: Race, Nation, Gender, Color and Class in the Anti-Racist Struggle.* New York: Routledge.

Antonio, Robert J., and Kellner, Douglas. (1994). "Postmodern Social Theory: Contributions and Limitations." In David Dickens and Andrea Fontana (Eds.), *Postmodernism and Social Inquiry.* (pp. 127–52). New York: Guilford.

Appiah, Kwame Anthony. (1985). "The Uncompleted Argument: Du Bois and the Illusion of Race." *Critical Inquiry* 12 (1), 21–37.

———. (1990). "Racisms." In David Theo Goldberg (Ed.), *Anatomy of Racism.* (pp. 3–17). Minneapolis: University of Minnesota Press.

———. (1992). *In My Father's House: Africa in the Philosophy of Culture.* New York: Oxford University Press.

———. (1995). "The Uncompleted Argument: Du Bois and the Illusion of Race." In Albert G. Mosley (Ed.), *African Philosophy: Selected Readings*. (pp. 199–215). Englewood Cliffs, NJ: Prentice Hall.

———. (1994). "Identity, Authenticity, Survival: Multicultural Societies and Social Reproduction." In Amy Gutmann (Ed.), *Multiculturalism* (pp. 149–65). Princeton: Princeton University Press.

———. (1996). "Race, Culture, Identity." In Kwame Anthony Appiah and Amy Gutman, *Color Conscious: The Political Morality of Race* (pp. 3–75). Princeton: Princeton University Press.

———. (1997). "'But Would That Still Be Me?': Notes on Gender, 'Race,' Ethnicity as a Source of Identity." In Naomi Zack (Ed.), *Race/Sex: Their Sameness, Difference, and Interplay*. (pp. 75–82). New York: Routledge.

Appiah, Kwame Anthony, and Gates, Henry Louis, Jr. (Eds.) (1999). *Africana: The Encyclopedia of the African and African American Experience*. New York: Basic/Civitas Books.

Appleby, Joyce; Covington, Elizabeth; Hoyt, David; Latham, Michael; and Snieder, Allison. (Eds.) (1996). *Knowledge and Postmodernism in Historical Perspective*. New York: Routledge.

Aptheker, Bettina. (1975). "W. E. B. Du Bois and the Struggle for Women's Rights: 1910–1920." *San Jose Studies* 1 (2), 7–16.

Aptheker, Herbert. (1948). "W. E. B. Du Bois: The First Eighty Years." *Phylon* 9, 58–69.

———. (1949). "The Washington–Du Bois Conference of 1904." *Science and Society* 13, 344–51.

———. (1961). "Dr. Du Bois and Communism." *Political Affairs* 40 (December), 13–20.

———. (1963). "To Dr. Du Bois—With Love." *Political Affairs* 42 (February), 35–42.

———. (1964). "Du Bois on Douglass: 1895." *Journal of Negro History* 49 (October), 264–68.

———. (1965). "Some Unpublished Writings of W. E. B. Du Bois." *Freedom* 5 (Winter), 103–28.

———. (1966). "W. E. B. Du Bois: The Final Years." *Journal of Human Relations* 14, 149–55.

———. (1971). "*The Souls of Black Folk*: A Comparison of the 1903 and 1952 Editions." *Negro History Bulletin* 34 (January).

———. (Ed.) (1973). *An Annotated Bibliography of the Published Writings of W. E. B. Du Bois*. Millwood, NY: Kraus-Thompson.

———. (1981). "W. E. B. Du Bois and Africa." *Political Affairs* 60 (March).

———. (1982). "W. E. B. Du Bois and Religion: A Brief Reassessment." *Journal of Religious Thought* 59 (Spring–Summer), 5–11.

———. (1983). *W. E. B. Du Bois and the Struggle Against Racism*. New York: United Nations Center Against Apartheid.

———. (1985). "Introduction to Du Bois's Creative Writings." In Herbert Aptheker (Ed.), *Creative Writings by W. E. B. Du Bois: A Pageant, Poems, Short Stories, and Playlets*. (pp. ix–xii). White Plains, NY: Kraus International.

——. (1989). *The Literary Legacy of W. E. B. Du Bois*. White Plains, NY: Kraus International.

——. (1990). "W. E. B. Du Bois: Struggle Not Despair." *Clinical Sociology Review* 8, 58–68.

——. (1997). "Personal Recollections: Woodson, Wesley, Robeson, and Du Bois." *Black Scholar* 27 (2), 42.

Arato, Andrew, and Gebhardt, Eike. (Eds.) (1997). *The Essential Frankfurt School Reader*. New York: Continuum.

Arnold, N. Scott. (1990). *Marx's Radical Critique of Capitalist Society*. New York: Oxford University Press.

Aronowitz, Stanley. (1990). *The Crisis of Historical Materialism*. Minneapolis: University of Minnesota Press.

——. (1996). *The Death and Rebirth of American Radicalism*. New York: Routledge.

Aronson, Ronald. (1995). *After Marxism*. New York: Guilford.

Arndt, Murray Dennis. (1970). "The *Crisis* Years of W. E. B. Du Bois, 1910–1934." Ph. D. dissertation, Duke University.

Arrington, Robert L. (Ed.) (1999). *A Companion to the Philosophers*. Malden: Blackwell.

Arroyo, Elizabeth Fortson. (1993). "Josephine St. Pierre Ruffin." In Darlene Clark Hine, Elsa Barkley Brown, and Rosalyn Teborg-Penn (Eds.), *Black Women in America: An Historical Encyclopedia*, 2 volumes (pp. 994–97). Brooklyn: Carlson.

Asante, Molefi Kete. (1987). *The Afrocentric Idea*. Philadelphia: Temple University Press.

——. (1988). *Afrocentricity*. Trenton: Africa World Press.

——. (1990). *Kemet, Afrocentricity, and Knowledge*. Trenton: Africa World Press.

Asante, Molefi K., and Karenga, Maulana. (Eds.) (2006). *The Handbook of Black Studies*. Thousand Oaks, CA: Sage.

Ashcroft, Bill; Griffiths, Gareth; and Tiffin, Helen. (1989). *The Empire Writes Back: Theory and Practice in Postcolonial Literatures*. New York: Routledge.

——. (Eds.) (1995). *The Post-Colonial Studies Reader*. New York: Routledge.

——. (Eds.) (1998). *Key Concepts in Postcolonial Studies*. New York: Routledge.

Awkward, Michael. (2000). "A Black Man's Place in Black Feminist Criticism." In Joy A. James and T. Denean Sharpley-Whiting (Eds.), *The Black Feminist Reader*. (pp. 88–108). Malden, MA: Blackwell.

Axelsen, Diana E. (1984). "Philosophical Justifications for Contemporary African Social and Political Values and Strategies." In Richard A. Wright (Ed.), *African Philosophy: An Introduction, Third Edition*. (pp. 227–44). Lanham, MD: University of America Press.

Azevedo, Mario. (Ed.) (1993). *Africana Studies: A Survey of Africa and the African Diaspora*. Durham: Carolina Academic Press.

Baber, Willie L. (1992). "Capitalism and Racism: Discontinuities in the Life and Work of W. E. B. Du Bois." *Critique of Anthropology* 12 (3), 339–64.

Babbitt, Susan E., and Campbell, Sue. (Eds.) (1999). *Racism and Philosophy*. Ithaca: Cornell University Press.

Bailey, Ronald. (1970). "Why Black Studies?" *The Education Digest* 35 (9), 46–48.

Baker, Houston A., Jr. (1972). "The Black Man of Culture: W. E. B. Du Bois and *The Souls of Black Folk*." In Houston A. Baker, *Long Black Song*. (pp. 96–108). Charlottesville: University of Virginia Press.

Baker-Fletcher, Karen. (1991). "A 'Singing Something': The Literature of Anna Julia Cooper as a Resource for a Theological Anthropology of Voice." Ph. D. dissertation, Harvard University.

———. (1994). *A Singing Something: Womanist Reflections on Anna Julia Cooper.* New York: Crossroads.

Balbus, Isaac D. (1982). *Marxism and Domination.* Princeton, NJ: Princeton University Press.

Bambara, Toni Cade. (Ed.) (1970). *The Black Woman: An Anthology.* New York: Signet.

Ba Nikongo, Nikongo. (Ed.) (1997). *Leading Issues in African American Studies.* Durham: Carolina Academic Press.

Bannerji, Himani. (1995). *Thinking Through: Essays on Feminism, Marxism, and Anti-Racism.* Toronto: Women's Educational Press.

Barkin, Kenneth. (1998). "W. E. B. Du Bois and the Kaiserreich Articles: An Introduction to Du Bois's Manuscripts on Germany." *Central European History* 31 (3), 155–71.

———. (2000). "'Berlin Days,' 1892–1894: W. E. B. Du Bois and German Political Economy." *Boundary 2* 27 (3), 79–101.

Barnett, Bernice McNair, and Mooney, Jessica. (2001). "W. E. B. Du Bois and Joe Feagin: Liberation Sociologists and Activist Intellectuals Affirming Diversity Along Race, Gender, and Class Lines." Paper presented at the annual meeting of the *Society for the Study of Social Problems*.

Barrett, Michele. (1980). *Women's Oppression Today: Problems in Marxist Feminist Analysis.* London: Verso.

Bartolovich, Crystal (2000). "Global Capital and Transnationalism." In Henry Schwarz and Sangeeta Ray (Eds.), *A Companion to Postcolonial Studies.* (pp. 126–61). Malden, MA: Blackwell.

Bates, Robert H.; Mudimbe, V. Y.; and O'Barr, Jean. (Eds.) (1993). *Africa and the Disciplines: The Contributions of Research in Africa to the Social Sciences and Humanities.* Chicago: University of Chicago Press.

Baulding, Lisa. (Producer). (1992). *W. E. B. Du Bois of Great Barrington.* [Documentary]. WGBY-TV Springfield, MA: PBS Video.

Bay, Mia. (1998). "'The World Was Thinking Wrong About Race': *The Philadelphia Negro* and Nineteenth-Century Science." In Michael B. Katz and Thomas J. Sugrue (Eds.), *W. E. B. Du Bois, Race, and the City: The Philadelphia Negro and Its Legacy.* (pp. 41–60). Philadelphia: University of Pennsylvania Press.

Beale, Frances. (1995). "Double Jeopardy: To Be Black and Female." In Beverly Guy-Sheftall (Ed.), *Words of Fire: An Anthology of African American Feminist Thought.* (pp. 146–56). New York: The Free Press.

Beavers, Herman. (2000). "Romancing the Body Politic: Du Bois's Propaganda of the Dark World." *Annals of the American Academy of Political and Social Science* 568 (March), 250–64.

Beck, Hamilton. (1996). "W. E. B. Du Bois as a Study Abroad Student in Germany, 1892–1894." *Frontiers: The Interdisciplinary Journal of Study Abroad* 2 (1), 45–63.

Bederman, Gail. (1995). *Manliness and Civilization: A Cultural History of Gender and Race in the United States, 1880–1917*. Chicago: University of Chicago Press.

Bell, Bernard W. (1985). "W. E. B. Du Bois's Struggle to Reconcile Folk and High Art." In William L. Andrews (Ed.), *Critical Essays on W. E. B. Du Bois*. (pp. 106–22). Boston: G. K. Hall.

———. (1996). "Genealogical Shifts in Du Bois's Discourse on Double-Consciousness as the Sign of African American Difference." In Bernard W. Bell, Emily R. Grosholz, and James B. Stewart (Eds.), *W. E. B. Du Bois: On Race and Culture*. (pp. 87–110). New York: Routledge.

Bell, Bernard W.; Grosholz, Emily R.; and Stewart, James B. (Eds.) (1996). *W. E. B. Du Bois: On Race and Culture*. New York: Routledge.

Bell, Derrick. (1995). "Racial Realism—After We're Gone: Prudent Speculations on America in a Post-Racial Epoch." In Richard Delgado (Ed.), *Critical Race Theory: The Cutting Edge*. (pp. 2–8). Philadelphia: Temple University Press.

Bell, Linda A., and Blumenfeld, David. (Eds.) (1995). *Overcoming Racism and Sexism*. Lanham, MD: Rowman & Littlefield.

Benhabib, Seyla. (1986). *Critique, Norm, and Utopia*. New York: Columbia University Press.

———. (1992). *Situating the Self: Gender, Community, and Postmodernism in Contemporary Ethics*. New York: Routledge.

Benhabib, Seyla, and Cornell, Drucilla. (Eds.) (1987). *Feminism as Critique: Essays on the Politics of Gender in Late-Capitalist Societies*. London: Polity Press.

Berman, Russell A. (1997). "Du Bois and Wagner: Race, Nation, and Culture Between the United States and Germany." *German Quarterly* 70 (2), 123–35.

Berman, Nathan. (2000). "Shadows: Du Bois and the Colonial Prospect, 1925." *Villanova Law Review* 45 (5), 959–70.

Bernasconi, Robert. (Ed.) (2001). *Race*. Malden, MA: Blackwell.

Bernasconi, Robert, and Lott, Tommy L. (Eds.) (2000). *The Idea of Race*. Indianapolis: Hackett.

Bernstein, Jay M. (Ed.) (1995). *The Frankfurt School: Critical Assessments*. London: Routledge.

Berry, Mary Frances. (1994). *Black Resistance, White Law: A History of Constitutional Racism in America*. New York: Allen Lane.

———. (2000). "Du Bois as Social Activist: Why We Are Not Saved." *Annals of the American Academy of Political and Social Science* 568 (March), 100–110.

Best, Steven. (1995). *The Politics of Historical Vision: Marx, Foucault, Habermas*. New York: Guilford.

Best, Steven, and Kellner, Douglas. (1991). *Postmodern Theory: Critical Interrogations*. New York: Guilford.

———. (1997). *The Postmodern Turn*. New York: Guilford.

———. (2001). *The Postmodern Adventure*. New York: Guilford.

Bienen, Henry. (1977). "State and Revolution: The Work of Amilcar Cabral." *Journal of Modern African Studies* 15 (4), 555–95.

Birt, Robert E. (Ed.) (2002). *The Quest for Community and Identity: Critical Essays in Africana Social Philosophy*. Lanham, MD: Rowman & Littlefield.

Blackey, Robert. (1974). "Fanon and Cabral: A Contrast in Theories of Revolution for Africa." *Journal of Modern African Studies* 12 (2), 191–209.

Blair, Karen. (1980). *The Clubwoman as Feminist: True Womanhood Redefined, 1868–1914*. New York: Holmes & Meier.

Blakely, Thomas D.; van Beek, Walter E. A.; and Thomson, Dennis L. (Eds.) (1994). *Religion in Africa*.

Blakeney, Ronnie F., and Snarey, John R. (2001). "The Ripples in Placid Lakes: W. E. B. Du Bois Revisited." *Theory and Research in Social Education* 29 (4), 742–48.

Blassingame, John. (Ed). (1973). *New Perspectives on Black Studies*. Chicago: University of Illinois Press.

Blau, Judith R., and Brown, Eric S. (2001). "Du Bois and Diasporic Identity: The Veil and Unveiling Project." *Sociological Theory* 19 (2), 219–33.

Blaut, James M. (1993). *The Colonizer's Model of the World: Geographical Diffusionism and Eurocentric History*. New York: Guilford.

Blee, Kathleen M. (1991). *Women of the Klan: Racism and Gender in the 1920s*. Berkeley, CA: University of California Press.

———. (2002). *Inside Organized Racism: Women in the Hate Movement*. Berkeley, CA: University of California Press.

Blight, David W. (1994). "W. E. B. Du Bois and the Struggle for American Historical Memory." In Genevieve Fabre and Robert O'Meally (Eds.), *History and Memory in African American Culture*. (pp. 73–92). New York: Oxford University Press.

———. (2001). "The Enduring Du Bois." *American Prospect* 12 (5), (March 12–26), 57–59.

Bloom, Harold. (Ed.) (2001). *W. E. B. Du Bois*. Broomall: Chelsea House Publishers.

Bobo, Jacqueline. (1995). *Black Women as Cultural Readers*. New York: Columbia University.

———. (Ed.) (2001). *Black Feminist Cultural Criticism*. Malden, MA: Blackwell.

Bobo, Lawrence D. (2000). "Reclaiming a Du Boisian Perspective on Racial Attitudes." *Annals of the American Academy of Political and Social Science* 568 (March), 186–202.

Bonilla-Silva, Eduardo. (2001). *White Supremacy and Racism in the Post-Civil Rights Era*. Boulder, CO: Lynne Rienner.

Bottomore, Tom. (1985). *The Frankfurt School*. New York: Tavistock.

Bouges, Anthony. (Ed.) (1983). *Marxism and Black Liberation*. Cleveland: Hera Press.

———. (2003). *Black Heretics, Black Prophets: Radical Political Intellectuals*. New York: Routledge.

Bourne, Jenny. (1983). "Towards an Anti-Racist Feminism." *Race & Class* 25 (Summer), 1–22.

Bowser, Benjamin, and Whittle, Deborah. (1996). "Personal Reflections on W. E. B. Du Bois: The Person, Scholar and Activist." *Research in Race and Ethnic Relations* 9, 27–65.

Boyd, Melba Joyce. (1994). *Discarded Legacy: Politics and Poetics in the Life of Frances E. W. Harper*. Detroit, MI: Wayne State University.

Boxill, Bernard. (1977–78). "Du Bois and Fanon on Culture." *Philosophical Forum* 9 (2–3), 326–38.

———. (1992). "Du Bois's Dilemma." In Boxill, *Blacks and Social Justice*. Lanham, MD: Rowman & Littlefield.

———. (1996). "Du Bois on Cultural Pluralism." In Bernard W. Bell, Emily R. Grosholz, and James B. Stewart (Eds.), *W. E. B. Du Bois: On Race and Culture*. (pp. 57–86). New York: Routledge.

———. (1997a). "Washington, Du Bois and Plessy vs. Ferguson." *Law & Philosophy* 16, (3), 299–330.

———. (1997b). "Two Traditions in African American Political Philosophy." In John P. Pittman (Ed.), *African American Perspectives and Philosophical Traditions*. (pp. 119–35). New York: Routledge.

———. (1997c). "Populism and Elitism in African American Political Thought." *Journal of Ethics* (Fall).

Braley, Mark Steven. (1994). "The Circle Unbroken: W. E. B. Du Bois and the Encyclopedic Narrative." Ph. D. dissertation, Princeton University.

Brewer, Anthony. (1980). *Marxist Theories of Imperialism*. London: Routledge & Kegan Paul.

Brewer, Rose. (1993). "Theorizing Race, Class and Gender: The New Scholarship of Black Feminist Intellectuals and Black Women's Labor." In Stanlie James and Abena Busia (Eds.), *Theorizing Black Feminism: The Visionary Pragmatism of Black Women*. (pp. 13–30). New York: Routledge.

Bridges, Charles Wesley II. (1973). "The Curriculum Theory Context of Activity Analysis and the Educational Philosophies of Washington and Du Bois." Ph. D. dissertation, Ohio State University, Columbus, OH.

Broderick, Francis L. (1955). "W. E. B. Du Bois: The Trail of His Ideas." Ph. D. dissertation, Harvard University.

———. (1958a). "The Academic Training of W. E. B. Du Bois." *Journal of Negro Education* 27 (Winter), 10–16.

———. (1958b). "German Influence on the Scholarship of W. E. B. Du Bois." *Phylon* 19 (December), 367–71.

———. (1958c). "The Tragedy of W. E. B. Du Bois." *Progressive* 22 (February), 29–32.

———. (1959). *W. E. B. Du Bois: Negro Leader in a Time of Crisis*. Palo Alto, CA: Stanford University Press.

———. (1974). "W. E. B. Du Bois: History of an Intellectual." In James E. Blackwell and Morris Janowitz (Eds.), *Black Sociologists: Historical and Contemporary Perspectives* (pp. 3–24). Chicago: University of Chicago Press.

Brodwin, Stanley. (1972). "The Veil Transcended: Form and Meaning in W. E. B. Du Bois's *The Souls of Black Folk*." *Journal of Black Studies* 2 (3), 303–21.

Bruce, Dickson D., Jr. (1992). "W. E. B. Du Bois and the Idea of Double Consciousness." *American Literature* 64 (June), 299–309.

———. (1995). "W. E. B. Du Bois and the Dilemma of Race." *American Literary History* 7 (2), 334–43.

Bubner, Rudiger. (1988). *Essays in Hermeneutics and Critical Theory.* New York: Columbia University Press.

Buhle, Mari Jo. (1981). *Women and American Socialism, 1870–1920.* Urbana: University of Illinois Press.

Buhle, Paul. (1991). *Marxism in the United States.* London: Verso.

Bulmer, Martin. (1991). "W. E. B. Du Bois as a Social Investigator: *The Philadelphia Negro,* 1899." In Martin Bulmer and Kevin Bales (Eds.), *The Social Survey in Historical Perspective, 1880–1940.* Cambridge: Cambridge University Press.

———. (1995). "The Challenge of African American Leadership in an Ambiguous World: W. E. B. Du Bois, Cater G. Woodson, Ralph Bunche and Thurgood Marshall in Historical Perspective." *Ethnic & Racial Studies* 18 (3), 629–47.

Burbridge, Lynn C. (1999). "W. E. B. Du Bois as Economic Analyst: Reflections on the 100th Anniversary of *The Philadelphia Negro.*" *Review of Black Political Economy* 26 (3), 13–31.

Burks, Ben. (1997). "Unity and Diversity Through Education: A Comparison of the Thought of W. E. B. Du Bois and John Dewey." *Journal of Thought* 32 (1), 99–110.

Busby, Margaret. (Ed.) (1992). *Daughters of Africa: An International Anthology of Words and Writings by Women of African Descent from the Ancient Egyptian to the Present.* New York: Pantheon.

Butler, Johnnella E. (1981). *Black Studies—Pedagogy and Revolution: A Study of Afro-American Studies and the Liberal Arts Tradtion Through the Discipline of Afro-American Literature.* Lanham, MD: University Press of America.

———. (2000). "African American Studies and the "Warring Ideals": The Color Line Meets the Borderlands." In Manning Marable (Ed.), *Dispatches from the Ebony Tower: Intellectuals Confront the African American Experience* (pp. 141–52). New York: Columbia University Press.

———. (Ed.) (2001). *Color-Line to Borderlands: The Matrix of American Ethnic Studies.* Seattle, WA: University of Washington Press.

Butler, Johnnella E., and Walter, John C. (Eds.) (1991). *Transforming the Curriculum: Ethnic Studies and Women's Studies.* Albany, NY: State University of New York Press.

Byrd, Rudolph P., and Guy-Sheftall, Beverly. (Eds.) (2001). *Traps: African American Men on Gender and Sexuality.* Indianapolis: Indiana University Press.

Byerman, Keith E. (1978). "Two Warring Ideals: The Dialectical Thought of W. E. B. Du Bois." Ph. D. dissertation, Purdue University.

———. (1981). "Hearts of Darkness: Narrative Voices in *The Souls of Black Folk.*" *American Literary Realism* 14, 43–51.

———. (1994). *Seizing the Word: History, Art, and Self in the Work of W. E. B. Du Bois.* Athens: University of Georgia Press.

Cabral, Amilcar. (1972). *Revolution in Guinea: Selected Texts.* New York: Monthly Review Press.

———. (1973). *Return to the Source: Selected Speeches of Amilcar Cabral.* New York: Monthly Review Press.

———. (1979). *Unity and Struggle: Speeches and Writings of Amilcar Cabral.* New York: Monthly Review Press.

Cahill, Susan. (Ed.) (1982). *Motherhood*. New York: Avon.

Cain, William E. (1990a). "W. E. B. Du Bois's *Autobiography* and the Politics of Literature." *Black American Literature Forum* 24, 299–313.

———. (1990b). "Violence, Revolution, and the Cost of Freedom: John Brown and W. E. B. Du Bois." *Boundary* 2 (17), 305–30.

———. (1993). "From Liberalism to Communism: The Political Thought of W. E. B. Du Bois." In Amy Kaplan and Donald E. Pease (Eds.), *Culture of United States Imperialism* (pp. 456–73). Durham: Duke University Press.

Calhoun, Craig. (1995). *Critical Social Theory: Culture, History, and the Challenge of Difference*. Malden, MA: Blackwell.

Callari, Antonio; Cullenberg, Stephen; and Biewener, Carole. (Eds.) (1995). *Marxism in the Postmodern Age: Confronting the New World Order*. New York: Guilford.

Capeci, Dominic J., Jr., and Knight, Jack C. (1996). "Reckoning with Violence: W. E. B. Du Bois and the 1906 Atlanta Race Riot." *Journal of Southern History* 62 (4), 727–67.

Caraway, Nancie. (1991). *Segregated Sisterhood: Racism and the Politics of American Feminism*. Knoxville: University of Tennessee.

Carbado, Devon W. (Ed.) (1999). *Black Men on Race, Gender, and Sexuality: A Critical Reader*. New York: New York University Press.

Carby, Hazel V. (1987). *Reconstructing Womanhood: The Emergence of the Afro-American Woman Novelist*. New York: Oxford University Press.

———. (1998). *Race Men*. Cambridge: Harvard University Press.

Carey, Stephen Anderson. (1992). "Black Men's Du Boisian Relationships to Southern Social Institutions in the Novels of John Oliver Killens." Ph. D. dissertation, University of Texas at Dallas.

Carr, Edward H. (1966). *The Bolshevik Revolution*, vols. 1–3. London: Pelican.

Carter, Cynthia Lorraine Jacobs. (1998). "Higher Education and the Talented Tenth at the New Millennium: A Study of Five Black Women of the African Diaspora." Ph. D. dissertation, George Washington University.

Cash, Floris Loretta. (1986). "Womanhood and Protest: The Club Movement Among Black Women, 1892–1922." Ph. D. dissertation, State University of New York, Stony Brook.

———. (2001). *African American Women and Social Action: The Clubwomen and Volunteerism from Jim Crow to the New Deal, 1896–1936*. Westport, CT: Greenwood Press.

Castle, George. (Ed.) (2001). *Postcolonial Discourse: An Anthology*. Malden, MA: Blackwell.

Castoriadis, Cornelius. (1988a). *Political and Social Writings, Volume 1, 1946–1955: From the Critique of Bureaucracy to the Positive Content of Socialism* (David Ames, Ed.). Minneapolis, MN: University of Minnesota Press.

———. (1988b). *Political and Social Writings, Volume 2, 1955–1960: From the Worker's Struggle Against Bureaucracy to Revolution in the Age of Modern Capitalism* (David Ames, Ed.). Minneapolis, MN: University of Minnesota Press.

———. (1991). *Philosophy, Politics, Autonomy* (David Ames, Ed.). New York: Oxford University Press.

——. (1993). *Political and Social Writings, Volume 3, 1961–1979: Recommencing the Revolution–from Socialism to the Autonomous Society* (David Ames, Ed.). Minneapolis, MN: University of Minnesota Press.

——. (1997). *The Castoriadis Reader* (David Ames, Ed.). Malden, MA: Blackwell.

Castronovo, Russ. (2000). "Within the Veil of Interdisciplinary Knowledge?: Jefferson, Du Bois, and the Negation of Politics." *New History* 31 (4), 781–804.

Cell, John W. (1982). *The Highest Stage of White Supremacy: The Origins of Segregation in South Africa and the American South.* Cambridge: Cambridge University Press.

Césaire, Aimé. (1972). *Discourse on Colonialism.* New York: Monthly Review Press.

Chabal, Patrick. (1981a). "The Social and Political Thought of Amilcar Cabral: A Reassessment." *Journal of Modern African Studies* 19 (1), 31–56.

——. (1981b). "National Liberation in Portuguese Guinea, 1956–1974." *African Affairs* 80 (318), 75–99.

——. (1983). *Amilcar Cabral: Revolutionary Leadership and People's War.* Cambridge: Cambridge University Press.

Chaffee, Mary Law. (1956). "William E. B. Du Bois's Concept of the Racial Problem in the United States." *Journal of Negro History* 41 (July), 241–58.

Chambers, Iain, and Curti, Lidia. (Eds.) (1996). *The Post-Colonial Question: Common Skies, Divided Horizons.* New York: Routledge.

Chandler, Nahum Dimitri. (1997). "The Problem of Purity: A Study in the Early Work of W. E. B. Du Bois." Ph. D. dissertation, University of Chicago.

Chatterjee, Partha. (1993). *The Nation and Its Fragments: Colonial and Postcolonial Histories.* Princeton: Princeton University Press.

Chilcote, Ronald H. (1968). "The Political Thought of Amilcar Cabral." *Journal of Modern African Studies* 6 (3), 373–88.

——. (1991). *Amilcar Cabral's Revolutionary Theory and Practice.* Boulder, CO: Lynne Rienner.

Childs, Peter and Williams, R. J. Patrick. (1997). *An Introduction to Postcolonial Theory.* New York: Prentice Hall.

Chrisman, Laura. (2003). *Postcolonial Contraventions: Cultural Reading of Race, Imperialism, and Transnationalism.* New York: Manchester University Press.

Christian, Barbara. (1985). *Black Feminist Criticism, Perspectives on Black Women Writers.* New York: Pergamon.

——. (1989). "But Who Do You Really Belong To—Black Studies or Women's Studies?" *Women's Studies* 17 (1–2), 17–23.

——. (1994). "Diminishing Returns: Can Black Feminism(s) Survive the Academy?" In David Theo Goldberg (Ed.), *Multiculturalism: A Critical Reader.* (pp. 168–79). Cambridge: Blackwell.

Clack, Beverly. (Ed.) (1999). *Misogyny in the Western Philosophical Tradition: A Reader.* New York: Routledge.

Clarke, John Henrik; Jackson, Esther; Kaiser, Ernest; and O'Dell, J. H. (Eds.) (1970). *Black Titan: W. E. B. Du Bois.* Boston: Beacon.

Coates, Rodney D.; Browning, Sandra Lee; and Beenah, Moshay. (1996). "Race, Class, and Power: The Impact of Du Bois's Scholarship and Revolutionary Agenda." *Research in Race & Ethnic Relations* 9, 211–39.

Coetzee, Pieter H., and Roux, Abraham P. J. (Eds.) (1998). *The African Philosophy Reader.* New York: Routledge.

Cole, Eve Browning. (1993). *Philosophy and Feminist Criticism.* New York: Paragon House.

Cole, George D. H. (1950–1965). *History of Socialist Thought*, vols. 1–4. New York: MacMillan.

Collier-Thomas, Bettye. (1980). *NCNW: National Council of Negro Women.* Washington, DC: National Council of Negro Women.

——. (1993). "National Council of Negro Women." In Darlene Clark Hine, Elsa Barkley Brown, and Rosalyn Teborg-Penn (Eds.), *Black Women in America: An Historical Encyclopedia*, 2 volumes (pp. 853–64). Brooklyn: Carlson.

——. (1997). "Frances Ellen Watkins Harper: Abolitionist and Feminist Reformer, 1825–1911." In Ann D. Gordon and Bettye Collier-Thomas (Eds.), *Afro-American Women and the Vote, 1837–1965*, Amherst, MA: University of Massachusetts Press.

Collins, Lee E. (2002). "Critical Race Theory: Themes, Perspectives, and Directions." In James L. Conyers, Jr. (Ed.), *Black Cultures and Race Relations* (pp. 154–68). Chicago: Burnham.

Collins, Patricia Hill. (1990). *Black Feminist Thought: Knowledge, Consciousness, and the Politics of Empowerment.* New York: Routledge.

——. (1993). "Feminism in the Twentieth Century." In Darlene Clark Hine, Elsa Barkley Brown, and Rosalyn Teborg-Penn (Eds.), *Black Women in America: An Historical Encyclopedia*, 2 volumes (pp. 418–25). Brooklyn: Carlson.

——. (1996). "The Social Construction of Black Feminist Thought." In Ann Garry and Marilyn Pearsall (Eds.), *Women, Knowledge, and Reality: Explorations in Feminist Philosophy.* (pp. 222–48). New York: Routledge.

——. (1998). *Fighting Words: Black Women and the Search for Social Justice.* Minneapolis: University of Minnesota Press.

——. (2000). *Black Feminist Thought: Knowledge, Consciousness, and the Politics of Empowerment*, 2nd ed. New York: Routledge.

——. (2005). *Black Sexual Politics: African Americans, Gender, and the New Racism.* New York: Routledge.

Collins, Randall. (2000). *The Sociology of Philosophies: A Global Theory of Intellectual Change.* Cambridge: Harvard University Press.

Cone, James H. (1975). *God of the Oppressed.* New York: Seabury Press.

——. (1999). *Risks of Faith: The Emergence of a Black Theology of Liberation, 1968–1998.* Boston: Beacon Press.

Contee, Clarence G. (1969a). "W. E. B. Du Bois and African Nationalism, 1914–1945." Ph. D. dissertation, American University, Washington, DC.

——. (1969b). "The Emergence of Du Bois as an African Nationalist." *Journal of Negro History* 54 (January), 48–63.

——. (1970). "W. E. B. Du Bois and *Encyclopedia Africana.*" *Crisis* 77, 375–79.

——. (1971). "A Crucial Friendship Begins: Du Bois and Nkrumah, 1935–1945." *Crisis* 78, 181–85.

——. (1972). "Du Bois, the NAACP, and the Pan-African Congress of 1919." *Journal of Negro History* 57, 13–28.

Conyers, James L. (Ed.) (1997). *Africana Studies: A Disciplinary Quest for Both Theory and Method*. Jefferson, NC: McFarland & Co.

———. (Ed.) (2003). *Afrocentricity and the Academy: Essays on Theory and Practice*. Jefferson, NC: McFarland & Co.

Cook, Mercer, and Henderson, Stephen E. (Eds.) (1969). *The Militant Black Writer in Africa and the United States*. Madison: University of Wisconsin Press.

Cooper, Anna Julia. (1998). *The Voice of Anna Julia Cooper: Including* A Voice From the South *and Other Important Essays, Papers, and Letters* (Charles Lemert and Esme Bhan, Eds.). Lanham, MD: Rowman & Littlefield.

Cortada, Rafael. (1974). *Black Studies in Urban and Comparative Curriculum*. Lexington, MA: Xerox College Publishing.

Cox, Oliver C. (1948). *Caste, Class, and Race: A Study in Social Dynamics*. New York: Monthly Review Press.

———. (1959). *The Foundations of Capitalism*. New York: Philosophical Library.

———. (1962). *Capitalism and American Leadership*. New York: Philosophical Library.

———. (1964). *Capitalism as a System*. New York: Monthly Review Press.

———. (1976). *Race Relations: Elements of Social Dynamics*. Detroit: Wayne State University Press.

———. (1987). *Race, Class, and the World System* (Herbert M. Hunter and Sameer Y. Abraham, Eds.). New York: Monthly Review Press.

———. (2000). *Race: A Study in Social Dynamics*. New York: Monthly Review Press.

Crenshaw, Kimberle; Gotanda, Neil; Peller, Gary; and Thomas, Kendall. (Eds.) (1995). *Critical Race Theory: The Key Writings That Formed the Movement*. New York: New Press.

Cross, Theodore. (1996). "Du Bois's *The Philadelphia Negro*: 100 Years Later." *Journal of Blacks in Higher Education* 11 (Spring), 78–84.

Crossley, Nick. (2005). *Key Concepts in Critical Social Theory*. Thousand Oaks, CA: Sage.

Crouch, Stanley, and Benjamin, Playthell. (2003). *Reconsidering the Souls of Black Folk*. Philadelphia: Running Press.

Croutchett, Larry. (1971). "Early Black Studies Movements." *Journal of Black Studies* 2, 189–200.

Cruse, Harold. (1967). *The Crisis of the Negro Intellectual: A Historical Analysis of the Failure of Black Leadership*. New York: Quill.

———. (2002). *The Essential Harold Cruse: A Reader* (William J. Cobb, Ed.). New York: Palgrave.

Daniels, Jessie. (1997). *White Lies: Race, Class, Gender and Sexuality in White Supremacist Discourse*. New York: Routledge.

Daniels, Phillip T. K. (1980). "Black Studies: Discipline or Field of Study?" *Western Journal of Black Studies* 4 (3), 195–99.

———. (1981). "Theory Building in Black Studies." *Black Scholar* 12 (3), 29–36.

Daniel, Walter C. (1990). "W. E. B. Du Bois's First Efforts as a Playwright." *CLA Journal* 33 (4), 415–27.

Darsey, J. (1998). "'The Voice of Exile': W. E. B. Du Bois and the Quest for Culture." *Communication Abstracts* 21 (6).

Davis, Angela Y. (1981). *Women, Race and Class*. New York: Vintage.

———. (1989). *Women, Culture, and Politics*. New York: Vintage.

———. (1995). "Reflections on the Black Woman's Role in the Community of Slaves." In Beverly Guy-Sheftall (Ed.), *Words of Fire: An Anthology of African American Feminist Thought*. (pp. 200–218). New York: The Free Press.

———. (1998). *The Angela Y. Davis Reader* (Joy A. James, Ed.). Malden, MA: Blackwell.

Davis, Elizabeth L. (1996). *Lifting as They Climb: The National Association of Colored Women*. New York: G. K. Hall.

Davis, William Allison. (1974). *Du Bois and the Problem of the Black Masses*. Atlanta: Atlanta University Press.

Deegan, Mary Jo. (1988). "W. E. B. Du Bois and the Women of Hull House, 1895–1899." *American Sociologist* 19 (4), 301–11.

———. (2001). "American Pragmatism and Liberation Sociology: The Theory and Praxis of Jane Addams, W. E. B. Du Bois, G. H. Mead, and Joe Feagin." Paper presented at the annual meeting of the *Society for the Study of Social Problems*.

D'Emilio, John. (2003). *Lost Prophet: The Life and Times of Bayard Rustin*. New York: Free Press.

Delgado, Richard. (Ed.) (1995). *Critical Race Theory: The Cutting Edge*. Philadelphia: Temple University Press.

Delgado, Richard, and Stefancic, Jean. (Eds.) (1997). *Critical White Studies: Looking Behind the Mirror*. Philadelphia: Temple University Press.

Delgado, Richard, and Stefancic, Jean. (2001). *Critical Race Theory: An Introduction*. New York: New York University Press.

DeMarco, Joseph P. (1974). "The Rationale and Foundation of Du Bois's Theory of Economic Cooperation." *Phylon* 35 (March), 5–15.

———. (1983). *The Social Thought of W. E. B. Du Bois*. Lanham, MD: University Press of America.

Dennis, Rutledge M. (1975). "The Sociology of W. E. B. Du Bois." Ph. D. dissertation, Washington State University.

———. (1977). "Du Bois and the Role of the Educated Elite." *Journal of Negro Education* 46 (4), 388–402.

———. (1996a). "Continuities and Discontinuities in the Social and Political Thought of W. E. B. Du Bois." *Research in Race & Ethnic Relations* 9, 3–23.

———. (1996b). "Du Bois's Concept of Double Consciousness: Myth and Reality." *Research in Race & Ethnic Relations* 9, 69–90.

———. (1997). "Introduction: W. E. B. Du Bois and the Tradition of Radical Intellectual Thought." *Research in Race & Ethnic Relations* 10, xi–xxiv.

Dews, Peter. (1987). *Logics of Disintegration: Post-Structuralist Thought and the Claims of Critical Theory*. New York: Verso.

Dickens, David R., and Fontana, Andrea. (1994). (Eds.) *Postmodernism and Social Theory*. New York: Guilford.

Dickson, Lynda Faye. (1982). "The Early Club Movement Among Black Women in Denver: 1890–1925." Ph. D. dissertation, University of Colorado at Boulder.

Digby, Tom. (Ed.) (1998). *Men Doing Feminism*. New York: Routledge.

Diggs, Irene. (1974). "Du Bois and Women: A Short Story of Black Women, 1910–1934." *Current Bibliography on African Affairs* 7 (Summer), 260–307.

———. (1976). "Du Bois and Children." *Phylon* 37 (December), 370–99.

Dill, Bonnie Thornton. (1979). "The Dialectics of Black Womanhood: Towards a New Model of American Femininity." *Signs: A Journal of Women and Culture in Society* 4 (3), 543–55.

———. (1983). "Race, Class, and Gender: Prospects for an All-Inclusive Sisterhood." *Feminist Studies* 9 (1), 131–50.

Dirlik, Arif. (1994). "The Postcolonial Aura: Third World Criticism in the Age of Global Capitalism." *Critical Inquiry* 20 (2), 328–56.

———. (1997). *The Postcolonial Aura: Third World Criticism in the Age of Global Capitalism*. Boulder: Westview.

Dobratz, Betty A., and Shanks-Melie, Stephanie L. (1997). *"White Power, White Pride!": The White Separatist Movement in the United States*. New York: Twayne.

Doherty, Thomas. (2003). *Cold War, Cool Medium: Television, McCarthyism, and American Culture*. New York: Columbia University Press.

Douglass, Frederick. (1950–1975). *The Life and Writings of Fredrick Douglass*, vols. 1–5 (Philip S. Foner, Ed.). New York: International.

———. (1992). *Frederick Douglass on Women's Rights* (Philip S. Foner, Ed.). New York: Da Capo Press.

———. (1994). *Autobiographies: Narrative of the Life, My Bondage and My Freedom, Life and Times*. New York: Library of America.

———. (1999). *Frederick Douglass: Speeches and Selected Writings* (Philip S. Foner, Ed., abridged and adapted by Yuval Taylor). New York: Library of America.

Dove, Nah. (1998a). *Afrikan Mothers: Bearers of Culture, Makers of Social Change*. Albany: State University of New York Press.

———. (1998b). "Africana Womanism: An Afrocentric Theory." *Journal of Black Studies* 28 (5), 515–39.

Dowdy, Lewis Carnegie, Jr. (1989). "The Impact of the Philosophies of the Presbyterian Church, U.S.A., Booker T. Washington, and W. E. B. Du Bois on the Educational Program of Johnson C. Smith University." Ph. D. dissertation, Rutgers State University of New Jersey, New Brunswick.

Drachler, John. (1975). *Black Homeland/Black Diaspora: Cross Currents of the African Relationship*. Port Washington, NY: Kennikat Press.

Drake, St. Clair. (1986–1987). "Dr. W. E. B. Du Bois: A Life Lived Experimentally and Self-Documented." *Contributions in Black Studies* 8, 111–34.

Drake, William Avon. (1985). "From Reform to Communism: The Intellectual Development of W. E. B. Du Bois." Ph. D. dissertation, Cornell University, Ithaca, NY.

Dred Scott vs. Sanford 1857: 60 US (19 How.).

Drummer, Raydora Susan. (1995). "Transformational Leadership in the Life of W. E. B. Du Bois: 1900–1930." Ph. D. dissertation, Michigan State University.

Duberman, Martin. (1968). "Du Bois as Prophet." *New Republic* (March 23rd), 36–39.

Dublin, Thomas; Arias, Franchesca; and Carreras, Debora. (2003). *What Gender Perspectives Shaped the Emergence of the National Association of Colored Women, 1895–1920?* Alexandria, VA: Alexander Street Press.

Du Bois, David Graham. (1978). "The Du Bois Legacy Under Attack." *Black Scholar* 9 (January–February), 2–12.

——. (1982). "W. E. B. Du Bois: The Last Years." *Race & Class* 24 (Autumn), 178–83.

——. (1998). "David Du Bois Reflects Upon His Father, W. E. B. Du Bois's Commitment to the Struggle of African People." *Crisis* 105 (3), 18.

Du Bois, W. E. B. (1898). "The Study of Negro Problems." *Annals of the American Academy of Political and the Social Science* 11 (January), 1–23.

——. (1906). *The Health and Physique of the Negro American*. Atlanta: Atlanta University Press.

——. (1911a). *The Quest of the Silver Fleece: A Novel*. Chicago: McClurg.

——. (1911b). "Writers." *Crisis* 1 (6), 20–21.

——. (1913). "The People of Peoples and Their Gifts to Men." *Crisis* 6, 7 (November), 339–41.

——. (1928). *Dark Princess: A Romance*. New York: Harcourt, Brace & Co.

——. (1930a). *Africa, Its Geography, People and Products*. Girard, KS: Haldeman-Julius.

——. (1930b). *Africa, Its Place in Modern History*. Girard, KS: Haldemen-Julius.

——. (1938). *A Pageant in Seven Decades, 1868–1938*. Atlanta: Atlanta University Press.

——. (1939). *Black Folk Then and Now: An Essay in the History and Sociology of the Negro Race*. New York: Henry Holt.

——. (1945). *Color and Democracy: Colonies and Peace*. New York: Harcourt Brace.

——. (1952). *In Battle for Peace: The Story of My 83rd Birthday*. New York: Masses & Mainstream.

——. (1954). *The Suppression of the African Slave Trade to the United States of America, 1638–1870*. New York: Social Science Press.

——. (1957). *The Ordeal of Mansart*. New York: Mainstream.

——. (1958). *Pan-Africa, 1919–1958*. Accra, Ghana: Bureau of African Affairs.

——. (1959). *Mansart Builds a School*. New York: Mainstream.

——. (1960a). *W. E. B. Du Bois: A Recorded Autobiography* [Compact Disc]. Washington, DC: Folkways.

——. (1960b). *W. E. B. Du Bois: Socialism and the American Negro* [Compact Disc]. Washington, DC: Folkways.

——. (1960c). *Africa in Battle Against Colonialism, Racism, and Imperialism*. Chicago: Afro-American Heritage Association.

——. (1961a). *Africa: An Essay Toward a History of the Continent of Africa and Its Inhabitants*. Moscow: Soviet Institute of African Studies.

——. (1961b). *Worlds of Color*. New York: Mainstream.

——. (1962). *John Brown*. New York: International Publishers.

——. (1963). *Colonial and Colored Unity: A Program of Action* (George Padmore, Ed.). London: Hammersmith.

——. (1964). *The Selected Poems of W. E. B. Du Bois*. Accra, Ghana: University of Ghana Press.

———. (1965). *The World and Africa: An Inquiry into the Part Which Africa Has Played in World History*. New York: International Publishers.

———. (1968a). *The Autobiography of W. E. B. Du Bois: A Soliloquy on Viewing My Life from the Last Decade of Its First Century*. New York: International Publishers.

———. (1968b). *Dusk of Dawn: An Essay Toward an Autobiography of a Race Concept*. New York: Schocken.

———. (1969a). *Darkwater: Voices from Within the Veil*. New York: Schocken.

———. (1969b). *The Souls of Black Folk*. New York: New American Library.

———. (1969c). *An ABC of Color: Selections from over a Half Century of the Writings of W. E. B. Du Bois*. New York: International Publishers.

———. (Ed.) (1969d). *Atlanta University Publications, 1896–1916*, Nos. 1–20, 2 volumes. New York: Arno Press.

———. (1970a). *The Negro*. New York: Oxford University Press.

———. (1970b). *The Gift of Black Folk: The Negro in the Making of America*. New York: Simon & Schuster.

———. (1970c). *W. E. B. Du Bois: A Reader* (Meyer Weinberg, Ed.). New York: Harper and Row.

———. (1970d). *W. E. B. Du Bois Speaks: Speeches and Addresses, 1899–1963*, 2 volumes (Philip S. Foner, Ed.). New York: Pathfinder Press.

———. (1970e). *The Selected Writings of W. E. B. Du Bois* (Walter Wilson, Ed.). New York: Mentor Books.

———. (1970f). "The Souls of White Folk." In Meyer Weinberg (Ed.), *W.E.B. Du Bois: A Reader* (pp. 298–305). New York: Harper and Row.

———. (1970g). "Of the Culture of White Folk." In Meyer Weinberg (Ed.), *W.E.B. Du Bois: A Reader* (pp. 309–20). New York: Harper and Row.

———. (1971a). *The Seventh Son: The Thought and Writings of W. E. B. Du Bois*, volume 1 (Julius Lester, Ed.). New York: Vintage Books.

———. (1971b). *The Seventh Son: The Thought and Writings of W. E. B. Du Bois*, volume 2 (Julius Lester, Ed.). New York: Vintage Books.

———. (1971c). *W. E. B. Du Bois: A Reader* (Andrew Paschal, Ed.). New York: Collier Books.

———. (1972a). *The Emerging Thought of W. E. B. Du Bois* (Henry Lee Moon, Ed.). New York: Simon & Schuster.

———. (1972b). *W. E. B. Du Bois: The Crisis Writings* (Daniel Walden, Ed.). Greenwich, CT: Fawcett.

———. (1972c). *The Reminiscences of W. E. B. Du Bois: An Oral History*. New York: Columbia University Libraries.

———. (1973). *The Education of Black People: Ten Critiques, 1906–1960* (Herbert Aptheker, Ed.). New York: Monthly Review Press.

———. (1977). *Book Reviews by W. E. B. Du Bois* (Herbert Aptheker, Ed.). Millwood, NY: Kraus-Thomson.

———. (1978). *W. E. B. Du Bois on Sociology and the Black Community* (Dan S. Green and Edwin D. Driver, Eds.). Chicago: University of Chicago Press.

———. (1980a). *Contributions of W. E. B. Du Bois in Government Publications and Proceedings* (Herbert Aptheker, Ed.). Millwood, NY: Kraus-Thomson.

———. (1980b). *Selection from Phylon* (Herbert Aptheker, Ed.). Millwood, NY: Kraus-Thomson.

———. (1980c). *Prayers for Dark People* (Herbert Aptheker, Ed.). Amherst: University of Massachusetts Press.

———. (1980d). *Selections from the Brownies Book* (Herbert Aptheker, Ed.). Millwood, NY: Kraus-Thomson.

———. (1980e). *The Papers of W. E. B. Du Bois, 1877–1963*. Sanford, NC: Microfilming Corporation of America.

———. (1982a). *Writings in Periodicals Edited by Others*, vol. 1 (Herbert Aptheker, Ed.). Millwood, NY: Kraus-Thomson.

———. (1982b). *Writings in Periodicals Edited by Others*, vol. 2 (Herbert Aptheker, Ed.). Millwood, NY: Kraus-Thomson.

———. (1982c). *Writings in Periodicals Edited by Others*, vol. 3 (Herbert Aptheker, Ed.). Millwood, NY: Kraus-Thomson.

———. (1982d). *Writings in Periodicals Edited by Others*, vol. 4 (Herbert Aptheker, Ed.). Millwood, NY: Kraus-Thomson.

———. (1982e). *Writings in Non-Periodical Literature Edited by Others* (Herbert Aptheker, Ed.). Millwood, NY: Kraus-Thomson.

———. (1983a). *Selections from The Crisis*, vol. 1 (Herbert Aptheker, Ed.). Millwood, NY: Kraus-Thomson.

———. (1983b). *Selections from The Crisis*, vol. 2. (Herbert Aptheker, Ed.). Millwood, NY: Kraus-Thomson.

———. (1985a). *Against Racism: Unpublished Essays, Papers, Addresses, 1887–1961* (Herbert Aptheker, Ed.). Amherst, MA: University of Massachusetts Press.

———. (1985b). *Creative Writings by W. E. B. Du Bois: A Pageant, Poems, Short Stories and Playlets* (Herbert Aptheker, Ed.). Millwood, NY: Kraus-Thomson.

———. (1985c). *Selections from Horizon* (Herbert Aptheker, Ed.). White Plains, NY: Kraus-Thomson.

———. (1986a). *Du Bois: Writings* (Nathan Irvin Huggins, Ed.). New York: Library of America Press.

———. (1986b). *Pamphlets and Leaflets* (Herbert Aptheker, Ed.). New York: Kraus-Thomson.

———. (1986c). *Newspaper Columns by W. E. B. Du Bois*, vol. 1 (Herbert Aptheker, Ed.). White Plains, NY: Kraus-Thomson.

———. (1986d). *Newspaper Columns by W. E. B. Du Bois*, vol. 2 (Herbert Aptheker, Ed.). White Plains, NY: Kraus-Thomson.

———. (1989). *The Souls of Black Folk*. New York: Bantam-Doubleday.

———. (1992). *The World of W. E. B. Du Bois* (Meyer Weinberg, Ed.). Westport, CT: Greenwood.

———. (1995a). *W. E. B. Du Bois Reader* (David Levering Lewis, Ed.). New York: Henry Holt.

———. (1995b). *Black Reconstruction in America, 1860–1880*. New York: Touchstone.

———. (1996a). *The Oxford W. E. B. Du Bois Reader* (Eric Sundquist, Ed.). New York: Oxford University Press.

——. (1996b). *The Philadelphia Negro: A Social Study*. Philadelphia: University of Pennsylvania Press.

——. (1996c). "The Talented Tenth Memorial Address." In Henry Louis Gates, Jr. and Cornel West, *The Future of the Race*. (pp. 159–79). New York: Alfred A. Knopf.

——. (1997a). *The Souls of Black Folk* (Robert Gooding-Williams and David W. Blight, Eds.). Boston: Bedford Books.

——. (1997b). *The Correspondence of W. E. B. Du Bois: Volume I—Selections, 1877–1934* (Herbert Aptheker, Ed.). Amherst, MA: University of Massachusetts Press.

——. (1997c). *The Correspondence of W. E. B. Du Bois: Volume II—Selections, 1934–1944* (Herbert Aptheker, Ed.). Amherst, MA: University of Massachusetts Press.

——. (1997d). *The Correspondence of W. E. B. Du Bois: Volume III—Selections, 1944–1963*. (Herbert Aptheker, Ed.). Amherst, MA: University of Massachusetts Press.

——. (1998a). "The Socialism of the German Socialists." *Central European History* 31 (3), 189–225 [Special Issue on "W. E. B. Du Bois and the Kaiserreich Articles"].

——. (1998b). "The Present Condition of German Politics—1893." *Central European History* 31 (3), 171–89 [Special Issue on "W. E. B. Du Bois and the Kaiserreich Articles"].

——. (1999). *Darkwater: Voices from Within the Veil*. Mineola, NY: Dover.

——. (2000a). "The Salvation of the American Negro Lies in Socialism." In Manning Marable and Leith Mullings (Eds.), *Let Nobody Turn Us Around: Voices of Resistance, Reform, and Renewal, An African American Anthology*. (pp. 409–19). Lanham, MD: Rowman & Littlefield.

——. (2000b). *Du Bois on Religion* (Phil Zuckerman, Ed.). Walnut Creek: Altamira.

——. (2000c). *W. E. B. Du Bois's Historic Lecture: "The Sufferings of Black Americans, Socialism, and the Arrogance of U.S. Capitalism"* [Compact Disc]. Durham, NC: Black Historic CD Series.

——. (2001). *The Negro*. Mineola, NY: Dover.

——. (2002). *Du Bois on Education* (Eugene F. Provenzo, Jr., Ed.). Walnut Creek: Alta Mira.

——. (2004). *The Social Theory of W. E. B. Du Bois* (Phil Zuckerman, Ed.). Thousand Oaks: Sage.

——. (2005a). *W. E. B. Du Bois on Asia: Crossing the World Color Line* (Bill Mullen and Cathryn Watson, Eds.). Jackson, MS: University Press of Mississippi.

——. (2005b). *Du Bois on Reform: Periodical-Based Leadership for African Americans* (Brian Johnson, Ed.). Lanham, MD: AltaMira Press.

Du Bois, W. E. B. and Washington, Booker T. (1970). *The Negro in the South*. New York: University Books.

duCille, Ann. (1994). "The Occult of True Black Womanhood: Critical Demeanor and Black Feminist Studies." *Signs* 19 (3), 591–629.

Duffy, Patricia A. (1997). "Philadelphia Stories: Studying W. E. B. Du Bois's Portrait of Family Life and the Impact of Changing Economics." Paper presented at the annual meeting of the *American Sociological Association*.

Dunn, Frederick D. (1991). "African American Philosophy and Philosophies of Education: Their Roots, Aims and Relevance for the 21st Century." Ph. D. dissertation, Columbia University Teacher's College.

During, Simon. (1987). "Postmodernism or Postcolonialism Today," *Textual Practice* 1 (1), 32–47.

Durr, Marlese. (2001). *The New Politics of Race: From Du Bois to the 21st Century*. Westport, CT: Greenwood.

Dussel, Enrique. (1985). *Philosophy of Liberation*. Maryknoll, NY: Orbis.

———. (1995). *The Invention of the Americas: Eclipse of the "Other" and the Myth of Modernity*. New York: Continuum.

———. (1996). *The Underside of Modernity: Apel, Ricoeur, Rorty, Taylor, and the Philosophy of Liberation* (Eduardo Mendieta, Ed.). New York: Prometheus.

Early, Gerald. (Ed.) (1993). *Lure and Loathing: Essays on Race, Identity, and the Ambivalence of Assimilation*. New York: Viking/Penguin.

Echeruo, Michael J. C. (1992). "Edward W. Blyden, W. E. B. Du Bois, and the 'Color Complex.'" *Journal of Modern African Studies* 30 (4), 669–84.

Edelin, Ramona Hoage. (1981). "The Philosophical Foundations and Implications of William Edward Burghardt Du Bois's Social Ethic." Ph. D. dissertation, Boston University Graduate School.

Edwards, Barrington Steven. (2001). "W. E. B. Du Bois: Empirical Social Research and the Challenge to Race, 1868–1910." Ph. D. dissertation, Harvard University.

Edwards, Brent Hayes. (2001). "One More Time: W. E. B. Du Bois as 'Ladies Man.'" *Transition* 11 (89), 88–118.

Efrat, Edgar S. (1967). "Incipient Pan-Africanism: W. E. B. Du Bois and the Early Days." *Australian Journal of Politics & History* 13 (3), 382–93.

Eisenstein, Zillah. (Ed.) (1979). *Capitalist Patriarchy and the Case for Socialist Feminism*. New York: Monthly Review Press.

Ekpo, Denis. (1995). "Toward a Post-Africanism: Contemporary African Thought and Postmodernism." *Textual Practice* 9 (1), 121–35.

Ellis, Mark. (1992). "'Closing Ranks' and 'Seeking Honors': W. E. B. Du Bois in World War I." *Journal of American History* 79 (June), 96–124.

———. (1995). "W. E. B. Du Bois and the Formation of Black Opinion in World War I: A Commentary on "the Damnable Dilemma." *Journal of American History* 81 (4), 1584–91.

Ellison, Ralph. (1980). *Invisible Man*. New York: Vintage Books.

English, Parker, and Kalumba, Kibujjo M. (Eds.) (1996). *African Philosophy: A Classical Approach*. Upper Saddle River, NJ: Prentice Hall.

Esedebe, P. Olisanwuche. (1994). *Pan-Africanism: The Idea and Movement, 1776–1991*. Washington, DC: Howard University Press.

Essed, Philomena, and Goldberg, David Theo. (Eds.) (2001). *Race Critical Theories: Texts and Contexts*. Malden, MA: Blackwell.

Everage, James H. (1979). "W. E. B. Du Bois, a Pioneer in American Sociology: *The Philadelphia Negro* Revisited." Paper presented at the annual meeting of the *Southern Sociological Society*.

Eze, Emmanuel Chukwudi. (Ed.) (1997a). *African Philosophy: An Anthology*. Malden, MA: Blackwell.

———. (Ed.) (1997b). *(Post) Colonial African Philosophy: A Critical Reader*. Malden, MA: Blackwell.

———. (Ed.) (1997c). *Race and the Enlightenment: A Reader*. Malden, MA: Blackwell.

———. (2001). *Achieving Our Humanity: The Idea of the Post-Racial Future*. New York: Routledge.

Fanon, Frantz. (1965). *A Dying Colonialism* New York: Grove.

———. (1967). *Black Skin, White Masks*. New York: Grove.

———. (1968). *The Wretched of the Earth*. New York: Grove.

———. (1969). *Toward the African Revolution*. New York: Grove.

———. (2001). "The Lived Experience of the Black." In Robert Bernasconi (Ed.), *Race* (pp. 184–202). Malden, MA: Blackwell.

Fargania, Sondra. (1995). *The Social Reconstruction of the Feminine Character*. Lanham: Rowman & Littlefield.

Fay, Robert. (1999). "Josephine Saint Pierre Ruffin." In Kwame Anthony Appiah and Henry Louis Gates, Jr. (Ed.), *Africana: The Encyclopedia of the African and African American Experience*. (pp. 1640). New York: Basic/Civitas Books.

Feldberg, Roslyn L. (1984). "Comparable Worth: Toward Theory and Practice in the United States." *Signs: Journal of Women in Culture and Society* 10 (2), 311–28.

Fegerson, Gerard. (1987). "Race, Science, and Medicine in the Late Nineteenth Century: W. E. B. Du Bois and the Health and Physique of the Negro American." M. A. thesis, Yale University, New Haven, CT.

Ferber, Abby L. (1998). *White Man Falling: Race, Gender, and White Supremacy*. Lanham, MD: Rowman & Littlefield.

———. (Ed.) (2004). *Home-Grown Hate: Gender and Organized Racism*. New York: Routledge.

Ferguson, Ann. (1986). "Motherhood and Sexuality: Some Feminist Questions." *Hypatia* 1 (2), 87–102.

———. (1998). "Socialism." In Alison M. Jaggar and Iris Marion Young (Eds.), *A Companion to Feminist Philosophy*. (pp. 520–40). Malden, MA: Blackwell.

Fitchue, M. Anthony. (1996–97). "Locke and Du Bois: Two Major Black Voices Muzzled by Philanthropic Organizations." *Journal of Blacks in Higher Education* 14 (Winter), 111–16.

Fitzpatrick, Sheila. (1982). *The Russian Revolution, 1917–1932*. New York: Oxford University Press.

Fletcher, Diorita C. (1973). "W. E. B. Du Bois's Arraignment and Indictment of White Civilization." *Black World* 22 (May), 16–23.

Foner, Philip S. (1964). *Frederick Douglass*. New York: Citadel.

———. (1992). "Introduction to *Frederick Douglass on Women's Rights*." In Philip S. Foner (Ed.), *Frederick Douglass on Women's Rights* (pp. 3–48). New York: Da Capo.

Fontenot, Chester. (Ed.) (2001). *W. E. B. Du Bois & Race: Essays Celebrating the Centennial Publication of* The Souls of Black Folk. Macon: Mercer University.

Ford, Nick Aaron. (1973). *Black Studies: Threat or Challenge*. New York: Kennikat.

Ford, Richard Thompson. (1995). "The Boundaries of Race: Political Geography in Legal Analysis." In Kimberle Crenshaw, Neil Gotanda, Gary Peller, and Kendall Thomas (Eds.), *Critical Race Theory: The Key Writings That Formed the Movement*. (pp. 449–64). New York: New Press.

Fossett, Judith Jackson, and Tucker, Jeffrey A. (Eds.) (1997). *Race Consciousness: African American Studies for the New Century*. New York: New York University Press.

Foster, Frances Smith. (1993). "Frances Ellen Watkins Harper." In Darlene Clark Hine, Elsa Barkley Brown, and Rosalyn Teborg-Penn (Eds.), *Black Women in America: An Historical Encyclopedia*, 2 volumes (pp. 532–36). Brooklyn: Carlson.

Foucault, Michel. (1977a). *Language, Counter-Memory, Practice: Selected Essays and Interviews by Michel Foucault* (Donald F. Bouchard, Ed.). Ithaca: Cornell University Press.

——. (1977b). *Power/Knowledge: Selected Interviews and Other Writings, 1972–1977* (Colin Gordon, Ed.). New York: Pantheon.

——. (1984). *The Foucault Reader* (Paul Rabinow, Ed.). New York: Pantheon.

——. (1988). *Politics, Philosophy, Culture: Interviews and Other Writings, 1977–1984* (Lawrence D. Kritzman, Ed.). New York: Routledge.

——. (1997). *The Essential Works of Michel Foucault, 1954–1984, volume 1 — Ethics: Subjectivity and Truth* (Paul Rabinow, Ed.). New York: New Press.

——. (1998). *The Essential Works of Michel Foucault, 1954–1984, volume 2 — Aesthetics, Method, and Epistemology* (Paul Rabinow, Ed.). New York: New Press.

——. (2000). *The Essential Works of Michel Foucault, 1954–1984, volume 3 — Power* (Paul Rabinow, Ed.). New York: New Press.

Fox, Bonnie. (Ed.) (1980). *Hidden in the Household: Women's Domestic Labor Under Capitalism*. Toronto: Women Educational Press.

Franklin, V. P. (1995). "The Autobiographical Legacy of W. E. B. Du Bois." In V. P. Franklin, *Living Our Stories, Telling Our Truths: Autobiography and the Making of the African American Intellectual Tradition*. New York: Scribner.

Fraser, Nancy. (1989). *Unruly Practices: Power, Discourse and Gender in Contemporary Social Theory*. Minneapolis: University of Minnesota Press.

——. (1991). "What's Critical About Critical Theory?: The Case of Habermas and Gender." In David Ingram and Julia Simon-Ingram (Eds.), *Critical Theory: The Essential Readings*. (pp. 357–87). New York: Paragon House.

Fredrickson, George. (1981). *White Supremacy: A Comparative Study in American and South African History*. New York: Oxford University Press.

——. (1987). *The Black Image in the White Mind: The Debate on Afro-American Character and Destiny, 1817–1914*. Hanover, NH: Wesleyan University Press.

Freedman, Martin Neil. (1975). "The Rhetorical Adaptation of Social Movement Leaders: Booker T. Washington and W. E. B. Du Bois." Ph. D. dissertation, Purdue University, Lafayette, IN.

Freundlieb, Dieter; Hudson, Wayne; and Rundell, John. (Eds.) (2004). *Critical Theory after Habermas*. Boston: Brill.

Frey, Raymond G., and Wellman, Christopher Heath. (Eds.) (2003). *A Companion to Applied Ethics*. Malden, MA: Blackwell.

Fritz, Jan M. (1990). "In Pursuit of Justice: W. E. B. Du Bois." *Clinical Sociology Review* 8, 15–26.

Fromm, Erich. (1947). *Man for Himself*. New York: Holt, Rinehart & Winston.

——. (1955). *The Sane Society*. New York: Holt, Rinehart & Winston.

——. (1970). *The Crisis of Psychoanalysis*. New York: Holt, Rinehart & Winston.

Frye, Charles A. (1978). *Towards a Philosophy of Black Studies*. San Francisco: R & E Research Associates.

Fulop, Timothy, and Raboteau, Albert J. (Eds.) (1996). *African American Religion: Interpretive Essays in History and Culture*. New York: Routledge.

Funk, Rainer. (1982). *Erich Fromm: The Courage to Be Human*. New York: Continuum.

Gabbidon, Shaun L. (1996). "The Criminological Writings of W. E. B. Du Bois: A Historical Analysis." Ph. D. dissertation, Indiana University of Pennsylvania.

——. (2000). "An Early American Crime Poll by W. E. B. Du Bois." *Western Journal of Black Studies* 24 (3), 167–74.

——. (2001). "W. E. B. Du Bois: Pioneering American Criminologist." *Journal of Black Studies* 31 (5), 581–99.

Gabel, Leona C. (1982). *From Slavery to the Sorbonne and Beyond: The Life and Writings of Anna Julia Cooper*. Northampton, MA: Smith College Studies in History.

Gaines, Kevin K. (1996). "Urban Pathology and the Limits of Social Research: W. E. B. Du Bois's *The Philadelphia Negro*." In Gaines, *Uplifting the Race: Black Leadership, Politics, and Culture in the Twentieth Century* (pp. 152–78). Chapel Hill: University of North Carolina Press.

Gaines, Stanley O., Jr. (1996). "Perspectives of Du Bois and Fanon on the Psychology of Oppression." In Lewis R. Gordon, T. Denean Sharley-Whiting, and Renee T. White (Eds.), *Fanon: A Critical Reader*. (pp. 24–34). Cambridge: Blackwell.

Gaines, Stanley O., Jr., and Reed, Edward S. (1994). "Two Social Psychologies of Prejudice: Gordon W. Allport, W. E. B. Du Bois, and the Legacy of Booker T. Washington." *Journal of Black Psychology* 20 (1), 8–28.

Gamble, Sarah. (Ed.) (2002). *The Routledge Companion to Feminism and Postfeminism*. New York: Routledge.

Gandhi, Leela. (1998). *Postcolonial Theory: A Critical Introduction*. Edinburgh: Edinburgh University Press.

Garry, Ann, and Pearsall, Marilyn. (Eds.) (1996). *Women, Knowledge, and Reality: Explorations in Feminist Philosophy*. New York: Routledge.

Gatens, Moira. (1991). *Feminism and Philosophy: Perspectives on Difference and Equality*. Indianapolis: Indiana University Press.

Gates, Henry Louis, Jr. (Ed.) (1990). *Reading Black/Reading Feminist: A Critical Anthology*. New York: Meridian.

——. (1996). "W. E. B. Du Bois and 'The Talented Tenth.'" In Henry Louis Gates, Jr. and Cornel West, *The Future of the Race*. (pp. 115–32). New York: Alfred A. Knopf.

——. (2000). "W. E. B. Du Bois and the Encyclopedia Africana, 1909–1963." *Annals of the American Academy of Political and Social Science* 568 (March), 203–19.

Gates, Henry Louis, Jr., and West, Cornel. (1996). *The Future of the Race*. New York:

Alfred A. Knopf.

Gatewood, William B. (1994). "W. E. B. Du Bois: Elitist as Racial Radical." *Georgia Historical Quarterly* 78 (2), 306–27.

Gbadegesin, Olusegun. (1996). "Kinship of the Dispossessed: Du Bois, Nkrumah, and the Foundations of Pan-Africanism." In Bernard W. Bell, Emily R. Grosholz, and James B. Stewart (Eds.), *W. E. B. Du Bois: On Race and Culture*. (pp. 219–42). New York: Routledge.

Geiss, Imanuel. (1974). *The Pan-African Movement: A History of Pan-Africanism in America, Europe, and Africa*. New York: Holmes & Meier.

Genovese, Eugene D. (1965). *The Political Economy of Slavery: Studies in the Economy and Society of the Slave South*. New York: Pantheon.

———. (1969). *The World the Slaveholders Made: Two Essays in Interpretation*. New York: Pantheon.

———. (1974). *Roll, Jordan, Roll: The World the Slaves Made*. New York: Vintage.

———. (1979). *From Rebellion to Revolution: Afro-American Slave Revolts in the Making of the Modern World*. Baton Rouge: Louisiana State University Press.

Gershoni, Yekutiel. (1995). "Contributions of W. E. B. Du Bois to Pan-Africanism." *Journal of Third World Studies* 12 (2), 440–43.

Gibson, Lovie Nancy. (1977). "Du Bois's Propaganda Literature: An Outgrowth of His Sociological Studies." Ph. D. dissertation, State University of New York-Buffalo.

Giddens, Anthony. (1971). *Capitalism and Modern Social Theory: An Analysis of the Writings of Marx, Durkheim and Max Weber*. Cambridge: Cambridge University Press.

Giddings, Paula. (1984). *When and Where I Enter: The Impact of Black Women on Race and Sex in America*. New York: Quill.

Gilkes, Cheryl Townsend. (1996). "The Margin as the Center of a Theory of History: African American Women, Social Change, and the Sociology of W. E. B. Du Bois." In Bernard W. Bell, Emily R. Grosholz, and James B. Stewart (Eds.), *W. E. B. Du Bois: On Race and Culture*. (pp. 111–41). New York: Routledge.

Gillespie, Michelle K., and Hall, Randal L. (2006). *Thomas Dixon Jr. and the Birth of Modern America*. Baton Rouge: Louisiana State University Press.

Gilroy, Paul. (1987). *There Ain't No Black in the Union Jack*. New York: Routledge.

———. (1993a). *The Black Atlantic: Modernity and Double Consciousness*. Cambridge: Harvard University Press.

———. (1993b). *Small Acts: Thoughts on the Politics of Black Cultures*. New York: Serpent's Tail.

———. (2000). *Against Race: Imagining Political Culture Beyond the Color Line*. Cambridge: Harvard University Press.

———. (2005). *Postcolonial Melancholia*. New York: Columbia University Press.

Gipson, Carolyn Renee. (1971). "Intellectual Dilemmas in the Novels of W. E. B. Du Bois." Ph. D. dissertation, University of Michigan, Ann Arbor.

Giroux, Henry. (1992). *Border Crossings: Cultural Workers and the Politics of Education*. New York: Routledge.

Glascoe, Myrtle G. (1996). "W. E. B. Du Bois: His Evolving Theory of Education."

Research in Race & Ethnic Relations 9, 171–88.

Goldberg, David Theo. (1987). "Raking the Field of the Discourse of Racism." *Journal of Black Studies* 18, 58–71.

———. (Ed.) (1990). *Anatomy of Racism*. Minneapolis: University of Minnesota Press.

———. (1993). *Racist Culture: Philosophy and the Politics of Meaning*. Cambridge: Blackwell.

———. (Ed.) (1994). *Multiculturalism: A Critical Reader*. Cambridge: Blackwell.

———. (1997). *Racial Subjects: Writing on Race in America*. New York: Routledge.

———. (2000). "Heterogeneity and Hybridity: Colonial Legacy, Postcolonial Heresy." In Henry Schwarz and Sangeeta Ray (Eds.), *A Companion to Postcolonial Studies*. (pp. 72–86). Malden, MA: Blackwell.

———. (2001). *The Racial State*. Malden, MA: Blackwell.

Goldberg, David Theo; Musheno, Michael; and Bower, Lisa. (Eds.) (2001). *Between Law and Culture: Relocating Legal Studies*. Minneapolis: University of Minnesota Press.

Goldberg, David Theo, and Quayson, Ato. (Eds.) (1999). *Relocating Postcolonialism: A Critical Reader*. Malden, MA: Blackwell.

Goldberg, David Theo, and Solomos, John. (Eds.) (2002). *A Companion to Racial and Ethnic Studies*. Malden, MA: Blackwell.

Golden, L. Hanga, and Milikan, Ov. (1966). "William E. B. Du Bois: Scientist and Public Figure." *Journal of Human Relations* 14, 156–68.

Goldman, Anita Haya. (1994). "Negotiating Claims of Race and Rights: Du Bois, Emerson, and the Critique of Liberal Nationalism." *Massachusetts Review* 35 (Spring–Summer), 169–201.

Goldstein, Stanley L. (1972). "The Influence of Marxism on the Educational Philosophy of W. E. B. Du Bois." Ph. D. dissertation, University of Texas at Austin.

Goodin, Patrick. (2002). "Du Bois and Appiah: The Politics of Race and Racial Identity." In Robert E. Birt (Ed.), *The Quest for Community and Identity: Critical Essays in Africana Social Philosophy* (pp. 73–83). Lanham, MD: Rowman & Littlefield.

Goodin, Robert E., and Pettit, Philip. (Eds.) (1993). *A Companion to Contemporary Political Philosophy*. Malden, MA: Blackwell.

Goodin, Robert E., and Pettit, Philip. (Eds.) (1997). *Contemporary Political Philosophy: An Anthology*. Cambridge: Blackwell.

Gooding-Willliams, Robert. (1987). "Philosophy of History and Social Critique in *The Souls of Black Folk*." *Social Science Information* 26, 99–114.

———. (1991). "Evading Narrative Myth, Evading Prophetic Pragmatism: A Review of Cornel West's *The American Evasion of Philosophy*." *American Philosophical Association Newsletter of the Black Experience* 90 (3), 12–16.

———. (1991–1992). "Evading Narrative Myth, Evading Prophetic Pragmatism: Cornel West's *The American Evasion of Philosophy*." *Massachusetts Review* 32 (December), 517–42.

———. (1994). "Du Bois's Counter-Sublime." *Massachusetts Review* 35 (Spring–Summer), 203–24.

———. (1996). "Outlaw, Appiah, and Du Bois's 'The Conservation of Races.'" In Bernard W. Bell, Emily R. Grosholz, and James B. Stewart (Eds.), *W. E. B. Du*

Bois: On Race and Culture. (pp. 39–56). New York: Routledge.

———. (2005). *Look, a Negro!: Philosophical Essays on Race, Culture and Politics.* New York: Routledge.

Gordon, Lewis R. (1993). "Racism as a Form of Bad Faith." *APA Newsletter on Philosophy and the Black Experience* 92 (2), 6–8.

———. (1995a). *Bad Faith and Anti-Black Racism.* Atlantic Highlands, NJ: Humanities Press.

———. (1995b). *Fanon and the Crisis of the European Sciences: An Essay on Philosophy and the Human Sciences.* New York: Routledge.

———. (Ed.) (1997a). *Existence in Black: An Anthology of Black Existential Philosophy.* New York: Routledge.

———. (1997b). *Her Majesty's Other Children: Sketches of Racism from a Neocolonial Age.* Lanham, MD: Rowman & Littlefield.

———. (1998). "African American Philosophy: Theory, Politics, and Pedagogy." *Philosophy of Education Yearbook: 1998* [On-line article]. Available at www. ed.uiuc .edu/EPS/PES-Yearbook/1998/gordon.htm [17 October 2001].

———. (1999). "A Short History of the 'Critical' in Critical Race Theory." *APA Newsletter on Philosophy and the Black Experience* 98 (2), 23–26.

———. (2000a). *Existentia Africana: Understanding Africana Existential Thought.* New York: Routledge.

———. (2000b). "What Does It Mean to Be a Problem?: W. E. B. Du Bois on the Study of Black Folk." In Lewis R. Gordon, *Existentia Africana: Understanding Africana Existential Thought* (pp. 62–95). New York: Routledge.

———. (2000c). "Du Bois's Humanistic Philosophy of Human Sciences." *Annals of the American Academy of Political and Social Science* 568 (March), 265–80.

———. (2002). "Sartrean Bad Faith and Anti-Black Racism." In Julie K. Ward and Tommy L. Lott (Eds.), (2002). *Philosophers on Race: Critical Essays.* (pp. 241–59). Malden, MA: Blackwell.

———. (2006a). *Disciplinary Decadence: Living Thought in Trying Times.* Boulder, CO: Paradigm.

———. (2006b). "African American Philosophy, Race, and the Geography of Reason." In Lewis R. Gordon and Jane Anna Gordon (Eds.), *Not Only the Master's Tools: African American Studies in Theory and Practice.* (p. 3–50). Boulder, CO: Paradigm.

Gordon, Lewis R.; Sharley-Whiting, T. Denean; and White, Renee T. (Eds.) (1996). *Fanon: A Critical Reader.* Cambridge: Blackwell.

Gordon, Lewis R., and Gordon, Jane Anna. (Eds). (2006a). *A Companion to African American Studies.* Malden, MA: Blackwell.

Gordon, Lewis R., and Gordon, Jane Anna. (Eds.) (2006b). *Not Only the Master's Tools: African American Studies in Theory and Practice.* Boulder, CO: Paradigm.

Gorman, William. (1950). "W. E. B. Du Bois and His Work." *Fourth International* 2 (May–June), 80–85.

Gotanda, Neil. (1995). "A Critique of 'Our Constitution Is Color-Blind.'" In Kimberle Crenshaw, Neil Gotanda, Gary Peller, and Kendall Thomas (Eds.), *Critical Race Theory: The Key Writings That Formed the Movement.* (pp. 257–75). New York:

New Press.

Gottlieb, Roger S. (1992). *Marxism, 1844–1990: Origins, Betrayal, Rebirth.* New York: Routledge.

———. (Ed.) (1989). *An Anthology of Western Marxism: From Lukács and Gramsci to Socialist-Feminism.* New York: Oxford University Press.

Gouldner, Alvin W. (1980). *The Two Marxisms: Contradictions and Anomalies in the Development of Theory.* New York: Seabury.

Graham, Maryemma. (1973). "The Threefold Cord: Blackness, Womanness and Art: A Study of the Life and Works of Frances Ellen Watkins Harper." M. A. thesis, Cornell University.

———. (1986). "Frances Ellen Watkins Harper." In Trudier Harris and Thadious M. Davis (Eds.), *Afro-American Writers Before the Harlem Renaissance.* Detroit: Gale.

Graham, Shirley. (1976). *His Day Is Marching On: A Memoir of W. E. B. Du Bois.* Chicago: Johnson.

Gramsci, A. (1967). *The Modern Prince and Other Writings* (Louis Marks, Ed.). New York: International.

———. (1971). *Selections from the Prison Notebooks of Antonio Gramsci* (Quintin Hoare and Geoffrey Nowell-Smith, Eds.). New York: International.

———. (1975). *History, Philosophy, and Culture in the Young Gramsci* (Pedro Cavalcanti and Paul Piccone, Eds.). St. Louis: Telos Press.

———. (1977). *Selections from the Political Writings, 1910–1920* (Quintin Hoare, Ed.). New York: International.

———. (1978). *Selections from the Political Writings, 1921–1926* (Quintin Hoare, Ed.). New York: International.

———. (1985). *Selections from the Cultural Writings* (David Forgacs and Geoffrey Nowell-Smith, Eds.). Cambridge: Harvard University Press.

———. (1992). *Prison Notebooks*, volume 1 (Joseph A. Buttigieg, Ed.). New York: Columbia University Press.

———. (1994a). *Antonio Gramsci: Pre-Prison Writings* (Richard Bellamy, Ed). New York: Cambridge University Press.

———. (1994b). *Letters from Prison*, 2 volumes (Frank Rosengarten, Ed.). New York: Columbia University Press.

———. (1995a). *Antonio Gramsci: Further Selections from the Prison Notebooks* (Derek Boothman, Ed). Minneapolis: University of Minnesota Press.

———. (1995b). *The Southern Question* (Pasquale Vericchio, Ed.). West Lafayette, IN: Bordighera.

———. (1996). *Prison Notebooks*, volume 2 (Joseph A. Buttigieg, Ed.). New York: Columbia University Press.

———. (2000). *The Antonio Gramsci Reader: Selected Writings, 1916–1935* (David, Forgacs, Ed.). New York: New York University Press.

Greco, Rose Dorothy. (1984). "The Educational Views of Booker T. Washington and W. E. B. Du Bois: A Critical Comparison." Ph. D. dissertation, Loyola University of Chicago.

Green, Dan S. (1973). "The Truth Shall Make Ye Free: The Sociology of W. E. B. Du

Bois." Ph. D. dissertation, University of Massachusetts.

———. (1977). "W. E. B. Du Bois's Talented Tenth: A Strategy for Racial Advancement." *Journal of Negro Education* 46 (3), 358–66.

Green, Dan S. and Driver, Edwin D. (1976). "W. E. B. Du Bois: A Case in the Sociology of Sociological Negation." *Phylon* 37 (4), 308–33.

Green, Dan S., and Smith, Earl. (1983). "W. E. B. Du Bois and the Concepts of Race and Class." *Phylon* 44 (December), 262–72.

Greer, Beatrice Tatum. (1952). "A Study of the Life and Works of Mrs. Frances Ellen Watkins Harper." M. A. thesis, Hampton Institute.

Gregg, Robert. (1998). "Giant Steps: W. E. B. Du Bois and the Historical Enterprise." In Michael B. Katz and Thomas J. Sugrue (Eds.), *W. E. B. Du Bois, Race, and the City: The Philadelphia Negro and Its Legacy.* (pp. 77–100). Philadelphia: University of Pennsylvania Press.

Griffin, Farah Jasmine. (2000). "Black Feminists and W. E. B. Du Bois: Respectability, Protection, and Beyond." *Annals of the American Academy of Political and Social Science* 568 (March), 28–40.

Grimshaw, Jean. (1986). *Philosophy and Feminist Thinking.* Minneapolis: University of Minnesota Press.

Grosholz, Emily R. (1996). "Nature and Culture in *The Souls of Black Folk* and *Quest of the Silver Fleece*." In Bernard W. Bell, Emily R. Grosholz, and James B. Stewart (Eds.), *W. E. B. Du Bois: On Race and Culture.* (pp. 177–192). New York: Routledge.

Gruesser, John Cullen. (2005). *Confluences: Postcolonialism, African American Literary Studies, and the Black Atlantic.* Athens, GA: University of Georgia Press.

Geuss, Raymond. (1981). *The Idea of Critical Theory.* Cambridge: Cambridge University Press.

Guettel, Charnie. (1974). *Marxism and Feminism.* Toronto: Women's Educational Press.

Guevara, Ernesto "Che." (1968). *Venceremos!: The Speeches and Writings of Che Guevara* (John Gerassi, Ed.). New York: Macmillan.

Guiner, Lani. (1995). "Groups, Representation, and Race-Consciousness Districting: A Case of the Emperor's Clothes." In Kimberle Crenshaw, Neil Gotanda, Gary Peller, and Kendall Thomas (Eds.), *Critical Race Theory: The Key Writings That Formed the Movement.* (pp. 205–34). New York: New Press.

Gunning, Sandra. (1997). "*The Woman's Era*." In William L. Andrews, Frances Smith Foster, and Trudier Harris (Eds.), *The Oxford Companion to African American Literature.* (pp. 786–787). New York: Oxford University Press.

Guy-Sheftall, Beverly. (1990). *Daughters of Sorrow: Attitudes Toward Black Women, 1880–1920.* Brooklyn, NY: Carlson.

———. (Ed.) (1995). *Words of Fire: An Anthology of African American Feminist Thought.* New York: The Free Press.

Guzman, Jessie P. (1961). "W. E. B. Du Bois—The Historian." *Journal of Negro Education* 30 (Fall), 377–85.

Gyekye, Kwame. (1995). *An Essay on African Philosophical Thought: The Akan Conceptual Scheme.* Philadelphia: Temple University Press.

———. (1996). *African Cultural Values: An Introduction.* Elkins Park, PA: Sankofa

Publishing.

———. (1997). *Tradition and Modernity: Philosophical Reflections on the African Experience*. New York: Oxford University Press.

Habermas, Jurgen. (1984). *Theory of Communicative Action*, volume 1. Boston: Beacon.

———. (1986a). *Theory and Practice*. Cambridge: Polity Press.

———. (1986b). *Knowledge and Human Interests*. Cambridge: Polity Press.

———. (1986c). *Toward a Rational Society*. Cambridge: Polity Press.

———. (1987a). *Theory of Communicative Action*, volume 2. Boston: Beacon.

———. (1987b). *The Philosophical Discourse on Modernity*. Cambridge: MIT Press.

———. (1988). *On the Logic of the Social Sciences*. Cambridge: MIT Press.

———. (1989a). *The Structural Transformation of the Public Sphere*. Cambridge: MIT Press.

———. (1989b.) *On Society and Politics: A Reader* (Steven Seidman, Ed.). Boston: Beacon.

———. (1990). *Moral Consciousness and Communicative Action*. Cambridge: MIT Press.

———. (1992a). *Autonomy and Solidarity* (Peter Dews, Ed.). London: Verso.

———. (1992b). *Postmetaphysical Thinking*. Cambridge: Polity Press.

———. (1993). *Justification and Application*. Cambridge: Polity Press.

———. (1994). *The Past as Future*. Lincoln: University of Nebraska Press.

———. (1995). *Between Facts and Norms: Contributions to a Discourse Theory of Law and Democracy*. Cambridge: MIT Press.

———. (1998). *On the Pragmatics of Communication* (Maeve Cooke, Ed.). Cambridge: MIT Press.

———. (2000). *On the Pragmatics of Social Interaction: Preliminary Studies in the Theory of Communicative Action*. Cambridge: MIT Press.

Hackney, James R., Jr. (1998). "Derrick Bell's Re-Sounding: W. E. B. Du Bois, Modernism, and Critical Race Scholarship." *Law & Social Inquiry* 23 (1), 141–64.

Hall, Perry A. (1999). *In the Vineyard: Working in African American Studies*. Knoxville: University of Tennessee Press.

Hamilton, Tullia K. Brown. (1978). "The National Association of Colored Women, 1896–1920." Ph. D. dissertation, Emory University.

Hamilton, Virginia. (1972). *W. E. B. Du Bois: A Biography*. New York: Crowell.

Hammond, Evelynn M. (1997). "Toward a Genealogy of Black Female Sexuality: The Problematic of Silence." In M. Jacqui Alexander and Chandra Talpade Mohanty (Eds.), *Feminist Genealogies, Colonial Legacies, Democratic Futures*. (pp. 170–81). New York: Routledge.

Hansberry, William Leo. (1970). "W. E. B. Du Bois's Influence on African History." In John Henrik Clarke, Esther Jackson, Ernest Kaiser, and J. H. O'Dell (Eds.), *Black Titan: W. E. B. Du Bois*. (pp. 98–114). Boston: Beacon.

Hansen, Jonathan M. (1997). "Fighting Words: The Transnational Patriotism of Eugene V. Debs, Jane Addams, and W. E. B. Du Bois." Ph. D. dissertation, Boston University.

Harding, Vincent. (1970). "W. E. B. Du Bois and the Black Messianic Vision." In John Henrik Clarke, Esther Jackson, Ernest Kaiser, and J. H. O'Dell (Eds.), *Black*

Titan: W. E. B. Du Bois. (pp. 52–68). Boston: Beacon.

Hare, Nathan. (1969). "W. E. Burghardt Du Bois: An Appreciation." In W. E. B. Du Bois, *The Souls of Black Folk*. New York: New American Library.

———. (1972). "The Battle of Black Studies." *Black Scholar* 3 (9), 32–37.

———. (1998). "The Challenge of a Black Scholar." In Joyce A. Ladner (Ed.), *The Death of White Sociology: Essays on Race and Culture*. (pp. 67–80). Baltimore: Black Classic Press.

Harper, Frances Ellen Watkins. (1988). *The Complete Poems of Frances E. W. Harper* (Maryemma Graham, Ed.). New York: Oxford University Press.

———. (1990). *A Brighter Coming Day: A Frances Ellen Watkins Harper Reader* (Frances Smith Foster, Ed.). New York: The Feminist Press at CUNY.

———. (1995). "Woman's Political Future." In Beverly Guy-Sheftall (Ed.), *Words of Fire: An Anthology of African American Feminist Thought*. (pp. 40–42). New York: The Free Press.

Harris, Cheryl I. (1995). "Whiteness as Property." In Kimberle Crenshaw, Neil Gotanda, Gary Peller, and Kendall Thomas (Eds.), *Critical Race Theory: The Key Writings That Formed the Movement*. (pp. 276–91). New York: New Press.

Harris, Joseph E. (Ed.) (1993). *Global Dimensions of the African Diaspora*. Washington, D.C.: Howard University Press.

Harris, Leonard. (Ed.) (1983). *Philosophy Born of Struggle: An Anthology of Afro-American Philosophy from 1917*. Dubuque, IA: Kendall/Hunt.

———. (Ed.) (1989). *The Philosophy of Alain Locke: Harlem Renaissance and Beyond*. Philadelphia: Temple University Press.

———. (Ed.) (1999a). *The Critical Pragmatism of Alain Locke: A Reader on Value, Theory, Aesthetics, Community, Culture, Race, and Education*. Lanham, MD: Rowman & Littlefield.

———. (Ed.) (1999b). *Racism: Key Concepts in Critical Theory*. Amherst, NY: Humanity Books.

Harris, Robert; Hine, Darlene Clark; and McKay, Nellie. (Eds.) (1990). *Black Studies in the Academy*. New York: The Ford Foundation.

Harris, Trudier. (1982). *From Mammies to Militants: Domestics in Black American Literature*. Philadelphia: Temple University Press.

Harrison, Faye V. (1992). "The Du Boisian Legacy in Anthropology." *Critique of Anthropology* 12 (3), 239–60.

Harstock, Nancy C. M. (1995). "The Feminist Standpoint: Developing the Ground for a Specifically Feminist Historical Materialism." In Nancy Tuana and Rosmarie Tong (Eds.), *Feminism & Philosophy: Essential Readings in Theory, Reinterpretation, and Application*. (pp. 69–90). Boulder, CO: Westview.

Hartmann, Heidi I. (1981). "The Unhappy Marriage of Marxism and Feminism: Towards a More Progressive Union." In Lydia Sargent (Ed.), *Women and Revolution: A Discussion of the Unhappy Marriage of Marxism and Feminism*. (pp. 1–41). Boston: South End.

Hayes, Floyd W. (Ed.) (1997). *A Turbulent Voyage: Readings in African American Studies*. San Diego, CA: Collegiate Press.

Held, David. (1980). *Introduction to Critical Theory: Horkheimer to Habermas*.

Berkeley: University of California Press.

Henderson, Lenneal J., Jr. (1970). "W. E. B. Du Bois, Black Scholar, and Prophet." *Black Scholar* 1 (January–February), 48–57.

Henderson, Robert M. (1972). *D. W. Griffith: His Life and Work.* New York: Oxford University Press.

Henderson, Vivian W. (1974). *Race, Economics, and Public Policy: With Reflection on W. E. B. Du Bois.* Atlanta: Atlanta University Press.

——. (1976). "Race, Economics, and Public Policy with Reflections on W. E. B. Du Bois." *Phylon* 37 (1), 1–11.

Hendricks, Wanda A. (1993). "Ida B. Wells-Barnett." In Darlene Clark Hine, Elsa Barkley Brown, and Rosalyn Teborg-Penn (Eds.), *Black Women in America: An Historical Encyclopedia*, 2 volumes (pp. 1242–46). Brooklyn: Carlson.

——. (1998). *Gender, Race, and Politics in the Midwest: Black Clubwomen in Illinois.* Bloomington, IN: Indiana University Press.

Hennessey, Alistair. (Ed.) (1992). *Intellectuals in the Twentieth-Century Caribbean*, 2 volumes. London: Macmillan, Caribbean.

Henton, Jennifer E. (2001). "Twain, Du Bois, Toomer, and Hurston: Reading American Literature and Reading Race." Ph. D. dissertation, University of Delaware.

Henry, Paget. (2000). *Caliban's Reason: Introducing Afro-Caribbean Philosophy.* New York: Routledge.

Higbee, Mark David. (1993). "W. E. B. Du Bois, F. B. Ransom, the Madam Walker Company, and Black Business Leadership in the 1930s." *Indiana Magazine of History* 89 (June), 101–24.

——. (1995a). "W. E. B. Du Bois and the Problems of the Twentieth Century: Race, History, and Literature in Du Bois's Political Thought, 1903–1940." Ph. D. dissertation, Columbia University.

——. (1995b). "Du Bois: The First Half Century." *Science & Society* 59 (1), 82–87.

Higginbotham, A. Leon, Jr. (1978). *In the Matter of Color: Race and the American Legal Process—The Colonial Period.* New York: Oxford University Press.

——. (1996). *Shades of Freedom: Racial Politics and Presumptions of the American Legal Process.* New York: Oxford University Press.

Higginbotham, Evelyn Brooks. (1989). "Beyond the Sound of Silence: Afro-American Women in History." *Gender & History* 1 (1), 50–67.

——. (1993). *Righteous Discontent: The Women's Movement in the Black Baptist Church, 1880–1920.* Cambridge: Harvard University Press.

Hill, Patricia L. (1978). "American Popular Response to W. E. B. Du Bois's *The Souls of Black Folk.*" *Western Journal of Black Studies* 2 (1), 54–59.

Hindess, Barry. (1993). "Marxism." In Robert E. Goodin and Philip Pettit (Eds.), *A Companion to Contemporary Political Philosophy.* (pp. 312–33). Malden, MA: Blackwell.

Hine, Darlene Clark. (Ed.) (1990). *Black Women in the United States 1619–1989*, 16 volumes. Brooklyn: Carlson.

Hine, Darlene Clark; Brown, Elsa Barkley; and Teborg-Penn, Rosalyn. (Eds.) (1992). *Black Women in America: An Historical Encyclopedia*, 2 volumes. Brooklyn: Carlson.

Hine, Darlene Clark; King, Wilma; and Reed, Linda. (Eds.) (1995). *We Specialize in the Wholly Impossible: A Reader in Black Women's History*. Brooklyn: Carlson.

Hine, Darlene Clark, and Thompson, Kathleen. (1998). *A Shining Thread of Hope: The History of Black Women in America*. New York: Broadway Books.

Hine, Darlene Clark, and Jenkins, Earnestine. (Eds.) (1999). *A Question of Manhood: A Reader in U.S. Black Men's History and Masculinity*, volume 1. Bloomington: Indiana University Press.

Hine, Darlene Clark, and Jenkins, Earnestine. (Eds.) (2001). *A Question of Manhood: A Reader in U.S. Black Men's History and Masculinity*, volume 2. Bloomington: Indiana University Press.

Hine, Darlene Clark; Hine, William C.; and Harrold, Stanley. (2002). *The African American Odyssey*, 2nd ed. Upper Saddle River, NJ: Prentice Hall.

Holmes, Eugene C. (1970). "W. E. B. Du Bois: Philosopher." In John Henrik Clarke, Esther Jackson, Ernest Kaiser, and J. H. O'Dell (Eds.), *Black Titan: W. E. B. Du Bois*. (pp. 76–81). Boston: Beacon.

Holt, Thomas C. (1982). "The Lonely Warrior: Ida B. Wells-Barnett and the Struggle for Black Leadership." In John Hope Franklin and August Meier (Eds.), *Black Leaders of the Twentieth Century* (pp. 39–62). Chicago: University of Chicago Press.

———. (1990). "The Political Uses of Alienation: W. E. B. Du Bois on Politics, Race, and Culture, 1903–1940." *American Quarterly* 42, 2 (June), 301–23.

———. (1998). "W. E. B. Du Bois's Archaeology of Race: Re-Reading "The Conservation of Races." In Michael Katz B. and Thomas J. Sugrue (Eds.), *W. E. B. Du Bois, Race, and the City: The Philadelphia Negro and Its Legacy*. (pp. 61–76). Philadelphia: University of Pennsylvania Press.

hooks, bell. (1981). *Ain't I a Woman: Black Women and Feminism*. Boston: South End.

———. (1984). *Feminist Theory: From Margin to Center*. Boston: South End.

———. (1989). *Talking Back: Thinking Feminist, Thinking Black*. Boston: South End.

———. (1990). *Yearning: Race, Gender, and Cultural Politics*. Boston: South End.

———. (1991). *Black Looks: Race and Representation*. Boston: South End.

———. (1994a). *Teaching to Transgress: Education as the Practice of Freedom*. Boston: South End.

———. (1994b). *Outlaw Culture: Resisting Representation*. New York: Routledge.

———. (1995). *Killing Rage: Ending Racism*. New York: Henry Holt.

———. (2000a). *Where We Stand: Class Matters*. New York: Routledge.

———. (2000b). *Feminism Is for Everybody: Passionate Politics*. New York: Routledge.

———. (2003a). *Teaching Community: A Pedagogy of Hope*. New York: Routledge.

———. (2003b). *Rock My Soul: Black People and Self-Esteem*. New York: Atria.

———. (2004a). *The Will to Change: Men, Masculinity, and Love*. New York: Atria.

———. (2004b). *We Real Cool: Black Men and Masculinity*. New York: Routledge.

Hord, Fred Lee, and Lee, Johnathan Scott. (Eds.) (1995). *I Am Because We Are: Readings in Black Philosophy*. Amherst: University of Massachusetts Press.

Horkheimer, Max. (1972). *Critical Theory*. New York: Continuum.

———. (1974a). *Eclipse of Reason*. New York: Continuum.

———. (1974b). *Critique of Instrumental Reason*. New York: Continuum.

———. (1978). *Dawn and Decline: Notes, 1926–1931 and 1950–1969*. New York:

Continuum.

Horkheimer, Max, and Adorno, Theodor W. (1995). *Dialectic of Enlightenment*. New York: Continuum.

Horne, Gerald. (1986). *Black and Red: W. E. B. Du Bois and the Afro-American Response to the Cold War, 1944–1963*. Albany: SUNY Press.

———. (2000). *Race Woman: The Lives of Shirley Graham Du Bois*. New York: New York University Press.

Hornsman, Reginald. (1986). *Race and Manifest Destiny: Origins of American Racial Anglo-Saxonism*. Cambridge, MA: Harvard University Press.

Horton, Robin. (1993). *Patterns of Thought in Africa and the West: Essays on Magic, Religion, and Science*. Cambridge: Cambridge University Press.

Hountondji, Paulin J. (1996). *African Philosophy: Myth and Reality*. Indianapolis: Indiana University Press.

Howard, Dick. (1972). *The Development of the Marxian Dialectic*. Carbondale and Edwardsville, IL: Southern Illinois University Press.

———. (1988). *The Marxian Legacy*. Minneapolis: University of Minnesota Press.

Howard, Dick, and Klare, Karl E. (Eds.) (1972). *The Unknown Dimension: European Marxism Since Lenin*. New York: Basic Books.

Hudson-Weems, Clenora. (1989). "Cultural and Agenda Conflicts in Academia: Critical Issues for Africana Women's Studies." *Western Journal of Black Studies* 13, 4 (Winter), 185–89.

———. (1992). "Africana Womanism." *Voice: The Caribbean International Magazine*, 37–8, 46.

———. (1995). *Africana Womanism: Reclaiming Ourselves*. Boston: Bedford.

———. (1997). "Africana Womanism and the Critical Need for Africana Theory and Thought." *Western Journal of Black Studies* 21, 2 (Summer), 79–84.

———. (1998a). "Africana Womanism: An Historical, Global Perspective for Women of African Descent." In Patricia Liggins Hill (Ed.), *Call and Response: The Riverside Anthology of the African American Literary Tradition* (pp. 1811–15). Boston: Houghton Mifflin.

———. (1998b). "Africana Womanism, Black Feminism, African Feminism, Womanism." In Obioma Nnaemeka (Ed.), *Sisterhood, Feminisms, and Power: From Africa to the Diaspora*. (pp. 149–62). Trenton, NJ: Africa World Press.

———. (1998c). "Self-Naming and Self-Defining: An Agenda for Survival." In Obioma Nnaemeka (Ed.), *Sisterhood, Feminisms, and Power: From Africa to the Diaspora*. (pp. 449–52). Trenton, NJ: Africa World Press.

———. (2000). "Africana Womanism: An Overview." In Delores Aldridge and Carlene Young (Eds.), *Out of the Revolution: The Development of Africana Studies*. (pp. 205–17). Lanham: Lexington Books.

———. (2001a). "Africana Womanism, Black Feminism, African Feminism, Womanism." In William Nelson, Jr. (Ed.), *Black Studies: From the Pyramids to Pan-Africanism and Beyond*. New York: McGraw-Hill.

———. (2001b). "Africana Womanism: Entering the New Millennium." In Jemadari Kamara and T. Menelik Van Der Meer (Eds.), *State of the Race, Creating Our 21st Century: Where Do We Go From Here*. Amherst: University of Massachusetts

Press.

Hufford, D. (1997). "The Religious Thought of W. E. B. Du Bois." *Journal of Religious Thought* 53–54 (2–1), 73–94.

Hull, Gloria T.; Scott, Patricia Bell; and Smith, Barbara. (Eds.) (1982). *All the Women Are White, All the Blacks Are Men, But Some of Us Are Brave: Black Women's Studies*. New York: The Feminist Press at CUNY.

Humm, Maggie. (Ed.) (1992). *Modern Feminisms: Political, Literary, Cultural*. New York: Columbia University Press.

Hunter, Jehron. (1996). "Du Bois Revisited." *Black Issues in Higher Education* 13 (5), 14.

Hunton, W. Alphaeus. (1970). "W. E. B. Du Bois: The Meaning of His Life." In John Henrik Clarke, Esther Jackson, Ernest Kaiser, and J. H. O'Dell (Eds.), *Black Titan: W. E. B. Du Bois*. (pp. 131–37). Boston: Beacon.

Hutchinson, Louise D. (1981). *Anna Julia Cooper: A Voice from the South*. Washington, DC: Anacostia Neighborhood Museum and Smithsonian Press.

———. (1993). "Anna Julia Haywood Cooper." In Darlene Clark Hine, Elsa Barkley Brown, and Rosalyn Teborg-Penn (Eds.), *Black Women in America: An Historical Encyclopedia*, 2 volumes (pp. 275–80). Brooklyn: Carlson.

Hwang, Hae-Sung. (1988). "Booker T. Washington and W. E. B. Du Bois: A Study in Race Leadership, 1895–1915." Ph. D. dissertation, University of Hawaii.

Idowu, E. Bolaji. (1975). *African Traditional Religions*. Maryknoll, NY: Orbis.

Ijere, Martin O. (1974). "W. E. B. Du Bois and Marcus Garvey as Pan-Africanists: A Study in Contrasts." *Presence Africaine* 79, 188–206.

Imbo, Samuel Oluoch. (1998). *An Introduction to African Philosophy*. Lanham, MD: Rowman & Littlefield.

Ingram, David. (1990). *Critical Theory and Philosophy*. New York: Paragon House.

———. (1995). *Reason, History, and Politics: The Communitarian Grounds of Legitimation in the Modern Age*. Albany: State University of New York Press.

Ingram, David, and Simon-Ingram, Julia. (Eds.) (1992). *Critical Theory: The Essential Readings*. New York: Paragon House.

Irele, F. Abiola. (1990). *The African Experience in Literature and Ideology*. Indianapolis: Indiana University Press.

———. (2001). *The African Imagination: Literature in Africa and the Black Diaspora*. New York: Oxford University Press.

Irele, F. Abiola, and Gikandi, Simon. (Eds.) (2004). *The Cambridge History of African and Caribbean Literature*. Cambridge: Cambridge University Press.

Jackson, Stevi. (Ed.) (1993). *Women's Studies: Essential Readings*. New York: New York University Press.

Jackson, Stevi, and Scott, Sue. (Eds.) (2001). *Gender: A Sociological Reader*. New York: Routledge.

Jacoby, Russell. (1981). *Dialectic of Defeat: Contours of Western Marxism*. Cambridge: Cambridge University Press.

Jaggar, Alison M. (1983). *Feminist Politics and Human Nature*. Totowa, NJ: Rowman & Allanheld.

Jaggar, Alison M., and Young, Iris Marion. (Eds.) (1998). *A Companion to Feminist*

Philosophy. Malden, MA: Blackwell.

James, C. L. R. (1963). *The Black Jacobins: Toussaint L'Ouverture and the San Domingo Revolution*. New York: Vintage Books.

——. (1977). *The Future in the Present: Selected Writings*. London: Allison and Busby.

——. (1980). *Spheres of Existence: Selected Writings*. London: Allison and Busby.

——. (1984). *At the Rendezvous of Victory: Selected Writings*. London: Allison and Busby.

——. (1992). *The C. L. R. James Reader* (Anna Grimshaw, Ed.). Cambridge: Blackwell.

——. (1993). *World Revolution, 1917–1936: The Rise and Fall of the Communist International*. Atlantic Highlands, NJ: Humanities Press.

——. (1994). *C. L. R. James and Revolutionary Marxism: Selected Writings of C. L. R. James, 1939–1949* (Scott McLemee and Paul Le Blanc, Eds.). Atlantic Highlands, NJ: Humanities Press.

——. (1995). *A History of Pan-African Revolt*. Chicago: Charles H. Kerr Publishing.

——. (1996). *C. L. R. James on the "Negro Question"* (Scott McLemee, Ed.). Jackson, MS: University of Mississippi Press.

——. (1999). *Marxism for Our Times: C. L. R. James on Revolutionary Organization* (Martin Glaberman, Ed.). Jackson, MS: University of Mississippi Press.

James, Joy A. (1996a). *Resisting State Violence: Radicalism, Gender, and Race in U.S. Culture*. Minneapolis: University of Minnesota Press.

——. (1996b). "The Profeminist Politics of W. E. B. Du Bois, with Respects to Anna Julia Cooper and Ida B. Wells Barnett." In Bernard W. Bell, Emily R. Grosholz, and James B. Stewart (Eds.), *W. E. B. Du Bois: On Race and Culture*. (pp. 141–61). New York: Routledge.

——. (1997). *Transcending the Talented Tenth: Black Leaders and American Intellectuals*. New York: Routledge.

——. (1999). *Shadow Boxing: Representations of Black Feminist Politics*. New York: St. Martin's Press.

——. (2000). "The Future of Black Studies: Political Communities and the 'Talented Tenth.'" In Manning Marable (Ed.), *Dispatches from the Ebony Tower: Intellectuals Confront the African American Experience* (pp. 153–57). New York: Columbia University Press.

James, Joy A., and Sharpley-Whiting, T. Denean. (Eds.) (2000). *The Black Feminist Reader*. Malden, MA: Blackwell.

James, Stanlie, and Busia, Abena. (Eds.) (1993). *Theorizing Black Feminism: The Visionary Pragmatism of Black Women*. New York: Routledge.

James, Winston. (1998). *Holding Aloft the Banner of Ethiopia: Caribbean Radicalism in Early Twentieth-Century America*. New York: Verso.

——. (2000). *A Fierce Hatred of Injustice: Claude McKay's Jamaica and His Poetry of Rebellion*. New York: Verso.

Jameson, Fredric. (1971). *Marxism and Form: Twentieth-Century Dialectical Theories of Literature*. Princeton, NJ: Princeton University Press.

——. (1975). "Notes Toward a Marxist Cultural Politics." *Minnesota Review* 5,

35–39.

——. (1979). "Marxism and Historicism." *New Literary History* 11, 41–73.

——. (1988). "Cognitive Mapping." In Cary Nelson and Lawrence Grossberg (Eds.), *Marxism and the Interpretation of Culture.* (pp. 347–60). Chicago: University of Illinois Press.

——. (1990). *Late Marxism: Adorno, or, The Persistence of the Dialectic.* London: Verso.

——. (1991). *Postmodernism, or, The Cultural Logic of Late Capitalism.* Durham: Duke University Press.

JanMohamed, Adul R. (1983). *Manichean Aesthetics: The Politics of Literature in Colonial Africa.* Amherst: University of Massachusetts Press.

Jardine, Alice, and Smith, Paul. (Eds.) (1987). *Men in Feminism.* New York: Methuen.

Jay, Martin. (1984). *Marxism and Totality: The Adventures of a Concept from Lukács to Habermas.* Berkeley: University of California Press.

——. (1996). *The Dialectical Imagination: A History of the Frankfurt School and the Institute of Social Research, 1923–1950.* Berkeley: University of California Press.

Jefferson, Paul. (1996). "Present at the Creation: Rethinking Du Bois's "Practice Theory." *Research in Race & Ethnic Relations* 9, 127–69.

Jennings, Patricia K. (1998). "The Lions and the Canon: The Formative Contributions of W. E. B. Du Bois and Frantz Fanon to Social Theory." *American Sociological Association.*

Johnson, Adolph, Jr. (1976). "A History and Interpretation of the William Edward Burghardt Du Bois-Booker Taliaferro Washington Higher Education Controversy." Ph. D. dissertation, University of Southern California, Los Angeles.

Johnson, Arthur L. (1949). "The Social Theories of W. E. B. Du Bois." M. A. thesis, Atlanta University, Atlanta, GA.

Johnson, Dennis L. (1995). "In the Hush of Great Barrington: One Writer's Search for W. E. B. Du Bois." *Georgia Review* 49 (3), 581.

Johnson, Jonathan. (2006). *Marxism and Social Theory.* New York: Palgrave Macmillan.

Johnson, Karen A. (2000). *Uplifting the Women and the Race: The Educational Philosophies and Social Activism of Anna Julia Cooper and Nannie Helen Burroughs.* New York: Garland.

Johnson, Vernon, and Lynne, Bill. (2002). *Walkin' the Talk: An Anthology of African American Studies.* Upper Saddle River, NJ: Prentice Hall.

Johnson-Feelings, Dianne. (Ed.) (1996). *The Best of the Brownies Book.* New York: Oxford University Press.

Jones, Atlas Jack. (1976). "The Sociology of W. E. B. Du Bois." *Black Sociologists* 6 (1), 4–15.

Jones, Beverly Washington. (1990). *Quest for Equality: The Life and Writings of Mary Eliza Church Terrell, 1863–1954.* Brooklyn, NY: Carlson.

——. (1993). "Mary Eliza Church Terrell." In Darlene Clark Hine, Elsa Barkley

Brown, and Rosalyn Teborg-Penn (Eds.), *Black Women in America: An Historical Encyclopedia*, 2 volumes (pp. 1157–59). Brooklyn: Carlson.

Jones, Gail. (1997). "W. E. B. Du Bois and the Language of the Color-Line." In Judith Jackson Fossett and Jeffrey A. Tucker (Eds.), *Race Consciousness: African American Studies for the New Century.* (pp. 19–35). New York: New York University Press.

Jones, Jacqueline. (1985). *Labor of Love, Labor of Sorrow: Black Women, Work and the Family from Slavery to the Present.* New York: Basic Books.

———. (1998). "'Lifework' and Its Limits: The Problem of Labor in *The Philadelphia Negro.*" In Michael B. Katz and Thomas J. Sugrue (Eds.), *W. E. B. Du Bois, Race, and the City: The Philadelphia Negro and Its Legacy.* (pp. 103–26). Philadelphia: University of Pennsylvania Press.

Jordan, Winthrop D. (1977). *White over Black: American Attitudes Toward the Negro, 1550–1812.* Chapel Hill, NC: University of North Carolina Press.

Juan, E. San, Jr. (2000). *Beyond Postcolonial Theory.* New York: Palgrave Macmillan.

Judy, Ronald T. (1994). "The New Black Aesthetic and W. E. B. Du Bois, or Hephaestus Limping." *Massachusetts Review* 35 (2), 249–82.

———. (2000). "Introduction: On W. E. B. Du Bois and Hyperbolic Thinking." *Boundary* 2 27 (3), 1–35.

Juguo, Zhang. (2001). *W. E. B. Du Bois: Quest for the Abolition of the Color Line.* New York: Routledge.

Kaiser, Ernest. (1970). "Cultural Contributions of Dr. Du Bois." In John Henrik Clarke, Esther Jackson, Ernest Kaiser, and J. H. O'Dell (Eds.), *Black Titan: W. E. B. Du Bois.* (pp. 69–75). Boston: Beacon.

Kaplan, Jeffrey, and Bjorgo, Tore. (Eds.) (1998). *Nation and Race: The Developing Euro-American Racist Subculture.* Boston: Northeastern University Press.

Karenga, Maulana. (1988). "Black Studies and the Problematic of Paradigm: The Philosophical Dimension," *Journal of Black Studies* 18 (4), 395–414.

———. (1997). "African Culture and the Ongoing Quest for Excellence: Dialogue, Principles, Practice." *The Black Collegian* (February), 160–63.

———. (2001). "Mission, Meaning and Methodology in Africana Studies: Critical Reflections from a Kawaida Framework." *Black Studies Journal* 3, 54–74.

———. (2002). *Introduction to Black Studies,* 3rd ed. Los Angeles: University of Sankore Press.

Katz, Michael B. (2000). "Race, Poverty, and Welfare: Du Bois's Legacy for Policy." *Annals of the American Academy of Political and Social Science* 568 (March), 111–27.

Katz, Michael B., and Sugrue, Thomas J. (Eds.) (1998). *W. E. B. Du Bois, Race, and the City: The Philadelphia Negro and Its Legacy.* Philadelphia: University of Pennsylvania Press.

Katznelson, Ira. (1999). "Du Bois's Century." *Social Science History* 23 (4), 459–74.

Kauffman, Linda S. (Ed.) (1993). *American Feminist Thought at Century's End.* Cambridge: Blackwell.

Keene, Jennifer D. (2001). "W. E. B. Du Bois and the Wounded World: Seeking Meaning in the First World War for African Americans." *Peace & Change* 26 (2), 135–52.

Keita, Maghan. (2000). *Race and the Writing of History: Riddle of the Sphinx*. New York: Oxford University Press.

Kelley, Robin D. G. (1990). *Hammer and Hoe: Alabama Communists During the Great Depression*. Chapel Hill, NC: University of North Carolina Press.

———. (1994). *Race Rebels: Culture, Politics, and the Black Working Class*. New York: The Free Press.

———. (1997a). *Yo' Mama's Disfunktional: Fighting the Culture Wars in Urban America*. Boston: Beacon.

———. (1997b). "Looking B(L)ackward: African American Studies in the Age of Identity Politics." In Judith Jackson Fossett and Jeffrey A. Tucker (Eds.), *Race Consciousness: African American Studies for the New Century*. (pp. 1–17). New York: New York University Press.

———. (2002). *Freedom Dreams: The Black Radical Imagination*. Boston: Beacon.

———. (Ed.) (1990). *Hermeneutics and Critical Theory in Ethics and Politics*. Cambridge: MIT Press.

Kellner, Douglas. (1984). *Herbert Marcuse and the Crisis of Marxism*. Berkeley: University of California Press.

———. (1989). *Critical Theory, Marxism, and Modernity*. Baltimore: Johns Hopkins University Press.

———. (1990a). "The Postmodern Turn in Social Theory: Positions, Problems, and Prospects." In George Ritzer (Ed.), *The Frontiers of Social Theory: The New Syntheses*. (pp. 255–86). New York: Columbia University Press.

———. (1990b). "Critical Theory and Ideology Critique." In Ronald Roblin (Ed.), *Critical Theory and Aesthetics*. (pp. 85–123). Lewistown: Edwin Mellen Press.

———. (1990c). "Critical Theory and the Crisis of Social Theory." *Sociological Perspectives* 33 (1), 11–33.

———. (1992). "Erich Fromm, Feminism, and the Frankfurt School." In Michael Kessler and Rainer Funk (Eds.), *Erich Fromm und die Frankfurter Schule*. (pp. 111–30). Tubingen: Francke Verlag.

———. (1993). "Critical Theory and Social Theory: Current Debates and Challenges." *Theory, Culture, and Society* 10 (2), 43–61.

———. (1995). "The Obsolescence of Marxism?" Bernard Magnus and Stephen Cullenberg (Eds.), *Whither Marxism?: Global Crises in International Perspective*. (pp. 3–30). New York: Routledge.

Kelly, Michael. (1982). *Modern French Marxism*. Baltimore: John Hopkins University Press.

Kemp, Sandra, and Squires, Judith. (Eds.) (1997). *Feminisms*. New York: Oxford University Press.

Kershaw, Terry. (1989). "The Emerging Paradigm in Black Studies." *Western Journal of Black Studies* 13 (1), 45–51.

———. (1992). "Toward a Black Studies Paradigm: An Assessment and Some Directions." *Journal of Black Studies* 22 (4), 477–93.

———. (2003). "The Black Studies Paradigm: The Making of Scholar Activists." In J. L. Conyers (Ed.), *Afrocentricity and the Academy* (pp. 27–36). Jefferson, NC: McFarland & Co.

Killian, Lewis M. (1999). "Generals, the Talented Tenth, and Affirmative Action." *Society* 36 (6/242), 33–40.

Kilson, Martin. (1973). "Reflections on Structure and Content in Black Studies." *Journal of Black Studies* 1 (3), 197–214.

———. (2000a). "Black Studies Revisited." In Manning Marable (Ed.), *Dispatches from the Ebony Tower: Intellectuals Confront the African American Experience.* (pp. 171–76). New York: Columbia University Press.

———. (2000b). "The Washington and Du Bois Leadership Paradigms Reconsidered." *Annals of the American Academy of Political and Social Science* 568 (March), 298–313.

Kim, Kyung-Man. (2005). *Discourse on Liberation: An Anatomy of Critical Theory.* Boulder, CO: Paradigm Publishers.

Kimbrough, Marvin Gordon. (1974). "W. E. B. Du Bois as Editor of *The Crisis.*" Ph. D. dissertation, University of Texas, Austin, TX.

King, Deborah K. (1995). "Multiple Jeopardy, Multiple Consciousness: The Contest of Black Feminist Ideology." In Beverly Guy-Sheftall (Ed.), *Words of Fire: An Anthology of African American Feminist Thought.* (pp. 294–318). New York: The Free Press.

King, Desmond. (1995). *Separate and Unequal: Black American and the U.S. Federal Government.* Oxford: Clarendon.

King, Martin Luther, Jr. (1970). "Honoring Dr. Du Bois." In Philip S. Foner (Ed.), *W. E. B. Du Bois Speaks: Speeches and Addresses, 1890–1919* (pp. 20–29). New York: Pathfinder.

Knupfer, Anne Meis. (1996). *Toward a Tender Humanity and a Nobler Womanhood: African American Women's Clubs in Turn-of-the-Century Chicago.* New York: New York University Press.

Kohlenbach, Margarete, and Geuss, Raymond. (Eds.) (2005). *The Early Frankfurt School and Religion.* New York: Palgrave Macmillan.

Kolakowski, Leszek. (1978a). *Main Currents of Marxism: I. The Founders.* New York: Oxford University Press.

———. (1978b). *Main Currents of Marxism: II. The Golden Age.* New York: Oxford University Press.

———. (1978c). *Main Currents of Marxism: III. The Breakdown.* New York: Oxford University Press.

Kostelanetz, Richard. (1985). "Fictions for a Negro Politics: The Neglected Novels of W. E. B. Du Bois." In William L. Andrews (Ed.), *Critical Essays on W. E. B. Du Bois.* (pp. 173–93). Boston: G. K. Hall.

———. (1991). *Politics of the African American Novel: James Weldon Johnson, W. E. B. Du Bois, Richard Wright, and Ralph Ellison.* Westport, CT: Greenwood.

Kourany, Janet A.; Sterba, James P.; and Tong, Rosemarie. (Eds.) (1999). *Feminist Philosophies: Problems, Theories, and Applications*, 2nd ed. Englewood, NJ: Prentice Hall.

Kramarae, Cheris, and Spender, Dale. (Eds.) (2000). *The Routledge International Encyclopedia of Women: Global Women's Issues and Knowledge*, 4 volumes. New York: Routledge.

Krell, David Farrell. (2000). "The Bodies of Black Folk: From Kant and Hegel to Du Bois and Baldwin." *Boundary 2* 27 (3), 103–34.

Kuhn, Annette, and Wolpe, Ann Marie. (Eds.) (1978). *Feminism and Marxism: Women and Modes of Production*. Boston: Routledge & Kegan.

Kwame, Safro. (Ed.) (1995). *Readings in African Philosophy: An Akan Collection*. New York: University Press of America.

Laclau, Ernesto, and Mouffe, Chantal. (1985). *Hegemony and Socialist Strategy: Toward a Radical Democratic Politics*. New York: Verso.

Laclau, Ernesto, and Mouffe, Chantal. (1987). "Post-Marxism Without Apologies." *New Left Review* 166, 79–106.

Lacy, Leslie Alexander. (1970). *Cheer the Lonesome Traveler: The Life of W. E. B. Du Bois*. New York: Dial.

Ladner, Joyce A. (Ed.) (1998). *The Death of White Sociology: Essays on Race and Culture*. Baltimore: Black Classic Press.

Lafollette, Hugh. (Ed.) (1999). *Blackwell Guide to Ethical Theory*. Malden, MA: Blackwell.

——. (Ed.) (2003). *Oxford Handbook of Practical Ethics*. New York: Oxford University Press.

Lancaster, Roger N., and di Leonardo, Micaela. (Eds.) (1997). *The Gender and Sexuality Reader*. New York: Routledge.

Lang, Jesse Michael. (1992). *Anticipations of the Booker T. Washington–W. E. B. Du Bois Dialectic in the Writings of Frances E. W. Harper, Ida B. Wells, and Anna Julia Cooper*. M. A. thesis, Georgetown University.

Lange, Werner J. (1982). "W. E. B. Du Bois, Franz Boas and the Rise of Antiracism in American Anthropology." Paper presented at the annual meeting of the *North Central Sociological Association*.

Langley, J. Ayodele. (1973). *Pan-Africanism and Nationalism in West Africa, 1900–1945: A Study in Ideology and Social Classes*. New York: Oxford University Press.

——. (1979). *Ideologies of Liberation in Black Africa, 1856–1970*. London: Collings Publishing Group.

Larue, H. C. (1971). "W. E. B. Du Bois and the Pragmatic Method of Truth." *Journal of Human Relations* 19, 76–83.

Lash, John S. (1957). "Thought, Research, Action: Dr. Du Bois and History." *Phylon* 18(April), 184–85.

Lawson, Bill E. (Ed.) (1992). *The Underclass Question*. Philadelphia: Temple University Press.

Lawson, Bill E., and Kirkland, Frank M. (Eds.) (1999). *Fredrick Douglass: A Critical Reader*. Malden, MA: Blackwell.

Lazarus, Neil. (Ed.) (2004). *The Cambridge Companion to Postcolonial Literary Studies*. New York: Cambridge University Press.

Lee, Jayne Chong-Soon. (1995). "Navigating the Topology of Race." In Kimberle

Crenshaw, Neil Gotanda, Gary Peller, and Kendall Thomas (Eds.), *Critical Race Theory: The Key Writings That Formed the Movement*. (pp. 441–48). New York: New Press.

Lee, Lenetta Raysha. (2000). "Whose Images: An Africological Study of the *Brownies Book* Series." Ph. D. dissertation, Temple University, Philadelphia.

Lee, M. (1999). "Du Bois the Novelist: White Influence, Black Spirit, and *The Quest of the Silver Fleece*." *African American Review* 33 (3), 389–400.

Lemelle, Sidney J., and Kelley, Robin D. G. (Eds.) (1994). *Imagining Home: Class, Culture, and Nationalism in the African Diaspora*. New York: Verso.

Lemert, Charles C. (1994). "A Classic from the Veil: Du Bois's *Souls of Black Folk*." *Sociological Quarterly* 35 (3), 383–96.

———. (1998). "Anna Julia Cooper: The Colored Woman's Office." In Anna Julia Cooper, *The Voice of Anna Julia Cooper: Including A Voice from the South and Other Important Essays, Papers, and Letters* (Charles Lemert and Esme Bhan, Eds.). (pp. 1–51). Lanham, MD: Rowman & Littlefield.

———. (2000). "The Race of Time: Du Bois and Reconstruction." *Boundary 2* 27 (3), 215–48.

Lemons, Gary L. (1997). "To Be Black, Male and 'Feminist'—Making Womanist Space for Black Men." *International Journal of Sociology and Social Policy* 17, 37–53.

———. (2001). "'When and Where [We] Enter': In Search of a Feminist Forefather—Reclaiming the Womanist Legacy of W. E. B. Du Bois." In Rudolph P. Byrd and B. Beverly Guy-Sheftall (Eds.), *Traps: African American Men on Gender and Sexuality*. (pp. 71–89). Indianapolis: Indiana University Press.

Leonhard, Wolfgang. (1971). *Three Faces of Marxism*. New York: Holt, Rinehart & Winston.

Lerner, Gerda. (Ed.) (1972). *Black Women in White America: A Documentary History*. New York: Vintage.

Lester, Julius. (1971). "Introduction." In *W .E. B. Du Bois, The Seventh Son: The Thought and Writings of W. E. B. Du Bois* (Julius Lester, Ed.). (pp. 1–153). New York: Random House.

Lewis, David Levering. (1993). *W. E. B. Du Bois: Biography of a Race, 1868–1919*. New York: Henry Holt.

———. (2000). *W. E. B. Du Bois: The Fight for Equality and the American Century, 1919–1963*. New York: Henry Holt.

Lichtheim, George. (1965). *Marxism*. New York: Praeger.

———. (1966). *Marxism in Modern France*. New York: Columbia University Press.

Lincoln, C. Eric. (1993). "The Du Boisian Dubiety and the American Dilemma: Two Levels of Lure and Loathing." In Gerald Early (Ed.), *Lure and Loathing: Essays on Race, Identity, and the Ambivalence of Assimilation*. (pp. 194–206). New York: Viking/Penguin.

Liss, Julia. (1998). "Diasporic Identities: The Science and Politics of Race in the Work of Franz Boas and W. E. B. Du Bois, 1894–1919." *Cultural Anthropology: Journal of the Society for Cultural Anthropology* 13 (2), 127–66.

Lloyd, Genevieve. (1984). *The Man of Reason: "Male" and "Female" in Western Philosophy*. Minneapolis: University of Minnesota.

Lloyd, Sheila Renee. (1999). "Plots on an Alternative Map: Emplotments of Pan-Africanism in the Writings of W. E. B. Du Bois, Langston Hughes, and Alice Walker." Ph. D. dissertation, Cornell University, Ithaca.

Locke, Alain L. (1983). *The Critical Temper of Alain Locke: A Selection of His Essay on Art and Culture* (Jeffrey C. Stewart, Ed.). New York: Garland Publishing, Inc.

———. (1989). *The Philosophy of Alain Locke: Harlem Renaissance and Beyond* (Leonard Harris, Ed.). Philadelphia: Temple University Press.

———. (1992). *Race Contacts and Interracial Relations: Lectures on the Theory and Practice of Race* (Jeffrey C. Stewart, Ed.). Washington, DC: Howard University Press.

Loewberg, Bert James, and Bogin, Ruth. (Eds.) (1976). *Black Women in Nineteenth Century American Life: Their Words, Their Thoughts, Their Feelings*. University Park: Pennsylvania State University Press.

Logan, Rayford W. (Ed.) (1971). *W. E. B. Du Bois: A Profile*. New York: Hill & Wang.

Loomba, Ania. (1998). *Colonialism/Postcolonialism*. New York: Routledge.

———. (Ed.) (2005). *Postcolonial Studies and Beyond*. Durham, NC: Duke University Press.

Lopez, Alfred J. (Ed.) (2005). *Postcolonial Whiteness: A Critical Reader on Race and Empire*. Albany, NY: State University of New York Press.

Lopez, Ian F. H. (1995). "The Social Construction of Race." In Richard Delgado (Ed.), *Critical Race Theory* (pp. 191–203). Philadelphia: Temple University Press.

———. (1996). *White by Law: The Legal Construction of Race*. New York: New York University Press.

Lorde, Audre. (1984). *Sister Outsider: Essays and Speeches by Audre Lorde*. Freedom, CA: The Crossing Press Feminist Series.

———. (1988). *A Burst of Light: Essays by Audre Lorde*. Ithaca, NY: Firebrand.

Lott, Tommy L. (1997). "Du Bois on the Invention of Race." In John P. Pittman (Ed.), *African American Perspectives and Philosophical Traditions* (pp. 166–87). New York: Routledge.

———. (Ed.). (1998). *Subjugation and Bondage: Critical Essays on Slavery and Social Philosophy*. Lanham, MD: Rowman & Littlefield.

———. (1999). *The Invention of Race: Black Culture and the Politics of Representation*. Malden, MA: Blackwell.

———. (2000). "Du Bois and Locke on the Scientific Study of the Negro." *Boundary 2* 27 (3), 135–52.

———. (2001). "Du Bois's Anthropological Notion of Race." In Robert Bernasconi (Ed.), *Race* (pp. 59–83). Malden, MA: Blackwell.

———. (Ed). (2002). *African American Philosophy: Selected Readings*. Upper Saddle River, NJ: Prentice Hall.

Lott, Tommy L., and Pittman, John P. (Eds.) (2003). *A Companion to African American Philosophy*. Malden, MA: Blackwell.

Lovell, Terry. (1996). "Feminist Social Theory." In Barry S. Turner (Ed.), (1996). *The Blackwell Companion to Social Theory*. (pp. 307–39). Malden, MA: Blackwell.

Lucal, Betsy. (1996). "Race, Class, and Gender in the Work of W. E. B. Du Bois: An

Exploratory Study." *Research in Race & Ethnic Relations* 9, 191–210.

Lyotard, Jean-Francois. (1984). *The Postmodern Condition*. Minneapolis: University of Minnesota Press.

Magnus, Bernard, and Cullenberg, Stephen, (Eds.) (1995). *Whither Marxism?: Global Crises in International Perspective*. New York: Routledge.

Magubane, Bernard Makhosezwe. (1987). *The Ties That Bind: African American Consciousness of Africa*. Trenton, NJ: African World Press.

Makang, Jean-Marie. (1993). "The Problem of Democratic Inclusion in the Light of the Racial Question: W. E. B. Du Bois and the Emancipation of Democracy." Ph. D. dissertation, Boston College.

Malos, Ellen. (Ed.) (1980). *The Politics of Housework*. London: Allison & Busby.

Mansbridge, Jane J., and Okin, Susan Mollier. (1993). "Feminism." In Robert E. Goodin and Philip Pettit (Eds.), *A Companion to Contemporary Political Philosophy*. (pp. 269–90). Malden, MA: Blackwell.

Marable, Manning. (1982). "Alain Locke, W. E. B. Du Bois, and the Crisis of Black Education During the Great Depression." In Russell J. Linnemann (Ed.), *Alain Locke: Reflections on a Modern Renaissance Man* (pp. 63–76). Baton Rouge, LA: Louisiana State University.

———. (1983). *How Capitalism Underdeveloped Black America*. Boston: South End.

———. (1983/84). "Peace and Black Liberation: The Contributions of W. E. B. Du Bois." *Science & Society* 47, 385–405.

———. (1985a). *Black American Politics: From the Washington Marches to Jesse Jackson*. London: Verso.

———. (1985b). "The Black Faith of W. E. B. Du Bois: Sociocultural and Political Dimensions of Black Religion." *Southern Quarterly* 23 (Spring), 15–33.

———. (1985c). "W. E. B. Du Bois and the Struggle Against Racism." *Black Scholar* 16 (May–June), 43–44, 46–47.

———. (1986). *W. E. B. Du Bois: Black Radical Democrat*. Boston: Twayne.

———. (1987). *African and Carribean Politics: From Kwame Nkrumah to Maurice Bishop*. London and New York: Verso.

———. (1991). *Race, Reform, and Rebellion: The Second Reconstruction in Black America, 1945–1990*. Jackson, MS: University Press of Mississippi.

———. (1992). *The Crisis of Color and Democracy: Essays on Race, Class and Power*. Monroe, MA: Common Courage Press.

———. (1993). *Blackwater: Historical Studies in Race, Class Consciousness, and Revolution*. Niwot, CO: University Press of Colorado.

———. (1995). *Beyond Black and White: Transforming African American Politics*. New York and London: Verso.

———. (1996). *Speaking Truth to Power: Essays on Race, Resistance and Radicalism*. Boulder, CO: Westview.

———. (1997). *Black Liberation in Conservative America*. Boston: South End.

———. (1998). *Black Leadership*. New York: Columbia University Press.

———. (Ed.) (2000). *Dispatches from the Ebony Towers: Intellectuals Confront the African American Experience*. New York: Columbia University Press.

———. (2002). *The Great Wells of Democracy: The Meaning of Race in American*

Life. New York: Basic/Civitas.

——. (Ed). (2005). *The New Black Renaissance: The Souls Anthology of Critical African American Studies*. Boulder, CO: Paradigm Publishers.

——. (2006). *Living Black History: How Re-Imagining the African American Past Can Remake America's Racial Future*. New York: Basic/Civitas.

Marable, Manning, and Mullings, Leith. (Eds.) (2000). *Let Nobody Turn Us Around: Voices of Resistance, Reform, and Renewal—An African American Anthology*. Lanham, MD: Rowman & Littlefield.

Marable, Manning; Ness, Immanuel; and Wilson, Joseph. (Eds.) (2006). *Race and Labor Matters in the New U.S. Economy*. Lanham, MD: Rowman & Littlefield.

Marcus, Judith, and Tar, Zoltan. (Eds.) (1984). *The Foundations of the Frankfurt School of Social Research*. New York: Transaction Books.

Marcuse, Herbert. (1958). *Soviet Marxism*. New York: Columbia University Press.

——. (1960). *Reason and Revolution*. Boston: Beacon.

——. (1964). *One-Dimensional Man: Studies in the Ideology of Advanced Industrial Society*. Boston: Beacon.

——. (1965a). "Socialism in the Developed Countries." *International Socialist Journal* 2 (8), 139–51.

——. (1965b). "Socialist Humanism?" In Erich Fromm (Ed.), *Socialist Humanism* (pp. 107–17). New York: Doubleday.

——. (1966). *Eros and Civilization*. Boston: Beacon.

——. (1967). "The Obsolescence of Marxism." In Nikolaus Lobkowicz (Ed.), *Marxism in the Western World* (pp. 409–17). Notre Dame: University of Notre Dame Press.

——. (1968). *Negations: Essays in Critical Theory*. Boston: Beacon.

——. (1969). *An Essay on Liberation*. Boston: Beacon.

——. (1970a). *Five Lectures: Psychoanalysis, Politics, and Utopia*. Boston: Beacon.

——. (1970b). "Marxism and the New Humanity: An Unfinished Revolution." In John C. Raines and Thomas Dean (Eds.), *Marxism and Radical Religion: Essays Toward a Revolutionary Humanism* (pp. 3–10). Philadelphia: Temple University Press.

——. (1971). "Dear Angela." *Ramparts* 9, p. 22.

——. (1972a). *Counter-Revolution and Revolt*. Boston: Beacon.

——. (1972b). *From Luther to Popper*. Trans. Joris De Bres. London: Verso.

——. (1973). *Studies in Critical Philosophy*. Boston: Beacon.

——. (1974). "Marxism and Feminism." *Women's Studies* 2 (3), 279–88.

——. (1976a). "On the Problem of the Dialectic" (Part 1). *Telos* 27, 12–24.

——. (1976b). "On the Problem of the Dialectic" (Part 2). *Telos* 27, 12–39.

——. (1997a). *Technology, War and Fascism: The Collected Papers of Herbert Marcuse*, volume 1 (Douglas Kellner, Ed.). New York: Routledge.

——. (1997b). "A Note on Dialectic." In Andrew Arato and Eike Gebhardt (Eds.), *The Essential Frankfurt School Reader*. (pp. 444–51). New York: Continuum.

——. (2001). *Towards a Critical Theory of Society: The Collected Papers of Herbert Marcuse*, volume 2 (Douglas Kellner, Ed.). New York: Routledge.

——. (2004). *The New Left and the 1960's: The Collected Papers of Herbert Marcuse*, volume 3 (Douglass Kellner, Ed.). New York: Routledge.

Mardorossian, Carine M. (2005). *Reclaiming Difference: Caribbean Women Rewrite Postcolonialism*. Charlottesville, VA: University of Virginia Press.

Marsh, James L. (1995). *Critique, Action, and Liberation*. Albany: SUNY Press.

——. (1998). *Post-Cartesian Meditations*. New York: Fordham University Press.

——. (1999). *Process, Praxis, and Transcendence*. Albany: SUNY Press.

——. (2001). "Toward a New Critical Theory." In William S. Wilkerson and Jeffrey Paris (Eds.), *New Critical Theory: Essays on Liberation*. (pp. 49–64). Lanham, MD: Rowman & Littlefield.

Marshall, Jessica. (1994). "'Counsels of Despair': W. E. B. Du Bois, Robert E. Park, and the Establishment of American Race Sociology." Ph. D. dissertation, Harvard University.

Marsh-Lockett, Carol P. (1997). "Womanism." In William L. Andrews, Frances Smith Foster, and Trudier Harris (Eds.), *The Oxford Companion to African American Literature*. (pp. 784–85). New York: Oxford University Press.

Martin, Michael, and Yeakey, Lamont. (1982). "Pan-African and Asian Solidarity: A Central Theme in W. E. B. Du Bois's Conception of Racial Stratification and Struggle on a World Scale." *Phylon* 43, 202–17.

Martin, Waldo E., Jr. (1984). *The Mind of Frederick Douglass*. Chapel Hill: University of North Carolina Press.

——. (1990). "Images of Frederick Douglass in the Afro-American Mind: The Recent Black Freedom Struggle." In Eric J. Sundquist (Ed.), *Frederick Douglass: New Literary and Historical Essays*. (pp. 271–86). New York: Cambridge University Press.

Marx, Anthony W. (1998). *Making Race and Nation: A Comparison of the United States, South Africa, and Brazil*. New York: Cambridge University Press.

Marx, Karl, and Engels, Friedrich. (1972). *On Colonialism*. New York: International.

Marx, Karl, and Engels, Friedrich. (1978). *The Marx-Engels Reader*, 2nd Edition (Robert C. Tucker, Ed.). New York: Norton.

Marx, Karl, and Engels, Friedrich. (1989). *Marx & Engels: The Basic Writings on Politics and Philosophy* (Lewis S. Feuer, Ed.). New York: Anchor.

Massey, Douglas S., and Denton, Nancy A. (1993). *American Apartheid: Segregation and the Making of the Underclass*. Cambridge: Harvard University Press.

Massiah, Louis. (Director). (1995). *W. E. B. Du Bois: A Biography in Four Voices* [Documentary]. San Francisco: California Newsreel.

Masolo, Dismas A. (1994). *African Philosophy in Search of Identity*. Indianapolis: Indiana University Press.

Matustik, Martin J. Beck. (1998). *Specters of Liberation: Great Refusals in the New World Order*. Albany: SUNY Press.

Mbiti, John S. (1975). *Introduction to African Religion*. London: Heinemann.

——. (1989). *African Religions and Philosophy*. London: Heinemann.

McCarthy, Thomas. (1991). *Ideal and Illusion: On Reconstruction and Deconstruction in Contemporary Critical Theory*. Cambridge: MIT Press.

McCarthy, Thomas, and Hoy, David Couzens. (1994). *Critical Theory*. Cambridge: Blackwell.

McClintock, Anne. (1992). "The Angel of Progress: Pitfalls of the Term 'Postcolonial.'" *Social Text* 31/32, 84–98.

———. (1995). *Imperial Leather: Race, Gender, and Sexuality in the Colonial Context*. New York: Routledge.

McCollester, Charles. (1973). "The Political Thought of Amilcar Cabral." *Monthly Review* (March), 10–21.

McCulloch, Jock. (1983). *In the Twilight of Revolution: The Political Theory of Amilcar Cabral*. London and Boston: Routledge and Kegan Paul.

McDaniel, Antonio. (1998). "*The Philadelphia Negro*, Then and Now: Implications for Empirical Research." In Michael B. Katz and Thomas J. Sugrue (Eds.), *W. E. B. Du Bois, Race, and the City: The Philadelphia Negro and Its Legacy*. (pp. 155–94). Philadelphia: University of Pennsylvania Press.

McDonnell, Robert W. (1979). *The Papers of W. E. B. Du Bois: A Guide*. Sanford, NC: Microfilming Corporation of America.

McFeely, William S. (1991). *Frederick Douglass*. New York: Norton.

McGary, Howard. (1999). *Race and Social Justice*. Malden, MA: Blackwell.

McGary, Howard, and Lawson, Bill E. (Eds.). (1992). *Between Slavery and Freedom: Philosophy and American Slavery*. Indianapolis: Indiana University Press.

McGee, B. R. (1998). "Speaking About the Other: W. E. B. Du Bois Responds to the Klan." *Communications Abstracts* 21, 6.

McGill, Ralph. (1965). "W. E. B. Du Bois." *Atlantic Monthly* (November), 78–81.

McGuire, Robert Grayson, III. (1974). "Continuity in Black Political Protest: The Thought of Booker T. Washington, W. E. B. Du Bois, Marcus Garvey, Joseph B. Danquah, and Kwame Nkrumah." Ph. D. dissertation, Columbia University, New York.

McKay, Nellie Y. (1985). "W. E. B. Du Bois: The Black Woman in His Writings— Selected Fictional and Autobiographical Portraits." In William L. Andrews (Ed.), *Critical Essays on W. E. B. Du Bois*. (pp. 230–52). Boston: G. K. Hall.

———. (1990). "The Souls of Black Women Folk in the Writings of W. E. B. Du Bois." In Henry Louis Gates, Jr. (Ed.), *Reading Black/Reading Feminist: A Critical Anthology*. (pp. 227–43). New York: Meridian.

McLemee, Scott. (1994). "Afterword—American Civilization and World Revolution: C. L. R. James in the United States, 1938–1953 and Beyond." In C. L. R. James, *C. L. R. James and Revolutionary Marxism: Selected Writings of C. L. R. James, 1939–1949* (Scott McLemee and Paul Le Blanc, Eds.). (pp. 209–83). Atlantic Highlands, NJ: Humanities Press.

McMurry, Linda O. (1998). *To Keep the Waters Troubled: The Life of Ida B. Wells* New York: Oxford University Press.

McNann, Carole, and Kim, Seung-kyung. (Eds.) (2002). *Feminist Theory Reader: Local and Global Perspectives*. New York: Routledge.

Meade, Homer Lee, II. (1987). "W. E. B. Du Bois and His Place in the Discussion of Racism." Ph. D. dissertation, University of Massachusetts.

Meehan, Johanna. (Ed.) (1995). *Feminists Read Habermas: Gendering the Subject of Discourse*. New York: Routledge.

Meier, August. (1954). "Booker T. Washington and the Rise of the NAACP." *Crisis* 60 (February).

———. (1959). "From 'Conservative' to 'Radical': The Ideological Development of W. E. B. Du Bois, 1885–1905." *Crisis* 75 (February), 527–36.

———. (1963). "The Paradox of W. E. B. Du Bois." In August Meier, *Negro Thought in America, 1880–1915: Racial Ideologies in the Age of Booker T. Washington*. Ann Arbor: University of Michigan Press.

Mendieta, Eduardo. (Ed.) (2005). *The Frankfurt School on Religion: Key Writings by the Major Thinkers*. New York: Routledge.

Mercer, Kobena. (1994). *Welcome to the Jungle: New Positions in Black Cultural Studies*. New York: Routledge.

Meyer, Arthur S. (1999). "W. E. B. Du Bois and the Open Forum: Human Relations in a 'Difficult Industrial District.'" *Journal of Negro History* 84 (2), 192–212.

Meyers, Diana Tietjens. (Ed.) (1997). *Feminist Social Thought: A Reader*. New York: Routledge.

Mezu, S. Okechukwu; Mezu, Rose Ure; and Bell, Bernard W. (1999). *Black Nationalists: Reconsidering Du Bois, Garvey, Booker T. and Nkrumah*. Randallstown, MD: Black Academy Press.

Mielke, David Nathaniel. (1977). "W. E. B. Du Bois: An Educational Critique." Ph. D. dissertation, University of Tennessee, Knoxville, TN.

Miller, Khadijah Olivia Turner. (2001). "Everyday Victories: The Pennsylvania State Federation of Negro Women's Clubs, Inc., 1900–1930." Ph. D. dissertation, Temple University.

Milligan, Nancy Muller. (1985). "W. E. B. Du Bois's American Pragmatism." *Journal of American Culture* 8 (2), 31–37.

Mills, Charles W. (1987). "Race and Class: Conflicting or Reconcilable Paradigms?" *Social and Economic Studies* 36 (2), 69–108.

———. (1997). *The Racial Contract*. Ithaca: Cornell University Press.

———. (1998). *Blackness Visible: Essays on Philosophy and Race*. Ithaca: Cornell University Press.

———. (1999). "The Racial Polity." In Susan E. Babbitt and Sue Campbell (Eds.), *Racism and Philosophy* (pp. 13–31, [endnotes] 255–57). Ithaca: Cornell University Press.

———. (2000). "Race and the Social Contract Tradition." *Social Identities: A Journal for the Study of Race, Nation and Culture* 6 (4), 441–62.

———. (2001). "White Supremacy and Racial Justice." In James Sterba (Ed.), *Social and Political Philosophy: Contemporary Perspectives* (pp. 321–37). New York: Routledge.

———. (2003). *From Class to Race: Essays in White Marxism and Black Radicalism*. Lanham, MD: Rowman & Littlefield.

Mills, Patricia. (1987). *Women, Nature and Psyche*. New Haven: Yale University Press.

Mishra, V. and Hodge, B. (1991). "What is Post(-)colonialism?" *Textual Practice* 5

(3), 399–415.

Mitchell, Ella Pearson. (1993). "Du Bois's Dilemma and African American Adaptiveness." In Gerald Early (Ed.), *Lure and Loathing: Essays on Race, Identity, and the Ambivalence of Assimilation.* (pp. 264–73). New York: Viking/Penguin.

Mizruchi, Susan. (1996). "Neighbors, Strangers, and Corpses: Death and Sympathy in the Early Writings of W. E. B. Du Bois." In Robert Newman (Ed.), *Centuries' Ends, Narrative Means.* Stanford: Stanford University Press.

Monteiro, Anthony. (2000). "Being an African in the World: The Du Boisian Epistemology." *Annals of the American Academy of Political and Social Science* 568 (March), 220–34.

———. (1994). "The Scientific and Revolutionary Legacy of W. E. B. Du Bois." *Political Affairs* 73 (2), 1–19.

Moon, Henry Lee. (1968). "The Leadership of W. E. B. Du Bois." *Crisis* 75 (February), 51–57. Moore, Jack B. (1981). *W. E. B. Du Bois.* Boston: Twayne.

Moore, Jack B. (1981). *W. E. B. Du Bois.* Boston: Twayne Publishers.

Moore, Percy L. (1996). "W. E. B. Du Bois: A Critical Study of His Philosophy of Education and Its Relevance for Three Contemporary Issues in Education of Significance to African Americans." Ph. D. dissertation, Wayne State University.

Moore, Richard B. (1970). "Du Bois and Pan-Africa." In John Henrik Clarke, Esther Jackson, Ernest Kaiser, and J. H. O'Dell (Eds.), *Black Titan: W. E. B. Du Bois.* (pp. 187–212). Boston: Beacon.

Moore-Gilbert, Bart. (1997). *Postcolonial Theory: Contexts, Practices, Politics.* London: Verso.

Morrison, Hugh James. (2000). "The Evolution of a Reform Plan: W. E. B. Du Bois's Sociological Research, 1896–1910." Ph. D. dissertation, Queen's University at Kingston, Canada.

Morrison, Toni. (1990). *Playing in the Dark: Whiteness and the Literary Imagination.* Cambridge: Harvard University Press.

Morrow, Raymond A. (with David D. Brown). (1994). *Critical Theory and Methodology.* Thousands Oaks, CA: Sage.

Morton, Patricia. (1991). *Disfigured Images: The Historical Assault on Afro-American Women.* New York: Praeger.

Moses, Wilson Jeremiah. (1975). "The Poetic of Ethiopianism: W. E. B. Du Bois and Literary Black Nationalism." *American Literature* 47 (November), 411–27.

———. (1978). *The Golden Age of Black Nationalism, 1850–1925.* New York: Oxford University Press.

———. (1990). "Sexual Anxieties of the Black Bourgeoisie in Victorian America: The Cultural Context of W. E. B. Du Bois's First Novel." In W. J. Moses, *The Wings of Ethiopia: Studies in African American Life and Letters.* Ames, IA: Iowa State University Press.

———. (1993a). "W. E. B. Du Bois's 'The Conservation of Races' and Its Context: Idealism, Conservatism, and Hero Worship." *Massachusetts Review* 34 (Summer), 275–94.

———. (1993b). "Du Bois's *Dark Princess* and the Heroic Uncle Tom." In W. J. Moses, *Black Messiahs and Uncle Toms: Social and Literary Manipulations of a*

Religious Myth. University Park, PA: Pennsylvania State University Press.
———. (1996). "Culture, Civilization, and the Decline of the West: The Afrocentricism of W. E. B. Du Bois." In Bernard W. Bell, Emily R. Grosholz, and James B. Stewart (Eds.), *W. E. B. Du Bois: On Race and Culture*. (pp. 243–60). New York: Routledge.
———. (1998). "W. E. B. Du Bois and Antimodernism." In W. J. Moses, *Afrotopia: The Roots of African American Popular History* (pp. 136–68). New York: Cambridge University Press.
Mosley, Albert. G. (Ed.) (1995). *African Philosophy: Selected Readings*. Englewood Cliffs, NJ: Prentice Hall.
Moss, Richard Lawrence. (1975). "Ethnographic Perspectives and Literary Strategies in the Early Writings of W. E. B. Du Bois." Ph. D. dissertation, State University of New York, Buffalo.
Mosse, George L. (1978). *Toward a Final Solution: A History of European Racism*. London: Dent & Sons.
Mostern, Kenneth. (1996). "Three Theories of the Race of W. E. B. Du Bois." *Cultural Critique* 34 (Fall), 27–63.
———. (2000). "Postcolonialism after W. E. B. Du Bois." *Rethinking Marxism* 12 (2), 61–80.
Mtima, Lateef. (1999). "African American Economic Empowerment Strategies for the New Millennium: Revisiting the Washington–Du Bois Dialectic." *Howard Law Journal* 42 (3), 391.
Mudimbe, V. Y. (1988). *The Invention of Africa: Gnosis, Philosophy, and the Order of Knowledge*. Indianapolis: Indiana University Press.
———. (1994). *The Idea of Africa*. Indianapolis: Indiana University Press.
Mullaney, Marie Marmo. (1983). *Revolutionary Women: Gender and the Socialist Revolutionary Role*. New York: Praeger.
Murray, Hugh. (1987). "Du Bois and the Cold War." *Journal of Ethnic Studies* 15 (3), 115–24.
Nagl-Docekal, Herta. (1998). "Modern Moral and Political Philosophy." In Alison M. Jaggar and Iris Marion Young (Eds.), *A Companion to Feminist Philosophy*. (pp. 58–65). Malden, MA: Blackwell.
Namasaka, Boaz Nalika. (1971). "William E. B. Du Bois and Thorstein Veblen: Intellectual Activists of Progressivism, a Comparative Study, 1900–1930." Ph. D. dissertation, Claremont Graduate School and University Center, Claremont, CA.
Neal, Larry. (1989). *Visions of a Liberated Future: Black Arts Movements Writings*. New York: Thunder's Mouth Press.
Neal, Terry Ray. (1984). "W. E. B. Du Bois's Contributions to the Sociology of Education." Ph. D. dissertation, University of Cincinnati.
Nealon, Jeffrey T., and Irr, Caren. (2002). (Eds.) *Rethinking the Frankfurt School: Alternative Legacies of Cultural Critique*. Albany, NY: State University of New York Press.
Nelson, Cary, and Grossberg, Lawrence. (Eds.) (1988). *Marxism and the Interpretation of Culture*. Chicago: University of Illinois Press.
Nelson, Truman. (1958). "W. E. B. Du Bois: Prophet in Limbo." *Nation* (January 25), 76–79.
———. (1970). "W. E. B. Du Bois as a Prophet." In John Henrik Clarke, Esther Jack-

son, Ernest Kaiser, and J. H. O'Dell (Eds.), *Black Titan: W. E. B. Du Bois*. (pp. 138–51). Boston: Beacon.

Nesbitt, Francis Njubi. (2004). *Race for Sanctions: African Americans Against Apartheid, 1946–1994*. Bloomington: Indiana University Press.

Newman, Louise M. (1999). *White Women's Rights: The Racial Origins of Feminism in the United States*. New York: Oxford University Press.

Newsome, Elaine Mitchell. (1971). "W. E. B. Du Bois's 'Figure in the Carpet': A Cyclical Pattern in the Belletristic Prose." Ph. D. dissertation, University of North Carolina, Chapel Hill.

Nicholson, Linda J. (Ed.) (1990). *Feminism/Postmodernism*. New York: Routledge.

Ngũgĩ wa Thiong'o. (1972). *Homecoming: Essays on African and Caribbean Literature, Culture, and Politics*. New York: Lawrence Hill.

———. (1983). *Barrel of a Pen: Resistance to Repression in Neocolonial Kenya*. Trenton, NJ: Africa World Press.

———. (1986). *Decolonizing the Mind: The Politics of Language in African Literature*. Portsmouth, NH: James Currey/ Heinemann.

———. (1993). *Moving the Center: The Struggle for Cultural Freedoms*. Portsmouth, NH: James Currey/Heinemann.

———. (1997). *Writers in Politics: A Re-Engagement with Issues of Literature and Society*. Portsmouth, NH: James Currey/EAEP/Heinemann.

Nkrumah, Kwame. (1962). *Towards Colonial Freedom*. London: Panaf Books.

———. (1964). *Consciencism: Philosophy and Ideology for Decolonization*. New York: Monthly Review Press.

———. (1965). *Neo-Colonialism: The Last Stage of Imperialism*. London: Panaf Books.

———. (1968). *The Handbook of Revolutionary Warfare*. New York: International.

———. (1970a). *Africa Must Unite*. New York: International.

———. (1970b). *Class Struggle in Africa*. New York: International.

———. (1973a). *Revolutionary Path*. London: Panaf Books.

———. (1973b). *The Struggle Continues*. London: Panaf Books.

Nnaemeka, Obioma. (Ed.) (1998). *Sisterhood, Feminisms, and Power: From Africa to the Diaspora*. Trenton, NJ: Africa World Press.

Noble, Jeanne. (1978). *Beautiful, Also, Are the Souls of My Black Sisters: A History of the Black Woman in America*. Englewood Cliffs, NJ: Prentice Hall.

Nonini, Donald. (1992). "Du Bois and Radical Theory and Practice." *Critique of Anthropology* 12 (3), 292–318.

Norment, Nathaniel, Jr. (Ed.) (2001). *The African American Studies Reader*. Durham, NC: Carolina Academic Press.

Novick, Michael. (1995). *White Lies, White Power: The Fight Against White Supremacy and Reactionary Violence*. Monroe, ME: Common Courage Press.

Nwankwo, Henry C. (1989). "The Educational Philosophy of W. E. B. Du Bois: A Nigerian Interpretation." Ph. D. dissertation, East Texas State University, Commerce, TX.

Nye, Andrea. (1988). *Feminist Theory and the Philosophies of Man*. New York: Croom Helm.

Nyerere, Julius Kambarage. (1966). *Freedom and Unity/Uhura na Umoja: A Selection from Writings and Speeches, 1952–1965.* New York: Oxford University Press.

———. (1968). *Freedom and Socialism/Uhuru na Ujamaa: A Selection from Writings and Speeches, 1965–1967.* New York: Oxford University Press.

———. (1973). *Freedom and Development/Uhuru na Maendeleo: A Selection from Writings and Speeches.* New York: Oxford University Press.

O'Dell, Jack H. (1970). "Du Bois and 'The Social Evolution of the Black South.'" In John Henrik Clarke, Esther Jackson, Ernest Kaiser, and J. H. O'Dell (Eds.), *Black Titan: W. E. B. Du Bois.* (pp. 152–63). Boston: Beacon.

Ofari, Earl. (1970). "W. E. B. Du Bois and Black Power." *Black World* 19 (August), 26–28.

Okere, Theophilus. (1971). "Can There Be an African Philosophy?: A Heremeneutical Investigation with Special Reference to Igbo Culture." Ph. D. dissertation, Louvain University.

———. (1991). *African Philosophy: A Historico-Hermeneutical Investigation of the Conditions of Its Possibility.* Lanham, MD: University of America Press.

Okin, Susan Moller. (1992). *Women in Western Political Thought.* Princeton, NJ: Princeton University Press.

Okolo, Okondo. (1991). "Tradition and Destiny: Horizons of an African Philosophical Hermeneutics." In Tsenay Serequeberhan (Ed.), *African Philosophy: The Essential Readings.* (pp. 201–11). New York: Paragon House.

Okoro, Martin Umachi. (1982). "W. E. B. Du Bois's Ideas on Education: Implications for Nigerian Education." Ph. D. dissertation, Loyola University of Chicago.

Olaniyan, Tejumola. (1992). "Narrativing Postcoloniality: Responsibilities." *Public Culture* 5 (1), 47–55.

———. (2000). "Africa: Varied Colonial Legacies." In Henry Schwarz and Sangeeta Ray (Eds.), *A Companion to Postcolonial Studies.* (pp. 269–81). Malden, MA: Blackwell.

Omi, Michael, and Winant, Howard. (1994). *Racial Formation in United States: From the 1960's to the 1990's.* New York: Routledge.

O'Neill, John. (Ed.) (1976). *On Critical Theory.* New York: Seabury Press.

Outlaw, Lucius. T., Jr. (1974). "Language and Consciousness: Foundations for a Hermeneutics of Black Culture." *Cultural Hermeneutics* 1 (February), 403–13.

———. (1983a). "Philosophy, Hermeneutics, Social-Political Theory: Critical Thought in the Interest of African Americans." In Leonard Harris (Ed.), *Philosophy Born of Struggle: An Anthology of Afro-American Philosophy from 1917* (pp. 60–88). Dubuque, IA: Kendall/Hunt.

———. (1983b). "Race and Class in the Theory and Practice of Emancipatory Social Transformation." In Leonard Harris (Ed.), *Philosophy Born of Struggle: An Anthology of Afro-American Philosophy from 1917* (pp. 117–29). Dubuque, IA: Kendall/Hunt.

———. (1983c). "Philosophy and Culture: Critical Hermeneutics and Social Transformation." In *Philosophy and Cultures: Proceedings of the 2nd Afro-Asian Philosophy Conference.* (pp. 26–31). Nairobi, Kenya: Bookwise Limited.

———. (1983d). "Critical Theory in a Period of Radical Transformation." *Praxis International* 3 (2), 138–46.

———. (1987). "On Race and Class, or, On the Prospects of 'Rainbow Socialism.'" In Marable Manning, Mike Davis, Fred Pfeil, and Michael Sprinker, (Eds.), *The Year Left 2: Toward a Rainbow Socialism—Essays on Race, Ethnicity, Class and Gender* (pp. 73–90). London: Verso.

———. (1990). "Toward a Critical Theory of 'Race.'" In David Theo Goldberg (Ed.), *Anatomy of Racism* (pp. 58–82). Minneapolis: University of Minnesota Press.

———. (1995). "On W. E. B. Du Bois's 'The Conservation of Races.'" In Linda A. Bell and David Blumenfeld (Eds.), *Overcoming Racism and Sexism.* (pp. 79–102). Lanham, MD: Rowman & Littlefield.

———. (1996a). *On Race and Philosophy.* New York: Routledge.

———. (1996b). "'Conserve' Races?: In Defense of W. E. B. Du Bois." In Bernard W. Bell, Emily R. Grosholz, and James B. Stewart (Eds.), *W. E. B. Du Bois: On Race and Culture.* (pp. 15–38). New York: Routledge.

———. (1997). "African, African American, Africana Philosophy." In John P. Pittman (Ed.), *African American Perspectives and Philosophical Traditions* (pp. 63–93). New York: Routledge.

———. (2000). "W. E. B. Du Bois on the Study of Social Problems." *Annals of the American Academy of Political and Social Science* 568 (March), 281–97.

———. (2001). "On Cornel West on W. E. B. Du Bois." In George Yancy (Ed.), *Cornel West: A Critical Reader.* Malden, MA: Blackwell.

———. (2005). *Critical Social Theory in the Interest of Black Folk.* Lanham, MD: Rowman & Littlefield.

Owen, Chandler. (1973). "Du Bois on Revolution." In Theodore G. Vincent (Ed.), *Voices of a Black Nation: Political Journalism in the Harlem Renaissance* (pp. 88–92). Trenton, NJ: Africa World Press.

Painter, Nell Irvin. (1993). "Sojourner Truth." In Darlene Clark Hine, Elsa Barkley Brown, and Rosalyn Teborg-Penn (Eds.), *Black Women in America: An Historical Encyclopedia*, 2 volumes (pp. 1172–76). Brooklyn: Carlson.

———. (1996). *Sojourner Truth: A Life, A Symbol.* New York: Norton.

Parry, Benita. (1987). "Problems in Current Theories of Colonial Discourse." *Oxford Literary Review* 9 (1), 2–12.

———. (2004). *Postcolonial Studies: A Materialist Critique.* New York: Routledge.

Paschal, Andrew G. (1971). "The Spirit of W. E. B. Du Bois." *Black Scholar* 20 (February), 38–50.

Pateman, Carole. (1988). *The Sexual Contract.* Stanford: Stanford University Press.

———. (1989). *The Disorder of Women: Democracy, Feminism, and Political Theory.* Stanford: Stanford University Press.

Pauley, Garth E. (2000). "W. E. B. Du Bois on Woman Suffrage: A Critical Analysis of His Crisis Writings." *Journal of Black Studies* 30 (3), 383–410.

Payne, James Chris, II. (1973). "A Content Analysis of Speeches and Written Documents of Six Black Spokesmen: Frederick Douglass, Booker T. Washington, Marcus Garvey, W. E. B. Du Bois, Martin Luther King, Jr. and Malcolm X." Ph. D. dissertation, Florida State University, Tallahassee.

Paynter, Robert. (1992). "W. E. B. Du Bois and the Material World of African

Americans in Great Barrington, Massachusetts." *Critique of Anthropology* 12 (3), 277–91.

Pearsall, Marilyn. (Ed.) (1986). *Women and Values: Readings in Recent Feminist Philosophy*. Belmont, CA: Wadsworth.

Peebles-Wilkins, Wilma, and Aracelis, Fran. (1990). "Two Outstanding Women in Social Welfare History: Mary Church Terrell and Ida B. Wells." *Affilia* 5 (Winter), 87–95.

Peller, Gary. (1995). "Race-Consciousness." In Kimberle Crenshaw, Neil Gotanda, Gary Peller, and Kendall Thomas (Eds.), *Critical Race Theory: The Key Writings That Formed the Movement*. (pp. 127–58). New York: New Press.

Pensky, Max. (Ed.) (2005). *Globalizing Critical Theory*. Lanham, MD: Rowman & Littlefield.

Perkins, Linda M. (1981). "Black Women and Racial 'Uplift' Prior to Emancipation." In Filomina Chioma Steady (Ed.), *The Black Woman Cross-Culturally*. (pp. 314–17). Cambridge: Schenkman.

———. (1997). "Women's Clubs." In William L. Andrews, Frances Smith Foster, and Trudier Harris (Eds.), *The Oxford Companion to African American Literature*. (pp. 787–88). New York: Oxford University Press.

Peterson, Charles. (2000). "Du Bois, Fanon, and Cabral and the Margins of Colonized Elite Leadership." Ph. D. dissertation, Binghamton University, Binghamton, NY.

Peterson, Dale. (1994). "Notes from the Underworld: Dostoyevsky, Du Bois and the Discovery of Ethnic Soul." *Massachusetts Review* 35 (Summer), 225–47.

Pfeffer, Paula F. (1990). *A. Philip Randolph, Pioneer of the Civil Rights Movement*. Baton Rouge: Louisiana State University Press.

Phillips, L. W. (1995). "W. E. B. Du Bois and Soviet Communism: *The Black Flame* as Social Realism." *South Atlantic Quarterly* 94 (3), 837–63.

Pittman, John P. (Ed.) (1992–1993). "African American Perspectives and Philosophical Traditions." (Special Triple Issue). *The Philosophical Forum* 24, 1–3.

———. (Ed.) (1997). *African American Perspectives and Philosophical Traditions*. New York: Routledge.

Poliakov, Leon. (1974). *The Aryan Myth*. New York: Basic Books.

Pollard, Alton B. (1993). "The Last Great Battle of the West: W. E. B. Du Bois and the Struggle for African America's Soul." In Gerald Early (Ed.), *Lure and Loathing: Essays on Race, Identity, and the Ambivalence of Assimilation*. (pp. 41–54). New York: Viking/Penguin.

Posnock, Ross. (1995). "The Distinction of Du Bois: Aesthetics, Pragmatism, Politics." *American Literary History* 7 (3), 500–524.

———. (1997). "How Does It Feel to Be a Problem?: Du Bois, Fanon, and the 'Impossible Life' of the Black Intellectual." *Critical Inquiry* 23 (2), 323–49.

———. (1998). *Color and Culture: Black Writers and the Making of the Modern Intellectual*. Cambridge: Harvard University Press.

Poster, Mark. (1975). *Existential Marxism in Postwar France: From Sartre to Althusser*. Princeton: Princeton University Press.

Prakash, Gyan. (Ed.) (1995). *After Colonialism: Imperial Histories and Postcolonial Displacements*. Princeton, NJ: Princeton University Press.

Price-Spratley, Townsand. (1996). "Negotiating Legacies: Audre Lorde, W. E. B. Du Bois, Marlon Riggs, and Me." *Harvard Educational Review* 66 (2), 216–30.

Pugh, Wesley C. (1974). "The Inflated Controversy: Du Bois vs. Washington." *Crisis* 81 (April), 132–33.

Puri, Shalini. (2004). *The Caribbean Postcolonial: Social Equality, Post-Nationalism, and Cultural Hybridity*. New York: Palgrave Macmillan.

Quainoo, Vanessa Wynder. (1993). *"The Souls of Black Folk*: In Consideration of W. E. B. Du Bois and the Exigency of an African American Philosophy of Rhetoric." Ph. D. dissertation, University of Massachusetts.

Quarles, Benjamin. (1966). "Frederick Douglass, Bridge-Builder in Human Relations." *Negro History Bulletin* 29 (5), 103–24.

———. (1991). *Black Abolitionists*. New York: Da Capo.

———. (1997). *Frederick Douglass*. New York: Da Capo.

Quayson, Ato. (2000a). *Postcolonialism: Theory, Practice or Process?* Malden, MA: Polity.

———. (2000b). "Postcolonialism and Postmodernism." In Henry Schwarz and Sangeeta Ray (Eds.), *A Companion to Postcolonial Studies*. (pp. 87–111). Malden, MA: Blackwell.

———. (2003). *Calibrations: Reading for the Social*. Minneapolis: University of Minnesota Press.

Rabaka, Reiland. (2001). "Africana Critical Theory: From W. E. B. Du Bois and C. L. R. James's Discourse on Domination and Liberation to Frantz Fanon and Amilcar Cabral's Dialectics of Decolonization." Ph. D. dissertation, Temple University, Philadelphia, PA.

———. (2002). "Malcolm X and/as Critical Theory: Philosophy, Radical Politics, and the African American Search for Social Justice." *Journal of Black Studies* 33 (2), 145–65.

———. (2003a). "W. E. B. Du Bois's Evolving Africana Philosophy of Education." *Journal of Black Studies* 33 (4), 399–449.

———. (2003b). "W. E. B. Du Bois and 'The Damnation of Women': An Essay on Africana Anti-Sexist Critical Social Theory." *Journal of African American Studies* 7 (2), 39–62.

———. (2003c). "'Deliberately Using the Word *Colonial* in a Much Broader Sense': W. E. B. Du Bois's Concept of 'Semi-Colonialism' as Critique of and Contribution to Postcolonialism." *Jouvert: A Journal of Postcolonial Studies* 7, (2), 1–32. Available on-line at: http://social.chass.ncsu.edu/jouvert/index. htm [23 February 2003].

———. (2003d). "W. E. B. Du Bois and/as Africana Critical Theory: Pan-Africanism, Critical Marxism, and Male-Feminism." In James L. Conyers (Ed.), *Afrocentricity and the Academy* (pp. 67–112). Jefferson, NC: McFarland & Co.

———. (2004). "The Souls of Black Female Folk: W. E. B. Du Bois and Africana Anti-Sexist Critical Social Theory." *Africalogical Perspectives* 1 (2), 100–141.

———. (2005a). "W. E. B. Du Bois and Decolonization: Pan-Africanism, Postcolonialism, and Radical Politics." In James L. Conyers (Ed.), *W. E. B. Du Bois, Marcus Garvey, and Pan-Africanism* (pp. 123–54). Lewistown, NY: Mellen Press.

———. (2005b). "W. E. B. Du Bois's Theory of the Talented Tenth." In Molefi K. Asante and Ama Mazama (Eds.), *The Encyclopedia of Black Studies*. (pp. 443–45).

Thousand Oaks, CA: Sage.

———. (2005c). "Booker T. Washington's Philosophy of Accommodationism." In Molefi K. Asante and Ama Mazama (Eds.), *The Encyclopedia of Black Studies.* (pp. 1–3). Thousand Oaks, CA: Sage.

———. (2005d). "African Worldview." In Molefi K. Asante and Ama Mazama (Eds.), *The Encyclopedia of Black Studies.* (pp. 56–57). Thousand Oaks, CA: Sage.

———. (2006a). "Africana Critical Theory of Contemporary Society: Ruminations on Radical Politics, Social Theory, and Africana Philosophy." In Molefi K. Asante and Maulana Karenga (Eds.), *The Handbook of Black Studies* (pp. 130–52). Thousand Oaks, CA: Sage.

———. (2006b). "The Souls of Black Radical Folk: W. E. B. Du Bois, Critical Social Theory, and the State of Africana Studies." *Journal of Black Studies* 36 (5), 732–63.

———. (2006c). "W. E. B. Du Bois's 'The Comet' and Contributions to Critical Race Theory." *Ethnic Studies Review: Journal of the National Association for Ethnic Studies* 29 (1), 22–48.

———. *(forthcoming). W. E. B. Du Bois, Black Radical Politics, and the Reconstruction of Critical Social Theory.* Lanham, MD: Lexington Books.

Rajan, Rajeswari. (1993). *Real and Imagined Women: Gender, Culture and Postcolonialism.* New York: Routledge.

Rajan, Gita, and Mohanran, Radhika, (Eds.) (1995). *Postcolonial Discourse and Changing Cultural Context: Theory and Criticism.* Westport, CT: Greenwood.

Rampersad, Arnold. (1989). "Slavery and the Literary Imagination: Du Bois's *The Souls of Black Folk.*" In Deborah E. McDowell and Arnold Rampersad (Eds.), *Slavery and the Literary Imagination: Selected Papers from the English Institute, 1987.* Baltimore: Johns Hopkins University Press.

———. (1990). *The Art and Imagination of W. E. B. Du Bois.* New York: Schocken.

———. (1996a). "Du Bois's Passage to India—*Dark Princess.*" In Bernard W. Bell, Emily R. Grosholz, and James B. Stewart (Eds.), *W. E. B. Du Bois: On Race and Culture.* (pp. 161–76). New York: Routledge.

———. (1996b). "W. E. B. Du Bois, Race, and the Making of American Studies." In Bernard W. Bell, Emily R. Grosholz, and James B. Stewart (Eds.), *W. E. B. Du Bois: On Race and Culture.* (pp. 289–305). New York: Routledge.

Randolph, A. Philip, and Owen, Chandler. (1971). "Du Bois Fails as a Theorist." In August Meier, Elliott Rudwick, and Francis L. Broderick (Eds.), *Black Protest Thought in the Twentieth Century* (pp. 91–94). New York: MacMillan.

Randolph, A. Philip, and Owen, Chandler. (1973). "Du Bois on Revolution: A Reply." In Theodore G. Vincent (Ed.), *Voices of a Black Nation: Political Journalism in the Harlem Renaissance* (pp. 88–92). Trenton, NJ: Africa World Press.

Rasmussen, David M. (Ed.) (1999). *The Handbook of Critical Theory.* Malden, MA: Blackwell.

Rasmussen, David M., and Swindal, James. (Eds.) (2004). *Critical Theory,* 4 Volumes. Thousand Oaks, CA: Sage.

Rath, Richard Cullen. (1997). "Echo and Narcissus: The Afrocentric Pragmatism of W. E. B. Du Bois." *Journal of American History* 84 (2), 461–95.

Rattansi, Ali. (1997). "Postcolonialism and Its Discontents." *Economy and Society* 26

(4), 480–500.

Rawls, Anne Warfield. (2000). "'Race' as an Interaction Order Phenomenon: W. E. B. Du Bois's 'Double-Consciousness' Thesis Revisited." *Sociological Theory* 18 (2), 241–74.

Ray, Benjamin C. (2000). *African Religions: Symbol, Ritual, and Community.* Upper Saddle River, NJ: Prentice Hall.

Ray, Larry. (1993). *Rethinking Critical Theory: Emancipation in the Age of Global Social Movements.* Thousand Oaks, CA: Sage.

Recht, J. J. (1971). "From W. E. B. Du Bois to Marcus Garvey: Shadows and Lights." *Revue Francaise d'Etudes Politiques Africaines* 62 (February), 40–59.

Redding, J. Saunders. (1949). "Portrait of W. E. B. Du Bois." *American Scholar* 18, 93–96.

——. (1970). "*The Souls of Black Folk*: Du Bois's Masterpiece Lives On." In John Henrik Clarke, Esther Jackson, Ernest Kaiser, and J. H. O'Dell (Eds.), *Black Titan: W. E. B. Du Bois.* (pp. 47–51). Boston: Beacon.

——. (1979). "The Correspondence of W. E. B. Du Bois: A Review Article." *Phylon* 40 (June), 119–22.

Reed, Adolph L., Jr. (1975). "The Political Philosophy of Pan-Africanism: A Study of the Writings of Du Bois, Garvey, Nkrumah, and Padmore and Their Legacy." M. A. thesis, Atlanta University, Atlanta, GA.

——. (1985). "W. E. B. Du Bois: A Perspective on the Bases of His Political Thought." *Political Theory* 13 (August), 431–56.

——. (1986). "Pan-Africanism as Black Liberation: Du Bois and Garvey." In W. Ofuatey-Kudjoe (Ed.), *Pan-Africanism: New Directions in Strategy.* Lanham, MD: University of America Press.

——. (1992). "Du Bois's 'Double-Consciousness': Race and Gender in Progressive Era American Thought." *Studies in American Political Development* 6, 132–37.

——. (1997). *W. E. B. Du Bois and American Political Thought: Fabianism and the Color Line.* New York: Oxford University Press.

Reed, Ishmael. (2000). "Eminent Contrarian: A Portrait of a Public Intellectual, W. E. B. Du Bois." *Village Voice Literary Supplement* (October–November), 146.

Reedom, John Anthony. (1977). "Du Bois and Washington: Opposite or Similar—An Evaluation of the Philosophies of Du Bois and Washington." Paper presented at the annual meeting of the *Southwestern Sociological Association.*

Rich, Adrienne. (1976). *Of Woman Born: Motherhood as Experience and Institution.* New York: Norton.

Richards, Paul. (1970). "W. E. B. Du Bois and American Social History: Evolution of a Marxist." *Radical America* 5 (November), 43–87.

Robinson, Armstead; Foster, Craig C.; and Ogilvie, Donald L. (Eds.) (1969). *Black Studies in the University: A Symposium.* New York: Bantam.

Robinson, Cedric J. (1977). "A Critique of W. E. B. Du Bois's *Black Reconstruction.*" *Black Scholar* 8 (7), 44–50.

——. (1990). "Du Bois and Black Sovereignty: The Case of Liberia." *Race & Class* 32 (2), 39–50.

——. (1994). "W. E. B. Du Bois and Black Sovereignty." In Sidney Lemelle and

Robin D. G. Kelley (Eds.), *Imagining Home: Class, Culture, and Nationalism in the African Diaspora*. New York: Verso.

———. (2000). *Black Marxism: The Making of the Black Radical Tradition*. Chapel Hill: University of North Carolina.

Rodgers-Rose, La Frances. (Ed.) (1980). *The Black Woman*. Beverly Hills: Sage.

Rodney, Walter. (1972). *How Europe Underdeveloped Africa*. Washington, DC: Howard University Press.

———. (1981). *Marx in the Liberation of Africa*. Georgetown, Guyana: People's Progressive Party Press.

———. (1990). *Walter Rodney Speaks*. Trenton, NJ: Africa World Press.

Roediger, David R. (1994). *Towards the Abolition of Whiteness: Essays on Race, Politics, and Working Class History*. New York: Verso.

———. (1999). *The Wages of Whiteness: Race and the Making of the American Working Class*. New York: Verso.

———. (2002). *Colored White: Transcending the Racial Past*. Berkeley: University of California Press.

Rogers, Ben F. (1955). "W. E. B. Du Bois, Marcus Garvey, and Pan-Africa." *Journal of Negro History* 40, 154–65.

Rogers, Mary F. (Ed.) (1998). *Contemporary Feminist Theory: A Text/Reader*. New York: McGraw-Hill.

Romero, Patricia W. (1976). "W. E. B. Du Bois, Pan-Africanists, and Africa, 1963–1973." *Journal of Black Studies* 6 (4), 321–36.

Roof, Maria. (1996). "W. E. B. Du Bois, Isabel Allende, and the Empowerment of Third World Women." *CLA Journal* 39 (4), 401–17.

Rosenau, Pauline Marie. (1992). *Postmodernism and the Social Sciences*. Princeton: Princeton University Press.

Rosenberg, Jonathan. (2000). "The Global Editor: Du Bois and *The Crisis*." *The New Crisis* 107 (4), 15.

Ross, Robert. (Ed.) (1982). *Racism and Colonialism: Essays on Ideology and Social Structure*. The Hague: Leiden University Press.

Royster, Jacqueline Jones. (1997). *Southern Horrors and Other Writings: The Anti-Lynching Campaign of Ida B. Wells, 1892–1930*. Boston: Bedford.

Ruddick, Sara. (1999). "Maternal Thinking as a Feminist Standpoint." In Janet A. Kourany, James P. Sterba, and Rosemarie Tong (Eds.), *Feminist Philosophies: Problems, Theories, and Applications*, 2nd ed. (pp. 404–14). Englewood, NJ: Prentice Hall.

Rudwick, Elliot M. (1956). "W. E. B. Du Bois: A Study in Minority Group Leadership." Ph. D. dissertation, University of Pennsylvania, Philadelphia.

———. (1957). "The Niagara Movement." *Journal of Negro History* 42, 177–200.

———. (1958). "W. E. B. Du Bois: In the Role of *Crisis* Editor." *Journal of Negro History* 18, 214–40.

———. (1959). "Du Bois Versus Garvey: Race Propagandists at War." *Journal of Negro Education* 28, 421–29.

———. (1960). *W. E. B. Du Bois: A Study in Minority Group Leadership*. Philadelphia: University of Pennsylvania.

——. (1968). *W. E. B. Du Bois: Propagandists of the Negro Protest*. New York: Antheneum.

——. (1969). "Notes on a Forgotten Black Sociologist: W. E. B. Du Bois and the Sociological Profession." *American Sociologist* 4 (4), 303–36.

——. (1974). "W. E. B. Du Bois as Sociologist." In James E. Blackwell and Morris Janowitz (Eds.), *Black Sociologists: Historical and Contemporary Perspectives*. Chicago: University of Chicago Press.

——. (1982). *W. E. B. Du Bois: Voice of the Black Movement*. Urbana: University of Illinois Press.

Ruffin, Josephine St. Pierre. (1895). "Address to the First National Conference of Colored Women." *The Woman's Era* 2 (5), 14.

Rustin, Bayard. (1971). *Down the Line: The Collected Writings of Bayard Rustin*. Chicago: Quadrangle Books.

——. (2003). *Time on Two Crosses: The Collected Writings of Bayard Rustin* (Devon W. Carbado and Donald Weise, Eds.). New York: Cleis Press.

Rutledge, Rebecka Rychelle. (2001). "Metaphors of Mediation: Race and Nation in Black Atlantic Literature—W. E. B. Du Bois, Ralph Ellison, Edourd Glissant, and Olaudah Equiano." Ph. D. dissertation, Washington University.

Sadar, Ziauddin. (1998). *Postmodernism and the Other: The New Imperialism of Western Culture*. London: Pluto Press.

Said, Edward W. (1999). "Traveling Theory Reconsidered." In Nigel C. Gibson (Ed.), *Rethinking Fanon* (pp. 197–214). Amherst, NY: Humanity Books.

——. (2000). "Traveling Theory." In Moustafa Bayoumi and Andrew Rubin (Eds.), *The Edward Said Reader* (pp. 195–217). New York: Vintage.

Salem, Dorothy. (1990). *To Better Our World: Black Women in Organized Reform, 1890–1920*. Brooklyn: Carlson.

——. (1993). "National Association of Colored Women." In Darlene Clark Hine, Elsa Barkley Brown, and Rosalyn Teborg-Penn (Eds.), *Black Women in America: An Historical Encyclopedia*, 2 volumes (pp. 842–51). Brooklyn: Carlson.

Sanchez, Lisa. (1991). "W. E. B. Du Bois: Clinical Sociologist." Paper presented at the annual meeting of the *Sociological Practice Association/ISA Working Group in Clinical Sociology*.

Sargent, Lydia. (Ed.) (1981). *Women and Revolution: A Discussion of the Unhappy Marriage of Marxism and Feminism*. Boston: South End.

Savage, Barbara Dianne. (2000). "W. E. B. Du Bois and 'The Negro Church.'" *Annals of the American Academy of Political and Social Science* 568 (March), 253–49.

Schechter, Patricia A. (2001). *Ida B. Wells-Barnett and American Reform, 1880–1930*. Chapel Hill: University of North Carolina Press.

Schickel, Richard. (1983). *D. W. Griffith: An American Life*. New York: Simon and Schuster.

Schneider, Paul Ryan. (1998). "Inventing the Public Intellectual: Ralph Waldo Emerson, W. E. B. Du Bois, and the Cultural Politics of Representing Men." Ph. D. dissertation, Duke University.

Schrager, Cynthia D. (1996). "Both Sides of the Veil: Race, Science, and Mysticism in W. E. B. Du Bois." *American Quarterly* 48 (4), 551.

Schrecker, Ellen. (1998). *Many Are the Crimes: McCarthyism in America.* Boston: Little, Brown.

Schwarz, Henry and Ray, Sangeeta. (Eds.) (2000). *A Companion to Postcolonial Studies.* Malden, MA: Blackwell.

Seidman, Steven. (1994). *Contested Knowledge: Social Theory in the Postmodern Era.* Oxford: Blackwell.

Seidman, Steven, and Wagner, David. (Eds.) (1992). *Postmodernism and Social Theory.* Oxford: Blackwell.

Sekyi-Otu, Ato. (1996). *Fanon's Dialectic of Experience.* Cambridge: Harvard University Press.

Self, Peter. (1993). "Socialism." In Robert E. Goodin and Philip Pettit (Eds.), *A Companion to Contemporary Political Philosophy.* (pp. 333–65). Malden, MA: Blackwell.

Sénghor, Leopold S. (1971). *The Foundations of "Africanité" or "Negritude" and "Arabité."* Paris: Présence Africaine.

———. (1995). "On Negrohood: Psychology of the African Negro." In Albert Mosley (Ed.), *African Philosophy: Selected Readings* (pp. 116–27). Englewood Cliffs, NJ: Prentice Hall.

Serequeberhan, Tsenay. (1990). "Karl Marx and African Emancipatory Thought: A Critique of Marx's Euro-Centric Metaphysics." *Praxis International* 10 (1–2), 37–53.

———. (Ed.) (1991). *African Philosophy: The Essential Readings.* New York: Paragon House.

———. (1994). *The Hermeneutics of African Philosophy: Horizon and Discourse.* New York: Routledge.

———. (1997). "The Critique of Eurocentrism and the Practice of African Philosophy." In Emmanuel C. Eze (Ed.), *(Post) Colonial African Philosophy: A Critical Reader* (pp. 141–61). Malden, MA: Blackwell.

———. (1998). "Africanity at the End of the Twentieth Century," *African Philosophy* 11 (1), 13–21.

———. (2000). *Our Heritage: The Past in the Present of African American and African Existence.* Lanham, MD: Rowman & Littlefield.

Serrano, Richard. (2005). *Against the Postcolonial: "Francophone" Writers at the Ends of French Empire.* Lanham, MD: Lexington Books.

Shapiro, Herbert. (1988). *White Violence and Black Response: From Reconstruction to Montgomery.* Amherst: University of Massachusetts Press.

Shaw, Stephanie J. (1991). "Black Club Women and the Creation of the National Association of Colored Women." *Journal of Women's History* 3 (2), 1–25.

Shiach, Morag. (Ed.) (1999). *Feminism and Cultural Studies.* New York: Oxford University Press.

Shipley, W. Maurice. (1972). "Reaching Back to Glory: Comparative Sketches in the Dreams of W. B. Yeats and W. E. B. Du Bois." *Crisis* 83, 195–98.

Shobat, Ella. (1993). "Notes on the 'Post-Colonial.'" *Social Text* 31/32, 99–113.

Siemerling, Winfried. (2001). "W. E. B. Du Bois, Hegel, and the Staging of Alterity." *Callaloo* 24, (1), 325–33.

Singh, Amritjit, and Schimdt, Peter. (Eds.) (2000). *Postcolonial Theory and the United States: Race, Ethnicity and Literature*. Jackson: University Press of Mississippi.

Singer, Peter. (Ed.) (1993). *A Companion to Ethics*. Malden, MA: Blackwell.

Slide, Anthony. (2004). *American Racist: The Life and Films of Thomas Dixon*. Lexington: University Press of Kentucky.

Smart, Barry. (1992). *Modern Conditions, Postmodern Controversies*. London: Routledge.

———. (1993). *Postmodernity*. New York: Routledge.

Smerdlow, Amy, and Lessinger, Hanna. (Eds.) (1983). *Class, Race, and Sex: The Dynamics of Control*. Boston: G. K. Hall.

Smith, Barbara. (Ed.) (1983). *Home Girls: A Black Feminist Anthology*. New York: Kitchen Table Press.

———. (1998). *The Truth That Never Hurts: Writings on Race, Gender, and Freedom*. New Brunswick: Rutgers University Press.

Smith, Eddie Calvin. (1975). "Educational Themes in the Published Work of W. E. B. Du Bois, 1883–1960: Implications for African American Educators." Ph. D. dissertation, University of Wisconsin–Milwaukee.

Smith, John David. (1980). "Du Bois and Phillips: Symbolic Antagonists of the Progressive Era." *Centennial Review* 24 (1), 88–102.

Speck, Beatrice F. (1974). "W. E. B. Du Bois: A Historiographical Study." Ph. D. dissertation, Texas Christian University, Fort Worth, TX.

Spickard, Paul, and Daniel, G. Reginald. (Eds.) (2004). *Racial Thinking in the United States: Uncompleted Independence*. Notre Dame, IN: University of Notre Dame Press.

Staton, Sandra Louise. (2001). "'They Have Girded Themselves for Work': The Emergence of the Feminist Argument in the Novels of William Edward Burghardt Du Bois." Ph. D. dissertation, Howard University, Washington, DC.

Steady, Filomina Chioma. (Ed.) (1981). *The Black Woman Cross-Culturally*. Cambridge: Schenkman.

———. (1987). "African Feminism: A Worldwide Perspective." In Rosalyn Terborg-Penn, Sharon Harley, and Andrea Benton Rushing (Eds.), *Women in Africa and the African Diaspora*. (pp. 3–24). Washington, DC: Howard University Press.

Stein, Judith. (2001). "The Difficult Doctor Du Bois." *Reviews in American History* 29 (2), 247–54.

Stephan, Nancy Leys. (1982). *The Idea of Race in Science: Great Britain, 1800–1960*. New York: MacMillan.

———. (1990). "Race and Gender: The Role of Analogy in Science." In David Theo Goldberg (Ed.), *Anatomy of Racism*. (pp. 38–57). Minneapolis: University of Minnesota Press.

Stepto, Robert B. (1985). "The Quest of the Weary Traveler: W. E. B. Du Bois's *The Souls of Black Folk*." In William L. Andrews (Ed.), *Critical Essays on W. E. B. Du Bois*. (pp. 139–72). Boston: G. K. Hall.

Sterba, James P. (Ed.) (1998). *Ethics*. Malden, MA: Blackwell.

———. (Ed.) (1999). *Feminism and Its Critics*. Lanham, MD: Rowman & Littlefield.

———. (Ed.) (2000). *Controversies in Feminism*. Lanham, MD: Rowman & Littlefield.

Sterling, Dorothy. (1979). *Black Foremothers: Three Lives*. Old Westbury, NY: Feminist Press.

———. (Ed.) (1984). *We Are Your Sisters: Black Women in the Nineteenth Century*. New York: Norton.

Stewart, James B. (1979). "Introducing Black Studies: A Critical Examination of Some Textual Materials." *Umoja* 3 (1), 5–17.

———. (1983). "The Psychic Duality of Afro-Americans in the Novels of W. E. B. Du Bois." *Phylon* 44 (2), 93–107.

———. (1984). "The Legacy of W. E. B. Du Bois for Contemporary Black Studies." *Journal of Negro Education* 53 (Summer), 296–311.

———. (1992). "Reaching for Higher Ground: Toward an Understanding of Black/Africana Studies." *The Afrocentric Scholar* 1 (1), 1–63.

———. (1996). "In Search of a Theory of Human History: W. E. B. Du Bois's Theory of Social and Cultural Dynamics." In Bernard W. Bell, Emily R. Grosholz, and James B. Stewart (Eds.), *W. E. B. Du Bois: On Race and Culture*. (pp. 261–88). New York: Routledge.

Stewart, Maria W. (1987). *Maria W. Stewart, America's First Black Woman Political Writer: Essays and Speeches* (Marilyn Richardson, Ed.). Indianapolis: Indiana University Press.

Stirk, Peter M. R. (2000). *Critical Theory, Politics and Society*. London: Pinter Press.

Stuart, Jack. (1997). "A Note on William English Walling and His 'Cousin' W. E. B. Du Bois." *Journal of Negro History* 82 (2), 270–75.

Stuckey, Sterling. (1987). "W. E. B. Du Bois: Black Cultural Reality and the Meaning of Freedom." In Stuckey, *Slave Culture: Nationalist Theory and the Foundations of Black America* (pp. 245–302). New York: Oxford University Press.

———. (1994). "Black Americans and African Consciousness: Du Bois, Woodson, and the Spell of Africa." In Stuckey, *Going Through the Storm: The Influence of African American Art in History* (pp. 120–40). New York: Oxford University Press.

Sumpter, Richard David. (1973). "A Critical Study of the Educational Thought of W. E. B. Du Bois." Ph. D. dissertation, Peabody College for Teachers of Vanderbilt University, Nashville, TN.

———. (2000). "W. E. B. Du Bois on Education: Its Socialistic Foundation." *Journal of Thought* 35 (1), 61–87.

———. (2001). "W. E. B. Du Bois: Reflections on Democracy." *Journal of Thought* 36 (2), 25–32.

Sundquist, Eric J. (Ed.) (1990). *Frederick Douglass: New Literary and Historical Essays*. New York: Cambridge University Press.

———. (1993). "W. E. B. Du Bois: African America and the Kingdom of Culture." In E. J. Sundquist, *To Wake the Nations: Race in the Making of American Literature*. Cambridge: Harvard University Press.

———. (1996). "W. E. B. Du Bois and the Autobiography of Race." In W. E. B. Du Bois, *The Oxford W. E. B. Du Bois Reader* (Eric Sundquist, Ed.). (pp. 3–36). New York: Oxford University Press.

Táíwò, Olúfémi. (1999a). "Cabral." In Robert L. Arrington (Ed.), *A Companion to the Philosophers* (pp. 5–12). Malden, MA: Blackwell.

———. (1999b). "Fanon." In Robert L. Arrington (Ed.), *A Companion to the Philosophers* (pp. 13–19). Malden, MA: Blackwell.

Tate, Claudia. (1997). "Woman's Era." In William L. Andrews, Frances Smith Foster, and Trudier Harris (Eds.), *The Oxford Companion to African American Literature*. (pp. 785–86). New York: Oxford University Press.

Taylor, Carl McDonald. (1971). "W. E. B. Du Bois: The Rhetoric of Redefinition." Ph. D. dissertation, University of Oregon, Eugene, OR.

Taylor, Carol M. (1981). "W. E. B. Du Bois's Challenge to Scientific Racism." *Journal of Black Studies* 11 (June), 449–60.

Taylor, Paul C. (2000). "Appiah's Uncompleted Argument: W. E. B. Du Bois and the Reality of Race." *Social Theory and Practice* 26 (1), 103–28.

Terborg-Penn, Rosalyn; Harley, Sharon; and Rushing, Andrea Benton. (Eds.) (1987). *Women in Africa and the African Diaspora*. Washington, DC: Howard University Press.

Terrell, Mary Church. (1932). *Colored Women and World Peace*. Philadelphia, PA: Women's International League for Peace and Freedom.

———. (1996). *A Colored Woman in a White World*. New York: G. K. Hall.

Therborn, Goran. (1996). "Critical Theory and the Legacy of Twentieth-Century Marxism." In Barry S. Turner (Ed.), (1996). *The Blackwell Companion to Social Theory* (pp. 53–82). Malden, MA: Blackwell.

Thiam, Awa. (1978). *Black Sister, Speak Out: Feminism and Oppression in Black Africa*. London: Pluto Press.

Thompson, John. (1990). *Ideology and Modern Culture: Critical Social Theory in the Era of Mass Communication*. Stanford: Stanford University Press.

Thompson, Mildred I. (1990). *Ida B. Wells-Barnett: An Exploratory Study of an American Black Woman, 1893–1930*. New York: Carlson.

Thompson, Robert Dee, Jr. (1997). "A Socio-Biography of Shirley Graham-Du Bois: A Life in the Struggle." Ph. D. dissertation, University of California, Santa Cruz.

Thompson, Vincent Bakpetu. (1969). *Africa and Unity: The Evolution of Pan-Africanism* London: Longman.

———. (1987). *The Making of the African Diaspora in the Americas, 1441–1900*. New York: Longman.

Tiffin, Helen. (1988). "Post-colonialism, Post-modernism and the Rehabilitation of Post-colonial History." *Journal of Commonwealth Literatures* 23 (1), 169–81.

Toomer, Jean. (1993). *Cane*. New York: Liveright.

Townes, Emilie Maureen. (1989). "The Social and Moral Perspectives of Ida B. Wells-Barnett as Resource for a Contemporary Afro-American Christian Social Ethic." Ph. D. dissertation, Northwestern University, Evanston, IL.

———. (1993). *Womanist Justice, Womanist Hope*. Atlanta, GA: Scholars Press, American Academy of Religion, Academy Series no. 79.

Towns, Saundra. (1974). "The Black Woman as Whore: Genesis of the Myth." *The Black Position* 3, 39–59.

Townsend, Kim. (1996). "'Manhood' at Harvard: W. E. B. Du Bois." *Raritan* 15 (4), 70–82.

Travis, Toni Michelle C. (1996). "Double Consciousness and the Politics of the Elite." *Research in Race and Ethnic Relations* 9, 91–123.

Trebilcot, Joyce. (Ed.) (1984). *Mothering: Essays in Feminist Theory.* Totowa, NJ: Rowman and Allanheld.

Tuana, Nancy. (1992). *Woman and the History of Philosophy.* New York: Paragon House.

Tuana, Nancy, and Tong, Rosemarie. (Eds.) (1995). *Feminism & Philosophy: Essential Readings in Theory, Reinterpretation, and Application.* Boulder, CO: Westview.

Turner, Barry S. (Ed.) (1996). *The Blackwell Companion to Social Theory.* Malden, MA: Blackwell.

Turner, Darwin W. (1974). "W. E. B. Du Bois and the Theory of a Black Aesthetic." *Studies in the Literary Imagination* 7, 1–21.

Turner, James, (Ed.) (1984). *The Next Decade: Theoretical and Research Issues in Africana Studies.* Ithaca, NY: Africana Studies and Research Center, Cornell University.

Turner, James, and McGann, Charles S. (1980). "Black Studies as an Integral Tradition in African American Intellectual History." *Journal of Negro Education* 49, 52–59.

Tursi, Renee. (2000). "The Force of Habit at the Turn of the Century: William James, Henry James, Edith Wharton, and W. E. B. Du Bois." Ph. D. dissertation, Columbia University, New York.

Tushnet, Mark. (1987). "The Politics of Equality in Constitutional Law: The Equal Protection Clause, Dr. Du Bois, and Charles Hamilton Houston." *Journal of American History* 74 (3), 884–903.

Tuttle, William M. (Ed.) (1957). *W. E. B. Du Bois.* Boston: Beacon.

———. (Ed.) (1973). *W. E. B. Du Bois: Essays and Explorations.* Englewood Cliffs: Prentice Hall.

———. (1974). "W. E. B. Du Bois's Confrontation with White Liberalism During the Progressive Era." *Phylon* 35 (3), 241–258.

Twine, Frances W., and Blee, Kathleen M. (Eds.) (2001). *Feminism and Anti-Racism: International Struggles for Justice.* New York: New York University Press.

Tyner, Jarvis. (1997). "From the Talented Tenth to the Communist Party: The Evolution of W. E. B. Du Bois." *Political Affairs* 76 (2), 5–9.

Urban, Wayne J. (1997). "W. E. B. Du Bois." *History of Education Quarterly* 37 (4), 441–44.

Vaz, Kim Marie. (Ed.) (1995). *Black Women in America.* Thousand Oaks, CA: Sage.

Velikova, R. (2000). "W. E. B. Du Bois vs. 'the Sons of the Fathers': A Reading of *The Souls of Black Folk* in the Context of American Nationalism." *African American Review* 34 (3), 431–42.

Venn, Couze. (2006). *The Postcolonial Challenge: Towards Alternative Worlds.* Thousand Oaks, CA: Sage.

Vincent, Theodore G. (Ed.) (1973). *Voices of a Black Nation: Political Journalism in the Harlem Renaissance.* Trenton, NJ: Africa World Press.

Vivian, John Donald. (1997). "The Making of a Radical: W. E. B. Du Bois's Turn to the Left." M. A. thesis, Florida Atlantic University.

Vogel, Lise. (1983). *Marxism and the Oppression of Women: Towards a Unitary Theory.* New Brunswick: Rutgers University Press.

Von Eschen, Penny M. (1997). *Race Against Empire: Black Americans and Anticolonialism, 1937–1957.* Ithaca, NY: Cornell University Press.

Walden, Daniel. (1963a). "NAACP Mourns the Passing of Dr. Du Bois, a Founder." *Crisis* 70 (October).

———. (1963b). "W. E. B. Du Bois: Pioneer Reconstruction Historian." *Negro History Bulletin* 26, 159–60, 164.

———. (1966). "W. E. B. Du Bois's Essential Years: The Link from Douglass to the Present." *Journal of Human Relations* 14, 28–41.

———. (1977). "W. E. B. Du Bois: A Renaissance Man in the Harlem Renaissance." *Minority Voices* 2 (1), 11–20.

Walker, S. Jay. (1975). "Du Bois's Uses of History: On Nat Turner and John Brown." *Black World* 24 (February), 4–11.

Wallace, Michele. (1990a). *Black Macho and the Myth of the Superwoman.* New York: Verso.

———. (1990b). *Invisibility Blues: From Pop to Theory.* New York: Verso.

Walters, Ronald W. (1993). *Pan-Africanism in the African Diaspora: An Analysis of Modern Afrocentric Political Movement.* Detroit: Wayne State University Press.

Walton, Sidney. (1969). *The Black Curriculum: Developing Programs in Afro-American Studies.* East Palo Alto: Black Liberation Publishers.

Ward, Julie K., and Lott, Tommy L. (Eds). (2002). *Philosophers on Race: Critical Essays.* Malden, MA: Blackwell.

Ware, Vron. (1992). *Beyond the Pale: White Women, Racism, and History.* New York: Verso.

Warren, Kenneth W. (2000). "An Inevitable Drift?: Oligarchy, Du Bois, and the Politics of Race Between the Wars." *Boundary 2* 27 (3), 153–69.

Warren, Nagueyalti. (1984). "The Contributions of W. E. B. Du Bois to Afro-American Studies in Higher Education." Ph. D. dissertation, University of Mississippi.

Washington, Mary Helen. (Ed.) (1987). *Invented Lives: Narratives of Black Women, 1860–1960.* Garden City, NY: Anchor.

Watts, Eric King. (1995). "Reconstituting 'The Message': An Exploration of Double Consciousness in Rap Artistry." Ph. D. dissertation, Northwestern University, Evanston, IL.

———. (2001). "Cultivating a Black Public Voice: W. E. B. Du Bois and "The Criteria of Negro Art." *Rhetoric & Public Affairs* 4 (2), 181–201.

Weate, Jeremy. (2001). "Fanon, Merleau-Ponty and the Difference of Phenomenology." In Robert Bernasconi (Ed.), *Race* (pp. 169–83). Malden, MA: Blackwell.

Weinbaum, Batya. (1978). *The Curious Courtship of Women's Liberation and Socialism.* Boston: South End.

Wellmer, Albrecht. (1974). *The Critical Theory of Society.* New York: Seabury.

Wells, Ida B. (1969). *On Lynchings.* New York: Arno Press.

———. (1970). *Crusade for Justice: The Autobiography of Ida B. Wells* (Alfreda

Duster, Ed.). Chicago: University of Chicago Press.

———. (1991). *The Selected Works of Ida B. Wells-Barnett* (Trudier Harris, Ed.). New York: Oxford University Press.

———. (1993). *A Red Record: Lynchings in the U.S.* Salem, NH: Ayer & Co.

———. (1995). *The Memphis Dairy of Ida B. Wells* (Miriam Decosta-Willis, Ed.). Boston: Beacon.

Werbner, Richard P. (Ed.) (2002). *Postcolonial Subjectivities in Africa.* London: Zed.

Wesley, Charles H. (1965). "W. E. B. Du Bois: Historian." *Freedomways* 5, 59–72.

———. (1984). *The History of the National Association of Colored Women's Clubs: A Legacy of Service.* Washington, DC: National Association of Colored Women.

Wesley, Dorothy Porter. (1993). "Sarah Parker Remond." In Darlene Clark Hine, Elsa Barkley Brown, and Rosalyn Teborg-Penn (Eds.), *Black Women in America: An Historical Encyclopedia*, 2 volumes (pp. 972–74). Brooklyn: Carlson.

West, Cornel. (1982). *Prophesy Deliverance! An Afro-American Revolutionary Christianity.* Philadelphia: Westminister.

———. (1988a). *Prophetic Fragments.* Grand Rapids: Eerdmans.

———. (1988b). "Marxist Theory and the Specificity of Afro-American Oppression." In Cary Nelson and Lawrence Grossberg (Eds.), *Marxism and the Interpretation of Culture* (pp. 17–34). Chicago: University of Illinois Press.

———. (1989). "W. E. B. Du Bois: The Jamesian Organic Intellectual." In *The American Evasion of Philosophy: A Genealogy of Pragmatism* (pp. 138–50). Madison: University of Wisconsin Press.

———. (1993a). *Keeping Faith: Philosophy and Race in America.* New York: Routledge.

———. (1993b). *Race Matters.* New York: Random House.

———. (1993c). *Beyond Eurocentricism and Multiculturalism, Volume One: Prophetic Thought in Postmodern Times.* Monroe, ME: Common Courage.

———. (1993d). *Beyond Eurocentricism and Multiculturalism, Volume Two: Prophetic Reflections: Notes on Race and Power in America.* Monroe, ME: Common Courage.

———. (1996). "Black Strivings in a Twilight Civilization." In Henry Louis Gates, Jr. and Cornel West, *The Future of the Race.* (pp. 53–114). New York: Alfred A. Knopf.

———. (Ed.) (1999). *The Cornel West Reader.* New York: Civitas.

———. (2004). *Democracy Matters: Winning the Fight Against Imperialism.* New York: Penguin.

White, Deborah Gray. (1999). *Too Heavy a Load: Black Women in Defense of Themselves, 1894–1994.* New York: Norton.

White, E. Frances. (1984). "Listening to the Voices of Black Feminism." *Radical America* 18 (2–3), 7–25.

———. (1995). "Africa on My Mind: Gender, Counter Discourse and African American Nationalism." In Beverly Guy-Sheftall (Ed.), *Words of Fire: An Anthology of African American Feminist Thought.* (pp. 504–24). New York: The Free Press.

Wiatrowski-Phillips, Lily. (1995). "W. E. B. Du Bois and Soviet Communism: *The Black Flame* as Socialist Realism." *Southern Atlantic Quarterly* 94 (3), 837–75.

Wiggerhaus, Rolf. (1995). *The Frankfurt School: Its History, Theories, and Political Significance*. Cambridge: MIT Press.

Wilkerson, William S., and Paris, Jeffrey. (Eds.) (2001). *New Critical Theory: Essays on Liberation*. Lanham, MD: Rowman & Littlefield.

Willet, Cynthia. (1995). *Maternal Ethics and Other Slave Moralities*. New York: Routledge.

———. (2001). *Soul of Justice: Social Bonds and Racial Hubris*. Ithaca, NY: Cornell University Press.

Williams, Eric. (1966). *Capitalism and Slavery*. New York: Capricorn Books.

Williams, Patrick, and Chrisman, Laura. (Eds.) (1994). *Colonial Discourse and Postcolonial Theory: A Reader*. London: Harvester Wheatsheaf.

Williams, Randall. (2001). *W. E. B. Du Bois: A Scholar's Courageous Life*. Montgomery: New South.

Williams, Robert C. (1983). "W. E. B. Du Bois: Afro-American Philosopher of Social Reality." In Leonard Harris (Ed.), *Philosophy Born of Struggle: An Anthology of Afro-American Philosophy from 1917* (pp. 11–20). Dubuque, IA: Kendall/Hunt.

Williams, Shirley. (1990). "Some Implications of Womanist Theory." In Henry Louis Gates, Jr. (Ed.), *Reading Black/Reading Feminist: A Critical Anthology*. (pp. 68–75). New York: Meridian.

Wilmore, Gayraud S. (Ed.) (1989). *African American Religious Studies*. Durham, NC: Duke University Press.

Wilson, Bobby M. (2002). "Critically Understanding Race-Connected Practices: A Reading of W. E. B. Du Bois and Richard Wright." *The Professional Geographer* 54 (1), 31–41.

Winant, Howard. (2001). *Racial Conditions: Politics, Theory, Comparisons*. Minneapolis, MN: University of Minnesota Press.

Wing, Adrien Katherine. (Ed.) (1997). *Critical Race Feminism: A Reader*. New York: New York University Press.

Wintz, Cary D. (1996). *African American Political Thought, 1890–1930: Washington, Du Bois, Garvey, and Randolph*. Armonk: M. E. Sharpe.

Wiredu, Kwasi. (1980). *Philosophy and an African Culture*. New York: Cambridge University Press.

———. (1991). "On Defining African Philosophy." In Tsenay Serequeberhan (Ed.), *African Philosophy: The Essential Readings* (pp. 87–110). New York: Paragon House.

———. (1995). *Conceptual Decolonization in African Philosophy: Four Essays*. Ibadan, Nigeria: Hope Publications.

———. (1996). *Cultural Universals and Particulars: An African Perspective*. Indianapolis: Indiana University Press.

———. (Ed.) (2004). *A Companion to African Philosophy*. Malden, MA: Blackwell.

Wolff, Robert Paul. (2005). *Autobiography of an Ex-White Man: Learning a New Master Narrative for America*. Rochester, NY: University of Rochester Press.

Wolin, Richard. (1992). *The Terms of Cultural Criticism: The Frankfurt School, Existentialism, and Poststructuralism*. New York: Columbia University Press.

———. (1995). *Labyrinths: Explorations in the Critical History of Ideas*. Amherst, MA: University of Massachusetts Press.

———. (2006). *The Frankfurt School Revisited: And Other Essays on Politics and Society*. New York: Routledge.

Wolters, Raymond. (2001). *Du Bois and His Rivals*. Columbia: University of Missouri Press.

Woodard, Frederic. (1976). "W. E. B. Du Bois: The Native Impulse—Notes Toward an Ideological Biography, 1868–1897." Ph. D. dissertation, University of Iowa, Iowa City, Iowa.

Wortham, John M. (1997). "The Economic Ideologies of Booker T. Washington and W. E. B. Du Bois: 1895–1915." Ph. D. dissertation, Boston University, Boston, MA.

Wright, Earl. (2001). "The Atlanta Sociological Laboratory: America's First Model of Urban Sociological Research." Paper presented at the annual meeting of the *Southern Sociological Society*.

Wright, Richard A. (Ed.) (1984). *African Philosophy: An Introduction, Third Edition* Lanham, MD: University of America Press.

Wright, William. (1978). "Du Bois's Theory of Political Democracy." *Crisis* 85, 85–89.

Wright, William D. (1985). "The Socialist Analysis of W. E. B. Du Bois." Ph. D. dissertation, State University of New York, Buffalo.

Yancy, George. (Ed.) (2004). *What White Looks Like: African American Philosophers on the Whiteness Question*. New York: Routledge.

Yee, Shirley J. (1992). *Black Women Abolitionists: A Study in Activism, 1828–1860*. Knoxville: University of Tennessee Press.

Yellin, Jean Fagan. (1973). "Du Bois's Crisis and Woman's Suffrage." *Massachusetts Review* 14 (2), 365–75.

Young, Iris Marion. (1980). "Socialist Feminism and the Limits of the Dual Systems Theory." *Socialist Review* 10 (2–3), 171–90.

———. (1981). "Beyond the Unhappy Marriage: A Critique of the Dual Systems Theory." In Lydia Sargent (Ed.), *Women and Revolution: A Discussion of the Unhappy Marriage of Marxism and Feminism*. (pp. 47–63). Boston: South End.

———. (1990). *Justice and the Politics of Difference*. Princeton: Princeton University Press.

Young, Kenneth Ray, and Green, Dan S. (1972). "Harbinger to Nixon: W. E. B. Du Bois in China." *Negro History Bulletin* 35 (October).

Young, Robert J. (1995). *Colonial Desire: Hybridity in Theory, Culture and Race*. New York: Routledge.

———. (1999). *Postcolonialism: An Historical Introduction*. Malden, MA: Blackwell.

———. (2003). *Postcolonialism: A Very Short Introduction*. New York: Oxford University Press.

Yuan, Ji. (1998). "W. E. B. Du Bois and His Socialist Thought." Ph. D. dissertation, Temple University, Philadelphia.

———. (2000). *W. E. B. Du Bois and His Socialist Thought*. Lawrenceville: Africa World Press.

Zack, Naomi. (1993). *Race and Mixed Race*. Philadelphia: Temple University Press.

———. (Ed.) (1995). *American Mixed Race: The Culture of Microdiversity*. Lanham, MD: Rowman & Littlefield.

———. (1996). *Bachelors of Science: Seventeenth Century Identity, Then and Now*. Philadelphia: Temple University Press.

———. (Ed.) (1997). *Race/Sex: Their Sameness, Difference, and Interplay*. New York: Routledge.

———. (1998). *Thinking about Race*. Albany, NY: Wadsworth.

———. (Ed.) (2000). *Women of Color and Philosophy: A Critical Reader*. Malden, MA: Blackwell.

Zack, Naomi; Shrage, Laurie; and Sartwell, Crispin. (Eds.) (1998). *Race, Class, Gender, and Sexuality: The Big Questions*. Cambridge: Blackwell.

Zahan, Dominique. (1979). *The Religion, Spirituality, and Thought of Traditional Africa*. Chicago: University of Chicago Press.

Zamir, Shamoon. (1994). "The Sorrow Songs"/"Song of Myself": Du Bois, the Crisis of Leadership, and Prophetic Imagination." In Werner Sollors and Maria Diedrich (Eds.), *The Black Columbiad: Defining Moments in African American Literature and Culture*. Cambridge: Harvard University Press.

———. (1995). *Dark Voices: W. E. B. Du Bois and American Thought, 1888–1903*. Chicago: University of Chicago Press.

Zinn, Maxine Baca, and Dill, Bonnie Thornton. (Eds.) (1994). *Women of Color in U.S. Society*. Philadelphia: Temple University Press.

Zinn, Maxine Baca; Cannon, Lynn Weber; Higginbotham, Elizabeth; and Dill, Bonnie Thornton. (1986). "The Cost of Exclusionary Practices in Women's Studies." *Signs* 11 (2), 290–303.

Index

abolitionism, 113, 138–40, 154, 172
Adorno, Theodor W., 11, 180n6. *See also* The Frankfurt School
Africa, xi, 43, 62, 94–95, 103, 121, 131–32n8, 160
Africana, 5–6, 9–12
Africana critical theory, 3, 5, 8–14, 16–19, 21–24, 26, 29n3, 32n11, 33n13, 68, 112, 138, 141–42, 146–47, 150–51, 162, 169, 178–79n2, 180–81n8, 196n7; as a social activist and political praxis-promoting theory, 17; as revolutionary theory, 18; as self-reflexive social theory, 17; conception of theory, 14–18; contraction and synthesis of black feminist and womanist theory, 177, 179n4, 180–81nn7–8; contraction of Amilcar Cabral's concept of "The Weapon of Theory," 14, 18–23; contraction of bell hooks's black feminist theory, 7, 137, 153, 182n11; contraction of Lewis Gordon's conceptualization of theory and philosophy, 19–20, 31n9; critical relationship with Africana philosophy, 9–14; critical relationship with Herbert Marcuse's conception of critical theory, 33n12, 88, 134n12,
146, 178–79n2, 179–80n6, 192, 195n1; critique of Africana philosophy's meta-philosophical character, 12; critique of Cornel West's conception of Afro-American critical thought, 12–13; critique of disciplinary dependency complex, 8; critique of the Frankfurt School, 10–11, 25, 27; critique of theoretical freeze-framing, 24; definition, 9–10, 13; emphasis on antithetical conceptual contraction, 14; emphasis on epistemic openness, 14–17; synthesis of a wide-range of classical and contemporary social theory, 16–18, 21–22; use of dialectics, 12, 17; utilization of Africana intellectual-activist ancestors, 11–12; utilization of Frantz Fanon's philosophy of liberation and discourse on decolonization, 7, 10, 13–14, 20–21; utilization of Lucius Outlaw's operationalization of Africana philosophy, 11–12; utilization of W. E. B. Du Bois as major paradigm and point of departure, xiv, 2–5, 11, 23–27, 39–40, 65, 85, 107, 140, 142–43, 169, 187–97

267

About the Author

Reiland Rabaka teaches Africana Studies in the Department of Ethnic Studies at the University of Colorado at Boulder, where he is also a research fellow at the Center for Studies of Ethnicity and Race in America (CSERA). He earned his M. A. and Ph. D. from Temple University in Philadelphia, Pennsylvania. During the 2003–2004 academic year he was a postdoctoral fellow at the Center for African American Studies (CAAS) at the University of Houston. His teaching and research interests include Africana philosophy, critical race theory, feminist theory, postcolonial theory, radical politics, critical social theory, critical pedagogy, and liberation theology. His research has been published in *Journal of African American Studies*, *Journal of Black Studies*, *Western Journal of Black Studies*, *Africana Studies Annual Review*, *Africalogical Perspectives*, *Ethnic Studies Review*, and *Jouvert: A Journal of Postcolonial Studies*, among others. He is the author of the forthcoming book, *W. E. B. Du Bois, Black Radical Politics, and the Reconstruction of Critical Social Theory*, which will be published by Lexington Books in 2008.